What Literature Teaches Us about Emotion

Literature provides us with otherwise unavailable insights into the ways emotions are produced, experienced, and enacted in human social life. It is particularly valuable because it deepens our comprehension of the mutual relations between emotional response and ethical judgment. These are the central claims of Patrick Colm Hogan's study that carefully examines a range of highly esteemed literary works in the context of current neurobiological, psychological, sociological, and other empirical research. In this work, he explains the value of literary study for a cognitive science of emotion and outlines the emotional organization of the human mind. He explores the emotions of romantic love, grief, mirth, guilt, shame, jealousy, attachment, compassion, and pity – in each case drawing on one work by Shakespeare and one or more works by writers from different historical periods or different cultural backgrounds, such as the eleventh-century Chinese poet Li Ch'ing-Chao and the contemporary Nigerian playwright Wole Soyinka.

Patrick Colm Hogan is a professor in the Department of English at the University of Connecticut. He is also on the faculty of the Cognitive Science Program, the Program in Comparative Literature and Cultural Studies, and the India Studies Program. He is the author of thirteen books, including *The Mind and Its Stories: Narrative Universals and Human Emotion* (Cambridge University Press, 2003), hailed by Steven Pinker of Harvard University as "a landmark in modern intellectual life," and the editor or coeditor of four books, including *The Cambridge Encyclopedia of the Language Sciences* (2011).

STUDIES IN EMOTION AND SOCIAL INTERACTION
Second Series

Series Editors

Keith Oatley
University of Toronto

Antony S. R. Manstead
Cardiff University

Titles published in the Second Series:

The Psychology of Facial Expression, edited by
   James A. Russell and José Miguel Fernández-Dols
Emotions, the Social Bond, and Human Reality: Part/Whole Analysis, by
   Thomas J. Scheff
Intersubjective Communication and Emotion in Early Ontogeny, edited by
   Stein Bråten
The Social Context of Nonverbal Behavior, edited by
   Pierre Philippot, Robert S. Feldman, and Erik J. Coats
Communicating Emotion: Social, Moral, and Cultural Processes, by
   Sally Planalp
Emotions across Languages and Cultures: Diversity and Universals, by
   Anna Wierzbicka
Feeling and Thinking: The Role of Affect in Social Cognition, edited by
   Joseph P. Forgas
Metaphor and Emotion: Language, Culture, and Body in Human Feeling, by
   Zoltán Kövecses
Gender and Emotion: Social Psychological Perspectives, edited by
   Agneta H. Fischer
Causes and Consequences of Feelings, by
   Leonard Berkowitz
Emotions and Beliefs: How Feelings Influence Thoughts, edited by
   Nico H. Frijda, Antony S. R. Manstead, and Sacha Bem
Identity and Emotion: Development through Self-Organization, edited by
   Harke A. Bosma and E. Saskia Kunnen
Speaking from the Heart: Gender and the Social Meaning of Emotion, by
   Stephanie A. Shields
The Hidden Genius of Emotion: Lifespan Transformations of Personality, by
   Carol Magai and Jeannette Haviland-Jones

(Continued after Index)

What Literature Teaches Us about Emotion

Patrick Colm Hogan
University of Connecticut

CAMBRIDGE
UNIVERSITY PRESS

CAMBRIDGE UNIVERSITY PRESS
Cambridge, New York, Melbourne, Madrid, Cape Town,
Singapore, São Paulo, Delhi, Tokyo, Mexico City

Cambridge University Press
32 Avenue of the Americas, New York, NY 10013-2473, USA

www.cambridge.org
Information on this title: www.cambridge.org/9781107002883

First published 2011

Printed in the United States of America

A catalog record for this publication is available from the British Library.

Library of Congress Cataloging in Publication data
Hogan, Patrick Colm.
  What literature teaches us about emotion / Patrick Colm Hogan.
    p. cm. – (Studies in emotion and social interaction)
  Includes bibliographical references and index.
  ISBN 978-1-107-00288-3 (hardback)
  1. Emotions in literature. 2. Philosophy of mind in literature. 3. Psychology
  and literature. 4. Philosophy of mind. I. Title.
  PN56.E6H64 2011
  809'.93353–dc22   2010037100

ISBN 978-1-107-00288-3 Hardback

For Lalita

Contents

ix

Figures

Acknowledgments

Most of Chapter 1 and part of the introduction appeared previously in *Emotion Review* 2.2 (2010): 184–195. I am grateful to the referees for their very helpful comments and suggestions. An earlier version of Chapter 7 was delivered as the keynote address at "Tagore in the Global Community," University of Illinois, Urbana/Champaign, October 2007. I am grateful to Rini Bhattacharya Mehta for inviting me and to the participants for the stimulating discussion that followed the presentation. Earlier versions of Chapters 2, 5, and 7 were delivered at the University of Aarhus in May 2009. I am grateful to Peer Bundgaard for organizing this series of talks and to the participants for their penetrating questions and comments. An earlier version of the discussion of *Macbeth* in Chapter 6 was presented at the University of Connecticut in November 2009. I am grateful to Martha Cutter and Liz Hart for setting up the talk and to the participants for their insightful and challenging discussion. An earlier version of the analysis of *Othello* benefited from the comments of participants in the Social Neuroscience seminar of the Shakespeare Association of America conference in March 2009. I am grateful to the organizers of that session, Paul Budra and Kirsten Uszkalo, and the other participants.

Simina Calin was, as usual, an invaluable resource at the Press, as was Jeanie Lee. Robert Swanson carefully indexed the book. I owe a particular debt to Keith Oatley for suggesting that I write the first chapter for *Emotion Review*, for encouraging the larger development of the project begun by that essay, and for providing valuable, challenging criticisms and suggestions throughout. Finally, my wife, Lalita Pandit Hogan, read carefully and aided kindly, as she always does.

Introduction: Studying Literature Studying Emotion

This book sets out to integrate literary insights with work from neuro-science, psychology, philosophy, and elsewhere in order to contribute to the ongoing interdisciplinary research program in emotion. Drawing on those sources, but stressing the particular value of literature, it treats the general structure of emotion, both egoistic and empathic, as well as particular emotions including romantic love, mirth, grief, guilt, shame, and jealousy. It also takes up the increasingly important connection between emotion study and ethics, proposing some general principles for understanding this connection both within and outside literary works.

Research in emotion has advanced remarkably in the past two or three decades. Our understanding of human feeling and motivation is incomparably greater than it was forty years ago. This advancement is due largely to the work of research scientists. These scientists have, to a great extent, been operating in the general context of cognitive science. One of the main lessons of cognitive science is that understanding the human mind requires the integration of work from a broad range of disciplines. For example, linguistics is advanced by the study of met-aphor while itself contributing to genetics; philosophical reflections orient anthropological investigations that themselves suggest topics for neurological study. Many of the great successes of cognitive sci-ence come from the fact that the research programs it has put forward are interdisciplinary. Cognitive science has forced researchers in tra-ditional disciplines to explore other techniques of examining a given topic, incorporating other data, other theories, other approaches, and other hypotheses. Yet verbal art is largely absent from this interdisci-plinary study of emotion – despite the fact that millennia of storytell-ing present us with the largest body of works that systematically depict and provoke emotion, and do so as a major part of human life.

1

In keeping with this final point, the first chapter argues that literature provides a vast and largely unexplored body of data for emotion research. On hearing this general idea, experimental psychologists sometimes reply that literature is not data. It is just anecdotes. But this is a bizarre response. Certainly, one cannot establish a science based on a researcher's private tales. But the existence and vast emotional influence of literary works are simply not private tales. Put crudely, saying, "There is a vast body of literature. It arises in all cultures at all time periods. It repeatedly produces emotions in readers. Some works have been particularly remarkable in their effects, provoking mirth or sorrow in readers or listeners from many times and places," is simply not comparable to saying, "I had an uncle once who cured his rheumatism with daily application of Jack Daniels." In fact, the dismissal of literature as a body of data is the unscientific view. It, in effect, says, "There is a vast area of human emotional life – real communicative products that both depict and induce emotional response, often across cultures and historical periods; however, we are going to ignore it."

Of course, a psychologist may respond that none of this means claims about emotion in literary works are necessarily correct. It does not even mean that the representations of emotions are "right." This is true. But this only means that in literary study, same as in psychology, neuroscience, and elsewhere, the data require interpretation. The depiction of Romeo and Juliet's love has been moving readers and audience members for centuries and in different countries. The data are that this particular play, with these words, these events, and these characters, has produced this recurring effect. Interpreting these data is the difficult part. Indeed, it would be a very bad interpretation to claim that the play is effective because it simply gets the emotion right. If that were true, then every well-done psychological survey of trauma would produce the effects of tragedy, and every report of an fMRI scan treating amygdala activation would thrill the reader like a horror film. Discounting literary data in the way just mentioned is really a matter of discounting an inadequate account of these data.

Such discounting is particularly unfortunate since (as argued in Chapter 1) literature is a body of data that is unusually well designed to solve problems that plague emotion research – problems with surveys, diary methods, interviews, mechanical tests (such as skin conductance), and so on. Indeed, it provides important data at several levels, some more abstract (such as genre), others more concrete (most importantly, individual literary works). One of these levels is (partially) explored in *The Mind and Its Stories*. That work isolates three cross-cultural narrative genres. It goes on to argue that these genres can be understood only by reference to cross-cultural emotion prototypes, and that those prototypes, in turn, tell us something about human emotion systems. The present work concentrates on individual works.

Of course, the value of discussing individual literary works is not entirely a matter of generating hypotheses about emotions generally. Though the theory of emotions is the main concern of the following pages, each chapter also aims at revealing some of the richness of individual literary works. Poets and playwrights are not (generally) scientists. Their insights into emotion are particular insights, insights about this character in these circumstances. Here, we return to interpretation. The interpretation an experimental scientist gives to his or her data serves to put those data into some sort of order. Or, rather, this interpretation serves to reveal an organization in the data that we would not have seen otherwise. The same point holds for literature. Our interpretation of *Romeo and Juliet* or *Hamlet* – that is, our analysis of the play in relation to hypotheses about emotion – should serve to reveal an organization in those works that we would not have seen otherwise. The difference between *Hamlet* and some experimental data, in this regard, is that the patterns of Shakespeare's play have human, experiential interest beyond their consequences for a theory of emotion. Literature is a part of human life. Indeed, literature is central to human life. Telling and hearing stories may take up as much or more of our time and as much or more of our emotional energy than our primary engagements in real life. Indeed, that centrality is part of what gives literature ecological validity in the study of emotion. For this reason, advancing our interpretive understanding of these influential and widely admired literary works is an important, if still secondary, goal of the following pages.

Given that the following chapters will be treating individual works, it is important to address a misunderstanding that some readers have had about using literature as data for an account of emotions. Specifically, there are two obvious ways in which one might approach emotion in relation to a single work. One way involves determining individual readers' responses to the text. The other involves interpreting the text itself.

Focusing on individual readers is certainly valuable. However, there are several problems with making this the single guiding approach. First, one could argue that its results are only as good as the interpretive skills of the individual test subjects. When I teach a work by Shakespeare – or one of the great Sanskrit dramatists, or a Persian poet – my students may begin with a response that is primarily a matter of disorientation and incomprehension. My hope is that this changes after we have finished studying the work. Would we say that their spontaneous incomprehension is a reasonable reflection of the emotional insights of the work? In these cases, it seems clear that a fuller understanding of the work is required to tell us anything useful about its emotional implications.

Even when we focus entirely on spontaneous reactions to a work, probably millions of people have responded to *King Lear* with emotion, people from different backgrounds, different societies, and in different historical periods. Test subjects are necessarily far fewer in number and far less diverse. Indeed, they are often a set of undergraduates from European or North American universities. This limitation is not insignificant or inconsequential. It is likely to bias our analysis toward the attitudes and propensities of a fairly narrow group.

More importantly, it is difficult to say just what the responses of these test subjects mean – or even precisely what their responses are, in the case of emotion. Specifically, even when testing spontaneous response, at least two problems arise. One comes in the representation of the emotion states of test subjects. The second concerns the isolation of the causes of those emotions. We are often somewhat inarticulate about our emotional states (when they go beyond simple cases of fear, anger, disgust, and a few others). Moreover, our objective tests are currently rather crude in such identifications. One may suspect, for example, that most readers feel something like hopeful enthusiasm and an empathic version of romantic longing when Romeo and Juliet meet and tentatively express their mutual affection. But just how is one to isolate this emotion, even as a mere label, either in self-reports (without biasing the study by introducing this complex idea) or in objective tests (e.g., fMRI scans)?

Moreover, if one comes up with a way of doing this, how is one to isolate the aspects of the text to which the response refers? Eye tracking is one option, but that does not tell us what the test subject was imagining at the point when he or she experienced the reported feeling. Even if we manage to fix the cause on some part of the text, we cannot be sure of precisely what the reader is getting out of the text. There are many subtleties, many complex connections in the text. These presumably have effects on readers. Few readers, however, are able to articulate anything like what these are. Our sensitivity in this case is not unlike our sensitivity to grammar. We understand sentences through grammar, but we find it almost impossible to formulate grammatical principles – or even to articulate features of language that bear on such principles. For example, in English, we form regular plurals by adding [əz] to words ending in sibilants, [z] to words ending in voiced nonsibilants, and [s] to everything else. Ordinary English speakers simply cannot tell us that this is what they are doing. They will add [z] to "dog" and [s] to "cat," but they won't be able to tell you what features of "dog" and "cat" determine this response. To do that, we need to analyze the words, and we need to analyze them with a certain sort of knowledge that is not simply a part of spontaneous understanding. In short, people find it almost impossible to interpret what guides their (fairly clear-cut) grammatical responses to such simple issues as regular plural formation. We have little reason to believe that people would, in general, be any better at interpreting what guides their complex emotional response to a literary work.

Again, the empirical study of reader response is very valuable. The point here is not at all to dismiss such research, but rather to suggest that interpretive study focusing on literary texts is at least as important. Indeed, if anything, it is more important, since it is more fundamental and its consequences are broader.

For these reasons, the following chapters will focus on the text itself, trying to reveal some of the subtleties of its "suggestions" or "dhvani" (as the Sanskrit theorists put it).[1] As just indicated, the presumption in these chapters is that such subtleties do affect readers' responses. Of course, not all the subtleties affect all readers' responses. Indeed, different readers will be affected by different resonances. However, again, these differences presumably balance out over large numbers. If they did not, the widespread emotional engagement produced by some works (e.g., *Romeo and Juliet* or *Hamlet*) would be anomalous. It would amount to a coincidence across sometimes millions of people. The noncoincidental basis for repeated emotional response is presumably to be found through careful interpretation of the work.

As already indicated, the first chapter articulates an argument for the value of literature in the study of emotion. The first half of the chapter presents reasons why literature may serve as a particularly valuable body of data in that it responds to some of the main problems with

---

[1] See Hogan 2003, 45–75, and Oatley "Suggestion."

standard research in the field. It is important to stress that this does not mean it displaces standard research. Rather, literature is a valuable site for interdisciplinary study that integrates psychological, sociological, neurological, and other approaches in the context of nuanced, complex depictions of human emotional experience – specifically, depictions that have had deep and enduring emotional impact across time periods and cultures.

As this reference to interdisciplinarity suggests, an understanding of literature and emotion cannot be derived from the literary works alone. Thus a researcher should generally invoke features of a story or character insofar as they at least partially converge with broader research trends.[2] Of course, the same point holds for psychological surveys or fMRI scans; they too are disambiguated in light of convergent research from a variety of fields using a variety of methods. Indeed, emotion research on any particular object, using any particular approach, can hardly produce advances in our understanding of emotion unless it is integrated with work on emotion treating on other objects and using other approaches. Thus the following chapters draw extensively on emotion research from a range of fields outside literary study. At the same time, however, the integration of literary features with this empirical research may challenge standard views in a number of ways. These challenges range from such simple matters as foregrounding under-researched emotions (e.g., mirth), to suggesting that ambivalence and conflict among emotion systems may be greater than researchers have commonly inferred, to differentiating the range of emotions (and emotional ambivalences) that operate in ethical response, to stressing aspects of emotional experience that are rarely recognized in mainstream empirical research (e.g., the effects of emotion on our experience and understanding of space and time). Moreover, literary narratives often provide frameworks for synthesizing the otherwise somewhat fragmented research findings on any given emotion. This synthesis itself should provide insights beyond the individual findings considered separately.

---

[2] Readers of this book have rightly pointed out that a concern for such convergence is increasingly emphasized in work by literary theorists and research scientists interested in literature. Widely cited figures in this area would include, most obviously, E. O. Wilson, as well as Brian Boyd and Denis Dutton. Such an emphasis is particularly pronounced among writers interested in literature and evolution. Evolution figures prominently in the following chapters, yet this does not mean that the following chapters themselves converge with evolutionary psychology. For some points of divergence, see Hogan "For Evolutionary" and chapter 8 of Hogan *Cognitive*.

In order to enhance the possibilities for convergent and synthetic theorization, Chapter 2 presents an account of emotion structure that draws extensively on current empirical research. This chapter articulates a multicomponent theory of emotion that – in keeping with the vivid particularity of stories (including, of course, performed stories) – stresses perceptual concreteness, both directly sensory and imaginative. This theory lays the groundwork for the following treatments of individual emotions. The chapter concludes with a brief discussion of the relation between ethics and emotion.

Chapters 3 through 8 take up a small number of individual literary works, examining them in connection with particular emotions. The first of these chapters treats romantic love, focusing on work by Li Ch'ing-Chao ("the greatest poetess of Chinese Literature" [Hu 28])[3] and Sappho,[4] as well as Shakespeare's *Romeo and Juliet*. This chapter considers what is almost certainly the most common emotion treated in enduring and popular literary works cross-culturally. This chapter also begins to suggest the central place attachment will hold in the course of the following analyses.

Chapters 4 and 5 address the two extremes of grief and mirth, also pervasive concerns in literature. The point is obvious in the case of mirth, owing to the proliferation of comedies and farces. As to grief, John Archer points out that "Whether a person lives in an individualistic or a collectivist society, the experience of bereavement generates a need to communicate thoughts and feelings to others." These lead to "the generation of the many literary works concerned with grief" (35). Chapter 4 explores grief in relation to writing by the highly influential, late-eighteenth/early-nineteenth-century Japanese poet, Kobayashi Issa, along with Shakespeare's *Hamlet*. The treatment of mirth begins with the tradition of Chinese joke telling, turning from there to Shakespeare's *The Comedy of Errors*.

---

[3] Treating work from China in this context has the advantage of opposing a common stereotype about Chinese society – that "the Chinese are uninterested in love," as Jankowiak puts it (166). Jankowiak points out that this mistaken view is bound up with the fact that "the remarkable continuity of romantic love found in Chinese literature has been little appreciated" (167). Jankowiak's comments are particularly valuable on the interrelation between literary imagination, personal aspirations and values, and practical behavior in China (see 182).

[4] The stature of Sappho is undoubtedly already well known to Western readers. Nonetheless, readers wishing to learn more about the extent of her influence may consult Robinson or Reynolds.

Up to that point, the ethical concerns raised in Chapter 2 have not been developed theoretically (though they do come up repeatedly in the particular literary analyses). The remaining chapters address the varieties of moral feeling. Chapter 6 focuses on guilt and shame. The chapter also gives some attention to jealousy. It considers guilt particularly in relation to Shakespeare's *Macbeth* and one of Wole Soyinka's plays. It then addresses shame in the fifteenth-century Noh drama, *Kagekiyo*, and in Shakespeare's *Othello*, taking up the relation of jealousy to shame in the latter.

Chapter 7 explores attachment in greater detail. Specifically, it examines the interrelations among attachment, disgust, and moral feeling in relation to a poem by Rabindranath Tagore and Shakespeare's *Measure for Measure*. This chapter moves from moral emotions bearing on oneself to moral emotions bearing on personal relations.

The final chapter addresses empathy more fully, extending the treatment of moral emotions to intergroup relations and politics. It begins with a brief discussion of ethics and evolution – a topic of active discussion in a number of fields. It goes on to analyze different varieties of empathy, focusing particularly on the difference between compassion and pity. In order to develop this analysis, the chapter focuses on Shakespeare's *The Tempest* and Aimé Césaire's rewriting of that play.

The afterword briefly takes up a distinctive aspect of the relation between literature and emotion. Rather than drawing on literature to explore a particular emotion, this chapter draws on literature to explore how literature and literary study themselves affect emotional propensities. Specifically, through an examination of Flaubert's *Madame Bovary*, it considers how literary stories may alter our spontaneous emotional responses to the world and to ourselves, and our imaginative elaboration of those responses. In each case, that response is mediated in important ways by the dialogues we enter into when sharing our emotional and interpretive responses to individual literary works. Literary criticism is itself part of that dialogue.

As is no doubt obvious, there is a pattern to the selection of literary works. First, the following chapters explore one Shakespeare play in connection with each emotion. There are three reasons for this. First, taking a work by a one author in each chapter helps provide continuity. Second, Shakespeare is simply the best-known writer in world literature. In this way, his work provides a useful reference point for a large number of readers. Focusing on any other author in all of the chapters would have limited the range of readers familiar with the literary texts being considered. Finally, Shakespeare does appear to have been uniquely celebrated for his insight into the human mind and social relations. This celebration is found among both literary critics and scientists – as in Keith Oatley's recent characterization of Shakespeare as "The Psychologist of Avon" (see "An Emotion's Emergence").

On the other hand, Shakespeare was obviously a European man writing in the late sixteenth–early seventeenth century. We presumably wish to draw conclusions about emotion that are broadly valid – not confined to a particular historical period and culture location. Given the focus on detailed interpretation, it is not possible to present a broad overview of works in each chapter. However, it is at least possible to select works that are from different periods or cultural traditions. As to temporal distribution, other examples range from the seventh or sixth century B.C.E. (Sappho) to the twentieth century C.E. (Soyinka, Césaire), including instances from the nineteenth century (Tagore, Issa), the fifteenth century (*Kagekiyo*), the twelfth century (Li), and a tradition extending back to at least the third century (Chinese jokes). The geographical distribution ranges from Japan (Issa and *Kagekiyo*), through China (Li and Chinese jokes), South Asia (Tagore), and Europe (Sappho), to the Americas (Césaire).

The only exception to this pattern occurs in the afterword, which draws on just a single work. There are two reasons for this. First, the afterword is necessarily more limited in its scope. It serves to outline some aspects of a research topic complementary to that treated in the main text. However, it necessarily cannot examine that topic in equal detail (without doubling the size of the book). Second, and more important, virtually every literary work depicts emotion, but very few deal with the effects of literature on emotion. Thus the choices were limited.

As already noted, recent decades have witnessed a remarkable flowering of research in and understanding of emotion. Some writers have even taken to speaking of an "affective turn." Literary study has certainly been drawn into this work. However, the vast pool of data supplied by literature remains underutilized in emotion research. It is my hope that this book – along with its precursors by Martha Nussbaum, Keith Oatley, and others – will make some contribution to changing that situation. More exactly, it is my hope that this book will have some effects on four levels. First, it will help advance our understanding of emotion in general and of the particular emotions it examines. Second, it will further clarify the nature of ethical emotion. Third, it will help contribute to the integration of literary research into emotion research (including the part that treats moral feeling). Finally, it will increase our understanding and appreciation of the particular literary works it takes up, most of which have already proven themselves to be emotionally and ethically significant for a broad range of people in different places and at different times.

1. Fictions and Feelings

On the Place of Literature in the Study of Emotion

In his recent, acclaimed book, *Proust was a Neuroscientist*, Jonah Lehrer argues that "any description of the brain requires both ... art and science" (x). He ends by urging the development of a "fourth culture" that "will freely transplant knowledge between the sciences and the humanities" (196). Lehrer discusses memory, vision, language, and other topics – including emotion – that have been well explored by the neurosciences. Unfortunately, he does not quite show that "any description of the brain requires both ... art and science." He discusses eight artists with insight and sensitivity. He explores neuroscientific research on a range of topics in a lucid and rigorous way. But it is never clear that the artists are contributing to the science. It is not even clear that Proust and others "had predicted" subsequent "experiments" or "anticipated the discoveries of neuroscience" (vii). After all, they were not designing experiments or formulating general theories. If the point is just that artists implicitly got the facts right about seeing, and other things, then we are all neuroscientists. We all get the facts right, for we are all living examples of how perceptual, memory, and emotion systems work.

On the other hand, as Lehrer shows, novelists, painters, and musicians sometimes depicted or appealed to aspects of human perception, thought, feeling, or memory in ways that were more complex and accurate than the standard views of their contemporaries, including scientists. In this way, they anticipated something about our more recent views, something important for science. They did not anticipate the science itself. But they did see something that science had not yet seen, at least not fully. In connection with this, Lehrer seems closer to the mark when he writes that "neuroscience is useful for describing the brain, and art is useful for describing our actual experience" (192). Perhaps the greatest value of Lehrer's book is in clarifying the – so to speak – human meaning of neuroscience. The cases from the arts serve to translate the sometimes alien, objectifying accounts of neuroscience into the realm of "what it feels like" to have certain memories or emotions (to allude to Nagel's essay on first-person experience).

But is the scientific value of literature solely a matter of allowing an experiential point of contact, a way of making hard science more accessible after the fact? If it is indeed the case that artists did comprehend something about the human mind before scientists, then the answer is "no." Again, it would be wrong to say that the artists formulated the science first. But it seems no less wrong to say that these artists were "neuroscientists" only in the sense that ordinary people are. They did not merely live their perception, memory, and so on. They *encoded* and *represented* it. Moreover, once they had done this, their representations were available to everyone. The value of these representations for scientific accounts need not remain hidden until after the scientific accounts are formulated. They can just as readily inspire or orient scientific research, even the design of experiments and the formulation of theories. Lehrer suggests as much when he writes that Kausik Si "began his scientific search [on memory] by trying to answer the question posed by [Proust's famous scene of] the Madeleine" (91).

This indicates that the encoding and representation of experience articulated in literary works could, perhaps even should, have a place in suggesting research or generating hypotheses – thus in the "context of discovery" – for at least certain sorts of psychological and neuroscientific investigation and theorization. This seems particularly clear in the case of emotion. Emotion is, after all, the primary stuff of literature. But that is not all. If the encoding and representation of experience in literature may be accurate to the point where they can contribute to discovery, it seems that they must have some validity as data as well. In this way, stories should have some place in our broad set of data – data that we understand as complex and open to different interpretations, but data nonetheless. Psychologists, neuroscientists, and literary theorists are rightly skeptical of any claims that literary portrayals are straightforwardly mimetically accurate in a simple and straightforward way. But this only means that we cannot always take the empirical significance of a story as self-evident – a point that applies equally to experimental research. In short, the arts – and the interpretation of the arts – should also have some place in the "context of justification" for some psychological and neuroscientific theorization, particularly regarding emotion.

We might consider the issue from the other side. As I have argued elsewhere (*The Mind*), storytelling has been pervasive in our lives and in the lives of people in other places and times. Suppose we have a theory of emotion that explains why we freeze or run in fear when we see a predator, why we feel disgust at the sight of feces, why we feel angry when pushed. But it has nothing to say about why cultures all over the world produce verbal art; why the depictions of emotions in those works are so emotionally powerful that we spend a great deal of our lives reading, watching, or listening to literary stories; and why those stories repeatedly manifest the same characteristics. We have a very poor cognitive science if it leaves aside this vast area of human life. The obvious place to seek explanations for the emotional engagement of literature – which, again, is pervasive in our actual lives – is, of course, in the literature itself.

In the following pages, we will consider in greater detail the idea that literature can, indeed should, play a role in the generation of hypotheses and research orientations, and that it even has probative value within research programs. However, before exploring these issues, we need to clarify the relations among emotional experience, encoding, and the representation of emotional experience. After addressing this, the chapter will consider how literature solves some problems with gathering data on emotion or generating a set of representations that may contribute to more adequate descriptions and explanations of emotion. Subsequent sections will then outline the levels of generality at which literature bears on emotion, concluding with a look at some points suggested by work at each level.

Representation

The beginning of a science of human emotion is in our individual experience of emotion – not merely its phenomenological tone, but also our sense of action readiness, our recognition of eliciting conditions, the ways we anticipate particular outcomes and imaginatively elaborate on the causes of a situation, and so on. If we discovered various sorts of activation of nuclei of the amygdala but had no experiences of the preceding sort, we would not understand those activations as emotions. Indeed, we would not even have an idea of emotions (as opposed to, say, reflexes) without the experiences just listed. We might say that we can *interpret* the amygdala activations only by reference to the experiences, even as we partially *explain* the experiences by reference to the activations.

On the other hand, the experience of emotions does not in itself constitute an idea of emotions. Experience must be mediated or objectified through an idea or concept. It must be *represented*. Whether we are engaging in casual conversation or doing neuroscience, we never think through an experience directly. Rather, we consider some representation of the experience. Indeed, experience itself is never "pure" and "direct." It is mediated by our sensory and cognitive architectures, the innate structures, the acquired processes and contents that shape what occurs in the world into what we think occurs. The fundamental operation here is encoding – the selection, segmentation, and structuration of input at various levels of processing.

Such encoding occurs most obviously through the activation of sensory neurons with particular sensitivities, associated lateral inhibition of some other neurons (producing, for example, sharper perceptual contrasts), the transmission of some information (activation) to emotion systems (e.g., through the "low road" pathway from the thalamus to the amygdala [LeDoux *Emotional* 164]), subsequent semantic categorization, and so on. But even this understates the mediated nature of emotional experience. As Phenomenologists emphasized, each momentary experience is compounded with a briefly remembered past and an anticipated future. There appear to be different time scales in the coordination of our actions and thoughts, perhaps related to different time scales of the basal ganglia and cerebellum.[1] Beyond these, there are larger-scale anticipations and memories that enter into our processing of current situations, our possible responses to those situations, and so forth. We may refer to this integration of memory and imagination (including both Phenomenological "horizons" of future and past) as "elaboration."

Needless to say, this too is not the end of the story, for the product of ongoing encoding and ongoing elaboration is some response. This response is itself encoded and elaborated. (We do not even experience our own actions without mediation.) It, in turn, alters the overall situation, producing further encoding and elaboration, and so forth.

Thus the experiential basis for the study of emotion is a rather messy complex of processes. It involves ongoing encoding of changing inputs

---

[1] See, for example, DeLong 866, on the timing operation of the basal ganglia in relation to movement and thought. On anticipatory time scales in relation to art, see Hogan "Sensorimotor."

with ongoing elaboration, plus ongoing responses that themselves change both the inputs (the worldly situation) and the elaboration, even certain aspects of encoding (through shifts in attention, thus selection, etc.). In this way, emotional experience itself is already representational. On the other hand, we should distinguish between representations that are formulated as objects of reflective scrutiny and the tacit representations that operate as part of unself-conscious processing. The word "representation" is commonly used for both sorts of mental content in "representational" (or "symbolic") accounts of mind (as opposed to Connectionist, or "sub-symbolic," accounts). For this reason, it seems best to retain the general usage of this word. We may reserve the word "depiction" or the phrase "depictive representation" for representations that are or may be the object of scrutiny or reflection. To distinguish the tacit representations, we may use the phrase "processing representations."

In a theory of emotion, we want to treat (among other things) the "experience" of emotion, with its encoding and elaboration of processing representations.[2] However, the only data we have regarding that experience are necessarily depictive representations.[3] How, then, do we gain access to or generate the most accurate set of such depictions?

Explanation and Interpretation

Before answering this question, we need to draw some basic distinctions between levels of analysis in any theoretical account of psychological, social, and related phenomena – phenomena that may be characterized as human, intentional (in the broad, Phenomenological sense of the term), embedded in "contexts of meaning" (as Habermas would put it [36]), and so on. Emotional experience is what we seek to explain by reference to mental architecture and psychological processes. For example, we explain the ongoing readjustment of our experiential response to an emotion-eliciting situation by reference to the working memory integration of emotional memory, long-term

---

[2] Of course, we also want to treat its social context and psychological and physiological substrates. My focus in this chapter, however, is on the experiential component, which bears most directly on literature.

[3] Let me stress again that I am speaking here of the *experience* of an emotion, "what it is like" to have the emotion. Various physical tests – such as fMRI scans – clearly serve as data in emotion study. But, to put it crudely, if asked "what is it like to be in love," showing an fMRI scan would not be a very helpful response.

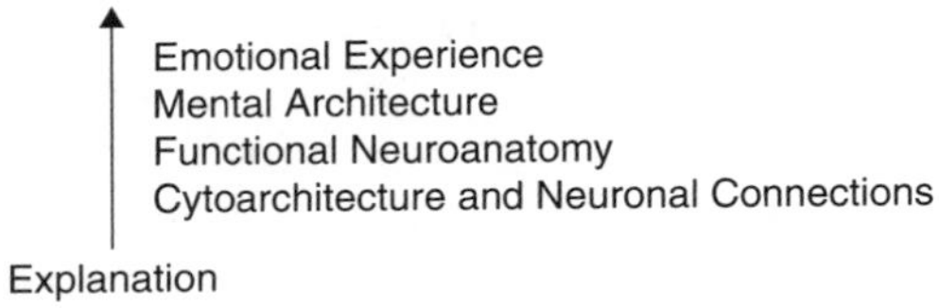

> ↑
> Emotional Experience
> Mental Architecture
> Functional Neuroanatomy
> Cytoarchitecture and Neuronal Connections
>
> Explanation

Figure 1.1. A simplified model of emotional explanation.

explicit memory, and changing perceptions. We then seek to explain this mental architecture of working memory, emotional memory, and the like, and these psychological processes (e.g., of integration) by reference to functional neuroanatomy. Thus we refer to processes in dorsolateral prefrontal cortex, their relation to activations of the amygdala and to sensory cortex. We explain functional neuroanatomy, in turn, by cytoarchitecture and neuronal connections, and so forth.

We could represent the general organization of the explanatory hierarchy as in Figure 1.1, with each lower level serving to explain the immediately higher level. However, this seems to make cytoarchitecture and neuronal connections basic, and emotional experience appears almost peripheral.

A parallel point holds if we shift to a second sort of explanation central to biological sciences and any sciences treating objects that emerge from biology. This is the explanation[4] that addresses the functions of properties and relations rather than their mechanics. We can explain functional neuroanatomy not only by reference to cytoarchitecture and neuronal connections, but also by reference to the evolution of the brain. In keeping with this, aspects of emotional experience may be explained by biological evolution. On the other hand, not all properties of emotional experience – not even all cross-culturally recurring properties – need to be explained in terms of evolutionary biology. For example, there are undoubtedly properties of human emotion that reflect functions operating at the level of human societies. Societies develop ways of limiting certain emotions and emotional relations (e.g., minimizing empathy with out-group members) and fostering other emotions and emotional relations (e.g., enhancing loyalty to in-group hierarchies). In some cases, these practices might have biological consequences. Given adequate plasticity in our innate propensities,

---

[4] More accurately, it is a form of approximative understanding. As I will discuss in Chapter 8, evolution itself operates by mechanisms that only approximate functions. Isolating the functions gives us an intuitive understanding of why the mechanisms spread genetically.

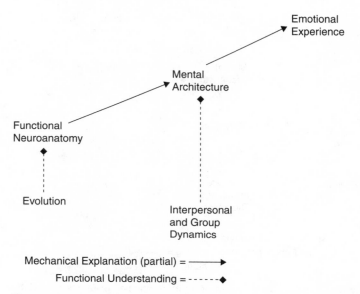

Figure 1.2. A simplified model of mechanical and functional explanation in emotion.

however, it seems that these biological consequences will be limited. In other words, societies may preserve these patterns not genetically, but socially.

This gives us a model of explanation along roughly the lines of Figure 1.2.

In this model, evolution functionally explains functional neuro-anatomy, and interpersonal and group dynamics functionally explain aspects of mental architecture (thus experientially acquired processes and contents) that are not explained by the evolution of functional neuroanatomy.

But, of course, this only worsens the initial problem. In both cases, we view something other than the emotional experience as basic – either the material constituents that form the mechanical explanation or the functions that yield the functional explanation. This is, in fact, the way we think of explanation, and it seems largely correct, as far as it goes.

However, this view of explanation leaves something out. Both the mechanical and the functional accounts are comprehensible only by reference to "higher" levels in the explanatory hierarchy. Specifically, any given level in this hierarchy wholly or partly explains the level immediately above (e.g., functional neuroanatomy explains psychological structure). However, any given level simultaneously allows us to

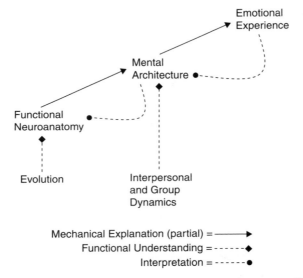

Figure 1.3. A simplified schema of emotion explanation and its interrelation with interpretation.

interpret the level immediately below. Activation of the dorsolateral prefrontal cortex (DLPFC) may be perfectly comprehensible as the causal result of activation along afferent projections. However, as such, it tells us nothing about psychology or about experience. It is only by connecting DLPFC with working memory that we may interpret this material finding in mental terms. Moreover, models of working memory themselves are comprehensible because we interpret them in relation to our experience of holding things in mind – how we do it, what limits we run up against, and so forth. The same points hold for emotion. We might represent this in a diagram along the lines of Figure 1.3.

Representation, Ecological Validity, and Simulation

As we have already noted, literature may play an interpretive role in an encompassing account of emotion, a role in communicating the experiential aspect of emotion. Indeed, this is precisely what makes Lehrer's project successful. The literary works he explores present us with detailed interpretive contexts for comprehending the mechanical explanations articulated by the scientists. By itself, however, this does not mean that literature should have any special role in either discovery or evaluation.

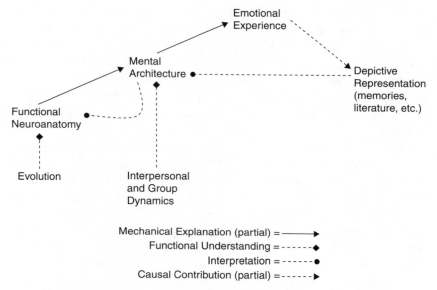

Figure 1.4. A schema of emotion explanation and interpretation that incorporates depictive representation.
Note: I leave aside the precise nature of the relation between emotional experience and depictive representations, assuming only that the latter are in part the causal result of the former, along with other factors.

To consider this issue, we need to begin with some simple and largely familiar points. Again, emotional experience is the fundamental phenomenon being explained by theories of emotion, whether they use a mental architecture including working memory, episodic memory, and so on; a neurobiological architecture of functional neuroanatomy; or some other alternative (e.g., a Connectionist model). Put simply, we do not typically consider amygdala activation or the release of dopamine as the final thing to be explained in an emotion theory. Rather, we consider the activation of the amygdala or the release of dopamine as means of understanding human experiences of fear, addiction, and so forth. However, as just discussed, we do not have access to such experiences directly. Thus the data we are explaining are not the experiences as such, but representations of the experiences. Moreover, these are not processing representations, but depictive representations. To accommodate this point, we need to add a further component to our schema (see Figure 1.4).

The set of depictive representations most obviously available as data are retrospective – memories of emotional experiences, either distant or recent. These are undoubtedly important, but they are far from infallible. First, our memories are reconstructions in light of current conditions (Schacter 8). Moreover, our ongoing judgments of emotional experience (e.g., our causal attributions [see Clore and Ortony 27]) are themselves inferential, thus fallible. In short, the memories we store are imperfect representations of the emotional experience, and the memories we recall are imperfect reconstructions of the (already imperfect) initial memories.

This is not to say that memories of emotional experiences are without probative value in the theorization of emotion. Survey-based studies of emotion, interviews, and similar methods rely in part on the recollection of memories, and they produce extremely useful results. The point is just that data based on such memories are not unproblematic.

One obvious response to this situation is to try to eliminate the time between the experience and the representation, perhaps even substituting some other depictive technique that bypasses the person's own articulation of the experience. For example, in one standard case, researchers will induce a certain emotion in test subjects by, say, showing them pictures. The assent to a label (e.g., "disgust") along with clear eliciting conditions (e.g., a photograph of feces) in effect serves to provide a depictive representation (e.g., roughly, "disgust at seeing feces").

Research of this sort corrects for problems with memory distortion. However, what it gains in directness, it tends to lose in precision, nuance, complexity, and ecological validity. For (apparently) uncomplicated motivational responses, such as disgust, this may not matter a great deal. Our emotional experience of a photograph of feces in a laboratory may not differ greatly from our emotional experience on encountering feces in the street. Moreover, both may be adequately captured by a simple label plus context (such as "disgust on seeing feces"). However, when it comes to more complex social emotions, such as guilt or romantic love, the limitations of the laboratory begin to appear more significant. This is not to say that well-designed experiments cannot tell us important things about complex social emotions. They certainly can. But they are clearly limited by the artificial context – the artificial eliciting conditions for the emotions, the artificial context of social feedback, the artificial restraints and opportunities for expressive and actional response, and so on. They may also be inhibited by the reduction of the emotional experience to brief, necessarily imprecise labels.

In very simple terms, we may distinguish the options thus far in the following way. We have spontaneous emotions in natural settings and we have prompted emotions in unnatural settings. The prompted emotions seem to translate relatively well into minimal depictive representations – usually, an emotion label plus the immediate context of elicitation. In complex cases, that minimal depiction is almost certainly inadequate. Even when the depiction is adequate, the emotional experience itself may not be a good case of the emotion as it occurs spontaneously. The test conditions artificially constrain all the components of emotion – eliciting conditions, expression, actional outcome, and so on. The spontaneous emotions, on the other hand, have the complexity of natural conditions for elicitation, expression, and so forth. However, they seem to translate rather uncertainly into depictive representations that may serve as data for theories of emotion.

Again, all these forms of research contribute to our understanding of emotion. Insofar as they converge on the same conclusions, we can feel fairly confident about our resulting theories. This is no reason, however, to eliminate other forms of emotional experience and its depictive representation, particularly if these seem to solve some of the problems with currently preferred methods (surveys, interviews, laboratory tests, etc.).

Literature is one such alternative. Literature is neither precisely spontaneous nor prompted in the sense of the earlier discussion. Thus it is not the momentary result of a confluence of contingent particulars that have real consequences in our daily lives. But it is also not an entirely artificial and limited provocation undertaken in entirely contrived circumstances. Indeed, one could make a case that literature is, in a certain sense, quite natural and spontaneous. Again, it appears that all societies have verbal art, that it is a part of the lives of people everywhere.[5] We probably have some (indirect) experience of intense cases of many emotions (e.g., romantic love) more often in stories than in life. Of course, our emotional response to stories is not the same as our actual engagement with events that have real consequences for our own practical existence. Nonetheless, such response is a part of our world and of our emotional lives. Beyond that, literature involves the complexity of real life. Moreover, it does so in a way that is already to a great extent available in a depictive representation.

[5] See Hogan *The Mind*.

More exactly, verbal art (e.g., fictional narrative) typically involves an elaborate set of "instructions" (Scarry 244) for simulating an emotional experience. When successful, a literary work produces a complex emotional experience in the reader. This experience is inseparable from the depictive content of the narrative, usually the representation of emotional experiences in the story. Of course, our response to literary depictions necessarily involves encoding and elaboration. These will vary somewhat across individuals and even for the same individual from reading to reading. This problem is partially mitigated, however, by the fact that some works are successful at producing emotional responses across many readers in different times and places – indeed, in different centuries and different continents. Across a large number of instances (probably millions in the case of many paradigmatic works), idiosyncrasies of encoding and elaboration should balance out, leaving the depictive content of the work along with the encoding and elaboration propensities shared by all or most readers. In this way, an emotionally successful work may present us with the closest thing we have to a full, ecologically valid depictive representation of emotional experience. As such, it is an eminently suitable source, not only for the interpretive clarification of explanatory claims (as Lehrer indicates), but for hypotheses about emotion and the partial evaluation of such hypotheses.

It may seem that there are still two types of problematic artificiality in literature. The first concerns the fact that the story need not have derived from an actual emotional experience of the author. Even if it does derive from such an experience, it is often altered beyond anything that commonly occurs in reconstructive memory. The relation of a literary work to an author's prior experiences, prominently including his or her emotional experiences, is a potentially important topic of research. However, the crucial point here is that the depictive validity of a literary work does not derive from its source in some prior experience. It derives from its *production* of such an experience.

The point is related to the second apparent artificiality of literary representations of emotion – their removal from the actual circumstances of life, thus the need for (or even possibility of) actional outcomes.[6] This is true and does indicate that literary works may vary somewhat from our actual experience of emotion in contexts where action is necessary. But, of course, literature does not even seem to provoke the sorts of egocentric emotions that are typically at issue in real-life contexts

---

[6] The restriction on action is stressed by Holland (*Literature*).

demanding action. Rather, they provoke *empathic* emotions.[7] They are directly parallel to the emotions we have when hearing about someone who experienced some joy or sorrow at a distance from us, someone that we can neither help nor harm. In this way, it is true that the probative value of literature is largely limited to empathic emotions. But it seems clear that, first of all, empathic emotions are closely related to egocentric emotions. For example, we typically feel compassion for someone if we would be likely to feel sorrow upon undergoing his or her experiences. Thus, even though there are some differences between empathic and egocentric emotions, simulative depictions that provoke the former should give us a reasonably good sense of the latter as well. Second, empathic emotions are themselves a crucial part of our emotional repertoire anyway and no less significant for a theory of emotion.

In short, depictive representation of emotional experience is crucial for our generation, evaluation, and interpretation of explanatory theories of emotion. But it is difficult to produce depictive representations that are complex, repeatable, and free of distortions due to artificiality, memory reconstruction, and other factors. The instructions for simulation given in literary works seem to be a primary case of such depictions, at least when these works are successful in producing empathic emotions across readers at different times and places. In this way, it seems that literary study should have an important role in the scientific study of emotion.

One might object to this conclusion on the following grounds. The source of the study of vision is visual experience, just as the source of the study of emotion is emotional experience. However, no one would conclude from this that "vision scientists would have to rely upon literary descriptions of visual experiences in order to gain access to the beginning of a science of vision" (as a colleague put it). Several points are important here. First, my claim is not that psychologists and neuroscientists need literature for the "beginning" of a science of emotion. I am not even saying that they *need* literature at all. I am merely saying that – like everything from statistical surveys to fMRI scans – literature could be a valuable part of research on emotion. (Note that research on emotion does not *need* fMRI scans and certainly did begin without them. That does not make these scans any less valuable.) Second,

---

[7] They also provoke aesthetic emotions, such as delight in the beauty of language. I leave these aside, however, because I assume the value of arts for research in aesthetics is uncontroversial.

the issue is not descriptions of visual experiences or descriptions of emotional experiences. The issue is, rather, descriptions or other depictions that are repeatedly successful in producing particular visual or emotional experiences. If a theory of visual processing has no way of accounting for how we see figures in drawings, then it is an inadequate theory. Indeed, if it has no way of accounting for how we envision objects or persons from descriptions, and why literary descriptions tend to be particularly vivid in this regard (as discussed at length by Scarry), then it is an inadequate theory. The same point holds for our emotional responses to art and literature. Finally, and most importantly, in real life, our emotional responses are bound up with complex and most often temporally extended experiential situations that are very difficult to capture depictively. Literature at least approximates that depictive complexity. The case of vision does not seem parallel in this crucial respect. Most obviously, we can create and thus control complex visual experiences in a laboratory. Visual recording equipment allows us to generate good depictive representations of those experiences, which are in effect momentary (at least in comparison with emotion).

Some Limits on the Depictive Accuracy of Literature

Of course, to say that literature should figure prominently in emotion research is not to answer the question of just how it should figure in that research. Nothing in the preceding argument indicates that literature must be taken at face value for research in emotion. Put differently, to say that a depictive representation provokes simulation that is emotionally effective is not to say that it represents real situations accurately in all details – even in all details that are effective for the emotion simulation.

First, a perhaps obvious point but one worth making explicit: The overt, literal claims made about emotion in literary works have no special theoretical status. Such statements may operate as part of the overall simulative effect of the work. But they are not, in general, comparable to scientific hypotheses about emotion. Indeed, my suspicion is that works of literature become less valuable for the study of emotion precisely to the degree that their composition was guided by prior theories of emotion.[8] Such guidance may be indicated by the explicit articulation of generalizations about emotion.

[8] For this reason, the literary analyses in the following chapters will not be concerned with treating theories of emotion that were current at the time Shakespeare, Li, Issa,

Second, even the events, character traits, causal relations, and other plot features of a literary story cannot be assumed to depict emotional conditions accurately. Of course, the success of a work does suggest that, on the whole, its depiction of events and other previously mentioned elements must be close enough to personal experience that the resulting simulation will provoke parallel empathic emotions (e.g., compassion for the suffering of the protagonist). But a crucial point here is that a successful work is a work that enhances the reader's emotional response. It is not necessarily the case that increased accuracy in the representation of an emotional experience produces such enhancement. Indeed, it may be the case that increased representational accuracy will, in certain respects, diminish empathic response. For example, it may be the case that romantic love is never unambivalent, that it is always somewhat wavering, that even the most devoted lovers remain aware of other possible sexual partners. However, it may also be the case that readers will experience less empathic intensity in response to Romeo if Romeo occasionally notices the alluring features of a passing Philomena. Thus the playwright is well advised to make Romeo's devotion to Juliet complete and entirely constant. Thus we might expect literature to deviate from depictive accuracy through *idealization*.[9]

Taking up one component of a standard theory of emotion, we might isolate two sorts of idealization here. Following LeDoux (*Emotional*) and others, we may distinguish two streams of emotional response. One, largely subcortical, involves the activation of emotion systems by external or internal stimuli (e.g., the sudden appearance of something bearlike). The other, cortical and largely prefrontal, involves modulation of that activation due to the availability of more information (e.g., that it is not a bear, but a doll), the recruitment of memories or other information in inferences (e.g., a memory that this type of bear

---

or others were writing. Exploring the relation of literary texts to contemporary medical and related discourses is certainly valuable and interpretively consequential. (For examples of this sort of research, see the essays in Paster, Rowe, and Floyd-Wilson; for a general approach of this sort to Shakespeare, see Paster *Humoring* and "Tragic.") However, it is a different project from the one undertaken here.

[9] There are various types of distortive emotional intensification, some of which will turn up in later chapters. For example, some emotions take time to develop. But it may be more effective in a given story to portray a particular emotion – such as romantic love – as arising very quickly. These are idealizations in the sense that they make depictive representations ideally emotionally effective for an audience. As this suggests, the term "idealization" should not be taken to imply that such depictive distortions are invariably moral improvements, as the case of Romeo's sustained fidelity may suggest – though idealization does often involve an ethical element.

only attacks moving targets, so I should inhibit my inclination to run), and so on. We may refer to these as the "arousal" and "modulation" components of emotional experience.[10] In referring to the constancy of Romeo, we have probably isolated a form of idealization in modulation (i.e., idealization bearing on audience members' modulation of their emotion). If Romeo seems interested in Philomena, we judge him and his emotional experience negatively, down-regulating our simulation of his attachment to Juliet, and thus limiting our empathic response to his hopes and sorrows. A case of arousal idealization may be found in depictions of sexual attractiveness in cases of romantic love. As the ancient Sanskrit theorists stressed, some emotional experiences are at least partially incompatible with others. For example, disgust tends to disrupt the experience of erotic love (see Chari 66). It is presumably no accident that, cross-culturally, depictions of the hero's beloved do not stress mucus or flatulence.

Thus we might expect literary depictions of emotion to be inaccurate in areas where either arousal or modulation idealization might enter. Of course, this does not mean that we merely dismiss such aspects of literary works. They bear on emotional response and are therefore relevant to a theory of emotion as well. However, we must approach the literary depictions with caution in areas where such idealization is likely.

Idealization is not the only distortive element here. A great deal of our emotional lives is bound up with group identifications, and our empathic responses are shaped by racial, ethnic, religious, national, gender, and other affiliations. For example, research shows that racial differences may inspire fear and/or anger, signaled by amygdala activation (see Ito, *et al.*, 196). Authors are undoubtedly affected by such group biases. Moreover, authors may enhance spontaneous biases, self-consciously or unself-consciously, by elaborating on them in ways that have political functions. These points suggest that, depending on the author and target audience of a work, there may be systematic distortions in keeping with the spontaneous experience of group affiliations (the arousal level) or ideological enhancements of such affiliations (the evaluation level). Thus we would expect works in patriarchal societies to treat male infidelity more indulgently than female infidelity. For instance, it seems perfectly innocuous that Romeo was in love with Rosaline before meeting Juliet. This does not seem to count against

---

[10] I realize that this is overly simple. The point is merely to isolate the two tendencies broadly in order to develop our understanding of idealization.

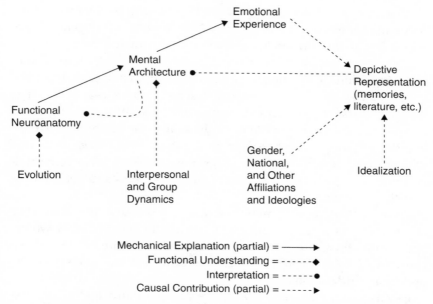

Figure 1.5 A final version of the explanation/interpretation schema that incorporates distorting factors.

him. However, it is not clear that the same point would hold if Juliet had a previous romantic attachment.[11] We may schematize the incorporation of these distorting factors as in Figure 1.5.

Three Levels of Literary Relevance to the Study of Emotion

If we remain aware of the biases in literary depictions of emotion, the preceding arguments indicate that literature should prove a valuable resource for emotion study. Of course, it already has proven to be such a resource, in works by Oatley (*Best*, "Why"), Nussbaum (*Upheavals*), and others. The obvious way of drawing on literature for emotion

[11] It is important to stress that I am counting this as part of patriarchal ideology, not part of some biologically determined double standard. On the serious problems with such a biological account, despite its popularity, see Harris; Russell and Harton; and DeSteno, Valdesolo, and Bartlett (627) and citations. As Harris points out, somewhat understating the case, "caution is warranted in treating laws, mores, and other cultural or societal phenomena" – including literary works – "as direct reflections of the emotional state of 'sexual jealousy' as experienced by an individual." These phenomena "in many societies were chiefly [composed and] enacted by men and, thus, are more likely to reflect the preferences and thoughts of men rather than women" (124).

theorization is to treat individual works. This will be the focus of the following chapters. However, there are two other levels of generality at which one might draw on literature to treat emotion.

The first level is the existence of literature itself, the systematic simulation of emotional experience. The bare fact of literature is so obvious and ubiquitous that it seems unremarkable. But it is highly remarkable. We actually spend time and effort reading about unknown – indeed, nonexistent – individuals who go through experiences that have no direct bearing on our lives. Sometimes we do this when it makes us sad. Yet we still enjoy the process and even come back for more. In this way, the mere fact of literature seems a valuable source of insight into emotion.

Second, there is an important level in between the generality of literature as a whole and the particularity of individual works. Specifically, there are widespread cross-cultural patterns in literary genre (see Hogan *The Mind*). These too provide a valuable source for understanding emotion.[12]

Because all the remaining chapters address individual works, the rest of this chapter considers the two more general topics, focusing on narrative.

The Generality of Verbal Art: On Stories

The first point to make about storytelling goes back at least to Aristotle, who maintained that we enjoy "mimesis" (14, 15). There is undoubtedly some truth in that. However, it is not clear that this is quite the right formulation of what we enjoy in verbal art. We do seem to enjoy the imitation of particular people, accents, and the like. But, with respect to verbal art, it is probably more accurate to say that we enjoy *simulation* (cf. Oatley "Why"). Of course, we do not enjoy every sort of simulation, just as we do not enjoy every sort of story. As a rough approximation,

---

[12] Royzman and Rozin implicitly recognize the value of such cross-story patterns in their treatment of symhedonia. Specifically, they explain that "sympathy may ... induce caring (emotional attachment)" (91), which may then allow for symhedonia (feeling joy for someone else). The sympathy and attachment are important because, according to their research, symhedonia is particularly difficult to provoke outside of attachment relations. They go on to suggest that this may "offer a partial explanation for the upward trajectory of many a popular narrative, from *Rocky* to *Harry Potter*, whose ultimately triumphant characters begin as underdogs mired in obscurity and defeat. Perhaps creators of such narratives are implicitly aware of and are intuitively exploring the attachment-building function of sympathetic sorrow" (92).

we might say that we enjoy stories (thus simulations) that present us with significant emotional experiences. This is unsurprising when the emotions are intrinsically pleasurable. We do not need a further explanation for human interest in comic works. But in fact, human stories contain a great deal of aversive emotion as well – such as pity and fear, in Aristotle's account of tragedy. This is more puzzling. This points to a research question that goes well beyond literature. Why is it that we engage in simulation of emotionally aversive situations?

The suggestion of literary experience is, again, that we experience some sort of pleasure in simulation as such. In terms of functional explanation, this makes sense. There is a clear survival function in imagining possible painful outcomes of our actions. For example, Glug might imagine going to gather berries in a place where there are lots of bears, and thus being mauled. As a result, he avoids those actions. In contrast, suppose Mutt avoids the displeasing imagination initially. As a result, he goes to gather berries, with tragic (and genetically consequential) results. In this way, experiencing pleasure in aversive imaginations and associated emotional elaborations is eminently adaptive.

At the same time, our experience of literature also suggests that there is a partial conflict between the aversive emotions in the simulation and the pleasure derived from them, and that we differ individually in our precise response to that conflict. Some people continue to feel pleasure even with high degrees of fear or disgust, whereas others have less tolerance for these feelings. We also begin to see a social and ideological function in the gender division that links male tolerance for aversive emotions to combative or other heroic situations (e.g., in war stories) and female tolerance for aversive emotions to bonding relations (e.g., stories of parental self-sacrifice).

Of course, here as elsewhere, the difficult part is isolating the mechanisms that underlie emotional responses. Even functional accounts must ultimately be based not only on behavioral manifestations, but on an algorithmic treatment of biological processes. Still, literature helps point us toward at least some preliminary functional hypotheses. Moreover, in the context of current emotion theories, it may point us toward research on substrates as well. For example, the pleasure in simulation may hint at some sort of reward system involvement.[13]

---

[13] The involvement of the reward system in compassion (see Kim and colleagues) suggests this as well, because compassion involves simulation of normally aversive feelings.

A second suggestion from the ubiquity of literature was also anticipated in critical traditions. This is usually referred to as "expressiveness." The European Romantic stress on literature as the expression of emotion is too well known to require comment.[14] But the idea turns up elsewhere as well. For example, the great tenth-to-eleventh-century Japanese novelist, Lady Murasaki, wrote that literary narrative "happens because the storyteller's own experience ... – not only what he has passed through himself, but even events which he has only witnessed or been told of – has moved him to an emotion so passionate that he can no longer keep it shut up in his heart" (501). As in the case of Aristotle, the critical formulations are close but not precisely right. It is not quite the expression of emotion that is at issue. After all, the poet does not go out alone in the woods and sing poems to nature. That is expressive, but it would not satisfy the craving isolated by Murasaki. Artists compose their stories for other people. They compose to be read or heard. This suggests that we have a deep need to share emotionally consequential experiences. The point applies not just to artists, but to readers as well. We want other people to read the books we like, see the movies we enjoyed. We want to discuss those books, communicating our enjoyment and hearing of our friends' enjoyment as well.

This is related to, yet distinct from, what Bernard Rimé has discussed in his path-breaking *Partage social des emotions* (see also Rimé "Emotion"). Rimé treats real emotional experiences that people directly and explicitly discuss with one another. Literature points us toward an attempt at actually re-creating the eliciting conditions of the emotion in such a way as to reproduce the emotional effect. We may refer to the former as "communicative" sharing and the latter as "experiential" or "simulative" sharing. Of course, communicative sharing of emotional experiences always involves some attempt at depicting the eliciting conditions of the experience. Depending on the literary skill of the speaker, this may come close to the simulative sharing that occurs in verbal art. The distinction is not absolute. But there is a clear difference in tendency.[15]

---

[14] For a discussion of the value of Romantic thought in the study of emotion, see Oatley, Keltner, and Jenkins 108–110.

[15] Rimé stresses that, in what I have called "communicative" emotion sharing, the addressee – or "sharee" – does experience emotion. This is the result of empathy with the speaker's – or sharer's – egocentric emotions. In experiential sharing, however, the sharer's emotions are not the source for the sharee's feelings. Rather, both the sharer and the sharee derive the (empathic) feelings from attention to a situation for

Although Rimé notes that happy experiences are widely shared, his account of the reasons for and effects of sharing – particularly his stress on social support – applies most obviously to emotions that are sorrowful, even traumatic.[16] Moreover, it applies to experiences that the speaker probably wants to communicate but probably does not want to share experientially with the addressee – at least not if he or she at all cares for the addressee and thus would not like to see him or her traumatized. In both ways, Rimé's explanations do not seem to cover the case of literature – either literature that authors wish to share with readers or literature that readers wish to share with one another. Indeed, Rimé's account raises the question of just why successful literary works appear to have beneficial emotional effects for readers, given that the effects of communicative sharing are generally experienced by the speaker rather than the listener. Finally, Rimé's account works well for personal interactions but not for relatively impersonal interactions, such as we find with an author and his or her readers. None of this indicates that Rimé's explanations are incorrect. They are rather compelling for the types of case he considers. However, it does suggest that they are incomplete. There is something else going on – something else suggested by literature.

There are two obvious evolutionary functions that we might hypothesize for experiential/simulative sharing of emotion. The first is that our emotion systems may require something like calibration. We have innate sensitivities to certain sorts of situation and we have experiences that form further emotional propensities. But these innate, then developmentally inflected sensitivities are not fixed at an absolute point for all people. For example, Cacioppo and Patrick emphasize that different degrees of social isolation are required to produce a sense of

which they are both observers (e.g., a literary work for which they are both readers). The point may be clarified by reference to developmental precursors of these types of sharing. The developmental roots of communicative sharing are presumably in such experiences as the child falling and tearfully reporting the fall to an attachment figure. In contrast, the childhood roots of experiential emotion sharing are probably in certain forms of joint attention of the child and caregiver.

[16] Rimé does not ignore the function of positive emotion sharing. Specifically, he points to a correlation between "relationship well-being" and "enthusiastic" response to a partner's positive emotion sharing. He concludes that "sharing positive emotions ... enhances ... social bonds" ("Emotion" 65). But the idea is left somewhat undeveloped and the correlation is not fully explained. One possibility is that a partner's enthusiastic, thus strongly mirroring, response to positive sharing shows his or her lack of envy or other empathy-blocking emotions. This, in turn, may serve to reinforce the sharer's sense of trust – a version of the pattern outlined further in this chapter.

loneliness in different individuals (15). Moreover, emotional sensitivities may vary temporarily even for a particular individual depending on the engagement of different emotional, perceptual, inferential, or other processes at a given time. An inclination to continually check our emotional responses against those of other people might help balance idiosyncrasies of our past or current experience, even perhaps of our own innate predispositions, by affecting elaborative or even encoding processes.

Of course, readers or viewers do not typically feel compelled to share movies or books with just anyone. Our pursuit of experiential sharing is particularly directed toward friends and family members (a point in keeping with research on emotion sharing generally, as discussed by Rimé). This suggests that our interest in the experiential sharing of emotions is particularly enhanced by attachment bonds.

This points toward a second possible function of emotion sharing. Sharing of important emotional experiences not only serves to test and calibrate our own emotional responses; it also serves to establish the degree to which another person has parallel or complementary responses to our emotions. One person's emotions tend to have emotional consequences for anyone with whom he or she is interacting. These consequences may be parallel – when Jones is sad, Smith becomes sad. But they may also be complementary – when Jones suffers grief, Smith overflows with *Schadenfreude*. It is well established that we feel more comfortable and friendly with someone who mirrors our expressions, actions, and the like (see Iacoboni 113–114). Sharing emotional experiences is one way of establishing a situation in which one can tacitly evaluate the degree and consequence of such mirroring beyond trivialities, such as repeating verbal idioms. In this way, the sharing of such experiences is a way of getting a feel for the depth of an attachment relation that already exists or the possibilities for developing an attachment relation where one does not already exist.[17]

Communicative sharing of personal experiences has the advantage of directly treating the particular relation of the sharer (or "narrator") and addressee to real events. But communicative sharing is necessarily limited in scope. Moreover, discrepancies in emotional attitudes may be

---

[17] As already noted, research by Royzman and Rozin suggests that empathic joy is more distinctive of attachment relations. This may suggest that the sharing of positive experiences, as in the sharing of literature, may be more consequential for particular aspects of attachment response. Note that, in sharing a literary work, we are typically sharing a work that we enjoy, even if it is tragic.

occluded by the fact that empathy in such situations is often obligatory. Put simply, one's partner may express compassion for one's situation, but have quite different (non-mirroring) responses to the events themselves. Sharing literary experiences, in contrast, may expose compatible or incompatible emotional responses more unconcealedly, and it will do so in a much broader range of possible cases. (Literary scenarios are not confined to one's actual experiences.) Finally, the development of an attachment relation may itself be bound up with the development of a repertoire of emotional memories based, most importantly, on shared experiences. When two people read the same book or see the same movie, they have, in effect, shared the experience of the book or movie. That is not the case when one person recounts events to the other.

The ideological operation of literature in such areas as gender also suggests a social function here. In sharing literary experiences, people do not necessarily appeal indifferently to everyone with whom they have bonding relations. Nor do they confine themselves to such relations. Rather, they often have a particular interest in what they take to be relevant identity groups. There are plenty of men who will not go to a movie that is labeled a "chick flick." If they happen to go to such a movie, then, by gender norms, they should find it boring or otherwise aversive. The sharing of emotional experiences in these cases is also, in a sense, corrective. But it is corrective not toward a reasonable or adaptive response (e.g., toward an appropriate degree of worry, given the situation). Rather, it is corrective toward ideologically defined gender norms.

Universal Genres: The Love Story

Related issues arise at the level of genre. In *The Mind and Its Stories*, I have drawn on a wide range of traditions in literature and orature to argue for the existence of three universal narrative prototypes – romantic, heroic, and sacrificial. Here, we might consider the romantic narrative. Many of the most widely admired or "paradigmatic" stories in the major literary traditions of East Asia, South Asia, the Middle East, Europe, and elsewhere converge toward a familiar pattern. Two people fall in love. They encounter an obstacle to their union, commonly in the form of some superior social authority. That authority is most often parental. However, it may also be religious or political. The opposition frequently results from the lovers belonging to identity groups that do not intermarry – different classes, castes, societies, and so on. There is often a rival (belonging to a group that is seen as appropriate for inter-marriage) who is preferred by the blocking social authority. This leads to the physical separation of the lovers. Commonly, one is confined and the other is exiled. During this separation, there may be death (in tragic versions) or imagery of death. There is also often some form of indirect communication that serves to sustain both the hope and the suffering of the lovers. The exiled lover may achieve social or spiritual success, which facilitates union with the beloved. The reunion often includes a reconciliation with family, though the rival often dies or is exiled.

This structure suggests many things. First, it is consistent with some common observations about the nature of love. The lovers' relation to one another strongly suggests a combination of sexual desire and attachment.[18] The intense longing of the lovers and pain in separation further suggests the involvement of the endogenous reward system.[19] But these points have not gone unremarked in the literature on roman-tic love. So what does knowledge about the genre add to our possible understanding of romantic love?

First, and most obviously, it suggests that commonplaces about the cultural relativity of romantic love are, at best, exaggerations. Undoubtedly, there are some differences in the precise working out of romantic relations – in different cultures and historical periods, but also in various individual conditions. But if these differences were pro-found and uniform, if (say) Chinese and European cultures differed fundamentally in the development of emotions, then we would not have paradigmatic works with the romantic structure (such as *Romance of the Western Chamber* and *Romeo and Juliet*) in each tradition. This illus-trates the leveling out of idiosyncrasies through the establishment of paradigms. Suppose one Chinese person at one time wrote a romantic story that only a handful of people read. That would tell us something (perhaps that, despite cultural differences, Chinese were not entirely impervious to romantic love). But it would not tell us very much. The appearance of the story and the response of its few readers could be aberrations within a broad cultural pattern. The interest of those indi-vidual readers need not even be due to the romantic elements of the

---

[18] On the integration of attachment and sexual desire in romantic love – along with care-giving, understood as a system distinct from attachment – see Shaver and Mikulincer. We will consider this integration further in Chapter 3.

[19] On the role of the ventral tegmental area and the nucleus accumbens, as well as the operation of dopamine and oxytocin – all involved in the endogenous reward system – see Fisher 90–91.

story. Indeed, these different readers may not even be responding to the same elements. Perhaps the heroine fondly reminds one reader of his or her sister, whereas another reader appreciates the cadence of the songs. However, when romantic narratives are read with great empathic engagement by a wide range of readers over many centuries, this suggests that the responses are not merely idiosyncratic, but share common features.

More importantly, the cross-cultural occurrence of this genre has implications for the interaction among certain emotive and cognitive systems. The often harsh behavior of parents toward children in such stories suggests that rage may have particularly close interrelations with the desire for attachment reciprocity. The relation here is particularly interesting because it appears to be triggered by the combination of sexuality and attachment (i.e., the child falling in love with someone else), even though the initial parent-child relation is not sexual. Moreover, this harsh behavior indicates that the activation of the anger system will inhibit attachment feelings, at least temporarily. All emotions here are also modulated by social hierarchies. One challenge for emotion theory is to give an algorithmic account of how the parental sense of entitlement tends to promote, or perhaps simply disinhibit, anger in a context of attachment.

Similarly, the frequently harsh treatment of the rival suggests complex processes of inhibition and enhancement across systems that interact in attachment and perhaps in sexual relations. Though the rival is often rather bland, he or she seems to inspire particular repulsion, which readers evidently accept (e.g., they do not reject the stories due to the fate of the rival). My conjecture here is that, first, attachment inhibits disgust regarding the attachment object (as sometimes noted in research; see Lieberman and Hatfield 291). Second, when the attachment object is also a sexual object, it enhances disgust toward other possible sexual objects (thus toward the rival). This hypothesis is undoubtedly overly simple. However, it may point to some of the emotion dynamics operating here.

Through exile and confinement, the romantic prototype also makes spatial organization a crucial part of the lovers' emotional experience. As such, it points toward ways of elaborating on the relation between our emotional organization of space and our attachment system (on the basic connection between person attachment and place attachment, see Panksepp *Affective* 265). Romantic stories indicate that we have an emotional organization of space that is neither the objective hippocampal organization nor the egocentric parietal organization (on these systems, see Clark, Boutros, and Mendez 43). Rather, it is a centering of space in the attachment object. Here, the object is the romantic beloved, but the point obviously extends to a child's relation to a caregiver.

We could continue teasing out particular psychological implications of the genre.[20] However, there are social aspects of emotion study that are indicated by the ubiquity of this genre as well. First, the genre suggests that societies commonly, perhaps invariably, form themselves into endogamous groups. However, individual attachment relations are not determined by these social divisions. Accidents of personal development and social interaction will invariably lead to situations in which feelings cross group boundaries – not only the feeling of sexual desire, but attachment and the dependency of reward system satisfaction. Empirical research indicates intergroup antagonism may be suppressed through self-conscious effort at one point, only to arise more intensely when that self-conscious effort is relaxed (see Kunda 345–346). The recurrence of intergroup attachments suggests that perhaps the reverse happens as well. Out-group members may be subjected to a form of effortful exclusion from sexual consideration, sometimes called "erotic discounting." When this effort is not made, however, desires and attachments may arise more forcefully.

Finally, the recurrence of the romantic plot suggests something about empathy. Again, empathy is at the basis of our emotional responses to literature. Some writers maintain that it is not just empathy; there is also suspense and other emotions. It is true that there are some emotions that arise in literary experience that are nonempathic. For example, our surprise at a new development in a literary work is our own surprise; it is not empathic surprise for a character. However, with only rare exceptions, these are not the emotions that sustain our reading of a literary work. If we do not have some empathic response to the characters and their concerns, it is very unlikely that we will be at all engaged by a story. Here, we might consider suspense. Suppose that, watching a movie, I feel suspense about whether or not the heroine will escape the serial killer. My suspense there is based almost entirely on my empathic connection with the heroine. It is not (again, with rare exceptions) a disinterested contemplation – nor is it an egocentric emotion, because I am not being pursued by the serial killer, nor is any of my friends or relatives.

---

[20] We will return to some of these implications in Chapter 3.

What is striking about the development of empathic response in romantic plots is that it almost invariably cultivates empathy for the lovers. Put differently, the "comic" conclusion involves the union of the lovers, not the triumph of the rival and the parents. Given the force of social ideology, we would have expected romantic plots to strongly favor social hierarchy and respect for in-group boundaries. But that is not what we find – although both the hierarchy and the group boundaries are stressed in such stories. This suggests that many of us have a strong emotional preference for attachment over group norms when the two are in conflict. This preference is shared by a significant number of people cross-culturally and holds empathically as well as egocentrically.

This last point may be extended and complicated by reference to other cross-cultural genres. For example, the recurrence of revenge stories in unrelated narrative traditions[21] may suggest that part of the preference here may be for "individuating" emotional relations over group divisions and social hierarchies, although the revenge stories are much more ambivalent than the love stories. Specifically, one of the hallmarks of attachment and revenge-inspiring hate is that both emotions are individuating. Most emotions operate by reference to general properties. For instance, certain *types* of properties are sexually arousing or frightening. But attachment is not a matter of general properties; rather, it is a matter of distinctive particularity. We are attached to a particular person. This is the reason that attachment leads us to focus on such unique properties as the beloved's voice. Similar points hold for vengeful hatred. Indeed, this similarity may suggest a relation between hatred and attachment, a relation further indicated by the connection of both with betrayal.

Conclusion

It may seem that neuronal structure and connections are fundamental and emotional experience is derivative. In an explanatory framework, this is true. But it is misleading. Simply to understand a particular amygdala activation as fear, we need to interpret the activation in relation to emotional experience. In that way, emotional experience is fundamental interpretively. When an fMRI researcher or developmental psychologist tries to understand fear, he or she cannot even start

---

[21] On the cross-cultural pattern of revenge plots, see chapter 4 of Hogan *Affective*.

without some intuitive sense of fear; fMRI studies on fear would not be done or would make no sense without being guided by – and then interpreted in relation to – such experience.

The issue then is just how we are to draw on this experience. Intuition alone is unanalyzed, vague, and various. As such, it is hardly an appropriate source for guiding and interpreting research. Rather, we need depictive representations – clearly articulated formulations of what fear (or love or anger) might be. There are different approaches to crafting such depictive representations. There are studies of perceptual responses (e.g., to images of snakes in various contexts), studies of personal memories (e.g., interviews or questionnaires bearing on grief and mourning), and so on. All the standard methods for orienting, developing, and evaluating emotion research have strengths and weaknesses. For example, what is gained in precision and replicability is often lost in ecological validity.

The main contention of this chapter is that literature presents a unique – in some ways – set of depictive representations of emotional experience. These representations are, in effect, instructions for the simulation of emotionally consequential experiences that, when successful, produce empathic emotional experiences in readers. As such, they not only have an important interpretive place in relation to explanatory theories of emotion. They also – and more importantly – provide objects for theoretical consideration, thus sources of information or data about emotion. Like other sources of data about emotion, they should therefore contribute to the generation of hypotheses or research orientations regarding emotion and to the evaluation of accounts of emotion.

This role of literature is enhanced by the fact that it avoids the simplification and artificiality that affect laboratory research. Literature also avoids distortive reconstruction from memory and researcher interference – problems that affect research embedded in natural settings. Of course, it is not perfect. Like all data, it requires interpretation and evaluation. Specifically, literature involves different types of idealization (based on arousal and modulation), in-group bias, and ideological revision. On the other hand, idealization, in-group bias, and ideological revision are also part of our emotional lives and thus relevant to a research program in emotion.

There are three obvious levels at which literature bears on the study of emotion – the level of the particular work, the level of generic or related patterns across works (particularly patterns that are cross-cultural), and the level of the most general conditions and properties of literature. We may find suggestions for possible research orientations and possible evidence for particular hypotheses at each level.

At the third, most general level, relevant data include the pleasure we experience in simulating even emotionally aversive situations, as well as our propensity to seek the experiential sharing of emotions. Both suggest possible evolutionary and social/ideological explanatory functions, with some hint of mechanical explanations as well.

At the next level, the cross-cultural romantic genre points toward an emotional organization of space bound up with attachment. It also indicates both inhibitory and disinhibitory relations involving the disgust system and the attachment system. It points toward a complex interaction between anger and attachment systems either initiated or exacerbated by the introduction of sexuality and further affected by discrepancies in social hierarchy. It suggests the importance of in-group/out-group divisions to the establishment of erotic discounting, but also ways in which such discounting may be unstable. Finally, it indicates that many people in different times and places have a preference for attachment relations over social norms in cases where the two are in conflict. This point is particularly striking because it appears to apply not only to egocentric but also to empathic emotions. This may result in part from the individuating quality of attachment (as opposed to other emotions, which tend to be triggered by repeatable properties). As such, this preference may extend – in a more limited and ambivalent way – even to negative individuating emotions, such as certain cases of hate.

2. What Emotions Are

The purpose of this chapter is to outline the basic principles of a theory of the general operation of emotion. This theory synthesizes and partially extends elements from the growing body of research on emotion, and at the same time anticipates some of the ideas drawn from literature in the following chapters. Integrating this work into a largely neurocognitive framework, it argues for a multicomponent yet still constrained – or "minimal" – account of emotion.

Specifically, the chapter presents a view of emotion episodes as initiated by concrete perceptual triggers (including remembered and imagined perceptions). These triggers have their effects in relation to particular receptive states on the part of the perceiver. The receptive states, in turn, result from innate sensitivities, critical period developments, and more diffuse experiences (the last stored as emotional memories). In this way, emotion episodes do not result from probability calculations, as commonly indicated in dominant appraisal-based theories of emotion. (The confinement of elicitors to perceptual features is what makes the account minimalist.) On the other hand, appraisals do enter into this account as part of elaborative processes that trigger emotions by recruiting images and memories. One contention of the present chapter is that such a multicomponent yet still minimal theory provides a better account of emotion than mainstream appraisal theory. This is in part because it seeks to integrate the insights of appraisal theory into a more rigorously algorithmic treatment of the onset and development of emotion episodes.

The Structural Components of Emotion: Neurons, Neuroanatomical Regions, and Systems

There are different levels at which one may approach emotion. As noted in the preceding chapter, we might distinguish the intentional or experiential level, the level of "objective" psychology, and the level of the neural substrate. Again, any psychology of emotion will ultimately have to be instantiated in neurological architecture. In other words, barring some radical revision of our understanding of the human brain, any psychological theory will ultimately have to make sense in terms of neuronal connections, neurochemistry, and so on. With this in mind, we may begin with some basic principles of emotional neurology that may help us understand the basic structures of a psychology of emotion.

Within neurocognitive architecture, the fundamental unit is the neuron. Above the neuron, we have interconnected neuron populations, most importantly the regions of gross functional neuroanatomy. Above that, we have systems, and above systems we have the relations among systems. We may take these as our starting point.

At the neuronal level, there may or may not be emotional specification for individual neurons. There is certainly some specialization at the neuronal level in some systems. For example, there are individual neurons that respond to particular visual phenomena. Downstream from these, there are neurons that respond to particular complexes of afferent (incoming) neuronal activation (thus, in effect, particular complexes of visual phenomena), and so on. Though my subsequent analyses will not strictly rely on the assumption, we might conjecture that there is at least something along the lines of neuronal specialization with emotion also. The specialization would bear not only on input (thus precisely what conditions activate the neurons) but also on outputs (thus, precisely what physiological, actional, attentional, or other processes follow from the inputs). The reason for this conjecture is simple. The inputs and outputs of individual neurons will be unique. As such, they should be differentiated in precisely what activates them and precisely what they activate. Translated into experiential terms, this should work its way out as different sensitivities (on the input side) and different consequences (on the output side).

The importance of the conjecture is that it allows in principle for a range of highly particularized emotion events that may not be fully correlated with the regional boundaries of gross functional neuroanatomy or emotion systems. Put simply, neuronal differentiation for emotion operation would seem to entail that two experiences of fear are not precisely the same if they involve distinct neuron populations. Indeed, since precise neuronal connections will not be identical across individuals, this suggests that there is inevitable individual diversity in emotion. This also opens the possibility of emotional experiences that do not really fit any of our usual emotion categories because they are the result of activation in unusually diverse neuron populations. Finally, this allows in principle for an integration of two seemingly opposed views of emotion. One view sees individual emotions as complexes of components. The other view posits discrete emotions as fundamental. As Husted, Shapira, and Goodman put it, the two views differ on whether "emotions truly stem from compartmentalized systems or arise from a multidimensional framework" (390). If there is neuron-level specialization, then we would expect there to be something componential going on in each emotion. The components (or some equivalent) would be, most basically, the specialized neurons, which can be part of somewhat different, activated populations at any given time. However, the idea of discrete emotions can still be accommodated by larger structures – primarily those of gross functional neuroanatomy. In this way, the two approaches can be combined in an algorithmically well-specified way.[1]

This leads us to the level of neuroanatomy. There appear to be broad tendencies for emotional specialization related to areas of the brain – largely, but not entirely, subcortical areas. As Husted, Shapira, and Goodman put it, "individual emotions may be controlled by distinct neural substrates" (389). For example, it appears to be well established now that the amygdala is crucially involved in fear (on the role of particular nuclei, see LeDoux *Emotional*, 157–178). There is evidence of an anterior insular cortical role in disgust (see Husted, Shapira, and Goodman for discussion) and some areas of the basal ganglia in trust (see King-Casas and colleagues). On the other hand, this sort of localization for emotions may be overly simple – or it may be overly simple for some emotions and not others. More exactly, we have reason to believe that there is some sort of regional specialization. This is most

---

[1] When discussing different views of emotion, I am invariably faced with the question, "Why can't all the approaches be correct?" It probably is the case that different theoretical accounts all tell us something about emotion, at least in pointing toward different data that an encompassing theory would need to treat. However, at least on the surface, these theories are usually incompatible. Saying that we will combine them often amounts to saying that we will not make an effort to formulate a coherent theory, thus to formulate a theory with explanatory force. One has successfully combined different theories only to the extent that the resulting theory involves an algorithmic specification of the explanatory principles involved in that reconciliation. Later sections of this chapter will try to reconcile appraisal and neurological accounts of emotional response in an algorithmically well-specified way.

obviously explained as the result of specialization of neurons that are densely interconnected in particular regions. If understood in this way, we would expect regional specialization to be, so to speak, fuzzier or more variable than the underlying neuronal specialization, because the precise activations could vary in any instance and the precise projections among neurons could vary across time. Moreover, we need not expect these regional specializations to correspond directly with the emotion words that occur in our languages – even in the case of putatively basic emotions. In some cases, regional activation patterns may correspond with a single emotion term. For example, it seems to be the case that, if you have a certain sort of amygdala activation, then you have fear. However, it may be that other sorts of localized regional activation do not fit particular emotion terms. For example, it may be that insular cortical activation is insufficient to constitute disgust.

This leads us beyond localized emotion regions to (nonlocalized) emotion systems and the relations among systems. Emotion systems are the complex interconnections of regions that are activated in concert during an emotion episode. In principle, these include the entire range of structures and processes that we will discuss in anatomizing emotion episodes further in this chapter. However, it is important to distinguish between regions that are active across emotion episodes generally and those that are specific to some subset of emotion episodes. For example, dorsolateral prefrontal (DLPF) processes of working memory probably come into play in any emotional experience. It is, therefore, important to count these processes as part of an emotion episode. However, it would be misleading to refer to DLPF cortex as part of the fear system, for example, because that would imply a particular DLPF function in fear.

This view of emotion systems allows for a second level at which we may locate the emotions corresponding to particular ordinary-language terms. Such emotions may be specified regionally (as in the case of fear) or as more complex activations of interconnected regions. The isolation of this level allows for something else as well. Some emotions may involve not only complexes of regional activation, but also complexes of regional inhibition. Disgust, for example, may require the activation of several regions including insular cortex. In addition, it might involve the reduction of the ordinary activation of some regions.[2]

---

[2] Depending on the independent activation of the disgust and hunger systems, either may inhibit the other. For example, Hoefling and colleagues explain that "disgust

This leads us to the interrelations of emotion systems. I take it that all the so-called basic emotions, along with fundamental motivations (which I will count as emotions, construing the term broadly), form fairly stable systems incorporating specialized regions along with excitatory or inhibitory inputs and excitatory or inhibitory outputs.[3] These systems include anger, fear, disgust, happiness, sadness, "reward," sexual desire, attachment, hunger, and others. Distinct systems have connections not only with perception, motor cortex (for action), and so forth. They also have interactions with one another.

More exactly, two emotion systems may have no mutual effects; they may be mutually activating; they may be mutually inhibiting; or there may be some combination of these relations. In some cases, particularly if the relations are only inhibitory, we would probably say that these interactions are simply part of having the activated emotion. For example, disgust inhibits both appetite for food and sexual desire. We would say that this is just part of disgust. In contrast, we might see, for instance, attachment and sexual desire as interrelated in more complex ways. To understand this, we may, first of all, isolate different components of both attachment and sexual desire. Most simply, both involve an urge for physical contact. In this way, the activation of one system may partially activate the other system through the shared component. There may also be more subtle interactions. For example, the enhanced empathy of attachment may, in specific cases, enhance sexual desire (e.g., when one's partner is exhibiting sexual desire) or inhibit it (e.g., when one's partner is exhibiting sorrow).[4]

---

toward unpalatable food is modulated automatically even by moderate levels of food deprivation" (55).

[3] As I have already indicated, there is a limiting case in which the emotion, thus the emotion system, is correlated with a single region. One could think of emotion systems as akin to houses and emotion regions as akin to rooms. Most houses have multiple rooms. But there are sometimes one-room houses, just as there are sometimes one-region emotion systems.

[4] This attachment-enhanced empathy is extremely important in our general emotional lives and in ethical response as well. It might be valuable, therefore, to isolate it more precisely through a distinct emotion term and concept. A good option would be the Ifaluk "*fago*, translated as 'compassion/love/sadness'." As Oatley, Keltner, and Jenkins explain, it is "the primary index of positive relationships, including those with children, relatives, and sexual partners. It is felt particularly when loved ones are in need in some way, including when they are absent, since in this absence they will be separated from those on whom they depend" (71–72). For reasons that are unclear to me, the Ifaluk isolation of this crucial, central emotional response is generally taken to show how "cultures can differ dramatically" (72). In my view, it comes closer to suggesting the opposite.

Furthermore, the relations between emotion systems or components of emotion systems may be symmetrical or asymmetrical. If symmetrical, then the two systems are equally likely to activate or inhibit one another. If two systems are asymmetrical, however, then one is more likely to activate or inhibit the other than vice versa. For example, it seems that disgust is more likely to inhibit the desire to taste when both are present (e.g., when a tasty looking treat has fallen in the gutter).[5] Thus these systems are asymmetrical.

Distinct systems may be coordinated in ways that produce relatively stable complexes of systemic interaction. This is commonly based on shared partial arousal and shared partial inhibition. For example, we may understand romantic love as a coordinated interaction of the attachment system and the sexual desire system (along with the endogenous reward system). In terms of mutual arousal, as just noted, attachment and sexual desire converge on longing for physical proximity and contact.[6] They also have shared inhibitory relations. For example, both tend to stand in inhibitory relations with disgust, though they may be asymmetrical in different directions. Specifically, disgust seems more likely to inhibit sexual desire,[7] whereas attachment seems more likely to inhibit disgust.[8] Indeed, physical disgust does not seem to have effects on attachment generally.

[5] There is a distinction here between the desire to taste on the one hand and hunger on the other. A distinction along these lines is common in neurolobiological studies of emotion and motivation. On some complexities of the two systems and their interrelations, see chapters 4 and 5 of Wong.

[6] For a range of ways in which these systems interact, see Gillath and Schachner.

[7] This is true insofar as the disgust is unusual, above some default threshold. As Lieberman and Hatfield point out, our basic disgust with other people's bodily fluids must be at least partially overcome "for sexual contact to take place" (291).

[8] This is not to say that it inhibits all varieties of disgust in all circumstances. Some issues include whether attachment inhibits disgust directly or indirectly, and whether the inhibition of disgust varies for different types of object. Attachment promotes proximity seeking (see, for example, Mikulincer and Shaver 161), which is directly opposed to the actional outcomes of disgust. It is therefore opposed to at least that component of disgust. On the other hand, Stevenson and Repacholi present evidence that disgust at fecal odors may be inhibited by familiarity, though not directly by attachment. At the same time, even this is not straightforward. The Stevenson and Repacholi study suggests an indirect relation between attachment and reduction in disgust, since the two are correlated (see 392). Perhaps attachment increases suppression of avoidance, which in turn increases exposure, which in turn decreases disgust. Moreover, there may be differences between disgust for contact with another person's skin and disgust for another person's feces, or between smell and the other sensory modalities (since smell does not involve the same thalamus-mediated processing circuit as the other senses [see, for example, Amaral 341]). These differences may bear on the inhibitory effects of disgust. (We will consider disgust again in Chapter 7.)

The Perceptual Causes of Emotion Circuit Activation

Through all these levels, the neurological substrate of emotion operates via sequences of activation. One neuron is linked to another, which is linked to another, and so forth, forming a circuit. The first neuron is activated; it, in turn, activates the second neuron, and so on. This chain of events is initiated by some starting activation. One contention of this chapter is that the initiator of these activations – thus the *eliciting conditions* of the emotion – must be one of three sorts. It must be a perception, a concrete imagination (thus an imagination that activates perceptual regions), or an emotional memory (which is also, ultimately, perceptual). The perception may be in any mode – visual, olfactory, somatosensory, and so on. Conversely, nonperceptual inferences (thus reasoning or other processes that do not involve concrete imagination or the recruitment of emotional memories) do not initiate the activation of emotion circuits. Thus this account rejects at least some versions of the dominant appraisal theory. Specifically, according to the account presented here, emotions are not produced by the evaluation of situations or events in relation to goals – which is the central idea of appraisal theory.[9] Rather, emotions are activated by concrete sensory phenomena. On the other hand, as we will see, evaluative thought – thus appraisal – does commonly involve direct perception, concrete imagination, and the activation of emotional memories. In this way, appraisals are crucial for emotion episodes and the two accounts may be reconciled in an algorithmically well-specified way. The crucial difference is that, in the view articulated here, appraisal does not produce emotion through its logic of probability calculations, nor even their conclusions, but through various incidentals that are commonly (though not invariably) involved with probabilistic estimations.[10]

There are three reasons for maintaining this position. First, all theories accept perceptual experiences, concrete imaginations, and emotional memories as initiating the activation of emotion circuits. It is

[9] For a rigorous and concise, but encompassing account of appraisal theory, see chapter 7 of Oatley, Keltner, and Jenkins.

[10] Perceptual emotion triggers bear some similarity to Oatley and Johnson-Laird's idea of an initial emotional response that is "automatic and unconscious." However, these do not involve "an appraisal of an event in relation to goals" (Oatley, Keltner, and Jenkins 173). As discussed further on, in the account presented here, a perception-based (or memory-based) emotional response has only a functional similarity to such an appraisal.

simpler to assume that these *alone* are the initiators of such activation. In other words, by Occam's Razor, we should only add further sources of activation if these commonly accepted sources prove inadequate.

Second, we have an emotion only on the condition that some emotion-specialized region is activated. These regions appear to be evolutionarily older than human neocortex. For example, LeDoux presents evidence that "the amygdala was selected as a key compo-nent of the defense system of the vertebrate brain before birds and mammals separated from reptiles" (*Emotional* 171). The activation of such regions will most obviously result from processes available in the brain before human prefrontal evolution – processes such as per-ception and long-term memory. If this were not the case, then such regions (e.g., the amygdala) would not have operated prior to that evolution. I am not saying that the emotion regions could not have evolved to accommodate input from subsequently evolved neocortex. But all accounts, it would seem, must assume the evolutionarily more basic arousal. Positing further arousal should be justified only on the basis of otherwise inexplicable data.

Finally, and most importantly, there is reason to believe that, as a matter of fact, inferences do not produce emotions without concrete perceptual experiences, whereas concrete perceptual experiences do produce emotions even when opposed to inferences. For example, no amount of statistical evidence is likely to make people less afraid of fly-ing than of riding in a car. Why is that? There are probably many expe-riential factors (including imaginations) involved in the former, such as the feeling of being unsupported at takeoff and landing, and the sense of being confined to a limited space during the flight. Statistics lack this concreteness. Similarly, it seems that body counts in war do rela-tively little to inspire people's feelings. But a single photograph of, say, a naked girl running in terror, may have enormous emotional impact.[11]

---

[11] Similarly, Harriet Beecher Stowe's Senator Byrd supports legislation against fugitive slaves when he has only "the idea of a fugitive" in mind. But he aids an escaped slave when his compassion is aroused by "the real presence of distress – the imploring human eye, the frail, trembling human hand" (101). Daniel Gardner presents a num-ber of cases of this general sort – some rather surprising. For example, in one study, 21% of psychiatrists said they would refuse to release a patient when told that the patient had "a 20 percent chance" of violence. The number of psychiatrists refusing release a patient climbed to 41% when the phrasing was changed to "20 out of every 100 patients similar to" this patient. The difference, Gardner explains, was that the former is "hollow, abstract," whereas the latter is "concrete" and "creates images" (80; Gardner gives an example of such images from one test subject).

Obviously, this is not to say that prefrontal areas have no function in emotion – quite the contrary. As we will discuss in the section on emotion episodes, working memory is extremely important in the unfolding of an emotion episode. Inference, imagination, and other "paraemotional" processes, as we might call them, may serve to sustain an emotion, or they may serve to inhibit an emotion, once the relevant system has been aroused.[12] Without these processes, emotional responses would be too brief, too erratic, and too contingent on external or somatosensory stimuli to motivate the sorts of long-term social projects that characterize human behavior.

Indeed, this account makes many of the same predictions as appraisal theory. For example, it suggests that anxiety disorders may result to a great extent from working memory processes that sustain fear system activation and thus that they should be treatable in part through cognitive-behavioral means. The specifics of the two accounts differ, however. By the account presented here, the effects of cognitive therapy do not result directly from the reasoning processes per se. They result, rather, from the different perceptions, concrete imaginations, and emotional memories recruited by working memory in pre-therapy and post-therapy thought. But both accounts suggest that cognitive-behavioral therapy should have at least some beneficial results.

The Origins of Eliciting Conditions

Needless to say, different emotion systems are activated by different objects. In appraisal theory, these differences are seen as the result of inferred causal relations to goals. But by the perceptual account just sketched, such case-by-case evaluation is not an option. Here, then, we need to consider why certain emotion systems are sensitive to certain concrete experiences.

I would isolate three sources for the responsiveness of emotion systems. First, we have some innate sensitivities. As Antonio Damasio put it, "we are wired to respond with an emotion, in preorganized fashion, when certain features of stimuli in the world or in our bodies are perceived, alone or in combination. Examples of such features include size (as in large animals); large span (as in flying eagles); type of motion

---

[12] The inhibitory function is stressed by LeDoux. As he writes at one point, referring to an evoked fear response from an activated amygdala, "The cortex's job is to prevent the inappropriate response rather than to produce the appropriate one" (*Emotional* 165).

(as in reptiles); certain sounds (such as growling)" (*Descartes'* 131). Arguably, the most crucial sensitivities are to the emotion expressions of other people. It is well known that we respond to the emotional expressions of others with parallel or complementary emotions (see Hatfield, Cacioppo, and Rapson 5), owing at least in part to our mirror neuron systems (for an introduction to mirror neurons, see Iacoboni). Mirror neuron systems are systems that fire either when one does something oneself or senses someone else doing it. Thus, a mirror neuron response to someone else's smile involves the activation of neurons that fire also when one smiles oneself. There appear to be bidirectional connections between emotion systems and the motor routines that express those emotions. Thus, we have projections from the emotion systems to motor systems that lead us to smile when happy. But we also have projections that partially activate happiness feelings when we smile. As Iacoboni explains, speaking more generally, "our mirror neurons fire when we see others expressing their emotions, as if we were making those facial expressions ourselves. By means of this firing, the neurons also send signals to emotional brain centers ... to make us feel what other people feel" (119).

This aspect of innate emotional sensitivities is crucial to the second source of emotional response – what we might refer to as "critical period experiences."[13] It seems clear that at least many emotion systems are initially rather plastic and come to be more fixed through early experiences. These early experiences seem to rely in part on the communication of emotion via emotion expression. Put simply, in early childhood, we learn how to feel not only through our own direct experiences (e.g., of pleasure or pain), but crucially by witnessing the emotion expressions of others. The general idea goes back at least to Albert Bandura. As Hatfield, Cacioppo, and Rapson summarize, "affective learning ... frequently occurs through vicariously aroused emotions. People can develop phobias merely by witnessing others respond fearfully .... They can learn to love and hate, or get angry or stay calm in the presence of others, in the same way" (46). Oatley, Keltner, and Jenkins point out that "Over time individual infants become more similar to

[13] Cf. Parkes 11 on the idea of "critical learning periods"; as will become clear, however, the notion of critical periods presented in the following pages does not entail the acquisition of "fixed action patterns." Rather, the conception of critical periods here is more similar to that found in linguistics, where the acquired practices are necessarily more flexible. (For a somewhat critical overview of the relevant work in linguistics, see Hyltenstam.)

their mothers in terms of their expressions of emotion" (303) and cite research showing that "mothers' reports of their own negative emotions predicted their children's negative emotions" (305). Martin Hoffman ("Empathy, Role-Taking") has pointed to the importance of caregivers' handling of infants in this process of learning what to feel.[14] Oatley, Keltner, and Jenkins note the early importance of the caregiver's vocal expression of emotion (202, 210). Tactile and vocal triggers are particularly consequential before children begin to scrutinize their caregivers' faces for emotional responses in preparation for "taking action with respect to an ambiguous elicitor" (Oatley, Keltner, and Jenkins 210).

Disgust provides a good example. Rozin, Haidt, and McCauley explain that, "For adults, feces seems to be a universal disgust substance." However, feces do not provoke this response in young children. Rozin, Haidt, and McCauley hypothesize that disgust "may be acquired by witnessing facial displays of emotions that elicit the experience of those emotions ..., perhaps engaging processes that involve mirror neurons" (765; see also Stevenson and colleagues 177). Or consider fear. Formerly, monkeys were thought to have an innate fear of snakes. However, further research suggests that the fear itself is not innate. Rather, monkeys acquire the fear by observing their mothers. When a monkey's mother shows a fear of snakes, the child begins to have that fear also (see Damasio *Looking* 47). As this suggests, in at least some cases, the learning is remarkably swift. We might suspect, therefore, that there is some sort of innate perceptual sensitivity that may enter here as well – perhaps a sensitivity to certain sorts of motion, in the case of snakes. Moreover, this perceptual sensitivity may already be linked to emotion activations. As Wong puts it, "animals may be pre-programmed through natural selection to acquire specific responses" (10).

Attachment gives another example of critical period development. Research indicates that early attachment patterns persist in later life. As Hatfield and Rapson explain, following attachment theory, "people's love schemas" are in part "shaped by children's early experiences and thus are relatively permanent" (656, though they are not immutable and may be modified by later experiences). For instance, according to the "considerable support" amassed by Shaver and Hazan, "anxious/ambivalent"

---

[14] I suspect that more active imitation has a role here as well. Indeed, certain sorts of play – particularly interactive play with a caregiver – might function to orient, specify, or attune emotion systems.

children are more likely "become anxious/ambivalent adults ... who are terrified they will be abandoned" (Hatfield and Rapson 656).

Indeed, attachment is probably particularly important here. Attachment may enhance our empathic sensitivity to emotions on the part of attachment objects. Thus, it may enhance emotion contagion between parents and children. If so, it could be an important factor in a child's development of other emotion systems. A child's enhanced sensitivity to his or her caregiver's fear, disgust, and so on could be of crucial importance for his or her developing systems for fear, disgust, and so forth. In this way, it seems that one's entire emotional make-up, across systems, may be profoundly affected by attachment feelings.

The final source of emotional response is emotional memories, as already mentioned. Emotional memories are "implicit" memories, which is to say they do not, in and of themselves, bring representational content into working memory. In this sense, they are not like "memories" as we ordinarily think of them. Our ordinary idea of memories is more or less equivalent to the technical concept of "episodic memories." These are "explicit" recollections of experiences – such as my memories of an oral exam in which I participated recently. When activated, an episodic memory brings those experiences explicitly to mind. In contrast, the activation of an emotional memory (roughly) leads one to re-experience the emotion. An emotional memory may be activated without a corresponding representational memory. In that case, we may experience the emotion but not understand why we are experiencing it. This is clear in cases of brain damage where the patient can form emotional memories but not episodic memories. In one well-known case, a patient had lost the ability to create new explicit, episodic memories. Thus, she never remembered her doctor when he entered her room. However, one day, he pricked her with a pin when shaking hands. The next day, "she still had no recognition of him, but she refused to shake his hand" (LeDoux *Emotional* 180–181), presumably because she had stored an emotional memory of the previous handshake.

These references to episodic and emotional memories lead in an obvious way to emotion episodes.

Emotion Episodes

Emotion episodes have a number of components. The first two are the subjective and objective conditions for the emotion. The subjective conditions include the background *motivational state* or *mood*, which is connected with the complete neurochemistry of the relevant emotion areas. More exactly, as we have discussed, emotion activation derives from the activation of neural circuits. Once initiated, the firing of these circuits is extremely rapid. Moreover, it may dissipate quickly. This gives rise to the "brief bursts" of emotional experience discussed by Greg Smith and others (see Greg Smith 36–40 and citations). I have been speaking up to this point of neurons and connections between neurons (thus synapses). However, neurochemistry is a key aspect of the activation of circuits. The transmission of activation from one neuron to another proceeds via neurochemical processes. Particular pathways of neuronal activation pass activation through neurochemical agents know as "neurotransmitters." (In some cases, neurochemicals inhibit activation rather than exciting it.) The presence of such neurotransmitters may increase (or decrease) the likelihood that, subsequently, arousal will be passed along the pathway. Subjectively, we may say that they make us more or less prone to certain sorts of emotion. Moreover, neurochemicals dissipate less quickly than the simple activation of an emotion circuit. Again, the arousal of an emotion circuit is a quickly passing, but possibly renewed spike of emotion. In contrast, neurochemicals may be associated with mood effects, the more enduring propensity to experience such bursts (cf. Greg Smith's discussion of mood and other aspects of the duration of emotion components, 36–40).[15]

It is important to note that, depending on the nature of a background mood state, we may have an inclination toward "mood repair" (see Forgas "Affect" 258 and citations) or "mood-congruent processing" (see Oatley *Best* 201 and Bower 389). When we are experiencing low levels of dysphoric emotions, such as fear, we commonly engage in unselfconscious strategies to limit our experience of that emotion. For example, we may divert attention from fear-producing objects. However, as the dysphoric emotion becomes stronger, such mood repair becomes increasingly difficult. At some point, we typically switch to the opposite, mood-congruent processing. In other words, we begin paying particular attention to fear-provoking objects, we recall frightening episodes in our past life, and so on (see Oatley, Keltner, and Jenkins 269). There are also differences in the way we process information, with

---

[15] These mood states form the subjective background for an emotion episode. In some cases, a disorder of neurochemical production results in emotional propensities that last beyond mood states. For example, depression is related to a low level of the neurotransmitter serotonin (Oatley, Keltner, and Jenkins 150).

some moods inclining us toward (roughly) inductive processes and others inclining us toward (roughly) deductive processes (see Forgas "Introduction" 15–17 and citations), and so forth.[16]

Again, this is the subjective side of an emotion episode. On the objective side, we have *eliciting conditions*. These are the emotion triggers discussed in the preceding section. As already stressed, the present account differs from mainstream appraisal theorists in seeing the elicitors as concrete, thus not as a function of probability calculations related to goals.

In fact, it seems that appraisals in this sense are a sort of functional idealization of our evolved mechanisms for emotional response. When we speak of evolution, we commonly talk as if organisms evolve to satisfy certain purposes. For example, we say that fear evolved to motivate us to escape dangerous situations. But this is merely a loose way of speaking. Instead, rather crude mechanisms are generated by complexes of genetic mutations. These mechanisms *approximate* the functions that we generally use in explaining evolution. In the case of emotion, we say that fear leads us to escape a dangerous situation. But clearly fear does not always begin when we are in fact in a dangerous situation. Moreover, fear often does begin when we are not in a dangerous situation at all. The *function* of emotions can be understood broadly in terms of appraisals. We have goals – such as maintaining bodily integrity, receiving enough nourishment, being cared for, and so on. Very often, our emotions are correlated with the pursuit of these goals and/or changes in the likelihood that we will achieve these goals. Thus, very often, we experience fear when, as a matter of fact, the likelihood of maintaining bodily integrity drops significantly. But, as with other evolutionary functions, it is enormously unlikely that our actual emotional responses are based on such functional appraisals. Rather, it is very likely that there is some simpler, evolved mechanism (or set of mechanisms) that has the same outcome as the functions in an adequate number of cases. One possible account of these mechanisms is given in the preceding section. If that account is correct, then those mechanisms had evolutionary success because they roughly approximated the goal-achievement functions treated in appraisal theory. For

[16] The cognitive effects can be more specific as well. As Bonanno, Goorin, and Coifman point out, sadness is connected with "more detail-oriented information processing, more accurate performance appraisals, and less overall reliance on heuristics and stereotyping for decision making." Indeed, sadness enhances "spatial memory while reducing verbal memory," whereas happiness does the opposite (799).

example, an innate fear sensitivity to snakes would serve to help preserve one's life, often leading to the same outcomes as an appraisal of the danger posed by a snake. But, again, the mechanisms are not at all identical with such appraisals.

Research conducted by Joan Kellerman, James Lewis, and James Laird provides a fitting example. Feelings of romantic love are connected with the mutual gaze of the lovers. Suppose John is feeling interested in Jane. He gazes at her eyes. If she gazes back, that suggests some sort of interest on her part. This leads him to positively appraise the likelihood of his interest leading to some relationship. This intensifies his interest, and so on. Jane, for her part, has similar goals and appraisals. By the perceptual account, the appraisals and other forms of elaborative processing serve only to facilitate the concrete triggers. (To use an analogy, they are like blood carrying hormones, not like the hormones themselves.) One possibility for a perceptual account is that the mutual gaze itself has emotional effects. This is just what the research suggests. Subjects were asked to gaze "into one another's eyes – but only in order to count how often the other was blinking." Compared with test subjects who did not engage in mutual gazing, these "subjects reported greater feelings of romantic love, attraction, interest, warmth, and respect for one another" (Hatfield, Cacioppo, and Rapson 56).

It is worth reiterating that the concrete eliciting conditions may be either directly perceptual or imagined. The effects of imagination are due to the fact that there is continuity between perception and perceptual imagination. For example, the brain reacts in much the same way to seeing a cup and imagining a cup (see Kosslyn 295, 301, 325 and Rubin 41–46, 57–59). The point has obvious bearing on literary study. Elaine Scarry's work on literary imagination suggests that the intensity of our response to imagined experiences may be in part a function of the vividness and detail of those imaginations, thus their approximation to actual perceptual experience. As Scarry indicates, this may be one reason for the emotional power of literature.

It is also important to note that the eliciting conditions of emotion include not only immediately present objects in their current conditions and locations. Our minds automatically project trajectories for object movement. For example, if I am crossing the street and see a car coming toward me, I do not freeze the scene and feel fine because the car is at a particular distance. My mind automatically projects a rough calculation of the car's arrival where I am (see, for example, van Leeuwen 272). My mind calculates trajectories of my own (real and possible) motion as well. It may be argued that these very short-term projections are of great importance for emotional response – indeed, central features of the eliciting conditions for emotion.[17]

In speaking of imagination and "sensorimotor projection" (the very short-term calculation of trajectories), we have already begun to point toward some of the other components of an emotion episode. Once the eliciting conditions activate emotion systems in a subject, a series of other things occurs. One of the earliest and most significant is the *reorienting of attention*. Emotion systems combine with the particulars of eliciting conditions to guide the direction and focus of our perceptual concerns. For example, if I see a car moving on the road in my direction, my fear system may direct my attention to the car briefly (to facilitate the calculation of its trajectory of motion). It may then redirect my attention to possible paths of escape – thus away from that trajectory. In other cases, my attention may be redirected toward aspects of my own bodily experience or toward memories.

Attentional reorientation is closely associated with *actional reorientation*. Actional reorientation involves the priming of motor routines and, often, the inhibition of ongoing actions in order to implement the new motor routines if necessary. Actional reorientation culminates in *actional outcomes*. Actional outcomes are behaviors that function (not always successfully) to alter aversive eliciting conditions or to sustain pleasurable eliciting conditions. Thus when I see the car barreling toward me, my actional reorientation may lead me to pause for a moment as I inhibit my ongoing action in preparation for replacing it with flight. The functional point of the flight is, of course, to alter the situation so that it no longer presents me with eliciting conditions for the aversive emotion of fear – specifically, so that my spontaneous calculation of the trajectory of the car does not involve a collision with me.

The actional outcomes are prepared in part by changes in the autonomic nervous system and skeletal muscles. For example, different emotions produce differences in heart and respiration rate, muscle tension, and so forth. These are referred to as the *physiological outcomes* of the emotion.

Physiological outcomes are in part subjectively perceived as the *phenomenological tone* or *feeling* of the emotion.[18] That phenomenological

[17] See Hogan "Sensorimotor."
[18] On the degree to which feeling an emotion is a function of physiological outcomes, see Oatley, Keltner, and Jenkins 124–131.

tone is not always unequivocal. It may be affected by the way we categorize our emotional experience (see, for example, Lindquist and Barrett), reflect on it, link it with emotional memories, and so on.

Physiological outcomes and feelings are related to a further component, already mentioned – *expressive outcomes*. These most obviously include facial expressions – ranging from changes in musculature (e.g., in smiles or frowns), to patterns in direction of gaze (e.g., lowered eyes), to degree of pupil dilation (more dilation being associated with greater interest [see Frijda 138–39]). However, they also include posture, gait, vocalizations (such as shrieking or sobbing), and other behaviors. Bachorowski and Owren argue that the primary function of vocalizations is not to give utterance to emotions but to alter the emotions of others. Their argument seems both compelling and generalizable. Thus expressive outcomes are external manifestations of an emotion that serve, not to change or maintain the eliciting conditions, but to affect the emotional states of other persons. Again, the effects of emotional expressions may be either parallel or complementary. In many cases, our emotional expressions serve to foster the same (thus parallel) emotions in others. This often occurs with laughing and crying. However, there are many cases of the opposite (complementary) sort as well. An angry growl has the basic function of producing, not anger (the parallel emotion), but fear (the complementary emotion).[19]

Another component of emotion episodes, already mentioned, is the *activation of emotional memories*. Clearly, the activation of memories, whether implicit or explicit, relies on some perceived parallel between the present eliciting conditions and the past experience. There are undoubtedly numerous factors contributing to the establishment of such a parallelism. These include emotion congruence (thus memories of fear, in the case of current fear), locational and personal identity (e.g., memories of the same place and memories of the same people), and emotionally defined perceptual sensitivities deriving from innate propensities (e.g., sensitivities to certain sorts of motion). But they

---

[19] Referring to "anger" as "parallel" somewhat oversimplifies the situation. Strictly speaking, anger may be a parallel – as when I share Jones's anger toward Smith – or reciprocal. Reciprocal response has some characteristics of parallel emotions (e.g., feeling tone) but some characteristics of complementary emotions (e.g., opposed actional outcomes). The distinction is important. However, the following discussions will largely leave it aside because our primary concern will be with parallel emotions or parallel components of emotions on the one hand and complementary emotions or complementary aspects of emotions on the other. This is the distinction that will be crucial for understanding emotion contagion, empathy, ethics, and related topics.

also include emotionally relevant categorizations, such as in-group/out-group divisions.

This last point suggests that *semantic memory* may play at least a limited role in emotion episodes. In part, this is a matter of categorization, particularly categorization of the objects or targets of an emotion. An apt illustration may be found in LeDoux's well-known example of glimpsing a stick at one's foot, jumping away because it seems to be a snake, then realizing it is a stick. As LeDoux explains, in this case, a low-information signal went from the thalamus to the amygdala causing the jump. At the same time, a more information rich signal went from the thalamus to the cortex. Presumably part of what occurred in cortical processing was the categorization of the object as a stick.[20]

Categorization also seems to have consequences for phenomenological tone. Ambiguous feeling states may occur in cases where the experience involves components shared by several emotions, such as a high heart and respiration rate, without disambiguating information. Categorization may serve to orient imagination and memory toward one of the alternatives. This was perhaps part of what occurred in research by Stanley Schachter. In a famous study, Schachter injected test subjects with a stimulant. He found that they attributed their increased physiological arousal to the emotion exhibited by a confederate of the researcher. Specifically, if the confederate exhibited anger, they categorized their emotion as anger. But if the confederate exhibited euphoria, they categorized their emotion as euphoria.

A great deal of what happens in an emotion episode bypasses self-conscious inference. But a great deal does not. In other words, there is considerable involvement of *working memory processes* in all this. Emotional response is highly complex, with many different components. We have been focusing on the distinct, automatic processes. But there are also processes that serve at a meta-level to coordinate more basic processes. These occur in working memory. Working memory

---

[20] In terms of the perceptual theory presented here, this process alters the eliciting conditions (from apparently seeing a snake to seeing a stick) primarily by incorporating further perceptual information. This information is, in part, what gives rise to the categorization ("This is a stick") in the first place. Insofar as that is the case, the categorization itself is not important. However, the categorization makes some other perceptual information salient, as my attention shifts to different aspects of the object. Moreover, my spontaneous perceptual projections change. My mind no longer expects the thing to lunge or slither. Thus, those projections no longer form part of the eliciting conditions. Finally, semantic categorization almost certainly involves different complexes of episodic and emotional memory activation as well.

is itself a complex system, including sensory components (at least for sound and vision) that maintain experiences, memories, and anticipations in an active state, as well as a multimodal area for integrating those experiences, memories, and anticipations. (For a full elaboration of working memory components, see chapter 3 of Baddeley, Eysenck, and Anderson.)

It is worth considering the inputs to and operations of working memory in more detail. We have many experiences even over the few moments in which an emotion episode begins to unfold. A first level of perceptual encoding and emotion system activation presents working memory with partially unified objects and conditions. It also presents working memory with a sort of preliminary causal attribution, in part simply by directing our attentional focus toward salient objects in the environment. Working memory serves to integrate all this with new incoming information from perception and memory. This integration is guided to a great extent by inferential routines – schemas or broad conceptual structures, prototypes or standard cases, scripts or standard sequences of actions and events, and so on. These inferential routines guide the ways in which working memory identifies objects, infers causes, and constructs anticipations.

In these ways, our working memory processes expand our immediate experience. These processes produce fuller causal accounts – what we might call *proximate causal inferences* (as opposed to the *minimal causal projections* of emotion systems). They also produce longer-term expectations – *working anticipations* (as opposed to the *sensorimotor projections* of emotion systems).[21] In addition, they modify our attentional focus and help specify our actions, thereby continually transforming the eliciting conditions for our emotional responses. Of course, the concrete perceptions, imaginations, and memories do not disappear. Embedded in the working memory processes, they continue to constitute the triggers for our emotional response.

---

[21] The differences I am pointing to here are manifest nicely in some empirical research on Theory of Mind. In a typical study, Jane and Sally are shown a doll in box A. Sally leaves and Jane watches while the researcher takes the doll from A and puts it in box B. When asked where Sally will look for the doll, two-year-olds do not say "Box A" and do not look at box A. Three-year-olds say "Box B," but look at box A. Four-year-olds say "Box A" and look at box A (see Doherty 27). As Doherty explains, "Younger children's correct looking … seems to be based on … knowledge [that] is implicit" (28). This implicit knowledge is a form of spontaneous causal and sensorimotor projection (as opposed to elaborative inference and anticipation). This may be found even with fifteen-month-olds (see Doherty 29–30).

As indicated in Chapter 1, we may refer to these various working memory operations collectively as the *elaboration* of an emotion episode. Thus we may distinguish between the initial emotion system activation and the elaboration of the emotion event through working memory. Elaborative processes, including appraisal, do not constitute the emotion-eliciting conditions per se. However, they do bear crucially on emotion elicitation by guiding perception, imagination, and memory activation.

A Minimal, Multicomponent Account of Emotion

All this adds up to what we might refer to as a "minimal, multicomponent" account of emotion. It is multicomponent in both description and explanation. Descriptively, it brings together a range of features that are part of an emotion episode, integrating them within a basically neurocognitive framework. As such, it systematizes and, in part, further develops a number of ideas that were available in the research, but were sometimes scattered and not fully brought into productive interaction.

This account addresses explanation at two levels. The first level is the explanation of an emotional experience, either an emotion episode or a longer-term emotional condition. This level involves reference to both subjective propensities and objective events or conditions. The other level is the explanation of emotional development, thus the explanation of how the propensities come about. Here, too, the account includes multiple components. Here, too, it brings together conclusions from other researchers, integrating, systematizing, and in some degree extending them. For example, innate sensitivities, critical periods, and emotional memories are all widely recognized. However, they are often discussed in isolation from one another. Thus they are not commonly brought together within the context of an encompassing, systematic account of emotion explanation and further explored as the three developmental components of emotional propensity. Similarly, the importance of attachment is widely accepted. However, it appears that other accounts have not brought this point into relation with the operation of critical periods in emotion acquisition.

The minimalism of the theory comes in the fact that it seeks to explain both emotional development and emotional experience by reference to a single type of emotion elicitor – concrete, perceptual experiences (current, remembered, or imagined). At the same time, it seeks to reconcile this limitation with the incorporation of appraisal or at least appraisal-like cognitive processes as one component of many emotion episodes. It does this through the idea of elaboration. In elaboration, probabilistic inferences may be developed and may contribute to the unfolding of an emotion episode. However, they do not do so through their logic of probability assessments. Rather, such inferential elaborations contribute to emotion episodes through their recruitment of perceptual representations (a species of "processing representations," to use the terminology introduced in the first chapter), specifically concrete imaginations and emotional memories.

This "perceptual elicitor" view does put the theory at odds with dominant appraisal approaches, a point stressed in the following chapters. However, it is important to note that this does not constitute a repudiation of appraisal theory. Indeed, appraisal theory is one of the key precursors of the present account. One main task of the present theory is to incorporate the insights of appraisal theory while giving an algorithmically well-specified treatment of just how appraisal processes produce emotions. Moreover, there are many different theories that go by the name "appraisal" and the present account is not incompatible with all of them. The challenge of the preceding account is aimed at theories that take emotion to be produced by estimated changes in the likelihood of goal achievement. (This includes both conscious and unconscious estimations.) That challenge does not apply to any "appraisal theories" that do not accept this view.

That said, it is important to stress that the emphasis on perceptual eliciting conditions is not an idiosyncratic feature of the present account. Though appraisal approaches remain dominant, perceptual approaches are not unheard of. For example, in her overview of theories of emotion causation, Moors isolates an entire set of "perceptual theories." The account presented earlier is consistent with these theories in "react[ing] against the ... view that emotion is a form of judgment" (652), even an unconscious one. Moreover, like the theories cited by Moors, the preceding account would underscore the importance of emotions that run counter to one's beliefs – and are not corrigible by reference to compelling logical inferences, as, for example, Döring discusses.

On the other hand, the account presented here diverges from Moors' perceptual theories in a number of ways. Perhaps most significantly, the present account would not assert that "processes involved in emotion have more in common with those involved in perception than those involved in judgment" and amount to "ways of seeing" (Moors 652). By the present account, perception, memory, and cognitive elaboration – often including judgment, as well as "propositional representations" (Moors 652) or at least categorizations – are mutually involved processes. Moreover, they are all similar in that they all involve concrete experiential elements. That is why "seeing as" is not a crucial feature of the present account. Any cognitive process – perception, judgment, memory, speculation – can elicit emotions, and "seeing as" is no more required than having a particular belief. For the account presented here, the only requirement is a relevant perceptual elicitor – sensation, imagination, or memory – along with an appropriate mood state. For example, if I think of a particular apartment where I lived in at a particular time, I have a feeling of loss, almost like a mild form of grief. I am not seeing anything relevant. I am not even adopting a "way of seeing" the apartment in imagination. Rather, the thought of the apartment activates a range of emotional memories. Those concrete memories give rise to the emotion, which is then enhanced or attenuated through elaborative processes that recruit other memories, and so on.

Of course, in these cases too, the divergence between the causes of emotion and the probability logic of appraisal remains. This divergence is perhaps particularly consequential in ethics, which is often viewed as necessarily bound by reasoning and judgment. This leads us to our final topic.

A Note on Ethics and Emotion

This is not a book on ethics. It is a book on literature and emotion. Thus it is not possible to give anything like a full account of ethics – neither a descriptive account of what ethics is nor a normative account of what it should be. However, ethical concerns enter centrally into both literature and emotion. As such, a treatment of those two topics should not leave ethics aside. I will be considering particular ethical issues in relation to particular emotions in the following chapters, especially Chapters 7 and 8. However, it is valuable to set out a few general considerations regarding ethics and emotion at the outset.

To a great extent, emotions are egoistic in the sense that, in experiencing an emotion, one's only object of hedonic concern is oneself.[22] I run

---

[22] One reader asked why one would say this, rather than "Among us humans most emotions are social." This is a rather baffling question. Perhaps he had in mind that

in fear to protect myself. I grab for food in order to feed myself. Ethics begins with constraint on egoistic emotion in favor of the well-being of others. However, despite centuries of insistence that this is a matter of ethical reason overcoming animal passion, this constraint cannot be solely intellectual. There must be some motivational component to it if it is going to result in behavioral changes. In keeping with the preceding account of emotion, that component must at some point involve the perceptual activation of emotion systems, even if it does so through working memory processes that guide the elaboration of an emotion episode. In other words, ethical action must be fostered through innate emotional sensitivities, critical period experiences, or emotional memories.

A number of authors have suggested that the origin and ultimate grounding of ethics is found in empathy. The preceding account of emotion fits well with this view. The fundamental source of nonegoistic emotion, by the preceding account, is almost necessarily the sensitivity to emotion expressions of others. That sensitivity is the first and most basic inclination that motivates us to act in ways not guided solely by our own emotional interests. In this way, the preceding account has a somewhat surprising implication. The basic sensitivities that form the groundwork for our ethical behavior are also the only emotion triggers that absolutely must be innate for us to be able to develop emotionally through critical period experiences.

On the other hand, those sensitivities do not, in and of themselves, lead directly to ethical empathic response. Indeed, their basic operation in critical periods is, in effect, egoistic. Take again the case of the baby monkey learning the fear of snakes from its mother. The baby perceives the mother's fear and therefore feels that fear. But this does not yet count as empathy. It is, rather, emotion contagion. It may seem that the difference between emotion contagion and empathy is that the former is self-relevant and the second is other-relevant. But this is not true. They are both self-relevant. If, as a result of empathy, I act to relieve someone else's distress, it is because that distress disturbs me.[23] In that

---

"social emotions" are not egoistic. But they generally are. If I feel ashamed or jealous or hateful, I act in such a way as to enhance my own pleasure and reduce my own pain. Being social does not make an emotion any less egoistic, in this sense.

[23] The point is not uncontroversial, as debates over empathy and altruism suggest. For discussion, see Batson and Shaw, Dovidio and Penner, and Hoffman ("Is Empathy"). It would seem that an act should count as altruistic if one's only personal gain is empathy-related (e.g., the relief of knowing that someone else is no longer in pain). It is difficult to make any sense out of any "purer" altruism. That would seem to involve

way, it is self-relevant. However, it is not egoistic in the technical sense (described earlier) because the empathizer's hedonic concerns are not confined to himself or herself. In empathic response, one object of my concern is someone else – his or her feelings and conditions. Indeed, my hedonic condition is partially dependent on that other person's hedonic condition. In contrast, in emotion contagion, I am responding solely to my own hedonic concerns as these are signaled by the other person.

The mechanisms here are simple. In emotion contagion, the activation of my emotion system bypasses the other person. In these cases, the reorienting of attention and action is toward the eliciting conditions of the other person's emotion. In empathy, in contrast, the reorienting of attention and action is initially toward the other person himself or herself. In order to be clear, we may say that the cause of the emotion in both cases is someone else's emotion. But our emotion systems select an *object* for the emotion. The object is the target for our attentional and actional orientation. In the case of empathy, that object is the feeling state of some other person. In the case of emotion contagion, the object is whatever we take to have caused that feeling state in the other person.

Here, we might consider two paradigmatic examples found with some frequency in heroic narratives (and in real wars): panic in battle and compassion for the wounded. When soldiers panic during battle, there is (apparently) a sort of chain reaction in which one or another soldier responds with terror to the conditions of the battle. Through facial expressions, vocalizations, and the manner of flight, one or more soldiers in the front lines communicate terror to other soldiers back from the front lines. These latter soldiers begin to feel terror also – terror of the enemy or the fighting. Their attentional focus is on what is happening at the front. Their actional response is flight away from the front. In other words, their emotional response takes the battle as its object, not the fleeing soldiers. Note that, at the inferential level, the

no human motivational system. To demonstrate the existence of a purer altruism, researchers would have to create a situation in which test subjects feel nothing at all about the pain of the other person – including no anticipated distress at imagining or remembering the person's pain after leaving the test situation. (Some studies show that people still help even when they face the option of leaving the test situation [see Batson and colleagues 248]. But this does not take account of post-test imagining/ remembering.) We would have a purer altruism if such a situation were created but the test subject engaged in helping behavior anyway. But altruistic action with no motivational urging would be very odd. After all, one does not engage in actions *for oneself* with no motivational urging.

soldiers may be perfectly capable of attributing causality correctly, saying, "I panicked when I saw other soldiers fleeing from the front lines." However, their emotion systems have oriented them toward the battle, not toward their fleeing comrades. In contrast, when one of these soldiers sees a wounded comrade, he feels sorrow for the wounded soldier. His emotion system reorients his attention to the comrade. If the emotion is strong enough, his actional reorientation draws him to the comrade – even when danger is still present. In short, the object of his emotional response is the feeling state of the fallen man. In the former case (of panic), we are dealing with emotion contagion; in the latter case (of a wounded soldier), with empathy.[24]

As this suggests, empathy may be the root of moral feeling, but emotion contagion is developmentally fundamental. How do we move from one to the other? How do we come to make someone else – more precisely, someone else's hedonic condition – the object of our emotional response?

To some extent, this is a matter of the particular emotion system being activated. Fear, for example, tends to be contagious. Sorrow, in contrast, tends to provoke empathy. When we hear a shriek of terror, our first impulse is to feel egoistic fear. We are inclined to isolate a danger and to place it in relation to our current position. In contrast, when we hear someone sobbing, our impulse is to feel "sorrow for" that person, to orient toward the person, to approach him or her.

On the other hand, this is not absolute. Suppose I feel empathy for Jones because he is grieving the death of his father. There is no issue of grief in my case, because the deceased person was not my father. Emotion contagion is unlikely here, and I will probably not shift my attentional focus from Jones. However, suppose I am at the hospital where my father is undergoing very dangerous surgery. After some moments of distracted conversation, my brother begins to cry. In those circumstances, it is very possible that I will be affected by emotion contagion rather than empathy. So the difference is not simply a matter of the emotion at issue.

Continuing with the second example, it is important to note that I might also feel empathy for my brother in this situation. Suppose,

---

[24] Sometimes the phrase "emotional contagion" is used more broadly, as in the case of Hatfield, Cacioppo, and Rapson. My claim is not that my usage is correct and theirs is wrong. Either usage is fine. Rather, my claim is that there are distinct emotional processes of this sort. I will be using the terms "emotional contagion" and "empathy" to refer to them.

for example, that I consider my brother more dependent on my father or otherwise more vulnerable due to some recent events in his life. Indeed, I may feel empathy rather than emotion contagion even if I do not consider my brother to be more dependent or vulnerable. In cases of this sort, the difference is presumably a matter of my elaboration of the outcomes, should the surgery be unsuccessful. In the emotion contagion case, I imagine my own routines in relation to my father and his absence at times when we would have been together. In the empathy case, however, I imagine relevant routines of my brother. For instance, in the first case, I might imagine my regular practice of calling my parents every weekend, now speaking only with my mother. In the second case, I might imagine the various sporting events of my nieces and nephew where my brother would no longer be sitting with our father.

As this suggests, there is both a spontaneous version of empathy and an elaborated version. The latter is more effortful. Both are more likely to occur when one's own emotional concerns are less immediately pressing (e.g., when I consider my brother more dependent and vulnerable). But they can occur even when one's own concerns are very strong. Elaborative empathy generally involves a self-conscious attempt to imagine the condition of the other person. As just explained, the elaborated version relies largely on concrete imagination. It also relies on emotional memories. These include memories that are empathic and memories that are egoistic. For example, my empathic emotional memories of my (much younger) brother as a dependent and vulnerable infant may contribute to my empathy with him now. At the same time, my egoistic emotional memories of physical illness may contribute to my empathy with my father. The egoistic memories can play a role in empathy because of the way in which their attentional and actional reorientations are determined in the new context, either as one spontaneously experiences it or as one elaborates on it through working memory.

The effortful nature of elaborative empathy suggests the possibility that we may be more or less motivated to engage in such a process and that we may be more or less skilled at it. It could, in principle, be the case that we are all equally motivated and that we are all equally competent. However, this does not generally appear to be the way effortful working memory processes operate. Indeed, there is fairly clear evidence that some people have greater empathic inclinations than others ("trait empathy," as it is called) and that some people are more skilled at understanding other people's emotions (see Salovey and colleagues).

A greater inclination to empathy is probably in part the result of a stronger initial parallel response to the emotion expressions of others. This could have a number of sources, ranging from innately high mirroring sensitivity to a breadth of experience stored in emotional memories. One possibility is that a great deal of the inclination derives from critical period experiences in which our empathic inclinations and capacities are developed and specified in the same way as our other emotion systems. More precisely, two possible sources of critical period empathy enhancement come to mind immediately. First, and most obviously, we would expect the usual imitative or "mimetic" emotional experiences. In these cases, the caregiver experiences and expresses an empathic emotion and the child experiences emotion contagion from the caregiver; in other words, the emotion contagion involves empathy for some third person (cf. Hoffman "Empathy and Prosocial Behavior" 448 on parental modeling). This extension of empathic response could be more or less confined to family members. It could be selective for identity groups. It could extend broadly to strangers. These variables should have consequences for the proneness toward empathy exhibited by the child in later life.

The second source would be the child's experience of the caregiver's empathic responses to the child himself or herself. In these cases, the child experiences the caregiver's change in emotion in response to his or her own emotion, the subsequent comforting (for dysphoric emotions) or mutual celebration (for euphoric emotions), and the effect of all this on his or her own initial emotion (attenuating it, in the case of dysphoric emotions; extending it, in the case of euphoric emotions). Though the developmental processes here are undoubtedly complex and interactive, one would expect the child's positive experiences of caregiver empathy as well as the associated secure attachment with the caregiver to be roughly correlated with a general inclination toward empathic responsiveness. It does seem that this is what we find. For example, as Mikulincer and colleagues report, studies "reveal that both dispositional and experimentally enhanced attachment security facilitate cognitive openness and empathy" (817). The point is also suggested by research indicating that "angry," thus markedly unsympathetic "responding to toddlers' anger," results in "a lower likelihood of empathic responding to others" (Lemerise and Dodge 732).

Again, differences in empathic response seem to bear not only on inclination to empathy, but also on differences in skills. In part, these are "theory of mind" skills, which is to say skills in understanding other people's mental states. Our "theory of mind" response to other people may be very theory-like, involving inferences about beliefs, emotions, and so on. Alternatively, it may be a matter of simulation, an imaginative recreation of the other person's interests, ideas, and so forth.[25] In these cases, too, it seems very likely that there are innate differences in relevant skills as well as critical period experiences that affect one's theory of mind capacities – thus one's sensitivity to emotion cues, one's ability to infer or simulate subjective states corresponding to those cues or resulting from observable eliciting conditions, and so on.

In both inclinations and in skills, however, it seems unlikely that our empathic capacities are fixed once and for all at the end of a critical period. Indeed, if empathic inclinations are in part a function of emotional memories (e.g., of having been in a similar situation oneself), we would expect them to alter continuously in the course of one's life. Moreover, empathic skills undoubtedly involve such matters as precision and accuracy of attentional orientation, ability to simulate point of view, and capacity for fine-grained emotion categorization or emotion modeling. By "emotion categorization," briefly introduced earlier, I mean our ability to class emotions under headings such as "anger," "irritation," "resentment," and so forth. By "emotion modeling," I mean our ability to relate new emotion episodes to other, previous, better understood emotion episodes – as when we think "Jones must be feeling like I did when ...." All these skills should be open to improvement (or the opposite) in the course of one's life. One may learn to encode more or different perceptual information, increasing the accuracy of one's attention to other people's emotion expressions (see, for example, Masumoto and colleagues 225). One may acquire more precise emotion categories (on the importance of complexity and nuance in emotion concepts for one's emotional understanding, see Lindquist and Barrett 522–523) and a greater wealth of emotion episodes that may serve as models.

Obviously, one source for developing such inclinations and skills is real-life interactions with real people. However, there is another source – indeed, a source that is more insistently empathic than real

---

[25] For an overview of these alternatives, see chapter 3 of Doherty. These are sometimes treated as two alternatives for how our theory of mind works. However, it seems fairly clear that we engage in both processes and thus that both bear on our understanding of other people's mental states. As Doherty notes, "After a lively debate about whether Theory Theory or Simulation Theory best describes mindreading, a consensus seems to be developing that it involves both" (48).

life. That source is literature. In real life, most of our activities and inter-actions either are egoistic or have an egoistic component. In contrast, our experiences of literary emotion are almost entirely empathic. There may be some political or other purpose we wish to see illustrated in a literary work, a purpose that touches our personal interests. But for the most part, we are engaged by the emotional interests of the characters. In this way, literature provides a remarkable source for affecting our inclinations toward empathy and our skills regarding empathy.

More exactly, literature is, to a great extent, founded on the simu-lation of the ideas, attitudes, and interests of characters, as Oatley has emphasized (in "Why Fiction" and elsewhere). Literary works repeat-edly present us with necessarily nonegoistic imaginations of emotion-rich situations. They present us with characters' minds, often in great detail and depth. In this way, literary works may foster an inclination to simulate people's minds in that detail. In any case, literary works indicate to us that we can engage in such simulation, thus opening it up as a possibility. Literary works draw our interest toward such simula-tions, involving our emotion systems in the fuller imagination of other people's subjective experience. More importantly, accomplished story-tellers direct our attention to nuances of emotional expression that we might ordinarily overlook. As such, they may serve to train our abil-ities to attend to and encode matters that we would otherwise have failed to notice – aspects of tone, gesture, phrasing, posture, and other external manifestations of people's internal experience. Literary works also provide us with multiple and complex instances of differentiated emotional experiences. The romantic love of Romeo and Juliet is not quite the same as that of Hamlet and Ophelia or Beatrice and Benedick (in *Much Ado About Nothing*). Indeed, the romantic love of Romeo is not precisely identical with that of Juliet. In this way, literary works can give us very fine-grained models for emotion.

In keeping with this, we might expect exposure to literature to enhance one's "emotional intelligence," as it is sometimes called. "Emotional intelligence" is a complex of inclinations and skills that bear on one's ability to understand and respond appropriately to emotional states, both one's own and those of others. Recent work by Keith Oatley and others indicates that literary reading does indeed enhance emo-tional intelligence (see Oatley "Communications" and references). The results are both short-term and long-term. In other words, those who have just recently engaged in literary reading are more likely to do well on emotional intelligence tasks. Moreover, those who have engaged in

literary reading for many years are likely to be in general more successful in such tasks, even without the immediately preceding exposure to
literature. If we only had the short-term result, we might think that literary reading merely serves to prime certain interests and sensitivities
that everyone has, but that people sometimes do not fully use. In other
words, we might judge the effects to be superficial and ephemeral. If we
only had the long-term result, we might conclude the students of literature are self-selecting. Those with the greatest empathic inclinations
and skills are simply the ones drawn to literary study. In this case, literary study would not really have any consequences. It would itself be a
consequence, not a cause. Given both the short-term and the long-term
results, however, it seems most likely that literature does indeed have
consequences for our empathic inclinations and our empathic skills (as
well as our skills in understanding and responding to our own emotions). This is just what one would expect from the preceding analysis.

Of course, here as elsewhere, I should caution against a too uncritical
view of the salutary effects of literature – in this case, a view that simply celebrates literature as a means of enhancing our empathic inclinations and skills. Both during and after a critical period, our empathic
capacities may either be enhanced or inhibited. In terms of inclinations,
the obvious and perhaps most common way in which our empathic
capacities may be limited is through the establishment of identity categories. Literature often plays an important role in this establishment.

To understand the inhibition of empathy through identity categories, we need to reconsider our response to other people's emotions. I
have mostly been speaking of these responses as parallel. When Jones
feels fear, then I feel fear, either through emotion contagion or through
empathy. However, there is another possibility. Instead of feeling a parallel emotion, I may feel a complementary emotion. When Jones feels
fear, I may feel disdain. When Jones feels anger, I may feel fear. When
Jones feels sorrow, I may feel delight. In many cases, my individual
relation to a particular person governs whether I have a parallel or complementary emotional response. However, there are other cases when
I have no relation to an individual person. When Smith feels fear at an
enemy soldier's enthusiasm for battle, it is not because he has any relation to that particular soldier. The same point holds when he feels joy at
an enemy soldier's fear, but panic on witnessing the fear of an unfamiliar soldier from his own side. Here, the difference may seem rational,
since the enemy is charged with attacking everyone on Jones's side. But
this is fundamentally a matter of identity categorization, which is not

in general so rational. Jones categorizes people as part of an in-group or an out-group. His initial response to in-group members is parallel; his initial response to out-group members is complementary. We see this more clearly in racial antagonism, when whites respond to blacks with fear and vice versa, a point well attested in neurological studies (see Oatley *Emotions* 73). This response occurs in the absence of any motivation based on some active, current conflict such as battle.

The same point holds for emotion skills. It is well established that white Americans interpret the emotions of whites and blacks differently when they are placed in the same situations and respond in the same ways. For example, in one study, a white person pushing a black person was understood as playful, whereas a black person pushing a white person in the same way was understood as aggressive (see Kunda 347). The suggestion of this research is that white observers are either encoding the events differently or interpreting the encoded information differently, or both. In other words, they are either paying attention to different details in the two cases, or they are using different principles to simulate subjective conditions based on those details, or both. For example, they may be focusing on some aspect of the facial expression when the white person makes the push, but focusing on some aspect of the action itself (e.g., the hand muscles) when the black person pushes. Alternatively, they may be simulating different subjective experiences as giving rise to particular facial expressions in the two cases – or they may simply be simulating only from the white person's point of view in both cases. In any event, the crucial point is that there is something wrong with this processing. Test subjects are presumably mistaken about the white person or about the black person, and the mistake appears to be based first of all on identity categorization. A more consequential case may be found in the different responses of white test subjects to white and black targets in video simulations of potentially lethal interactions. As Ito and colleagues explain, "Participants were faster and more accurate in 'shooting' armed blacks compared with armed whites. By contrast, they were faster and more accurate in 'not shooting' unarmed whites than unarmed blacks" (198).

In-group/out-group divisions are, of course, pervasive in real life. But they are also pervasive in literary works. Racial, religious, ethnic, national and other ideologies are widespread in literature. Thus literary works may not only foster an openness to empathy; they may also foster an inhibition of empathy through identity categorization. Such categorization may involve directing our attention to different properties of emotion expression in different groups. More significantly, literary works may foster the use of different principles for simulation for different groups (e.g., through highly distorted depictive representations of the emotional lives of out-group members – for example, hateful, violent Muslims). They may more generally inhibit our tendency to simulate some people's experiences at all.

On the other hand, the nature of literary creation does seem to tend much more toward expanding rather than contracting our empathic inclinations and skills. It would take us away from the main concerns of the book to treat this topic. However, as discussed in *The Mind and Its Stories*, any attempt to create and develop an individual character almost inevitably leads an author away from simple out-group reduction and toward elaborated individualization, away from mere rejection of empathy in complementary emotional response and toward at least partially parallel, empathic response (see 145ff.). We could hardly expect all accomplished works of verbal art to overcome all forms of empathy-constraining ideology. However, we might expect such works to exhibit more complex responses to identity categorization, often including both ideological and counterideological tendencies.

In any case, it seems clear that both literature and emotion are closely intertwined with empathy and ethics. Thus one can hardly discuss the former without connecting it with the latter. We will see the importance of these connections repeatedly and concretely in the following chapters.

Conclusion

In discussing the neurological substrates of emotion or the underlying structural organization of our emotional architecture, we must distinguish different levels of specificity. First, there is the level of individual neurons, which may be specialized for different aspects of emotion initiation or response. Above this, there is the level of neuron populations, particularly those densely interconnected in emotionally specialized regions of functional neuroanatomy. These regions are, of course, not isolated, but linked with regions governing motor routines, attentional focus, autonomic nervous activity, and so on. We may refer to these large, interconnected networks as "systems." Finally, above the level of systems, we have relations among systems. These relations may be excitatory, inhibitory, or neutral. Moreover, they may be symmetrical or asymmetrical. In other words, two systems may affect one another equally (symmetrical); alternatively, one system may arouse or inhibit the other more than the reverse. Our emotion terms may isolate phenomena at the second or third level. In addition, our emotion terms are often ambiguous or vague with respect to these systems and relations among systems. Moreover, we invariably lack terms for some emotions. In part, this results from the possible idiosyncrasy of particular emotional episodes, with their potentially diverse populations of activated neurons.

In referring to emotion systems, we may incorporate components of different functional areas, including areas that are not emotional per se. For example, we may include the activation of flight-related motor routines in the emotion system for fear. In these cases, there is some distinctive relation between a specific emotion and the affected aspect of the other system. There are, in addition, some systems that interact with emotion systems in more general ways. Working memory is a prominent case of this sort. Working memory serves to integrate various sorts of information coming from the different activated systems – different modes of perception, actional orientations and motor routines, and so forth. Working memory also serves to sustain emotional experience over longer periods of time. The arousal of a particular emotion circuit may dissipate fairly quickly. The residual neurochemical changes will linger for somewhat longer, enhancing sensitivity to triggers for such arousal. But it is through working memory that those triggers are sustained as objects of attentional focus (e.g., in mood-congruent processing), thus potentially reactivating relevant circuits (e.g., sustaining fear even when the immediate trigger for the fear is no longer physically observed). By the same token, working memory may serve to divert attention from current triggers or otherwise operate to inhibit spontaneous emotional response (e.g., in mood repair).

An emotion episode begins with some mood state on the part of a subject plus some eliciting conditions. The eliciting conditions may be external or internal. Appraisal theorists see these eliciting conditions as relying on (usually unconscious) inference about changes in the likelihood of goal achievement. In the account presented here, however, emotion systems are understood as responding to perceptual experiences, not probabilistic inferences. Moreover, the variables that affect intensity of emotional response are concrete – proximity, speed and type of movement, direction, line of sight (for animate objects), and so on. Even the timescales are different. In this account, very-short-term perceptual projections (a fraction of a second) and working anticipations (of perhaps a couple of seconds) are crucial. The long-term expectations stressed in appraisal theory have emotional impact only insofar as they incorporate perceptual projections and working anticipations, as well as current experiences and emotional memories. In each case, the relevant elicitors must be directly perceived, remembered, or imagined vividly.

The precise triggers of emotion systems have three sources. Some are innate. The most important innate triggers are emotion expressions. These allow children to learn emotion triggers through the emotional responses of their caregivers. The most important of these learned triggers are acquired during critical periods when the emotion systems develop. Finally, some triggers are the result of emotional experiences, stored as emotional memories, which continue to be acquired throughout one's life.

Other components of an emotion episode include attentional and actional reorientation. These involve an implicit, simplified causal attribution for the emotional experience. Actional reorientation leads eventually to actional outcomes that serve to affect the eliciting conditions, changing aversive conditions or sustaining pleasurable conditions. Actional outcomes are distinct from expressive outcomes. Rather than affecting the eliciting conditions, expressive outcomes serve to alter the emotional responses of others, largely by signaling the emotional state of the subject issuing the expressions. Both expressive and actional outcomes are closely related to the set of physiological outcomes – such as increased respiration rate – that prepare one for action and/or expression. These physiological outcomes may be the somatic substrate for what we experience as the phenomenological tone or feeling of an emotion.

Emotion episodes also involve certain cognitive processes, prominently the integration of a wide array of information in working memory. Much of the information entering working memory derives initially from the emotion systems. Moreover, certain working memory processes are affected by the already triggered emotion state (e.g., inductive versus deductive orientation in inference). But working memory also synthesizes a great deal of information that does not simply derive from emotion systems. As such, it produces new imaginations, reconstructs episodic memories (see Schacter 8, 104–113), activates emotional memories, and in other ways produces an ongoing series of new eliciting conditions for emotion. This complex of working processes constitutes emotional *elaboration*. (For a partial schematization of this account of emotion, see Figure 2.1.)

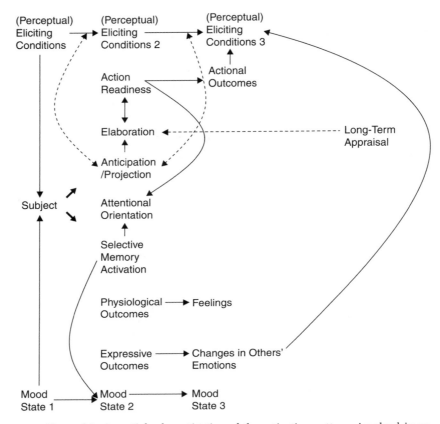

Figure 2.1. A partial schematization of the activation patterns involved in an emotion episode.
Note: Solid arrows mark causal connections. Dotted arrows indicate inclusion (e.g., anticipation and projection are part of eliciting conditions).

Emotional response is, first of all, egoistic in the sense of bearing only on one's own hedonic concerns. We may say that ethical consider- ations enter at the point when egoistic emotional response is qualified by some nonegoistic motivation. Empathy appears to be at the root of nonegoistic emotion. It is closely related to, but also distinct from, emo- tion contagion. In both cases, the immediate cause of one's emotion is someone else's emotion, usually communicated through an expression of that emotion. The difference is a matter of how we isolate the *object* of our emotion, thus what our reference point is for attentional and actional reorientation. Emotional contagion involves a parallel emo- tion directed at the eliciting conditions of the other person's emotion (e.g., the bear that caused the other person to shriek in fear). Empathy involves a parallel emotion directed at the other person's hedonic state (e.g., the person's experience of being near the bear, in the bear's line of sight, etc.). Either may occur spontaneously through attentional processes triggered by mirroring responses. Alternatively, either may occur through elaborative processes in working memory.

Elaborative processes for empathy involve two components – first, an openness to parallel emotional experience; second, skills at attending to, simulating, categorizing or modeling, and otherwise understanding the other person's emotional experience. As with other emotion processes, both spontaneous and elaborative empathy include innate components (presumably bound up with mirror neuron operation), critical period developments (presumably involving caregiver responses to others and to the child himself or herself), and emotional memories. In the case of elaborative empathy, there seem to be further, trainable skills involved as well (e.g., the development of encoding strategies or multiple and complex models for particular emotions).

Literature may play a role in fostering openness to empathic response. In any case, it appears to help readers develop skills for empathic understanding. It focuses attention on emotion-relevant nuances of expression and action, often subtly differentiating details of eliciting conditions, and so on. Of course, literature may also play the opposite role. Through ideologies bearing on identity groups, literature may inhibit empathic openness or foster the use of mistaken strategies for simulation and inference. Nonetheless, there is a strong tendency for authors who are exploring characters to specify those characters in ways that are at least partially inconsistent with identity group divisions. Thus, literary works often end up cultivating some empathy even for out-group members and at least partially challenging empathy-inhibiting ideologies.

3. Romantic Love

Sappho, Li Ch'ing-Chao, and *Romeo and Juliet*

Romantic Spaces: Desire, Attachment, and Dependency

Twenty-six hundred years ago, the Greek poet, Sappho, rejoiced in the return of her beloved and blessed her for putting an end to the time of separation and "longing" (Edmonds 249). Nine hundred years ago, the great Chinese poet, Li Ch'ing-Chao, wrote a poem about spring. The bulk of the poem concerns the transition from winter – the new grass, the buds of plum blossoms. Despite the change of season, however, the poem is ambivalent. "Spring has come," she explains, but "Plum blossoms are slightly broken" (Hu 87). By the end of the poem, we understand the ambivalence. Addressing her husband, she explains, "Twice in three years you missed the spring," and implores, "Do come back" (Hu 88). Here, she counts time not simply in seasons, but in the presence or absence of her beloved. As both poets suggest, time and space are not only fundamental to our epistemic relation to the world; they are equally fundamental to our emotional relation to the world. Our sense of both time and space is structured by feeling.

As to our sense of space, distances appear small or vast depending on our interests in bridging them. The most obvious coordinates of distance are bodily proximity. We might think of them as organized around the poles of disgust and desire. Disgust wants us to keep someone "at arm's length," beyond the space of possible touch – ideally, beyond the range of smell. Desire makes us wish to bring the full length of skin against skin. This is clearly part of romantic love. Li suggests the point subtly when she calls to her husband to "celebrate an incomparable flower" which is "Half-open ... In the middle of the garden," "like beauties just coming out of a bath" (Hu 42). The images suggest the opposites of disgust triggers – beauty, fragrance, cleanliness. In another poem, touch enters with her "skin, delicate, smooth" (Hu 100), which she reveals to her husband.

But, of course, there is more to romantic love than desire. A fragment from Sappho suggests this when she explains how she "ran ... like a little girl/after her mother" (Barnard 54; see also Edmonds 279), presumably following her beloved. That is, of course, attachment. It is almost a commonplace of research on romantic love that such love fuses lust with the tenderness of attachment (see, for example, Shaver and Hazan 482[1]). Indeed, as Sappho implies, it is not merely that romantic love involves the same type of feelings, the same psychological system, the same neurochemistry or neuron populations as parental and filial bonds. Rather, the precise nature of our early associations shapes how we experience romantic love later on.

Clearly, the manifestations of attachment bonds are not confined to our sense of space. Those bonds, however, are closely bound up with space. For the child, space is, in some ways, first of all defined simply by the presence or absence of Mom. There are, of course, other axes of familiarity and security. But a fundamental division is, roughly, "with Mom" and ... everything else. The child's geography is not unlike that of the ancient cartographers who distinguished between the known

---

[1] Following Bowlby, Shaver and Hazan distinguish caregiving from attachment and see both as contributing to romantic love. There are, of course, differences in the general behavior of parents and children and this may suggest that we should distinguish attachment from caregiving. However, by the account of emotion presented in Chapter 2, we would expect different situations to activate emotion systems in different degrees, with somewhat varying neuron populations (including those of other emotion systems, with which the attachment system stands in excitatory or inhibitory relations), somewhat different expressive or actional outcomes, and so forth. Thus, we would expect the situations of children to give rise to (attachment-based) need more often than (attachment-based) solicitude and the situations of parents to give rise to solicitude more often than need, given attachment on both sides. All the same, it seems clear that, in the right circumstances, attachment provokes even heroically protective solicitude from children toward parents and terrible separation anxiety from parents toward children. This suggests that the system is the same.

Sometimes, authors distinguish attachment from affiliation, on the grounds that the parent/child bond is not simply a matter of protection and security. This is certainly true, but it means that attachment itself is not a matter of protection. (Technically, it is only functionally similar to protection in its results.) It is, of course, true that someone (e.g., a child) may feel deeply reliant on someone else (e.g., a parent) for personal security. Frightened by a dog, a small child may jump into the arms of an adult he or she barely knows. In those circumstances, the child would probably feel panic if the adult tried to leave. This is a real emotion and it undoubtedly occurs between children and parents. However, it is not attachment.

world, centered in their own capital, and the unknown world, marked by the legend, "There Be Monsters." For the child, there is the safe space of home, centered in mother's arms, and, surrounding it on all sides, an alien space marked with the same legend as those yellowing maps.

Of course, this makes sense for the child, for whom much of the unknown world does hold the equivalent of monsters. But adults in love feel just the same. Sappho may not chase after her lover whenever she leaves the room. But her pursuit of her beloved over longer and sometimes perhaps even shorter distances manifests the same worry. Here, then, is where "attachment style" enters, the persistence of attachment patterns developed in childhood. Perhaps most importantly, as empirical research has indicated, a child may have more or less security of attachment with his or her caregiver.[2] That security or insecurity is likely to carry over into his or her later relationships.[3]

In keeping with this, a child may respond to these two spaces (i.e., with Mom and anywhere else) in different ways. Indeed, some writers distinguish a third space in the child's emotional geography, a sort of borderland between the security of Mom and the dangers of the Dark Beyond. To continue our metaphor, it is a sort of borderland, a frontier. The child's sense of security gives location and extent to that borderland. If a child's security of attachment is great, then the borderland may be deep, extending far from the caregiver. If the child's security of attachment is slight, then the borderland may barely extend beyond the length of the caregiver's arms.

This reference to the caregiver's arms points to another aspect of our emotional geography. Our fundamental bodily space is the space of our action, the space of what we can touch, take, or repel. It is bound up with the frontal and parietal systems that produce our "peripersonal space map" (Iacoboni 16), the map of *"potential actions"* (16), along with our own "body schema" (132). (These are differentiated from the hippocampal system, which gives us objective, rather than subject-relative representations of space; see Clark, Boutros, and Mendez 43.) In social emotions, this sense of bodily space is doubled. At least when we have

---

[2] For a concise outline of attachment patterns, see Parkes 13–15; see also Mikulincer 28–29 and Fitness, Fletcher, and Overall 229. (Treatments of attachment types, though closely related, are not entirely uniform.)

[3] On the complex persistence and alteration in attachment patterns, see Waters, Weinfield, and Hamilton, as well as the entire issue of *Child Development* (71.3 [May/June 2000]) in which this appears. For a more recent discussion, see Holland and Roisman.

some interest in another person's physical relation to us, we spontaneously place ourselves in his or her position, simulating his or her sense
of bodily space.[4] We know, in a bodily way, not only whether we can
reach others, but whether they can reach us. Our attitude toward that
bodily space varies radically depending upon our feeling about that
other person.

There are two obvious axes governing our response to these interrelated bodily spaces, these actional or existential spaces (as we might
call them) of self and other. The first is the axis of disgust and desire,
already mentioned. The second is the axis of trust and fear. The former
bears more obviously on sexuality; the second bears more clearly on
attachment. In each case, we have a sort of default case and a change in
that default case that results from the interaction of different emotion
systems.

We will consider disgust in Chapter 7. However, it is worth making
a few basic observations here. Generally, we do not find the appearance
of other people disgusting. But we do, as a default, find their bodily
products disgusting and we find bodily contact with them disgusting
in proportion to its intimacy (e.g., contact of clothing is less disgusting
than contact of skin). Moreover, we find others more disgusting to the
degree that they are ill – or, of course, when they die.

Desire is the opposite pole of an axis here in the sense that it leads us
to wish for intimate physical contact that is rejected in disgust. However,
it is important to recognize that disgust/desire ambivalence is not only
possible, but common. Disgust and desire remain opposites because
the objects of both disgust and desire are not people, but rather aspects
of people. Jones may find Smith both attractive and disgusting because
he finds Smith's shape attractive and Smith's breath sour. He does not
simultaneously find Smith's shape or Smith's breath both attractive and
disgusting. The point is important, because it bears on the reality as
well as the (literary or other) idealization of romantic love.

Before considering this point further, we should turn to the second
axis, that of fear and trust. Here, the default is mild fear – hence the
fact that seeing a stranger's face causes amygdala activation, suggesting
apprehension (see Oatley *Emotions* 73). One's first impulse is to say that
attachment involves trust as a fundamental component. However, that

---

[4] Of course, here as elsewhere, the simulation is not absolute. We still do distinguish
between our own actions and those of others – perhaps by way of our mapping of our
own bodies (see Iacoboni 132).

does not appear to be true. If Sappho trusted her beloved, would she run after her like a panicked child? Or, for that matter, would a panicked child run after his or her mother if he or she fully trusted her? Rather, trust seems to vary with the security of the attachment. Indeed, security of attachment could be understood as trust in the attachment object. But what does that trust comprise? The most obvious component is the opposite of what we tacitly assume in fear. We fear someone due to an implicit assumption of their malevolence. To trust someone is to implicitly assume their benevolence. The strongest guarantor of their benevolence is, of course, their own attachment. Put differently, malevolence (which might otherwise be merely temporary and incidental) reaches its most extended form in personal antipathy, whereas benevolence (which might otherwise be merely temporary and incidental) reaches its most extended form in attachment. One's own feeling of attachment does not necessarily entail trust, for attachment may be insecure. However, the ideal of attachment is trust, and the ideal of trust involves the other person's reciprocated attachment.[5]

What does this suggest about attachment generally and romantic love particularly? It suggests that we should strongly wish for our attachment objects to reciprocate our feelings. Moreover, if someone feels that his or her attachment is not reciprocated, we would expect him or her to feel insecure – not precisely fearful (for there is not necessarily any particular danger that would trigger fear), but afflicted by a more diffuse anxiety. With respect to romantic love, one would expect that this need for reciprocity, and the corresponding anxiety, would be proportionate to the force of the attachment and the degree of insecurity lingering from childhood.

But trust is not contingent on reciprocal attachment only. It involves at least two other components. A child may fully trust the mother's feelings and yet feel great anxiety when entering another room where Mom is not present, when going beyond the "borderland" of relative security. The reasons for this are simple and obvious. The benevolence of the caregiver does no good if he or she is not in a position to help should some threat arise – or, worse still, if he or she is not in a position even to know about such a threat. Of course, the distance a child

[5] The ideal is, of course, eminently reasonable, given the practical importance of trust in a love relationship (see Clark and Monin 212–216). Moreover, it is not neurologically implausible, but facilitated by neurochemistry. As Oatley, Keltner, and Jenkins point out, "oxytocin release correlated significantly with the occurrence of displays of love." Research also shows that "oxytocin is involved in trust" (162).

is willing to wander is not solely dependent on trust in caregivers. It is in part dependent on self-confidence as well – self-confidence related to the child's sense of his or her own abilities, his or her familiarity with the place, and so on. At least initially, however, even this self-confidence is partially underwritten by the child's trust in the caregiver's ability to intervene when the child cannot successfully cope with the new place or what happens there. This returns us to space. The crucial aspect of space here is the distance at which the caregiver can know and act, the distance at which he or she can, for example, hear the child cry and come to help or comfort.

The worries of adults are typically not physical, but social and emotional. A child wants Mom around in case he or she falls and gets scraped. An adult is more likely to worry about job insecurity or mortgage payments. Moreover, our precise delimitation of space changes vastly. Yet something stays the same. We still need our attachment figures to give us their attention and to know what troubles us, or what makes us happy. As Rimé stresses, and as discussed in Chapter 1, we share our emotions with attachment figures. This is part of attachment. There is a painful contradiction between loving and being unable to communicate what we feel – unless we are inhibiting the communication for some higher purpose that itself serves attachment, such as protecting the beloved from anxiety. Moreover, we need the beloved to give comfort and indeed to receive comfort from us – comfort that often assumes the bodily form of caresses.

The fundamental spatial organization of attachment, then, is one of accessibility. In emotional geography, distance is a matter of how far we need to go to hear the voice or feel the touch of the beloved. Thus, we would expect that separation would disturb and disorient us. It means that the beloved can neither know nor act on what concerns us. Moreover, we cannot know or act on what concerns him or her. There is a double failure of trust. This is not a loss of trust in the person's intentions. We may have no doubt about his or her feelings. It is, rather, a loss of trust in his or her capacity. Again, the result is diffuse anxiety.

Li expresses the feeling nicely in a poem about the end of autumn. Just as spring was beginning in the other poem, here, winter is imminent. There is no specific threat, but all of nature is somber; "Flowers are few.... Lotus leaves are faded" (Hu 57). The herons have hidden their heads – the image suggests shame over their emotion or worry over what they might see. Why? They "grudg[e]" the departure of the husband and wife (Hu 57) or "regret" that her husband must leave "so soon" (Rexroth and Chung 12). The change of season and the behavior of the herons – Li's characteristic "fusion of emotion and scene" (Hu 121) – serve to represent the anxiety felt by Li at the prospect of this separation. Put differently, the entire space around her is suffused with the anxiety of an alien place as the departure of her husband approaches.

Yet it seems clear that the hurt of separation goes beyond anxiety. Even more clearly, the joy of reunited lovers surpasses relief. There is a sort of ecstasy in union that is more than both the renewed sense of security and the physical pleasure of carnal fulfillment. When Sappho is separated from her beloved, her response is much deeper than a sort of wariness about an alien world. It is a pain so severe that she wishes for her own death (Page 76).[6] The bliss of reunion is just as extreme. This suggests that the deepest source of our sense of joy and loss are part of romantic love as well. This is presumably the endogenous reward system, the system that, for example, addicts men and women to drugs. In keeping with this, Fisher notes that romantic love is "associated with elevated activity of dopamine in the reward pathways of the brain" (90; see also 94). She also notes the involvement of the nucleus accumbens and the ventral tegmental area (90–92), both part of the reward system (see Kupfermann, Kandel, and Iversen 1009–1012). Love is not only sexual desire and attachment; it is a relation to the beloved that makes

---

[6] There is disagreement as to whether the person wishing to die in this poem is the speaker of the poem or the addressee (see, for example, Williamson 144). Either interpretation fits the following analysis of the feeling. I have chosen to attribute the feeling to the speaker ("Sappho") because I find Page's interpretation of the complex meanings of the poem to be compelling (see Page 82; Stehle also attributes the line to the speaker – see 147). In either case, the wish to die is the result of the usual distress over separation from one's beloved. I am therefore somewhat baffled by Snyder's claim that critics attribute this despair to Sappho because of a bigoted feeling that she must be "unhappy" because her love is "unnatural" (59). Indeed, the point is precisely the opposite. The lesbian love expressed in the poems, and rightly emphasized by Snyder, is no different from nonlesbian love in this respect.

The issue of who is speaking this particular line, however, is related to a larger issue in Sappho interpretation. Critics emphasize Sappho's place as the leader of a group of young women. They therefore stress the communal purposes of her poetry. For example, Hallett writes that "Sappho's verses were basically intended as public, rather than personal, statements." Thus "even those written in the first person may not express her own feelings" (139; see also Williamson 146 on this particular poem). This is probably true, but not crucial for purposes of the present analysis. When Shakespeare writes in the voice of Romeo or Juliet, he is not expressing his own actual feelings for Juliet or Romeo. This does not make the speech any less emotionally compelling for the reader nor does it make its insights into the emotion any less valid. Moreover, as Williamson point out, "it would be perverse to argue that there is nothing of the poet herself in her love poetry, even if the voice may sometimes be mediated by poetic personae or may express loves other than her own" (132).

our physical well-being neurochemically dependent on him or her.[7] We may refer to this as "reward dependency."

This account fits with another feature of romantic love. Reunion after separation is joyous. But we habituate to togetherness; it becomes ordinary (though shared touch may still provoke opiate release, with beneficial calming effects [see Oatley, Keltner, and Jenkins 161]). This does not prevent subsequent separation from being deeply painful. In keeping with this, Wong points out that dopamine systems are bound up with "motivational value" rather than "hedonic properties" (229), thus "striving," rather than "the experience of pleasure" (231). He discusses this in the context of drug addiction, where the drug is sought even in the absence of "euphoric effects" (231).

But just what is it that addicts us – not to love (as the adage has it), but to the beloved? Literature, of course, cannot provide us with the neurological details, but it does suggest some things. The first noteworthy thing about this dependency is that it is individualized. In other words, it is not substitutable. If I am hungry, I can satisfy my hunger with different sorts of food, even though I may prefer one over others. If I am thirsty or have sexual desire, parallel points hold. But if I am feeling the dependency-based effects of separation, then only the beloved will relieve the pain. Love, so to speak, accepts no substitutes. We tend to view the beloved as somehow unique. (Attributing uniqueness to the beloved is a standard feature of romantic love; see Fisher, et al.) But it is, in fact, our emotional response that is unique.

This situation seems to have resulted from the linking of reward dependency and attachment. Addiction is not generally tied to a unique object. Attachment is (see Parkes 3). The integration of the two systems seems to explain the particularity of reward dependency in this case. On the other hand, these systems already had shared properties that facilitated their integration. Thus, as Panksepp notes, "attachments and addictive dependencies share ... key attributes" ("Affective" 54).[8]

---

[7] This is not unrelated to sexual desire and attachment. Indeed, as one would expect, the systems are interrelated. As Stein and Vythilingum point out, "When attraction is high, there may be significant overlap of and interaction between the neurocircuitry involved in mediating bonding and that involved in mediating reward." Moreover, "Dopaminergic fibers originate in the VTA [ventral tegmental area]," which is involved in "[b]oth maternal and romantic love," and "dopamine plays a key role in both attachment states and in reward processing" (240).

[8] See also Oatley, Keltner, and Jenkins 161, and citations on the relation between "affiliative bonding" and dopamine, as well as Stein and Vythilingum, quoted in the preceding note.

In any event, because both attachment and, in this case, reward dependency are individual, romantic love tends to be strongly linked with individuating features of the beloved. The most obvious of these features is the beloved's face. But the point applies no less to the beloved's voice, posture, touch, gait – "the dear sound of your footstep,"[9] as Sappho put it (Barnard 41). The experience of these unique features is an experience of the beloved's presence – producing, when most intense, the joy of (neurochemical) reward, along with sexual arousal and the calming of anxiety.

Delight in the beloved's uniqueness is obviously, in most cases, bound up with seeing the beloved. But, as with so much else in romantic love, this seeing involves a need for reciprocity. We see the beloved and, generally, wish to be seen by them as well. Indeed, we want to see the "brightness of her beaming face" (Edmonds 209; "the bright radiance of her changing face" in Page [53]) on seeing us.[10] We want the beloved to see us with the same joy as we see them, the same sense of reward.

In its most extreme forms, this concern for the beloved's perception and response can lead the lover to evaluate his or her relation to the world at large almost entirely through the reception given by the beloved. Thus, when apart from her husband, Li cannot bring herself even to comb her hair, for, without him, "All effort would be wasted" (Rexroth and Chung 49). Indeed, as we would expect, the point extends to her relation to space. She does not fix the furniture for the same reason.

With respect to being seen, then, the lover's only concern is to appear his or her best to the beloved. The lover turns a critical eye on him- or herself, to enhance the pleasure of the beloved. But, with respect to seeing the beloved, the lover may be almost entirely uncritical – at least at those points when love is most intense. Put differently, our sense of reward and attachment leads us to experience the beloved as beautiful. We experience a certain complex joy on seeing the beloved and, as a result, judge him or her to be beautiful. Why might this happen?

---

[9] Or "lovely step" (Carson 29), to stress the relation of the Greek *eraton* to "love" (see Carson 28 and Snyder 70).

[10] A standard interpretation of this line is as a comparison and contrast with the flash of weapons in an army (see Page 57), since Sappho is contrasting what she sees as most beautiful with what other people see as most beautiful. That is certainly plausible. Even so, however, the comparison suggests the beloved's presence and her awareness of the speaker.

Normally, our judgments of beauty are guided at least in part by averaging. Studies have repeatedly shown that the most average face is seen as the most beautiful face (see Langlois and Roggman). But whatever serves as a marker of the beloved's uniqueness can serve as a trigger for reward and for attachment-based relief. Thus, the very features of the beloved that deviate from the average – which is to say, features that we would normally see as violating aesthetic standards – may be features that mark their uniqueness the most fully. In consequence, those features may be the very features that we respond to most strongly, which is to say, with the greatest sense of beauty. As Sappho put it, some people think that ships or cavalry are the most beautiful things on the "dark earth." But she believes it is "whatever one loves" (Barnard 41). Indeed, the point finds an unlikely supporter in Kant's aesthetics. Kant emphasized that a genuine judgment of the beautiful is singular (*Critique of Judgment* 154), and that beauty cannot follow a rule (79). In Kantian terms, the beloved is an ideal case of beauty, for we judge him or her to be beautiful precisely in his or her singularity.

Thus, as other writers have remarked, one does not so much love someone because he or she is beautiful; one finds someone beautiful because one loves him or her. Indeed, the point generalizes. What one feels in response to the beloved's presence can easily become the source of a wide range of evaluative judgments – concerning the intelligence, virtue, or other properties of the beloved. This leads to the general "overvaluation" or "idealization" of the love object, as Freud famously put it (*Group* 112; my account of this is obviously different from Freud's). The point is nicely expressed in a legend about the paradigmatic lover of the Arabic and Persian traditions, Majnun. As Zia Inayat Khan explains, someone "tried to dissuade Majnun from his obsessive love of Layla, arguing that she was really rather plain. However, Majnun answered that 'My Layla must be seen with my eyes'" (xxi).

The physical aspect of this overvaluation is particularly important. This allows us to return to the disgust/desire axis. We saw earlier that sexual desire appears to be inversely related to disgust. In certain respects, it is clear that sexual desire inhibits disgust reactions. For example, sexual desire may involve an active interest in engaging in acts where one shares saliva with another person – generally, a thoroughly repulsive idea. Attachment appears to inhibit disgust as well. Insofar as attachment leads me to see someone's identifying features as beautiful, I am less likely to see that person's features as disgusting. On the other hand, it is clear that the disgust system is not at all disabled in romantic love. When faced with disgust triggers, sexual arousal can be dampened and approach behaviors associated with attachment or dependency (such as caressing) may be inhibited. One result of this is that, in romantic love, we generally feel that we should inhibit the disgust we impose on our partners. At the same time, we feel that the beloved should be able to suppress disgust when that is physically or emotionally necessary – for example, at times of caretaking and at times of emotion sharing.

Romantic Time: Durations and Trajectories

We began this outline of romantic love with the idea that both space and time are organized and oriented by feeling. We have considered space, and this has led us to a range of other observations about the nature of romantic love, particularly its components of sexual desire, attachment, and reward dependency. We should now turn to time.

Clearly, our subjective sense of time is as much governed by feeling as our subjective sense of space. Indeed, it is as governed by the component feelings of romantic love. It is as much a matter of desire, addiction, and attachment.

In treating the subjective experience of time, it is important to begin with several distinctions. First, we have a default sense of time, a gauge that we use in judging when to begin and end certain activities, when to return to tasks left aside. There is usually a rough correspondence between our default sense of time and the objective passage of time as recorded on clocks. I put fish in the oven, then go to check my e-mail. I return to the kitchen when I sense that it is about time for the fish to be done. I talk for a while in class. When I have the sense that we are nearing the end of the class period, I check my watch. My timing is never perfect, but it is close enough.

There are, however, periods when we do not operate with the default pacing of time. Rather, we check our watches and find that far more or far less time has passed than we tacitly anticipated. We may refer to this as our experience of temporal *duration*. In some cases, our experience of temporal duration is greatly extended beyond the default; in some cases, it is greatly reduced.

In addition, we have a sense of how long it will take to achieve some goal – to arrive at a destination, to finish a project. This is our anticipated temporal *trajectory*. Here it is important to make a further subdivision. There is a temporal trajectory that we can, in effect, imagine as a sort of experience. Then there is a temporal trajectory that is a mere number, a calculation beyond our imaginative capacities. Or perhaps there is a scale of imaginability. I feel that I have a very clear imaginative sense of what it means that I will see my wife in two hours; a fairly clear imaginative sense of what it means that I will see her in two days; a marginal imaginative sense of what it means that I will see her in two weeks; and really no imaginative sense at all of what it means that I will see her in two months. The division here is, I believe, related to three things. First, it is related to our sense of duration. The closer an anticipated trajectory comes to a unit of experiential duration, the more it is concretely imaginable. Second, it is related to our emotional constitution. An anticipated trajectory is more "experiential" to the extent that it coincides with the time of some possible emotional state – most importantly, a mood, rather than an emotional episode. Finally, it is related to an important division between *fantasy* and *planning*.

By "fantasy," I mean the imagination of any desirable or undesirable state or event. Fantasy, so to speak, takes no stand on the actual possibility of that state or event. In contrast, planning is the determination of concrete steps that may be undertaken to pursue such a state (if it is desirable) or to prevent it (if it is undesirable), beginning from one's current condition. We may add *enactment* as the putting into practice of the plan.

Our sense of duration becomes bloated when we are in pain. It dwindles when we are in a state of joy. That is unremarkable in itself. But it tells us that we should expect the reward dependency of love to drag out time in the pain of separation and to condense it in the delight of union. This is not the pleasure of sexuality or the pain of frustration, though those of course contribute to our sense of time. This is predominantly a matter of the craving for presence – for touch, voice, scent – that goes along with the particularity of love. In one of her most famous poems, Li expresses this both by referring to the passing of seasons, and by creating a sense of the slow passage of every moment through the imagery and sound of her verse. Her use of repetition is particularly haunting. The poem begins "xún xún mì mì/lěng lěng qīng qīng/qī qī cǎn cǎn qī qī," "search search seek seek/cold cold clear clear/miserable miserable sad sad sorrowful sorrowful." Subsequently, she refers to the rain, "diǎn diǎn dī dī," "drop drop drip drip" (Cai 274). The monosyllables mark the constantly repeating moments of pain, separation isolating and extending each of these instants.

As this example suggests – through its references to searching and seeking – our durative experience of time is inseparable from our anticipatory trajectories.[11] Specifically, it seems that our durative experience is inseparable from our sense of planning.[12] Other things being equal, insofar as lovers can formulate and enact plans bearing on their union or separation, their experience of duration will tend to regress toward the default. However, insofar as they are unable to do this, the discrepancy between experienced and real duration will be enhanced. Times of union and joy will seem still briefer, and painful separations will stretch out, seemingly without end (like the dripping of water in Li's poem).

To consider the crucial temporal trajectories for lovers, let us return for a moment to children. The security of the child is a function of Mom's spatial location primarily insofar as that determines Mom's access to knowledge and ability to act. In other words, space here is, in effect, a proxy for an anticipated trajectory – a trajectory of communication, a trajectory of comfort, or whatever. For the child, the key aspect of the attachment object's location is how that location will affect sharing of feelings (e.g., pain or pride) and how this will inhibit or allow contact. In other words, it is a matter of the temporality of possible plans. These plans are, of course, reciprocal. They concern how the child will make it to the caregiver and equally how the caregiver will make it to the child.

---

[11] There are obviously many aspects to this in the case of romantic love. For example, one, which we will not be considering here, involves our sense of prototypical relationship stages. For a discussion of some of these other issues, see Honeycutt and Cantrill.

[12] The approach here is obviously different from the more standard account of "scalar timing theory." In that theory, experiences of duration are accounted for by three mechanisms – a pacemaker (marking time units by pulses), a switch (marking the start and finish of the relevant time period), and an accumulator (yielding the total sum of pulses, thus the experiential duration). Gil, Rousset, and Droit-Volet draw on this model to argue that "when the internal clock runs faster than normal, time passes faster, and the individual is ready to produce an action earlier, for example, to give immediate first aid to an accident victim" (462). The account presented here differs from that of Gill, Rousset, and Droit-Volet not only in cognitive architecture (not including such structures as an "accumulator"). It also differs in viewing the duration of time as bound up with the interaction of motivation to act with ability (or inability) to engage in action, along with hedonic quality and intensity or reward system involvement, and other factors. On the other hand, the two accounts are not entirely mutually exclusive. For example, the present account also suggests some sort of default system of bodily timing along the lines of a pulsing "pacemaker," and the account of Gil, Rousset, and Droit-Volet stresses attention, which would necessarily figure in a full development of the present account.

The infantile anticipatory temporality of attachment is, first of all, the time of that planned trajectory – the time of reaching the attachment figure, by sound, by sight, by touch.

Or, rather, this is one primary mode of anticipatory temporality. This is the mode of possible action. A second mode occurs when the child cannot envision any plan that will end the separation. He or she does not know where the caregiver is or knows but cannot reach or communicate with the place. This results in panic.

There is a third mode as well, a lull between the realization of separation and either enactment of a plan or panic in the face of impossibility. This is the "in-between" time, parallel to the "in-between" or frontier space; it is the period of waiting when the pain of separation can be deferred. The child calls "Mom!" and looks about expectantly. He or she calls again, turning more vigorously. After a moment, he or she gets up and toddles to the other room (enactment) or begins to cry (panic).

Lovers are remarkably similar. The periods across which they can defer pain are much longer, just as their organization of space is more elaborate. But the modes of response are fundamentally the same. Lovers organize time by reference to how quickly they can hear, see, or touch. They defer the pain of separation through the usual mechanisms of emotion regulation, such as distraction (see Gross). In the interim, their sense of the duration of time is distorted in the usual way, depending on just how successful the emotion control happens to be. When faced with the impossibility of action, they may panic or fall into a sense of despair, a sense that there is no hope for a future in which they will be able to take steps to end the pain of separation. This is the despair that led to Sappho's death wish.

Romeo and Juliet

The points we have been considering manifest themselves abundantly in *Romeo and Juliet*.[13] The play, however, has the advantage of integrating

---

[13] Readers of *Romeo and Juliet* may be surprised to find that relatively little criticism on the play treats romantic love. The tendency of most critics who might have treated this issue has been, rather, to take up an approach influenced by psychoanalysis and refer only to desire. Thus Belsey asserts that *"Romeo and Juliet* is about desire" (53). Writers such as Lloyd Davis refer to "love," but do so in the context of Lacanian "lack," which defines desire. Other psychoanalytic approaches rely on dubious accounts of love that do not seem consistent with recent research on the topic. For example, Kristeva insists

these properties into a life story. Moreover, that story is at once particular and structured by a pervasive narrative prototype, romantic tragi-
comedy.[14] Indeed, part of the force of the story comes from the ways
it both manifests and varies that structure. For that reason, it may be
valuable to recall the standard structure (briefly outlined in Chapter 1)
before entering into the play itself.

A prototypical romantic plot begins with two people falling in love.
This love is, however, problematic. Specifically, it involves some conflict
with social hierarchy – commonly familial, though sometimes religious
or political. There are two recurring reasons for the problem. It may
simply violate the preferences of the authority. For example, the woman's parents may prefer another groom. It may also be the case that the
lovers are from groups that are antagonistic (e.g., warring nations) or
hierarchized (e.g., different classes), thus from groups between which
marriage is socially taboo. This conflict leads to the separation of the
lovers. Here we see the space of the narrative shaped by the emotional
geography of romantic love. The separation often sends the man into
exile and confines the woman to the home. A brief experience of despair
may be followed by the intervention of helpers – often versions of social

on "the intrinsic presence of hatred in amatory feeling," for "the relation with an
other, hatred ... is more ancient than love." Specifically, "As soon as an *other* appears
different from myself, it becomes ... hated" (79).

[14] On the cross-cultural and transhistorical pervasiveness of this prototype, see chapter three of Hogan *The Mind*. Some influential Shakespeare critics dismiss the idea
that the play manifests "a universal legend of love ... characteristic of the human
condition in every age and culture" (Callaghan 87). In fact, empirical evidence suggests that the view derided by such critics is more or less correct, leaving aside the
tendentious phrasing (e.g., it is not *the* human condition, but a recurring part of
human experience). Moreover, I hope it is clear from the preceding discussion of
Sappho that there is nothing in the idea of romantic love that "relegates homosexuality to the sphere of deviance," and that both Sappho and Li would challenge the
contention that romantic love is bound up with "women's submission" (Callaghan
86). Of course, individual works may certainly use romantic or other plots toward
patriarchal ends. On the other hand, the general tendency of romantic emplotment
is to develop sympathy for the lovers and against figures of authority. Thus, due both
to its genre and its particular development of that genre, it is difficult to understand
Callaghan's view that the play "produces the required subjectivities and harnesses
them for the state" (92). One problem here is that many interpretations of the play
seem to be based on a rejection of any emotional response to the play. It is difficult to
see how someone could view the play as affirming hierarchy, given readers' general
sympathy with the lovers. Similarly, it is difficult to understand the idea that critics
"expose the misogyny" of *Romeo and Juliet* (Goldberg 226), unless one suppresses
any sense of readers' feelings for the women and men in the play. For example, how
many readers' feelings are consistent with the idea that the play is hateful toward
Juliet and admiring toward her father?

authorities themselves, also familial, religious, or political. This allows
the lovers to make plans to be reunited. The association of separation
with deep pain and a desire for death, along with a sense of despair,
may be developed into the actual death of one or both lovers. If this
occurs, we have a tragic version of the plot. In cases where there is no
actual death, there is often a rumor or possibility of death. Following
this, comic versions of the plot allow the lovers' plans to succeed, such
that they are reunited. The enduring quality of the comic ending –
where the lovers live "happily ever after" – is a standard idealization.

Romeo and Juliet opens with a curious prologue that seems to establish the play not as romantic, but as sacrificial. In the sacrificial tragi-
comedy (another cross-culturally recurring structure[15]), society has
committed some violation of moral, usually divine law. In a Christian
context, the prototype of this violation is the Fall of Adam and Eve – a
violation that not only prefigures, but allows for all subsequent violations. In the Judeo-Christian story and elsewhere, the sin results in
communal devastation. Commonly, that devastation involves famine
or disease, though it may be of other sorts as well. To compensate for
the initial sin, the devastated society must sacrifice. Often, the devastation may be ended only with the sacrifice of some innocent member of
the society, who gives up his or her life for the well-being of the larger
community. Here, of course, the Christian prototype is Jesus.

As a sacrificial plot, *Romeo and Juliet* is not very prototypical. First of
all, the devastation is neither famine nor disease, but a sort of civil war.
Moreover, this devastating conflict is not divine punishment for a prior
crime. It is, rather, both the crime and the punishment, worked out in
cycles of cruelty and retribution. The people's "hands" are "unclean"
(thus sinful) precisely because they are stained with "blood" (l.4). In
this way, Shakespeare presents us with a secular version of the sacrificial plot. The general sacrificial structure is preserved, however, for
there is a Jesus-like innocent who must die. Or, rather, there are two
such innocents – Romeo and Juliet, who "with their death bury their
parents' strife" (l.8).

Needless to say, the doubling of the innocent victim into a boy and
a girl from the different, warring houses is crucial to the development
of this as a romantic plot. This embedment of a romantic plot in a sacrificial one inflects the characterization of the group division that so
often makes the lovers' union difficult or even impossible. Here, that

---

[15] See chapter 6 of *The Mind*.

division is a scourge on society – again, both a sin and a punishment. This further stresses the innocence of the lovers, and indeed of romantic love – an innocence that is part of the idealization of love in the play, and also part of the play's ethical suggestiveness.

The first scene of the play introduces the conflict between the Montagues and the Capulets. Two servingmen of the Capulets enter. One, Sampson, boasts of his violent contempt for the Montagues and his inclination to fight with the men and violate the women. The scene is important not only in establishing the conflict between the two families, but in representing its absurdity. The contempt of the two sides for one another seems to be based entirely on the division into two sides, a division that is, therefore, wholly arbitrary – unlike the class-based division to which the second servant, Gregory, seems to allude, when he says that "The quarrel is between our masters and us their men" (I.i.21–22). Sampson could just as readily have been a servant of the Montagues as of the Capulets. The point obviously tells in favor of the lovers. It does this in part simply by opposing the in-group/out-group division. But it also suggests, perhaps, that romantic attachment in some way involves a superior discernment of individuality in contrast with arbitrary group membership – something one might expect from the particularizing quality of romantic love. The scene also serves to highlight the different sorts of sexuality that may cross group boundaries. Sampson's boastful sexuality is a form of intergroup violence. The sexuality of Romeo and Juliet, in contrast, is conciliatory – precisely because it is linked, not with contempt, but with attachment.

On the other hand, the Montagues and the Capulets are not wholly equal in this scene. Differences in personality weigh one side more heavily toward violence and the other more heavily toward peace. Samson provokes the fight with the Montague servants. Benvolio, a Montague, enters and tries to make peace. He is followed by Tybalt, a Capulet, who professes a "hate" of the very word "peace" (I.i.72).

More importantly, when the patriarchs enter, ready to fight, we find that their wives restrain them. This could suggest that women are generally less warlike than men – and it probably does suggest this. It also suggests, however, that attachment is a force against conflict or war – a point that is amply developed in union of the two main lovers.

The aftermath of the battle allows Benvolio and the Montagues to speak about Romeo. It is clear that Romeo is in a state of melancholy, though the cause is not yet clear. When Romeo enters, his first exchange with Benvolio reveals the predictable consequences of emotion on our experience of temporal duration. When told it is only nine o'clock, Romeo complains that he thought it much later, explaining that "Sad hours seem long" (I.i.164). When questioned further, he explains that, if he had that for which he longed, then the hours would be "short" (I.i.168). Benvolio rightly ascertains that the cause of this temporal disorder is love. Romeo makes it clearer. His love is not reciprocated. This is, perhaps, the fundamental fault in love, and one often bypassed in romantic plots.

A series of jokes following the exchange serves to suggest that Romeo may not be feeling the pain he expresses, that he may be primarily playing the role of a suffering lover. His spirits are not as bleak as he pretends, and his joy does not seem so dependent on his beloved. Nonetheless, he plays the part well. He goes on to assert that he has "lost" himself (I.i.200). He is not where he appears to be, but somewhere else – presumably with the beloved. The idea here is based on the lover's desire for reciprocity. As we noted, Li saw no point in combing her hair unless she was going to be seen by her husband. Similarly, Romeo's own sense of himself has no relation to the responses of Benvolio (thus where he is). His sense of himself – his value, interest, the aptness or advantage of his self-presentation – is a function of her response only. He goes on to make the broad claim that his beloved is beautiful. But in this, too, Romeo seems false or self-deceived, for there is nothing particular about this beauty. It is merely general, even when he elaborates on it subsequently.

Our sense of a problem is furthered when Romeo presents the specifics of his dissatisfaction. The beloved Rosaline is "in strong proof of chastity well armed" (I.i.213). Romeo feels an intense sexual attraction for Rosaline. But despite his melancholy humor, there is little reason to believe that his feelings for her go much beyond such sexual desire. This is not to say that his sexual desire per se shows his lack of attachment and dependency. The desire may be there and quite urgent even with the most sincere attachment. Indeed, the attachment and the desire may be mutually arousing. There is no evidence, however, that Romeo has attachment. Indeed, despite his initial indication that his feelings are not reciprocated, it seems clear that the only reciprocation he requires is an agreement to have sex. In other words, his desire for reciprocation is purely instrumental. If he can make it to Rosaline's bed without her reciprocal feelings, that is perfectly fine with him – as he indicates quite clearly by his complaint that she will not "ope her lap to saint-seducing gold" (I.i.217).

Romeo goes on to complain that he has fallen into "despair" (I.i.225) as Rosaline has sworn to live the life of a nun. What Romeo says is fitting, for Rosaline's choice leaves him with no possibilities for making plans whereby he might overcome his separation. This is precisely the condition that should give rise to despair. Again, however, there is no indication here that Romeo's feelings involve genuine attachment, thus it is unlikely that the pain of separation would overwhelm all other aspects of his life and give rise to true despair.

Still, this does perhaps indicate that Romeo is in a condition of receptivity to love. In other words, the subjective conditions for the emotion may be in place. Benvolio implies that Romeo may be in such a state when he suggests that Romeo consider other possible mates. Romeo rejects the suggestion. But, as we will see, he soon follows Benvolio's advice and does indeed fall in love.

The following scene introduces us to Juliet's position as a possible bride. Capulet discusses the topic with Paris, who has come to seek her hand. Having introduced one part of the romantic conflict – group antagonism – Shakespeare begins to introduce the other – parental preference for a rival. In this scene, Capulet appears somewhat benevolent. He tells Paris that "My will to her consent is but a part" (I.II.17), suggesting that the conflict with familial authority may not be an issue here. Indeed, earlier, the Prince had outlawed the civil strife between Montagues and Capulets, which might be taken to hint that a marriage alliance between these groups would be viewed favorably by political authority as well.

Of course, readers familiar with the play know that these expectations are not fulfilled. The following scene introduces both Juliet herself and a sort of alternate family for Juliet. The Nurse is in all ways the opposite of the proper Capulets. She is unabashedly sexual, open-minded, and, despite all her flaws, genuinely affectionate. Her sexuality, though crude, has a sort of innocence, at least when compared with Romeo's attempt to turn the aspiring nun, Rosaline, into a prostitute. More importantly, the first real sense of attachment in the play comes in this scene, when the Nurse speaks of her dead daughter and dead husband, and of Juliet's infancy. She recalls a scene when Juliet fell. Her husband made a bawdy joke, and the child stopped crying. It is just the sort of event that suggests a secure environment that would promote security of infantile attachment – a quality evident in Juliet's daring later in the play.

The contrast is striking when Lady Capulet stiffly introduces the topic of marriage – "How stands your dispositions to be married?" (I.iii. 65). She urges Paris, the clear parental preference. Yet she apparently leaves the final choice to her daughter, who at this point seems pliable to her parents' will.

Of course, everything changes two scenes later when the lovers meet. Romeo first sees Juliet and is moved immediately to extravagant praise of her unique beauty – and, indeed, her exalted spiritual status. Though overly quick, the feelings expressed by Romeo already evidence that his response is predominantly one of attachment rather than lust. For example, the content of his speech on Juliet contrasts strikingly with the overtly sexual images he used – and aims he expressed – in discussing Rosaline. Thus, he speaks of how he will touch Juliet's hand and thereby "make blessed my rude hand" (I.v.53). The phrase is significant for two reasons. First, it suggests the sort of contact associated with attachment more than that associated with sexual desire. Second, it suggests the sort of complete idealization that results from a strong feeling of attachment.

Romeo realizes that he was simply pretending to be in love before – even if he was pretending to himself as well as others. He asks himself, "Did my heart love till now?" (I.v.54). The answer is clearly "no."

Immediately following this moment of self-realization, we are reminded of the group conflict. Tybalt wishes to attack Romeo, recognizing his voice though he is masked. Capulet calms him and speaks well of Romeo. This too suggests that we might expect parental authority to be less of an obstacle than is commonly the case in romantic plots.

The first meeting of Romeo and Juliet follows. The meeting is marked by the sort of distorting depictive idealization that we noted in Chapter 1 – in this case, by making the attachment immediately reciprocal. (The speed of Romeo's initial response was an idealization of this sort as well.) Part of the attachment involves the other sort of idealization we have considered – not the idealization of the emotion by the author, but the idealization of each lover by the other.[16] In keeping with this, both Romeo and Juliet use spiritualized imagery to characterize their touch. They then extend from touch of hands to the more clearly sexual touch of lips. But they maintain the spiritualized imagery. In part,

---

[16] For clarity, I will refer to the former as "depictive idealization" and the latter as "attachment idealization," except when context already makes clear which sort of idealization is at issue.

the word play is comic. But it is in part serious as well, suggesting the attachment-based idealization that each engages in – and at the same time suggesting the innocence of this love, including its sexual aspects. As already noted, the sacrificial embedding of the love story hints at a link between the lovers and the paradigmatic sacrificial victim, Jesus. Given this – or, indeed, simply given the sacrificial context generally – we would expect their love to be spiritualized to some degree.

Immediately after this meeting, Romeo and Juliet separately learn each other's identities. Juliet reflects that, for her, Romeo was "Too early seen unknown, and known too late!" (I.v.141). This points to a further aspect of romantic love. One falls in love with someone from the set of possible love objects (cf. Fisher 102). In other words, one is open to certain possible partners. But one does not give others a second look. Again, the latter is sometimes referred to as "erotic discounting," our setting aside some people as possible objects of desire or, in this case, love. Categorization of individuals as members of an antagonistic out-group serves the function of erotic discounting by reducing them to instances of their group category rather than establishing them as individuals. Such categorizations are widely associated with responses of fear and disgust (amygdala and insula activation in fMRI studies) – the opposites of trust and desire – thus just what we would expect to forestall romantic love.

The prologue to act two indicates that Romeo's first love, for Rosaline, was "desire," while the new love, for Juliet, is "affection" (II.1, 2), as we have inferred. It also stresses that the feelings are reciprocal – "Now Romeo is beloved and loves" (l. 5). It then poses the lovers' dilemma. Since their families are enemies, they do not have the opportunity to meet. But they do not despair. They plan what they can do – for, at this point, they are still within the same, mutually accessible space.

The second act opens with Romeo speaking in effect about emotional geography. He refers to Juliet's location as his "center" (II.i.2). Moreover, earlier, Romeo had engaged in witty exchanges with his friends over Rosaline. But now, he retires, rejecting their "jests" (II.ii.1). The famous balcony scene follows.

Despite its renown, most of what Romeo says in this scene is adolescent nonsense (e.g., that her eyes have gone to heaven to twinkle in the place of stars – a bizarre image). But it does serve to communicate two things. First, it repeats his idealization of Juliet, in keeping with attachment, while at the same time stressing the sexual aspect of the relation. Second, and far more importantly, it indicates his careful attention to details of her facial expression and her gestures. This attention to detail – "See how she leans her cheek upon her hand!" (II.ii.23) – is part of his individuating affection, the same sort of feeling that led Sappho to celebrate her beloved's "footstep" (Barnard 41). Moreover, in this case, the attention points toward emotionally expressive features that Romeo is presumably not only witnessing, but mirroring. When her hand touches her cheek, he envisions himself too "touch[ing] that cheek" (II.ii.25). This is precisely what occurs in mirroring, and it points toward a further consequence of attachment. Specifically, it suggests that mirroring is enhanced in attachment relations. This is what one would expect from the empirical research on attachment and empathy. As Royzman and Rozin report, the "intensity of both sympathy [empathic sorrow] and symhedonia [empathic joy] was significantly higher when the target person" was an attachment figure (90).[17]

These evident increases in mirroring and empathy give rise to an almost paradoxical aspect of love. On the one hand, lovers feel that they know and understand each other more fully than they know and understand anyone else. Moreover, they feel that this is reciprocated, that they are known and understood as well (see Hatfield and Rapson on lovers feeling "fully understood" [658]). At the same time, however, there is always the inaccessibility of consciousness that makes lovers uncertain that they are truly loved. Interestingly, in this speech, Romeo reverses this typical concern of the lover, again suggesting an enhanced empathy. Rather than worrying that he cannot know if Juliet loves him, he worries that she does not fully comprehend that he loves her. On seeing her, he remarks with the expected delight, "O, it is my love!," then continues, "O, that she knew she were!" (II.ii.10–11).

Again, though the last-quoted comment shows off Romeo's sensitivity to advantage, most of what he says is muddled. Juliet's reflections are far more sensible.[18] They return us to the practical concern of the warring

---

[17] See also Iacoboni 126–129. In keeping with this, Kim and colleagues note that "administration of oxytocin increases the ability to empathize with others" (2079). Oxytocin is connected with attachment. Oatley, Keltner, and Jenkins explain that oxytocin is "involved in ... maternal bonding" (161). Panksepp reports that it "serves to facilitate maternal moods and related action tendencies" (*Affective* 250); similarly, "evidence ... indicates that ... oxytocin may mediate the attachment of an infant to the mother" (*Affective* 256).

[18] For many years, critics (somewhat incomprehensibly) viewed Juliet as "naïve, immature ... and uncomplicated." With the advent of feminist criticism, however, critics began to recognize that she is "a multifaceted character who transcends Romeo in maturity, complexity, insight, and rhetorical dexterity," to quote Carolyn Brown (333).

families and the larger, normative issues suggested by this conflict. Her crucial statement here is "'Tis but thy name that is my enemy./ Thou art thyself" (II.ii.38–39). The antagonism between Montagues and Capulets is a matter of categories, identifications that reduce particulars to groups. The individuating character of attachment operates to lead Juliet to this recognition – and, with her, the audience, at least for the time of the play. She elaborates on the point, explaining to a fantasized Romeo that the name of Montague "is no part of thee" (II.ii.48) and has no force to affect his "dear perfection" (II.ii.46) – which is to say, the perfection she attributes to him because of her delight even at imagining this attachment object.

Juliet concludes that, just as she will "no longer be a Capulet" (II. ii.36), Romeo should cast off his name. Juliet offers in exchange, "Take all myself" (II.ii.49). The offer extends the particularity of love to the sheer singularity of one's self. Indeed, it points toward the lovers' sense – bound up with enhanced mirroring – that they are really one. Juliet does not merely adjure Romeo to take hold of her body, though that idea is surely there. She urges him to take her very self – precisely what he can never experience, precisely what is always separate. Later, Romeo suggests the same complete and profound identity. When Juliet calls his name, he thinks, "It is my soul that calls upon my name" (II.ii.164).

At last, Romeo speaks. When she is able to hear distinctly, she recognizes his voice. Her particularization of Romeo here is not especially noteworthy because it does not go beyond ordinary human capacities. However, there is a hint of further mirroring. Specifically, Juliet says she has "drunk" the "words/Of thy tongue's uttering" (II.ii.58–59). The image of drinking conveys the event of taking in something from the outside – what she does in hearing Romeo's words. But it indicates that this is done, not by the ear, but by the mouth, throat, and tongue, thus by what Romeo uses to utter those words, not what she uses to hear them. The word "drunk" may also hint at the intoxication both feel at the union, an intoxication suggesting that reward dependency may already have developed. This is indicated further by Romeo's complete indifference to the threat against his life.

Of course, this is not to say that the uncertainties of our necessarily separate human consciousnesses are absent. Juliet asks Romeo directly, "Dost thou love me?" But then she reflects, "I know thou wilt say 'Ay';/ And I will take thy word. Yet, if thou swear'st,/Thou mayst prove false" (II.ii.90–92).

The scene ends with the suggestions of emotional space and time that we would expect. Romeo will call for her by nine the next morning. "'Tis twenty years till then" (II.ii.169), Juliet observes. Despite the danger of the Capulets, they linger, simply delighted by the experiential sharing of their mutual presence. Romeo speaks of "Forgetting any other home but this" (II.ii.175). Presumably, he does not mean the dwelling of the Capulets. Rather, he is referring to the center of his emotional geography – wherever Juliet is, is home. In the closing lines of the scene, he longs for a complete union, wishing he were the peace in Juliet's breast.

Romeo approaches Friar Lawrence in the following scene. He confesses his new love and begs the Friar's help to marry. When reminded of Rosaline, Romeo emphasizes the reciprocal nature of this new attachment. More importantly, Friar Lawrence confirms the earlier indications that Romeo's response to Rosaline was not love so much as a mimicry of love. In that case, "Thy love did read by rote" (II.iii.88), he explains. He then gives his consent to aid the couple. Thus, we find a helping figure who is also a religious authority. This further contributes to the association of the couple with innocence and sanctity, a connection first suggested by the sacrificial frame (though, in this case, perhaps rendered somewhat equivocal for Shakespeare's audience by the fact that the religious figure is Catholic).

In the following scene, we meet Juliet's nurse again, who serves the same helper role as the Friar. Through the nurse, Romeo arranges for his marriage and his wedding-night access to Juliet, thus enacting his plan for their union. Friar Lawrence and the nurse are certainly not idealized characters. They are, in fact, deeply flawed. Nonetheless, they represent a sort of alternative to the more official authority figures in the play. They are, in effect, alternative parents. They provide the "secure base" of "availability, noninterference, and encouragement" that are so important for the autonomous development of children, adolescents, and adults (Feeney and Thrush 57). Perhaps most importantly, they are figures with whom the lovers can share their emotions and whom they can trust with that sharing. Moreover, this occurs within a larger social context of distorted restrictions on emotion sharing. It is, for example, far easier to share feelings of hate in this society than feelings of love. Indeed, in some ways, one could see *Romeo and Juliet* as a play about the devastating consequences of social failures in the sharing of emotions.

The lovers are brought together for marriage in the final scene of the second act. First, Romeo alludes to the reward dependency that is part of a lover's intense craving for the mere presence of the beloved. Speaking as if he has in mind the brief bliss of some addictive drug, he says that he will accept any future "sorrow" in "exchange" for the "joy/That one short minute gives me in her sight" (II. Vi. 3–5). Friar Lawrence rightly characterizes these as "violent delights" (II.vi.9).

The following scene intensifies the group antagonism by crystallizing it in an actual incident. Here, again, the Capulets are at fault. This is primarily because of the hot-headed Tybalt, who kills Mercutio – not a Montague, but a friend of Romeo and a relative of the Prince. Romeo does whatever is in his power to prevent the violence, and Shakespeare makes it clear that Romeo is motivated here by his love of Juliet. The importance of this is the suggestion that attachment does not serve only to make the beloved a single exception to group antagonism. Rather, it softens that group antagonism generally. Because Romeo loves a Capulet, he can say to Tybalt that "Capulet" – the marker of this arbitrary group division – is a "name I tender/As dearly as mine own" (III.i.2–73).

In general, *Romeo and Juliet* does not stress gender ideology. But it is there – largely as an object of implicit criticism. Women and men differ systematically in the play. Most importantly, the men are more violent – in both conflict and in love, as Friar Lawrence's reference to "violent delights" (II.vi.9) suggests. We have already seen that the patriarchs are ready to plunge into battle and are restrained only by their wives. Moreover, Romeo is more liable than Juliet to fanciful, untempered, and imprudent love madness – even beyond his proneness to muddled poetic conceits. Tybalt, the villain of the play, is the most stereotypically masculine character as well. His villainy and his masculinity are inseparable. Now, with Mercutio on the verge of death, Romeo brings up the ideological issue directly. "O sweet Juliet," he complains, "Thy beauty hath made me effeminate" (III.i.115–116). Of course, we had not witnessed much of a fighting spirit in Romeo before he saw Juliet. In a sense, however, the point is true. Romantic love has inhibited Romeo's combativeness. The statement suggests the point of an ideology that links love with femininity, and that blames the woman for that love (though, of course, it was Romeo who first wooed Juliet, not the reverse). Any ideology that readies men for war will almost necessarily oppose their inclinations toward attachment – and particularly any attachment across the boundaries of group antagonism. Juliet's beauty did not make Romeo effeminate. However, his attachment to Juliet did encourage him to violate ideological norms of masculine combativeness.

Overcome by anger at Tybalt's act, Romeo now manifests all the violent manliness he "lacked" before. It happens that Tybalt returns just then. In the heat of the moment, filled with "fire-eyed fury" (III.i.126), Romeo fights with Tybalt and slays him.

The ideological point here is complex and ambivalent. Tybalt had taken advantage of Romeo's peacemaking efforts, stabbing Mercutio under Romeo's arm. The fight was not fair – and the unfairness was due to Romeo's interference. There was something wrong here. Perhaps love of Juliet had made Romeo too protective of Tybalt, thus endangering Mercutio. Moreover, it is difficult to view Tybalt's death in a fair fight as anything other than just retribution for his treacherous and cowardly murder of Mercutio. Most members of the audience are probably as caught up as Romeo in the vengeful anger of the moment. Most probably feel pleased that Tybalt dies. But it is difficult to sustain this pleasure. Just after Tybalt dies, a citizen enters seeking "Tybalt, that murderer" who "killed Mercutio" (III.i.140, 139). It is impossible to believe that Tybalt would not have been punished for killing the Prince's relative. Moreover, it is clear that this sort of manly rashness is what caused the problems to begin with.

In a surprising development, the scene is followed by a sudden reversal of gender roles. This suggests that we are not to take seriously Romeo's idea that love had made him effeminate. Rather, again, there are gender ideologies of what is proper masculine behavior and what is proper feminine behavior. These ideologies serve to support a certain distribution of violence within and between groups. By placing a reversal of the gender roles so soon after Romeo's declaration, Shakespeare suggests that there is nothing necessary in the ideologically gendered distribution of violence. Lady Capulet finds herself in the position of Romeo. Just as Romeo lost a friend, she has lost a relative. In her case, the death was not due to deceit and treachery. Nonetheless, she is, if anything, more violent than Romeo, and far more fixated on the arbitrary categories of group identity. Specifically, she cries out "For blood of ours shed blood of Montague" (III.i.131). Later, learning the whole story, she insists to the Prince that "Romeo must not live" (III.ii.183). In contrast, Capulet pleads that Romeo has done only what the law would have done anyway – killed Tybalt for killing Mercutio.

The Prince recognizes both sides of the argument. Romeo's fault was less than Tybalt's. But it was nonetheless a fault, and a serious one. Thus, the Prince will give a punishment, but one less than death. This leads to the prototypical exile of the lover. But Shakespeare has developed the causes of the exile in such a way as to make them bear on larger issues of gender ideology as well as group definition and inter-group antagonism, particularly because these are related to ideologies of social violence.

Juliet soon learns of Tybalt's death. At first, there is some confu-sion as to precisely who has died. In keeping with a common motif in romantic plots, Juliet initially believes that Romeo has been slain. Drawing on standard imagery from the romantic plot, she calls for her own confinement to "prison" (III.ii.58). Soon enough, however, she learns the truth. This leads to a momentary break in the idealization of the beloved. Seeing Romeo as the murderer of her cousin, Juliet sud-denly feels ambivalent. She sees him as a "Fiend" who merely appears "angelical" (III.ii.75). More significantly for our purposes, she experi-ences a sudden disinhibition of disgust in his regard. Stressing the oral nature of disgust and the prototype of feces, she contrasts his "sweet flesh" with the "vile matter" it contains (III.ii.82, 83). I say "disinhibi-tion" because the suggestion here is that Juliet's attachment to Romeo had not completely eliminated her natural ambivalence toward another person and particularly her natural disgust toward another human body. Rather, the systems activated by attachment and her experi-ence of endogenous reward in his presence (or even the thought of his presence) had simply inhibited other systems, which would otherwise continue to respond in the spontaneous way.

Here something curious occurs. The Nurse expresses the hope that "Shame come to Romeo" (III.ii.90). The wish should be fully in keeping with Juliet's feelings at that moment. She has just experienced physi-cal and moral disgust with Romeo. The public exposure of his hidden "vile matter" is precisely what would provoke the shame called for by the Nurse. In context, then, the Nurse would seem to be voicing Juliet's own unuttered inclination. But Juliet reacts with outrage, cursing the Nurse and berating herself as a "beast" (III.ii.95) for having criticized Romeo. In short, she sees herself as an object of disgust just as she had formerly seen Romeo.

At one level, Juliet's change is unsurprising. It is a more extreme version of the mother who criticizes her child for misbehaving but will not tolerate criticisms of that same child from anyone else, even for the same misbehavior. This is a tendency we all share. But it is none-theless puzzling. Just what is going on in these cases? Juliet's quick shift from disgust with Romeo to disgust with herself suggests one possibility. We may take different perspectives in any relationship. In an attachment relation, our inclination to adopt the perspective of the beloved is enhanced. However, it is enhanced only in certain circumstances. When a lover is considering only herself and her beloved, her point of view is most obviously that of herself. Intensified focus on expressive features of the beloved and enhanced mirroring certainly allow and even facilitate shifts in perspective. But the "dual situation" tends to foster a sort of egocentric fixation in point of view. In contrast, once a third person is introduced, the lover's point of view shifts with the object of public focus. If the public focus is on the beloved – at least in cases where that focus causes or would cause distress to the beloved – then the lover's perspective is likely to shift out of egocentrism toward the beloved. This may even involve the lover taking herself as an object (thus a trigger for anger or disgust). Here Juliet begins by thinking only of her relation with Romeo. However, the Nurse takes up Juliet's feelings of disgust and shares them in a wish that explicitly calls for making Romeo the object of public ridicule. This shifts Juliet out of a dyadic framework and into an awareness of the larger society, with its focus on and antipathy toward Romeo. Due in part to this shift, Juliet correspondingly shifts her point of view. In this new configuration, she sees herself as having betrayed Romeo with her words. As a result, she experiences the same disgust, but with herself as its object.

This is followed by Juliet's memory that there was something "worser than Tybalt's death" (III.ii.108), something that she tried to forget. Indeed, there is a suggestion here that her initial anger with and disgust at Romeo may not have been due wholly to the killing of her cousin. Rather, it may have been due, at least in part, to this graver consequence of the fight. Now she remembers. It is a deep injury to both of them. Romeo has been banished. The suffering that results from this is the equivalent of "ten thousand Tybalts" (III.ii.114) dead. In a dyadic framework, this is an injury to herself for which Juliet would blame Romeo. But now she is in the public framework. Therefore, she – at first, incomprehensibly – seems to feel guilt over the events rather than an inclination to blame. Thus, Romeo's banishment "presses to my memory/Like damnèd guilty deeds to sinners' minds!" (III.ii.111). We can infer several possible reasons for this. First, she identifies so strongly with Romeo that it is as if she herself had committed the punished offense. Second, in a mutual attachment relation, she feels responsible for any injury to her beloved, that is, any injury from which she failed to protect him. Finally, and most obviously, she feels guilt for having reviled Romeo just at the moment when he was most downcast.

Again, even though he was not present, she had been disloyal to him in public. In this way, her sense of guilt is continuous with her immediately preceding sense of self-disgust.

These points all suggest further aspects of romantic love. It is not that lovers are never disloyal to one another or that they always do or can protect one another. But a commitment to such loyalty and protection are part of romantic love. They are part of its fundamental orientation toward reciprocity, part of its empathic enhancement, part of its cognitive and affective division between dyadic and public contexts.

Now, seeing nothing that can be done to prevent Romeo's exile, seeing no way of devising and enacting plans to bridge the distance that will separate them, Juliet contemplates suicide. But the nurse, in her role as helper, quickly devises a plan for bringing the lovers together. She leaves to seek Romeo, who is with Friar Lawrence.

Romeo is in the same condition as Juliet. He follows the usual principle of emotional geography, dividing the world into the place where the beloved is – in this case, not merely home, but "Heaven" (III.iii.29) – and the place where she is not, which is to say, "purgatory, torture, hell itself" (III.iii.18). Like Juliet, he considers death preferable and even makes "to stab himself" (III.iii.106). It is noteworthy that his behavior is much like that of Juliet, but it provokes a different response from others – in keeping with gender ideology. The nurse urges him to "be a man" (III.iii.88). The Friar questions if he is a man, chides him for shedding "womanish" tears (III.iii.110), and claims that his male appearance conceals a woman. It is clear that emotional expression revealing vulnerability, but also deep attachment and reward dependency, are here marked as female – by the nurse and Friar Lawrence, if not by Shakespeare himself. The linking of men with steely coolness and women with yielding warmth is challenged again two scenes later, when Lady Capulet opposes continued sorrow for her nephew's death and recommends instead hiring a killer to do in Romeo. It is, of course, only when Friar Lawrence begins to formulate plans that may lead to the reunion of the lovers that Romeo recovers – suggesting again that the despair he exhibited was not a matter of gender, but of practical possibilities for action.

The first step of the Friar's plan is to consummate the marriage. Here, Shakespeare returns us to the rival and Juliet's father. Just as Romeo and Juliet are making their marriage final, Juliet's parents are agreeing to the marriage with Paris. This highlights not only the usual role of parental authority in romantic plots, but also the complete emotional divide between parent and child in this particular case. Once more, Friar Lawrence and the nurse have shared the feelings of the lovers, whereas the real parents are entirely unaware. Capulet is assuring Paris of "my child's love" (III.iv.13) at the very moment when she is sharing that love with Romeo – her "husband-friend" (III.v.52).

The parting of the lovers manifests the concerns we have witnessed already many times. For example, anticipating their separation, Juliet recurs to emotional temporality, explaining, "in a minute there are many days" (III.v.45). It seems unnecessary to repeat these points.

Following this departure, Lady Capulet informs Juliet of her betrothal to Paris. Juliet refuses, explaining that she feels "hate" (III.v.148). Though it is not explained in the play, hate is perhaps best understood as a complex emotion that includes both anger and disgust.[19] The disgust is important here. It suggests that, at least at this moment of intense romantic love for Romeo, the thought of any other man is particularly disgusting to Juliet. The romantic inhibition of disgust toward Romeo may be connected with an intensification of disgust toward other possible partners. The response of Juliet's parents is violent and shows a complete inability to empathize with her – suggesting a profound flaw in the attachment relations here. The act concludes with Juliet considering her alternatives. Either she will learn some plan from Friar Lawrence or she will use her own "power to die" (III.v.244).

With Friar Lawrence, Juliet makes explicit the religious elevation of the lovers and their love, an idea already suggested at various points, as we have seen. Specifically, she explains that "God joined my heart and Romeo's" (IV.i.55). Friar Lawrence unfolds his notorious plan of a false death. Here, Shakespeare takes a device used by storytellers – the false suggestion of one lover's demise – and makes it a device used by one of the characters. Juliet agrees, explaining that she will do anything "without fear" in order "To live an unstained wife to my sweet love" (IV.i.87–88). The phrase is revealing. First, her fear has narrowed to a single object – the loss of Romeo. All other dangers fade to insignificance by comparison. But at the same time, her sensitivity to disgust has been focused as well. Again, just as her disgust for Romeo is inhibited, her disgust for other men is enhanced. Part of that disgust is a worry about contamination. Thus, she can withstand such profoundly repulsive conditions as being "O'ercovered quite with ... reeky

---

[19] Indeed, for Johnson-Laird and Oatley, to feel hate is "to feel intense disgust" (Oatley *Best* 428n.15). On anger in hatred, see Panksepp *Affective* 191.

shanks and yellow chapless skulls" (IV.i.82–83) if it will result in her reunion with Romeo. But she could not bear the touch of Paris. It is only by avoiding that touch that she will remain "unstained." Ever ready with gender clichés, the friar worries that Juliet may suffer "womanish fear" (IV.ii.119). But Shakespeare shows that the cliché is wrong, when Juliet calls for the medicine that will make her seem dead – "Give me, give me! O, tell not me of fear!" (IV.ii.121). In *Romeo and Juliet*, bravery is not the monopoly of one sex, and it is enhanced by attachment, not diminished by it.

Again, this bravery does not arise because the fear and disgust systems have been disabled by romantic love. They are still fully operational, still subject to activation by experience or imagination. Indeed, it would hardly be brave to undertake dangerous actions if one were insensible of the danger. We see this clearly when Juliet is alone the night before her wedding to Paris, thus the night when she must take the poison. She feels "a faint cold fear" (IV.iii.15) and imagines the "foul" (IV.iii.34) air of the tomb, the "green ... fest'ring" (IV.iii.42–43) body of Tybalt. Filled with terror and disgust at the prospect, she suffers doubts. But we know from the prologue that her death is necessary to save the society. In that context, her doubts are parallel with those of Jesus in Gethsemane the night before his death. As is well known, Jesus analogized his acceptance of death and resurrection to drinking from a cup (see Matthew 26:42). In Juliet's case, this imitation of death and resurrection are the literal result of accepting the drink given by her spiritual father. Finally, she downs the draft. In the morning, the family finds her evidently dead.

The final act brings us to the failure of Friar Lawrence's plans. In tragedy, we are accustomed to necessity, to the downfall of the hero resulting from the faults of his or her own character, from some excess or deficiency, or from the inexorable laws of society. But this is, in part, an idealization. In real life, plans go awry by chance. Indeed, this is one aspect of emotion central to the account of Oatley. As Oatley puts it, "emotions are part of a solution to problems of organizing knowledge and action in a world that is imperfectly known and in which we have limited resources" (*Best* 3). Nussbaum too stresses the relation of emotion to being "vulnerable to events that we do not control" (*Upheavals* 12). The eruption of chance into Shakespeare's play may make it less successful as a tragedy. However, it may by the same token make it truer to our emotional experience, as less idealized.

By chance, Romeo learns that Juliet has died. This faces him with the absolute impossibility of planning their union. This despair leads to the only plan compatible with despair. "Juliet," he says, addressing her memory, or the spirit he hopes she has become, "I will lie with thee tonight" (V.i.34). Events conspire to this end. The friar's letter explaining Juliet's case goes undelivered. The apothecary is poor, with "Famine" in his "cheeks" (V.i.69), and therefore agrees to sell Romeo the poison.

Showing disdain for the vileness of the tomb, Romeo goes to join Juliet. Now, too, he praises her unmatched beauty – his feeling of reward is still so great even in the presence of her mere soulless form. He drinks the poison and dies kissing the body he believes to be dead, clearly free of disgust at Juliet even as a corpse.

The friar enters and, despite his insistence on manly bravery in others, flees in fright ("I hear some noise" [V.iii.131]) and disgust over "death" and "contagion" (V.iii.132). The irony is obvious and once again plays against the gender ideology he has helped purvey. I do not believe, however, that Shakespeare is primarily exposing a hypocrite. The friar is less deceitful than simply wrong. Bravery and fortitude are not manly virtues, diminished by the more yielding emotions. Rather, they are the result of those yielding emotions. The friar, for all his good will, lacks adequate attachment to overcome the fear and disgust that press on him.

When Juliet awakes, she is now in the position of Romeo. Her beloved is dead. She knows there is no plan that she can imagine and enact in life that will make any difference now. She plunges a dagger in her breast.

As the Watchman explains, she had lain in the tomb for two days (V.iii.377). Then she awoke from death. Again, we see the association with Jesus. This has a number of implications. For our present purposes, however, it is sufficient to note that Shakespeare is once more stressing the value of this deep love – both affectionate and sexual – perhaps particularly because it is a love that crosses the boundaries of antagonistic groups. The point is brought out beautifully by Harriett Hawkins, who discusses how, in *Romeo and Juliet*, as well as *Othello* and *Antony and Cleopatra*, "men and women alike put love before tribal, military and political priorities (I here use 'tribal' to cover familial, national, racial, and religious tribalism), and although they pay the highest price for doing so, even at the moment of death they never regret that they did." [20] In the end, the families are reconciled and the "discords" of their "hate" (V.iii.294, 292) are ended, the society redeemed by the "sacrifices" (V.iii.504) of these lovers.

Conclusion

In sum, paradigmatic literary works – in this case, works by Sappho, Li, and Shakespeare – converge with psychological and other empirical research on romantic love. At the same time these works help lead us beyond the more standard empirical approaches. For example, the latter tend to isolate emotions from one another, focusing on a single emotion, or even a single emotion component, at a time. The study of literary works points toward the ways in which emotion systems interact in mutually enhancing or inhibiting ways. In keeping with this, literary works provide integrative frameworks in which we can synthesize findings about aspects of an emotion. This allows us to produce a more nuanced and ecologically valid understanding of that emotion as a whole.

More exactly, the literary works and the empirical research may be integrated to suggest an account along the following lines. First, romantic love appears to interweave sexual desire, attachment, and reward dependency. Sexual desire clearly involves a craving for sexual gratification. But it also involves a broader desire for physical contact, a desire that inhibits certain sorts of disgust response (though remaining susceptible to inhibition by other, stronger disgust triggers). Attachment, too, involves a desire for physical contact and involves some disgust inhibition, making the two emotional responses compatible in these respects. This is not to say that the disgust system is disabled. Perhaps most importantly, disgust responses may actually be enhanced for possible sexual partners other than the beloved.

Attachment and its associated reward dependency involve delight in the presence of the attachment object, a presence signaled by individuating properties of that object, such as face, voice, posture, and movement. At its most intense, this delight in the particularity of the beloved tends to foster a sense that the beloved is physically ideal or perfectly beautiful. That idealization may also be extended to distinctive personality features of the beloved.

---

[20] Hawkins also discusses how Shakespeare's lovers "have historically evoked more outraged cries of critical condemnation than mass murderers or serial killers such as Tamburlaine, Macbeth, or Iago," at least in part for this reason (116).

This is not to say that the lovers' feelings about one another are uniform across contexts. There appears to be a particularly significant difference between lovers' responses to one another in dyadic, or private, and triadic, or public, contexts. In the former context, lovers' emotional responses to one another may be egocentric. In public contexts – at least contexts that are threatening or painful for the beloved – the lover's emotional response may become "allocentric," empathically centered on the beloved. This is related to the enhanced attentional focus and apparently enhanced mirroring and empathy between lovers. Indeed, in many cases, this includes an expanded sense of the self as including the beloved.

Attachment and reward dependency organize and orient not only our response to social relations, but even our experience of space and time. Our sense of temporal duration in the present is in part a function of the delight of union or the pain of separation. Our imagination of the future is inseparable from a visceral response to when union or separation can or might occur – for instance, how long it would take to hear the voice or feel the touch of the beloved. This anticipatory response differs depending on whether we can experience the outcome only as fantasy or can take concrete steps to achieve (or prevent) it through planning. Our emotional response to the inability to enact plans bearing on anticipated trajectories may give rise to panic (perhaps particularly in the case of impending separation) or despair (perhaps particularly in the case of enduring separation). On the other hand, these may be moderated by emotion regulation for certain periods, particularly when the ability to enact plans may arise in the future. They also may be affected by attachment security.

For adult lovers, the security of attachment is a function of critical period experiences in childhood and of experiences in the current relationship. In both cases, a crucial part of this security is the sense that the attachment bond is (or is not) mutual. Attachment leads us to want not only the presence of the beloved, but their attachment to us. This mutual attachment entails not only the (directly functional) properties of the beloved's enhanced attention and benevolence, but also the (indirectly functional) property of their delight in our presence as well.

Finally, romantic love is interwoven with ideological issues. First, it is connected with the definition of group identities. This operates for potential partners through erotic discounting. More importantly, it operates through social disapproval of romantic love that crosses boundaries between antagonistic or hierarchized groups. This disapproval is a central issue in literary narratives across cultures. Ideological concerns may also enter with respect to gender. For example, in opposing attachment to putatively genuine masculinity, a given social order may seek to enable belligerence against out-groups. In fact, attachment may enhance "masculine" virtues such as bravery and fortitude. But it may do so in ways that violate social hierarchies or oppositions.

Many of the properties of romantic love are brought out poignantly in the verses of Li and Sappho. Many of these properties are movingly depicted, with their complex interactions, in Shakespeare's play. In addition, the play represents, and criticizes, gender ideologies with great sensitivity.

4. Grief

Kobayashi Issa and *Hamlet*

Chronicle of a Death

Kobayashi Issa (1763–1827) is "one of the three towering figures" of Japanese *haikai* poetry. His popular verses are "incised into rocks and stone slabs all over Japan" (Bolitho 61). At the age of fourteen, he "was turned out by his father and sent off to Edo" to work "as a domestic servant" (63). He visited home in 1791, then again in 1801. As it happened, his father fell ill and died during the latter visit. Issa recorded the events, and resulting grief.

From the moment his father falls ill, we can see certain patterns emerging in Issa's narrative. The first and most obvious is the centrality of attachment. We would be sad to see anyone become sick and infirm. But of course it is no accident that Issa's mourning is specifically for his father. Indeed, the link between attachment and grief has been a central feature of recent theories of mourning.[1]

When he first discovers that his father has fallen face-down in the garden, he seems to make light of the situation, not taking it seriously. But he consults a doctor. The prognosis is bad. What he experiences then is akin to panic – indeed, it is a form of panic. He explains that he was "Overwhelmed, and not knowing what to do" (Issa 65). He was filled with fear, but he could devise no plan, short- or long-term, that would change this situation. There was no possible actional outcome that would respond to this condition.

After this, he watches his father reading sutras aloud "as he always used to do." But now he feels "sad" because his father's voice is "weak" and his "bearing" is "unsteady" (65). This begins to suggest something

---

[1] For an overview of some current theories of grief, with a particular emphasis on attachment, see Shaver and Tancredy.

111

about attachment. There is a formative period in which an attachment relation is established. With a parent, this is usually the critical period, the fundamental time in childhood when the pattern is set for one's subsequent attachment relations. But it seems that there is something comparable for the subsequent relations as well. One forms an attachment to one's spouse or a friend at a certain time in one's own biographical history and in theirs. In all these cases, that initial period of attachment seems to serve as a defining point of comparison for what follows – particularly a point of emotional comparison. We see this in the use of flashback montages in melodramas. While John is sitting at Jane's deathbed, we cut to a series of brief recollections of those early days of joy and hope when they first met. The effect is often cheaply sentimental in movies. But it can be cheaply sentimental precisely because it is part of how we feel. The emotional time of attachment is not uniform. The early period rises up as a landmark. In an attachment relation, we often define our present emotional place by its distance from that beginning. One part of that definition involves judging the appearance, the physical strength or weakness, youthfulness or age, of the attachment object – particularly when that appearance is related to a trajectory that ends in separation. Issa's sadness here, then, is a foretaste of grief. Indeed, his attention was undoubtedly drawn to the weakness of his father's voice and the unsteadiness of his bearing precisely because of the doctor's prognosis and the imagination of decline that prognosis outlined. Note that such a trajectory will be in part self-conscious, but it will also occur spontaneously. Our minds calculate such patterns and implications even when they are unwarranted. In a case such as this, it was far from unwarranted.

We have noted the obvious centrality of attachment in grief. In Issa's case, this was intensified by the history of the relationship, particularly the long separation. Issa suggests that he and his father had been quite close when he was very young, before his stepmother entered the house. His father apologetically explains that he sent his son away in the hope that this would be best. Issa urges his father to recover and, referring to his pet name when he was a boy, assures his father that "Once you are well again I will be the Yatarō I used to be" (71). Here, both have in effect retreated to the initial attachment period. Issa in particular is trying to assure both his father and himself that things will eventually be like they were in that formative time. In this case, it is a way of fending off his grief, a method of mood repair.

In connection with this, Issa reflects miserably on the time they were apart. He thinks of "my obligation to him – deeper than snow on Mt. Fuji, unmelting even in summer" (70). He feels deep regret, even guilt over the separation. "Living apart from my father until my hair was covered with frost," he explains, "was a far graver offence" than any other (71). The imagery is suggestive here. Death and grief are associated with perceptual conditions, including cold. When Issa says that his obligation is deeper than the snow, he at once expresses the extent of his duties to his father and hints at the coldness that will soon mark his father's body. Indeed, it will mark his own grief as well, and his own sense of remorse and guilt, which may also be spoken of as "unmelting even in summer." The frost on his own hair takes up this image, and also marks strikingly the change that has occurred since that initial period of attachment.

Not long after this, Issa once again experiences the sense of hopelessness, the inability to act, a sort of panic – this time combined with a sense of guilt. The issue is trivial. His father wanted pears and Issa could not find any for him. He bitterly complains that "Heaven must have forsaken me" and explains that "I shall always regret" this (73). Why would such an insignificant point become so weighty that Issa would invoke the will of heaven? It is because there is so little that he can do. He feels his father's pain with a profound empathy. Indeed, from the start, he "felt far worse than if the suffering had been my own" (65). But his feeling cannot issue in any action. Now, at last, there is something he can do – but he fails.

Thus far, Issa's chronicle suggests that grief is built up from a number of feelings in addition to sadness – prominently attachment, with its particular, uneven temporality. The attachment intensifies the feeling of empathy with the person who is dying (and, as we will see, even with the person who is dead). In addition, grief is marked by moments of panic, when one wishes more than anything to take some action to change things, but cannot. This is bad enough when the loved one is still alive. It becomes worse when he or she has died – for then the impossibility of action is not merely contingent, but necessary. In both cases, it may be bound up with regret and guilt, which extend beyond the panic as well.

Given the intensity of Issa's pain and the impossibility of changing the situation, we might expect mechanisms of mood repair to enter. The most obvious method of mood repair involves a shift in attentional focus. As his father's caregiver, this is not possible. Another option might be the recruitment of a sorrow- and guilt-inhibiting emotion system. Of course, this is not, in most cases, planned. Rather, it operates spontaneously, in the usual manner of mood repair. Anger is an obvious case in point. The decline and death of a loved one invariably entail many impulse frustrations for everyone involved. Thus, they provide ample eliciting conditions for anger. In keeping with this, our response to the decline and death of some attachment figure will almost invariably alternate between episodes of (mutually enhancing) sorrow and guilt on the one hand and anger on the other hand. The anger will occur initially without any mood-repair function. But insofar as the human mind has mechanisms to produce mood repair, it is at least possible that anger will be recruited for that function.

To be most effective in mood repair, anger must issue in some sort of action. Anger will only substitute one aversive emotion for another if I am just as feckless in fury as in sorrow. The first condition for effective action is causal attribution or blame. After all, my actional response in anger involves addressing the cause – for instance, by confronting another agent who is to blame for the angering situation. We are notoriously bad at attributing causes to our emotions, particularly when those causes are diffuse and not directly perceivable. Thus Clore and Ortony explain that "people tend to experience their affective feelings as reactions to whatever happens to be in focus at the time" (27). In Zajonc's words, "If the person is unable to specify either the origin or the target of affect he or she is experiencing, then this affect can attach itself to anything that is present at the moment" (48). In the case of a parent's death, the causes of anger might range from the inevitability of aging to the operation of certain bacteria in the parent's body. For the most part, these are not helpful to mood repair. More importantly, they are not salient objects of attentional focus. As such, they are unlikely candidates for causal attribution. In contrast, when there are several caregivers or simply a number of people around, it is likely that there will be conflicts among them. These contribute to the bereaved person's anger. Though usually far less important than other causes, they are nonetheless highly salient. As such, they become prominent candidates for causal attribution or blame. In this context, then, dissention among the remaining family members may become more likely. Indeed, they may even blame one another for the suffering and death of the loved one.

I have phrased this almost as a purely logical deduction from the principles of emotional response and mood repair. However, I was actually first pointed in the direction of this conclusion by reading Issa and Shakespeare. Indeed, there is some unclarity in the literature on mood repair. For example, Klaus Fiedler notes that the phrase "mood repair" suggests "deliberate attempts to improve one's own aversive affect" (171). Moreover, research by Erber and Erber shows that there is no simple and straightforward process of changing one's negative mood (see 276–279). Indeed, one reader of this manuscript commented that the idea of mood *repair*, a "fixing" of aversive emotions, is inconsistent with research showing that the suppression of expressive outcomes has deleterious effects (see Butler and colleagues). However, when the research on mood repair is combined with literary depictions, such as that of Issa, and with the account of emotion given in Chapter 2, a different account might emerge.

Specifically, we might make four points about mood repair. First, a simple terminological note – "repair" here only means "mitigate aversive experience." In evolutionary terms, mood repair may have had adaptive benefits (or it may simply result from the general structure of our emotion systems). But this hardly means that it does not have deleterious consequences as well. Second, mood repair is not suppression anyway. If one feels angry and suppresses the anger, one has not mitigated the feeling. The two are distinct and even opposed processes. Thus, the research on suppression of expressive outcomes is not relevant to mood repair.

The third point about mood repair is that, in keeping with the account of emotion in Chapter 2, it is not an evaluative process, particularly a deliberate one.[2] Rather, it is a set of mechanisms (perhaps adaptive) triggered in particular circumstances. Issa's memoire suggests three elements of these circumstances for one particular mechanism that we may refer to as "mood shift" (the change from one, more aversive emotion to another, less aversive emotion – for example, grief to anger). First, the situation allows no actional outcome that will alter the eliciting conditions of the initial (more aversive) emotion. Second, one's ongoing ambivalence includes the activation of inhibitory emotion systems that are less aversive (e.g., mild anger, which is less aversive than grief and inhibitory of grief) and that do allow actional outcomes. Third, possible

---

[2] Of course, we can self-consciously engage in processes to alter our emotions. In general, however, this cannot be how mood repair operates, because deliberate thought about changing one's mood is actually likely to prolong the mood ("Whatever I do, I'm going to avoid remembering that my father has died. I'm going to keep the memory of my father's death far away from my thoughts....").

causes for those inhibitory emotions are salient even in relation to the initial, aversive emotion. These are not the only conditions in which a mood repair mechanism is triggered, but they appear to be one set of such circumstances.

The final point to make about mood repair is that the mechanisms involved are closely related to those of mood-congruent thought. In other words, they are a type of processing that guides the elaborative component of emotional experience. Thus, in mood-congruent processing, excitatory emotional memories are aroused (e.g., sorrowful emotional memories in connection with grief) and automatically incorporated into elaborative thought. In contrast, with mood repair, inhibitory emotional memories are aroused (e.g., angry emotional memories in connection with grief) and automatically incorporated into elaborative thought. As this suggests, at least in the case of mood shift, mood repair is not so much the opposite of mood-congruent processing as its complement. In effect, mood shift requires mood-congruent processing. The two processes merely operate on different emotions.

Again, the preceding reflections on mood repair and anger derive to a great extent from reading Issa and Shakespeare. Given this, it should come as no surprise that Issa soon reports conflict with his family. The conflict may have been real and significant in this case, but its place in the unfolding of events was undoubtedly intensified by the human propensity for reductive causal attribution and for the recruitment of that causal attribution in mood repair. In this case, Issa's father wants cold water. Issa believes that this will harm him, and, according to his report, the doctor concurs. Nonetheless, other members of the family insist on fulfilling his father's wish. Issa is deeply angry. He views his family as giving his father "poison" and not truly wishing for his recovery (75). He says that "On the surface they seemed solicitous of father, but this was simply to hide the fact that secretly they would be happier if he died" (76). Unfortunately, in this case, the anger is relatively ineffective as mood repair because it does not point to any actional outcomes. As Issa explains, "there was nothing I could do," for he was "unable to condemn the wrongs staring me in the face" (75).

This situation changes only after his father's death, when he can oppose these scheming relatives in conflict over inheritance. Thus, he confronts "those who were driven by greed" (85). Obviously, conflicts over inheritance are largely a matter of actual financial interest. Moreover, appeals to higher principles of fairness are, to a great extent, a matter of rationalizing one's own greed. There are other motives as well, however – motives related to grief. One of these derives from anger that has diffuse sources but is likely to be blamed entirely on those other people who are salient in the bereaved person's current environment – the relatives. Real conflicts over finances only increase the likelihood of such attributions. There is, in addition, a sense that these material things are all that remain of the loved one – particularly all that remain of the security one expected from that person. This is true most obviously and perhaps most intensely of a deceased parent. A parent's home is a place where the child can go even in times of disaster. A parent's wealth can help the child in times of need. The point is not purely rational and economic. One might never seek a parent's real financial help, even when experiencing great distress. But it is, so to speak, a sign of one's security, an extension of the parent's physical proximity during the formative attachment period of early childhood.[3] To receive the house or the money is no compensation for the loss of that security with the death of the loved one. But to be deprived of the home and financial benefits only worsens the sense of insecurity. In short, greed is undoubtedly a central component of inheritance disputes, but grief is a crucial component as well.

There are many moments of "anticipatory" grief in the three weeks of Issa's father's illness. (On the idea of anticipatory mourning, see Rando.) Nonetheless, there is a striking change in the tone and content of his reflections once he realizes that his father is about to die. He feels more intensely the sense that "there was nothing I could do" (81). But this feeling of "action paralysis," as we might call it, is now accompanied by very short-term expectations that present us with another, crucial component of grief. After a person dies, we are not constantly self-conscious about his or her death. Indeed, we have countless cognitive routines and associations that lead us to anticipate interaction with that person. For example, I remember one day, many years ago, a few days after my grandmother died. I came downstairs and found my mother weeping. She explained that she had seen something on the television that she thought would interest her mother. She picked up the phone and began dialing the number before she realized

---

[3] I am speaking here as if the attachment bond is "secure." But the same points hold, sometimes even more forcefully, when it is insecure or anxious. Exceptions may occur in cases where there is a high degree of avoidance (for a discussion of attachment styles and bereavement, see Stroebe, Schut, and Boerner), but the dismissal of bonds with the deceased person in these cases may be more apparent than real. In any case, the loss almost certainly has continuing emotional consequences, despite the dismissal.

that her mother was no longer alive. The sequence of events involved a very short-term anticipation of the sensory presence (the voice) of an attachment figure, along with the sense of security that such an experience carries with it. The anticipation was abruptly reversed. The regular knowledge of her mother's death was, of course, sorrowful enough. But this event was still more painful because it involved a sudden and sharp shift from anticipated security to the complete loss of that sense of security, from anticipated comfort, warmth, and so on to the complete loss of these. Such violated expectations may be part of the reason for the tendency of grief to "occur in waves," as Bonnano, Goorin, and Coifman put it (803).[4]

Before the death actually occurs, Issa realizes that it will occur. In a brief poem, he anticipates no longer performing a task that has now become routine: "Can this be the last time/I brush flies away/As you sleep?" (81). The pathos of this brief poem comes from a very profound realization. Even though Issa has the sense that there is nothing he can do, there are, in fact, many things he can do while his father is alive. Moreover, he is doing them. They are small things and, as he performs them, they seem like nothing. But the pain he will experience after his father's death will not afford him even these slight opportunities for action. Moreover, when he looks at his father's corpse later and has the impulse to shoo the flies, he will remember that now it is pointless; now there is no longer a person there whom the flies might wake or irritate.

The final night, he fights against his own expectations. His father always had a "happy face at dawn." For this reason, Issa "looked forward" to daybreak. This time, however, he dreaded it. He was "sick at heart" (82) and wanted that night to drag on forever. He would not see the happy face that had greeted him on other days, but only the same unexpressive mask.

Frustrated short-term anticipations and their associated despair come more forcefully after his father's death. He enters the sickroom

---

[4]   Of course, I am not the first person to have noticed such automatic anticipations. At a basic, descriptive level, Tomasini notes that "the grieving often talk about their expectations of loved ones being there in the familiar everyday pattern of lives once shared" (445). Parkes has discussed these anticipations with particular insight. My account of the way such anticipations operate and the way they produce emotion is quite different from that of Parkes. Nonetheless, my account very strongly supports his conclusion that altering these tacit expectations actually constitutes "[m]uch of the work of relearning which follows a major loss and which, in the past, has been termed 'grief work'" (32).

and "felt briefly as if I were waiting for my father to awaken" (85). He recalls his father, in particular the expressions of his emotion – the "suffering face," the "sound of his voice calling to me" (85).

The point is made even more poignantly when, just after his father's death, Issa remarks, "there was no longer anyone to whom I could turn" (81). In grief, our first response is to turn for comfort to someone else with whom we have an attachment relation. We face them, sharing our expressions of grief, embracing – our sense of warmth and security temporarily restored in their arms. In such a time, Issa could turn only to one person – his father. But even the slightest suggestion of this reminds him that his father is precisely the person to whom he cannot turn. After the ceremonies, he repeats the idea. "I came back home depending on my father" – thus anticipating the warmth, security, aid of his father. Now he is as vulnerable as an abandoned child – "to whose protection could I turn now?" (84). This is why the room is now so "lonely" (82), why he was "alone" and "vulnerable as a bubble." Whoever may be present, there is not that one source of comfort and care. Indeed, his entire sense of place is changed. He not only lacks a family, but a home – for the home was defined by his personal attachment to his father. Now, he is "a lonely exile in a strange land" (85).

Underlying this sense of lost comfort and security is another sense of loss – the loss of someone with whom Issa could share the entire range of emotional experience. Though the two had been apart for many years, Issa could, until then, always imagine sharing with his father whatever was important to him – not only extraordinary difficulties, but daily joys. Now that too is gone. Issa ends his account of his father's death with a poem noting precisely this. "Were father here/We could see these green fields at dawn/Together" (86). Even such simple possibilities of experiential sharing are lost forever. The sentiment of the poem is still more resonant because we know about his father's happiness at dawn, and about Issa's joy in seeing that happiness. Now, it is not simply that Issa cannot share his delight with his father. The delight itself is lost – for sharing with his father was the source of that delight.

Another aspect of grief is brought out by Issa's sense that he will lose not only a source of comfort and a partner in sharing of emotional experience, but also a source of admiration, thus a crucial foundation for his self-esteem. After his father's death, he finds himself not only "alone" and "vulnerable," but also "insignificant as dust" (84). The image is apt. As his father has been reduced to dust in death, Issa has lost the one person whose attachment made him (i.e., Issa himself) more than dust. He recalls his father in the prime of life, a quarter-century earlier. Issa himself was just a boy and leaving home. Now any resentment is gone, and Issa remembers only his father's encouragement. In this memory, his father fully expects him to make his "fortune" and anticipates the day when he will return. Issa's father looks forward to that day and the wondrous sight of his son's "shining face." As he walks away, he tries to suppress any sign of his anxiety, so that his father would not see him "falter" (83). His self-pride is deeply connected with his father's pride in him. The loss of paternal appreciation – along with the sense of guilt[5] – threatens that self-pride.

Longer-term imaginations – with their embedded short-term projections and anticipations – enter into grief as well. He recalls how, just the previous day, his father had spoken of the future. He "laughed" and shared with his son a vision of "what was to come" (82). But now he was "an empty husk," not something that will grow into a future. Sometimes these long-term imaginations are bound up with regret and guilt. Before, he could imagine somehow in the future making up for the lost time and fulfilling in part the duties he owed as a son. But now his recent "vows of lifelong devotion would remain forever unfulfilled" (82).

Finally, grief is bound up with memory. We have already seen that it is connected with distant memories, memories of a time when the loved one was vigorous, before the decline that led to death. One's working memory, one's ongoing recollection of the present, is crucial in grief as well. This is true in two ways. First, when one is not thinking of the death, one is prone to the anticipations and painful frustrations already mentioned. Second, one often is thinking of the death. One's thoughts repeatedly turn toward the deceased, toward the recent past, toward the life that is no longer there. The imagination is sometimes so vivid that one feels as if the deceased person is present, right there before one. "Dozing, I would see him in my dreams; awake, his image stood before me," Issa explains (84). (As Archer reports, "the bereaved person" may believe "that the deceased has actually visited them." He cites one study according to which "14 per cent said that they had seen" the deceased [79].) In contrast, the actual world seems flimsy and insignificant, less substantial than the aery nothing of one's imagination.

---

[5] Feelings of guilt are common among caregivers after the death of loved ones. See, for example, Jacinto.

The actual world is, at moments, reduced to fancy, and fancy takes the place of reality. Speaking of the funeral, Issa reports that "It all seemed unreal to me as I held my incense in nerveless fingers" (84). Even what he grasps with his hand does not seem palpable.

It is unsurprising in this context that, in addition to cold, Issa (like others) should experience grief as darkness. When his father died, he writes, "I felt that a light had gone out in the darkness" (81). The metaphor has many implications – most obviously, relating to fear and to a sense of being lost (thus not being in a familiar, homey place)[6]. One of these implications is that he can no longer see what is there in front of him. This is true even though his eyes register things. Indeed, part of the "derealization" of his world involves an actual sense that it is darker. "[E]ven the lamplight seemed dimmer," he tells us (82).

Hamlet, Mourning, and Mood Repair

Needless to say, the features we have noted in Issa's mourning are not idiosyncratic to him, nor are they somehow distinctively Japanese. They are the ordinary ways in which we all respond to the death of someone we love. We find them in *Hamlet* as well.

Of course, there is a difference. *Hamlet* is fictional. Yet, as a number of writers have noted, the grief expressed in the play appears to be related to Shakespeare's mourning over his own son, Hamnet. Indeed, for much of the play, it is valuable to take up the perspective, not of the character, Hamlet, but of the author. The link has been argued with great insight by Stephen Greenblatt (*Will* 311–322). Indeed, Greenblatt suggests why Shakespeare may have felt particularly intense mourning at the time. In our terms, the action paralysis of grief had recently been enhanced by changes brought in during the Reformation.[7] Specifically, Catholic rituals had permitted mourners a way of acting productively in grief. Technically, these rituals presented possible actional outcomes that put the bereaved person in some contact with the deceased, and

---

[6] This is related to the sense of separation distress that marks bereavement and is manifest in amygdala activation (see Freed and colleagues; see also Stein and Vythilingum 240).

[7] In addition, the age of Shakespeare's son is relevant here. Research by Gamino, Sewell, and Easterling indicates that "the younger the decedent, the greater the negative grief affect" (344). This is further complicated by parental guilt (349) and an increase in grief when the "relationship quality" is problematic (344). This fits Shakespeare's situation in that he was away from his family for such long periods (a point also stressed by Greenblatt).

which allowed the former to give aid to the latter. These ceremonial practices were eliminated in the English Reformation. This change left the populace with an enhanced desire for productive action in response to grief (since people remained aware of the Catholic ceremonies). At the same time, however, the change rigorously excluded any such action. Shakespeare, Greenblatt suggests, turned to theater as a substitute.

In keeping with this, the most significant emotions, for many aspects of the work, are perhaps not those of the hero, but those of the writer. Extending Greenblatt's insight, we may say that much of the play in effect operates as a sort of literary attempt at mood repair. Like any work of fiction, it is a sort of tempered fantasy. In this case, the tacit function of the fantasy is to ease the pain of loss suffered by the author. We will consider the point in relation to the details of this particular play. But it is presumably not unique to *Hamlet*. As such, it suggests that for the author, the emotive function of fictional storytelling may often be a matter of repairing – or, in other cases, sustaining – an emotional state.

The fundamental, generative fact about the story-world of *Hamlet* is that the King, Hamlet's father, died unexpectedly, and Hamlet is grieving for his loss.[8] Moreover, he is grieving in a world that seems to

---

[8] Needless to say, the point has not been ignored by Shakespeare critics. (For a useful overview of the enormous body of *Hamlet* criticism, see Wofford.) However, it has been explored relatively little in terms of recent research on mourning. Rather, the focus of critics treating Hamlet's grief has tended toward the historical specificity of ideas about grief, mourning, or "melancholy." This work can be very valuable. However, it does not tell us much about the nature of grief generally, since its project is to explore cultural and historical particularities. Codden, for example, relates melancholy to the early modern ideas about madness and explores the interrelation between discourses of madness and both political and gender ideologies.

This historical orientation is found even in cognitive approaches to Shakespeare. For example, Mary Crane is concerned with the way *Hamlet* manifests "early modern cognitive theory." The resulting interpretations are insightful. But the degree to which Crane's analysis is historically constrained may be seen in her reference to Hamlet's view that "associates" "blushing … with outward manifestation of inwardly felt shame" (134). One might have thought that Shakespeare was simply recording an ordinary fact about human nature. Crane, however, ties this to a historically particular belief expressed in Timothy Bright's *Treatise of Melancholie* – which, she earlier explained, served as a source for Shakespeare (116).

Certainly, many literary ideas about emotion may have resulted from the influence of medical or other theories. However, many resulted from the author's observation of human action, expression, experience, and so forth. As stressed in the first chapter, to be successful beyond a small circle of readers familiar with historically particular theories – and somehow emotionally affected by those theories – a work must manifest something that is more in keeping with the actual operation of people's emotions.

have forgotten that the king lived at all, though only four months have passed – hardly any time in grief. In some ways, everything in the play follows from this fact.

Yet Shakespeare does not begin with Hamlet, his mourning, his anger. He begins, rather, with a ghost. Moreover, it is a ghost witnessed, not by the grieving Hamlet, but by men who have no ongoing emotional state and no working memory preoccupation that would lead to such a hallucination. Later, before Horatio and the others tell him about the ghost, Hamlet evidences the same propensities that we found in Issa. His working memory is so taken up with the imagination of his father that the imagination becomes almost more vivid and real than what is actually there. Thus, Hamlet tells Horatio, "My father, methinks I see my father" (I.ii.183). Horatio asks where and Hamlet replies, "In my mind's eye" (I.ii.185). But the initial phrasing suggests something else. Hamlet does not *think* he sees his father in his "mind's eye," or imagination. He *does* see his father there. The qualification, "methinks," suggests that Hamlet's imagination verges on actual perception.

Again, one part of grief results from the sharp conflict between reality and spontaneous expectation derived from imagination. Specifically, we often spontaneously anticipate seeing, hearing from, speaking with a person. This anticipation does not automatically stop once the person has died. Rather, it occurs, but is interrupted when we suddenly remember that we can never see, hear from, or speak with that person again. It may be argued that one function of a belief in God and the immortality of the soul is to dull the pain of this realization.[9] We cannot speak with the person here and now, but eventually, in the future, we will be able to do so. These religious beliefs, then, have the function of mood repair.[10]

Work that is not historically oriented has tended to be psychoanalytic. For example, Marjorie Garber's influential analysis does touch on mourning, but it does so in the context of such Freudian notions as the uncanny and the repetition compulsion – along with Lacanian and Derridean ideas – not in relation to a neurocognitive architecture. Janet Adelman treats Hamlet's feelings in terms of the maternal body. The point is, of course, related to attachment, and thus to our analysis of grief. One would expect there to be some convergence in psychoanalytic and neurocognitive accounts because they are discussing many of the same phenomena. The particulars are obviously different, however, especially in the interpretive principles, which allow Adelman to infer a range of psychoanalytic themes from imagery that does not appear related to the maternal body, except when considered in the context of psychoanalysis.

9 See Hogan "Literature."

10 Here one might be tempted to ask just what the function of grief might be. In fact, this seems to me a perfect case of the excesses of evolutionary psychology. Attachment has clear evolutionary functions. Various forms of sadness have evolutionary functions

But just how does this mood repair operate? Who is it that survives, that continues life in the next world? What form of the beloved is there, waiting for us? Is it the decrepit old man, wasted by disease? Is it the child, the vigorous youth, the man at thirty, forty, fifty? In our imaginations, it is probably some combination, something like a prototypical version of the loved one, a kind of average across our memories. But, like all prototypes, it is a weighted average, an average for which some instances count more powerfully than others. Given that the significance of this prototype is a function of attachment, we might expect that the imagination of this transcendental and eternal beloved would derive most fully from memories of that initial period when the attachment was fixed.

When Hamlet sees his father in his mind's eye, then, just what does he see? Does he imagine the corpse, "barked about ... with vile and loathsome crust" (I.v.71–72)? Of course, Hamlet is not a person, so there is no real answer to this question. But we and Shakespeare respond to Hamlet as a person, and a person would imagine his or her dead father in a prototypical way. On the one hand, the imagined figure would be the father Hamlet was accustomed to only five months earlier – the one whose hair was turning gray. At the same time, however, we would expect it to be the father transformed by childhood memories from the initial period of attachment. Those memories stretch back three decades to Hamlet's birth. We know from the gravedigger when that was. It was at the time of King Hamlet's battle with Fortinbras (V.i.146–150). That time was, then, the crucial period of the King's physical prowess and strength, the time we would expect to figure prominently in Hamlet's imagination of his father.

Of course, in some ways, this change in the beloved's remembered image, the shift toward a more vigorous past at the time of initial attachment, may worsen the pain of broken anticipation. As Hamlet expects to see his father, he is confronted with the realization that his father has died and with the memory of his father's disfigured corpse, so horribly different from the vigorous young man who defeated the young Norway (himself now "impotent and bedrid" [I.ii.29]). Again,

(e.g., in relation to discouraging separation from attachment figures). Memories and anticipation have evolutionary functions. Once these are in place, grief seems to be a necessary result. It may end up having some sort of function, particularly as taken up in a social context. But grief itself is not anything additional to the components just mentioned. As such, it does not require any evolutionary account beyond the accounts of those components.

the mere thought that this reinvigorated figure still lives spiritually has a function in mood repair. But the hope it holds out is distant, abstract, uncertain. The most profound and effective sort of mood repair would involve some actual communication from that spirit, something to confirm the idea that yes, indeed, he is still alive – visible in his particular self, endowed with the same memories and affections, able to speak and listen. This is something the bereaved person longs for. It is part of what he or she imagines and part of what makes those imagined images almost real.

After the death of his son, Hamnet, one can only guess that Shakespeare was like everyone else. He longed to speak with the lost child, to see him in blossoming youth. But if he alone saw the boy, that would not give him any assurance. It could be merely his overwrought imagination playing tricks, or his memory, or some confusion of dreaming and seeing. He would need not only to have the experience, but to share it concretely and experientially with others. In writing *Hamlet*, Shakespeare puts Hamlet in his own position – or, rather, he is both the bereaved person and the deceased. In *Hamlet*, Shakespeare has examined both his own grief and his grieving wish that he had died rather than his son, for he switches the death from the son to the father. In any case, his first step in this process is to establish unequivocally the continuing life of the deceased. Thus the play can operate as a sort of mood repair in which the author reassures himself of the life of the beloved son who has died.[11]

The opening scene of the play occurs at night, thus in the darkness that is such a common model for the condition of the bereaved. It is also "bitter cold" – aptly, for a play concerning grief. The guard who reports also speaks as if the coldness is as much a matter of emotion as of physical temperature, for he explains that he is "sick at heart" (I.i.7, 8), as if the chill and the despondency are inseparable.

In this context, Shakespeare introduces us to a skeptical Horatio. Hamlet's school friend doubts the appearance of a ghost. Indeed, his "ears" are "fortified against" the story that a ghost has appeared (I.i.31, 32). But he, along with Barnardo and Marcellus, soon sees and recognizes the dead king. All three bear witness that this is "something more than fantasy" (I.i.34). Yet, the fantastical quality of the scene is emphasized by the nature of the king's appearance. He does not walk

[11] Such a change in elaborative future possibilities is, of course, a different form of mood repair than the ambivalence-based mood shift discussed above.

out in his cerements. Rather, Horatio reports, he wears "the very armor he had on/When he the ambitious Norway combated" (I.i.60–61). In other words, he appears now, as a ghost, in the way he appeared at the most vigorous and physically powerful time of his manhood – the time of young Hamlet's infancy (V.i.146–150), the formative period of Hamlet's attachment with him. Later, Horatio explains that the ghost's beard "was as I have seen it in his life,/A sable silvered" (I.ii.241–242). The suggestion is that the ghost fuses different properties, as we would expect from a prototype – some from his recent appearance, but others from his prime during Hamlet's initial attachment period.

Horatio's recognition and description give us a particular clue that this is mood repair. It would make sense if, say, the aging Polonius recognized the link between the Ghost and King Hamlet thirty years earlier. But how could Horatio, Hamlet's schoolmate, recognize this? Of course, one can imagine explanations. For example, there could have been a portrait of the king from the period in question. But the play does not provide any such explanations. It is a bit of an anomaly. The function of Horatio's recognition, then, is to confirm the sense of the bereaved person that the vigorous beloved, whom he or she remembers, is still alive. In this way, we might suspect that it comes more from Shakespeare's own grief over his son (and perhaps anticipatory mourning for his father [see Greenblatt 317–318]) than from the logic of the plot. On the other hand, this only enhances its emotional impact on the audience that necessarily shares with Shakespeare these same propensities of grief.

But this does not entirely convince Horatio – for he only sees the image. He does not hear the Ghost speak. He does not converse with it. He therefore cannot recognize it as bearing the mind of the King. When the Ghost appears a second time, he shouts, "Stay, illusion" (I.i.127), suggesting a lingering disbelief, signaled by the word "illusion" – but, at the same time, a suspicion that this is a real agent, for otherwise there would be no reason to command it with the word, "Stay." Later, the Ghost speaks privately with Hamlet. This too fits with mood repair. The bereaved person may long for a communal recognition that the deceased person is still alive and accessible. This does not mean, however, that he or she wishes for everyone to share the same intimate relation with the deceased. If I have lost a loved one, I want other people to confirm my hopes about his or her continued existence. However, I want him or her to direct that continued existence particularly toward me.

This brings us to another aspect of grief. For the bereaved person, nothing in the world is as important as the beloved's death. Indeed, all other matters of life pale to insignificance. Of course, he or she will, at times, experience other emotions and other interests. But when experiencing the mood-congruent processing of grief episodes, he or she is likely to find all other interests trivial. As such, he or she is likely to feel that the entire world should recognize this triviality. Of course, people in mourning realize that this is an unreasonable feeling and modulate it. But there are qualifications in this case. Hamlet's father was a king. As such, his death actually had larger worldly significance. In other words, it really is consequential in just the way all of us tend to feel that our individual losses are consequential. Second, we more strongly empathize with attachment figures than with others – and, most often, we more strongly crave their empathy for us. This occurs even when the attachment figure is dead. Even when they are dead, we engage in a sort of hypothetical empathy, imagining their feelings as if they were alive – or imagining them as living and observing us with the ordinary feelings of embodied souls. In consequence, we expect a certain level of grief and remembrance from all those people to whom the deceased person was attached. Our empathy with the deceased person gives rise to our sense that there are duties of mourning – our own duties, but also the duties of other attachment figures, such as the deceased person's siblings, children, spouse, and friends.

Thus, Hamlet has every reason to be distressed that the mourning for his father has been so brief. The period of grief for a king, a husband (in Gertrude's case), a brother (in Claudius's case), should have driven out all banal thoughts of self-interest, and certainly such frivolities as remarriage within four months of the husband's death. The point is particularly painful in the case of Gertrude, for she has not only forgotten, but actually replaced her husband. The focus of Horatio on the Ghost contrasts strikingly with the relative indifference, even callousness of Gertrude and Claudius.

This also suggests why Hamlet grows so attached to Horatio so quickly. They were friends at school. But Horatio has been at Elsinore for some time without even meeting Hamlet. Later, Horatio becomes Hamlet's only confidant. Had there been such a relation between the two before, Hamlet surely would have known about Horatio's presence much earlier. Their new bond is based on the sharing of Hamlet's attachment-based focus on his father.

Indeed, this points to another aspect of grief that could partially mitigate the behavior of Gertrude and even Claudius. The loss of one attachment object prompts us to seek a replacement. We want someone with whom we can share that sense of mutual cherishing that has been lost. Hamlet finds this figure, in part, in Horatio. He also seeks such a substitute in Ophelia. But, of course, both are different from Gertrude and Claudius. Had the king still been alive, Hamlet could have become close friends with Horatio and wooed Ophelia. But if King Hamlet had not died, then Gertrude could not have married Claudius, and Claudius would not be king and husband to Gertrude. Put differently, one can imagine the dead king feeling betrayed and forgotten by the marriage of Gertrude and Claudius but happy for an engagement between Hamlet and Ophelia.

One aspect of Claudius and Gertrude's marriage is particularly painful to Hamlet. This is that Claudius has tried to replace the dead king not only with respect to his wife, but also with respect to his child. Thus, Claudius refers to Hamlet as "my son" (I.2.64). Hamlet rejects this substitution unequivocally. He judges it to be a betrayal of his father.

Of course, just as Hamlet makes ethical judgments of Gertrude and Claudius, Gertrude and Claudius make judgments of Hamlet. Needless to say, the bases of the judgments are entirely different. When Claudius first introduces his marriage, he does so in connection with characterizing Denmark as "this warlike state" (I.ii.9). The phrase may seem incidental, but it is not. It introduces the issue of ideology in relation to mourning. This particular characterization of Denmark suggests that his marriage, like his assumption of the throne, is bound up with the governing of Denmark as a militarily powerful nation. In keeping with this, the first order of business after the talk of marriage concerns the threat from Norway – a threat revived by the decease of King Hamlet.

But what precisely is the ideology of mourning here? Claudius soon articulates it. He characterizes Hamlet's mourning as a matter of "duties to your father" (I.ii.88) and "filial obligation" (I.ii.91). Of course, Hamlet agrees that there are such duties. He stresses, however, that he *feels* the grief. Specifically, he not only wears mourning clothes, sighs, and weeps, thus manifesting the conventional practices and the universal expressive outcomes of bereavement. He also has "that within which passes show" (I.ii.85) – the emotion itself. Indeed, for Hamlet, with his ethics tacitly based on empathy, this is precisely what his duty is. His father wants love, not mere "show." In contrast, this is precisely what Claudius rejects. Hamlet, he explains, is manifesting "unmanly grief"

(I.ii.94). The gender ideology of any "warlike state" is likely to take the same view – at least if men are the regular combatants in war. Grief, with its basis in attachment and its enhancement of empathy, is not an inclination that the leaders of any such state would care to see cultivated in their men. Needless to say, the gender ideology of a warlike state allows men to express emotion. But the emotions it fosters and prizes in men are anger and ambition, not tenderness and affection. The yielding and sympathetic feelings are apportioned to women. Thus, grief for men must both appear and be a matter of duty, not of womanly softness. It is and should be a matter of show – except insofar as it leads to anger, as we will see. To complete the argument, Claudius marshals the usual ideological associations, including religion. Thus Hamlet's "unmanly grief" is also "impious" and "incorrect to heaven" (I.ii.94, 95).

When Claudius and Gertrude leave, Hamlet reflects on his situation. He begins by wishing for death – indeed, complete annihilation, his flesh melting like ice. This is common in grief. All of life seems to be given meaning and purpose by the lost attachment figure. The deceased beloved defines home, thus the origin and end of other actions and interests. Even more importantly, he or she constitutes the primary person with whom one wishes to share emotions, both communicatively and experientially. Now, after this person's death, there is no experience worth having, because there is no experience that can be shared, directly or indirectly, with the beloved. In keeping with this, Hamlet turns to his construal or encoding of the world. It is "weary, stale, flat, and unprofitable" (I.ii.133). The weariness is, of course, his own – not due to prior exertion, but due to a lack of any animating motivation for action. The staleness means that he sees nothing as new and surprising. Novelty engages us, draws our attention and interest. It does this, of course, for ourselves. But it does this also with respect to others. Often our first impulse on seeing something novel is to share it, to point it out. The oldness of the world for Hamlet reflects that there is nothing he can share as novel. Flat is a version of the same idea, transposed from taste to landscape. It also suggests that there is no place Hamlet could go that would be different, because all points are the same. Unprofitable is perhaps the most obvious, but also the most interesting. It indicates that Hamlet sees no valuable result deriving from any course of action. In sum, his mourning yields no actional outcome that would ameliorate the situation. There is nothing Hamlet can do to alter the eliciting conditions of his grief, nothing that will change the death of his father.

In connection with this, Hamlet reflects on his mother's and uncle's marriage. His clear repulsion at this "incestuous" union (I.ii.157) indicates not only his abstract moral disapproval and feeling that his father has been betrayed. His references to "Things rank and gross in nature" (I.ii.136) suggest that Hamlet feels disgust for the world in general, more particularly for Claudius and Gertrude, and perhaps most intensely for Gertrude. This points to another feature of grief. The sight, touch, smell of the parent's decaying body – and subsequently the memory of that body – almost necessarily give rise to disgust. Yet the grieving child either finds that sense of disgust overwhelmed by attachment feelings or, what seems more likely, modulates it due to a sense of obligation. As already noted, feelings of racial antipathy, which include disgust, may be modulated. One risk of such modulation, however, is that these feelings will reappear, perhaps more intensely, later and in another context (see Kunda 344–345). This may be the case with disgust in grief, as well (i.e., it seems unlikely that this cognitive process would be confined to the context of racism). As we have already seen, there appears to be an intensified inclination toward anger at those who are around the dead person (e.g., relatives), thus salient objects of possible causal attribution for the anger. A parallel point may hold for disgust.

Hamlet's grief and despair prepare us for the reintroduction of the ghost. Horatio enters and explains to Hamlet that the Ghost has appeared. Remarkably, Shakespeare has Horatio describe the Ghost's attitude in terms that fit more with Hamlet's enhanced empathy than with the martial ideology of Claudius. Specifically, he explains that the Ghost had a "countenance more in sorrow than in anger" (I.ii.232). On the other hand, Hamlet is himself not entirely averse to the manliness advocated by Claudius. Indeed, anger would serve well to temper his grief. In connection with this, Hamlet dwells not on the sorrow, but on the martial display of his father's spirit, his bearing of arms. He concludes that there has been "foul play" (I.ii.256).

The next scene brings us to Ophelia, her brother Laertes, and her father Polonius. For our purposes, the importance of this scene is simply that it indicates how Hamlet has been pursuing Ophelia's love. In context, this seems best understood as an expression of his need for an attachment substitute, someone with whom he can feel trust, warmth – someone with whom he can share feelings and experiences, particularly those of his current loss. But Laertes warns Ophelia against Hamlet, and Polonius forbids her from interacting with him. We can anticipate that the result will be far more painful to Hamlet than it would normally have been.

Hamlet begins scene four with the apt announcement that "it is very cold" (I.iv.1). He is waiting with Horatio and Marcellus. The Ghost appears and draws him away. Now the Ghost begins to have a function of mood repair for Hamlet. He adjures his son, "Pity me not" (I.v.5), diminishing the empathic enhancement linked to grief. Instead, he urges "revenge" (I.v.7), thus anger. In keeping with the propensities of grief, the blame falls on other family members. The Ghost claims that his brother poisoned him when he lay napping in the orchard. It is, of course, curious that the King knows this, since he was asleep at the time. The story is, therefore, more in keeping with the misattributions and mood-regulation needs of grief than with rigor in plot development. Indeed, through the injunction to revenge, the Ghost not only provides Hamlet with a means of emotion modulation (through the activation of sorrow-inhibiting anger). He also provides him with a possible action, a way of doing something to (apparently) ameliorate the situation of death and grief.

Anger is not the only emotion that King Hamlet tries to introduce here. He also seeks to cultivate disgust for the same targets – again, in line with the inclinations of grief. Specifically, he characterizes the marriage of Gertrude and Claudius not only as "damned incest," but "lust" that "sate[s] itself ... on garbage" (I.v.83, 55–57). Interestingly, he also recalls the "vile and loathsome," leperlike condition of his own body at death (I.v.72). Ordinarily, this would be a clear source of disgust for Hamlet. However, the modulation of such disgust is, again, part of grief – a modulation that seems likely to result in intensified disgust elsewhere, as in this case.

Finally, the Ghost links all this with his desire to be remembered. Hamlet could be describing precisely the circular, self-regenerating operation of working memory in grief when he asserts that his father alone will appear in "the table of my memory" (I.v.98). Everything else will be erased. Words, "forms," impressions will all be "wipe[d] away" (I.v.100), leaving only his father – or, rather, his father's commandment for revenge, the commandment that might substitute for the fixated, ruminative sorrow that has until now preoccupied his thought.

Here the famous problem of Hamlet's tardiness arises. Once anger, disgust, and revenge have been introduced, why doesn't he get on with the business and kill Claudius? But things are not that simple. We may wish to feel something other than grief – something more admired, more manly, and less painful. But that does not mean that we will succeed. Again, Hamlet's mourning is not merely a matter of appearances or forced and temporary feeling. He suffers "that within which passes show" (I.ii.85), the genuine feeling of grief. Such feeling is not so easy to modulate. Indeed, just as anger would inhibit the sorrow, lethargy, and hopelessness of grief, so too this sorrow, lethargy, and hopelessness may serve to inhibit anger in turn.[12]

When we next see Hamlet, he seems only deeper in grief, not more fired up by anger. He appears with "fouled" stockings, "Ungartered" and "Pale as his shirt" (II.i.79–81). This not only suggests a generally miserable emotional state, but a specific sort of misery – the misery of attachment loss. We may care about our appearance for anyone, but we particularly tend to see ourselves through the eyes of those we love. Our enhanced empathy with them carries over even to their perception of us. At a time of attachment loss, the bereaved person may neglect his or her appearance not only because it seems trivial in comparison with the overwhelming fact of the beloved's death. He or she may do so also due to a painful and persistent awareness that the beloved is no longer there to appreciate that appearance (as in Li's inability to comb her hair in the absence of her husband). In Hamlet's case, the effect is enhanced because he has now lost Ophelia as a possible attachment substitute as well. Indeed, she has directly affronted his attempts at emotion sharing. Following Polonius's command, she "did repel his letters and denied/ His access" to her (II.i.109–110).

Also in keeping with grief rather than anger, Hamlet makes repeated references to his desire for death. He tells Polonius that he would walk "Into my grave" (II.ii.209) and explains that, of all things, he would most "willingly part" with his "life" (II.ii.218). He manifests the sense that now his home is lost. Denmark to him is not a familial place, but "a prison" and, indeed, "one o'th'worst" (II.ii.247, 251). As if illustrating the concept of mood-congruent processing, he explains to Rosencrantz and Guildenstern how he encodes only the sorrowful – and disgusting – aspects of his world. The earth seems "sterile"; the air is nothing but "a foul and pestilent congregation of vapors" (II.ii.307, 311). Given various possible encodings of the world – which, so to speak, includes both roses and sewers – Hamlet, in grief, spontaneously encodes only

---

[12] There is, of course, also the issue of the trustworthiness of the ghost. The issue was perhaps more weighty to Shakespeare than it is to many modern readers. On the historical concerns suggested by the play, see chapter 3 of Greenblatt's *Hamlet*.

the sewers, not the roses. Although Hamlet's anger does not appear to be greatly aroused by the Ghost's admonishments, his already developing disgust is. This is unsurprising, for disgust does not have the same sharp conflict with grief that anger does. Indeed, the two appear largely compatible, as long as the disgust is directed away from the attachment object.

At the end of the second act, Hamlet chides himself for inaction. Indeed, he tries to enhance his anger. Moreover, he does so by an appeal to militarist and gender ideologies. He questions whether he is "a coward" (II.ii.582). He lists a series of taunts that should serve as eliciting conditions for anger, complaining of his own passivity in the face of such affronts. He subsequently complains that he is like a "whore" or "drab" (II.ii.597, 598) who relieves his emotional pain "with words" (II.ii.597). Put differently, he is a woman who seeks emotion sharing, not a man who makes his deprivation an occasion for violence.

At the start of the third act, Hamlet has made no progress in regulating his grief with anger. In the first scene, we have the famous "To be, or not to be" soliloquy in which he contemplates suicide. There is military imagery in the speech, but even that has its primary function in recounting Hamlet's inability to do anything, to take any action that would alter the conditions of his grief. He asks if he should "take arms against a sea of troubles" (III.i.59). In context, "taking arms" certainly points toward the pursuit of revenge against Claudius. He conjectures a positive outcome for that option – "And by opposing end them" (III.i.60). But the imagery – the "sea of troubles" – suggests something else. One can go out and oppose one's sword to the waves of the sea, as in the Irish story of Cuchulain (see, for example, Gregory 241). But one cannot end the sea. Its waves continue. The precise correlate of the waves in Hamlet's life is vague, but an obvious connection is with the recurring bouts of longing and sorrow that characterize mourning. Indeed, the next words suggest that "taking arms" is not a matter of taking revenge. It is rather committing suicide; it is "To die, to sleep" (III.i.60). Just as taking arms would "end" the "sea of troubles," death, he says, would "end/The heartache, and the thousand natural shocks" (III.i.59–62). Here, the correlations are clearer. "Heartache" is his enduring emotional state. The "thousand natural shocks" are the momentary pangs of grief – perhaps particularly those moments of abruptly interrupted anticipation, where he spontaneously expects his father only to realize that such an expectation can never be fulfilled again.

Hamlet's famous dialogue with Ophelia follows this contemplation of suicide. The initial interaction with Ophelia is an outstanding example of how violated expectations may have a powerful effect on emotional response. Specifically, Ophelia apparently expresses concern that she has not seen him in so long. For Hamlet, in the context of his recent suicidal thoughts, this interest would almost certainly suggest solicitude. Ophelia then begins, "I have remembrances of yours/That I have longed long to ... " (III.i.93–94). It is difficult to imagine that anyone in Hamlet's position would not spontaneously project some positive conclusion – for example, "to answer with my own." What he undoubtedly does not expect is "to redeliver." In the context of positive expectations, Ophelia's abrupt rejection of both his attachment and his emotion sharing provokes anger. Briefly, Hamlet is no longer melancholy. Moreover, all his disgust surfaces, now directed at Ophelia, manifest in his condemnation of her as a potential "breeder of sinners" (III.i.122), his question as to whether she is "honest" (III.i.103), and his assertion that "beauty will ... transform honesty ... to a bawd" (III.i.111–112). He even seems to feel a sudden surge of manliness as he claims that he is "very proud, revengeful, ambitious" (III.i.125). The claim is not a remorseful self-accusation, despite the phrasing. It is a boast. Indeed, he has only recently berated himself for the lack of precisely these manly "vices."

However, his anger has abated in the following scene. His need for an attachment substitute is manifest again. He freely takes up feminine imagery in asserting that Horatio now has this place. Specifically, he explains, "Since my dear soul was mistress of her choice ... S'hath sealed thee for herself" (III.ii.65, 67).

Yet, despite this return to attachment, something seems to have changed in Hamlet, precipitated perhaps by the apparently complete loss of Ophelia. In his next scene with Ophelia, Hamlet's anger is barely concealed in his repeated sexual taunts. More significantly, his anger toward Claudius has sharpened as well. Specifically, the players have performed *The Murder of Gonzago*. Claudius has responded with outrage. Hamlet asserts that this is proof of Claudius's guilt. But, of course, it is not. The play performed for the royal audience clearly suggested that King Hamlet was murdered by Claudius and said directly that a widow who remarries "kills" her first husband a second time (III.ii.190–191). There was more than enough material to give "offense," as Claudius says (III.ii.239), even to the most innocent king. We in the real audience learn that Claudius is in fact guilty, because we are given access to his thoughts. Hamlet, however, has no better reason to suspect Claudius of murder now than he did before. If he could doubt the Ghost, then he could surely doubt the results of this "test." Yet he is willing to accept the play's results as proof. The reason has less to do with the merits of the evidence than with his own state of mind, which, it seems, has now begun to shift from mourning to more "manly" preoccupations.

Following this, Hamlet at last has a private meeting with his mother, a meeting at which they can share their feelings over what has happened in recent months. From the start of the interview, it is clear that Hamlet's predominant emotional state at that moment is not grief, but anger. (We see subsequently that there is disgust as well.) This fits perfectly with the attribution of blame and direction of anger at those who are salient figures around the loved one's death, often relatives. But, of course, there are particular conditions here, as is always the case. Again, Hamlet's anger appears to be bound up with the definitive loss of Ophelia as an attachment substitute. This may relate to a curious feature of Hamlet's behavior in this scene. His anger and general level of arousal incline him toward action. When he kills an unseen man behind the arras, we see that only the slightest provocation (the most minimal eliciting conditions) now may lead to an actional outcome. But something is strange here. Polonius cries out, "What, ho! Help!" (III.iv.23). Hamlet stabs through the arras, then asks, "Is it the King?" (III.iv.27). But shouldn't he have been able to distinguish Polonius's voice from Claudius's? Hamlet's response to the cry is so swift that we may assume he did not engage in any reflection on the identity of his victim before he acted. At that time and place, he certainly would have expected Claudius more than Polonius. In this way, he was no doubt inclined to take any hidden figure as his uncle. But one would imagine that the voice of Polonius must have entailed some unself-conscious recognition, no matter how fleeting. In that case, it is at least possible to conjecture that this recognition played a role in Hamlet's action, that one source of his anger was the loss of Ophelia, for which Polonius was responsible. Of course, once again, Hamlet is not a real person, so there is no precise fact here. Nonetheless, this is the sort of process one might expect in a person faced with these events.

Hamlet's subsequent discussion with Gertrude involves the usual idealization of the lost love object and the not unexpected disgust response to other salient figures in the environment – specifically, King Hamlet's wife and brother. Thus, rather than recalling the leprous figure of his father's corpse, Hamlet extols his beauty, comparing him to Hyperion, Jove, Mars, and Mercury (III.iv.57–59). In contrast, he characterizes Claudius as "a mildewed ear" (III.iv.65). He elaborates on the sexual relations of his mother and uncle, stressing the disgust of "the rank sweat of an enseamèd bed ... stewed in corruption," a "nasty sty" (III.iv.93–95).

But a peculiar thing happens after this. The Ghost appears again. Hamlet immediately conjectures that the Ghost comes to encourage his vengeful action. Yet he pleads with his father, "Do not look upon me,/ Lest with this piteous action you convert/My stern effects" and substitute "tears ... for blood" (III.iv.128–129, 131). Seeing the Ghost does not inspire Hamlet's anger, but his grief – which will inhibit anger and lead Hamlet to shed his own tears rather than Claudius's blood. The idea is strange in the context of the story's logic, for the point of the Ghost's appearance is to inspire anger. It is, however, not strange emotionally. Emotionally, this is just the sort of moment when – alone with his mother in her room – Hamlet might spontaneously anticipate his father's presence. The unexpected appearance of the Ghost, unseen by Gertrude, suggests just such a spontaneous anticipation. The resulting danger of renewed grief likewise suggests the almost invariable result of such an anticipation.

There may also be something like a psychoanalytic suggestion here. One may not accept an infantile Oedipal scenario in which the child wishes for the father's death (i.e., his elimination as a rival for the mother's love). It seems clear, however, that everyone feels some ambivalence toward attachment figures, experiencing moments of hostility, even rage. We have seen how grief tends to promote an idealization of the deceased and a modulation of disgust. It also promotes a modulation of anger – including, we may assume, anger at past acts, thus continuing resentments. Thus, we find Issa recalling his exile from home in a way that places no blame on his father. This is presumably not the way Issa recalled that scene even a few weeks earlier. As with disgust, we would expect the modulated anger to turn up elsewhere. This too may have contributed to Hamlet's hasty murder of the intruder in this scene. (Moreover, guilt resulting from momentary spikes of unmodulated anger – and disgust – may be a factor in the depression suffered by Hamlet and others in mourning.)

The fourth act begins with a substantially changed situation. Polonius is dead, and Claudius realizes that Hamlet is capable of vengeance. Indeed, in this short period, Hamlet's episodic anger seems to have become a more enduring hatred, possessing his mind with the same tenacity now as grief did formerly. This is fitting because it is

only through such constant anger that grief may be consistently controlled. When being sent off to England, Hamlet pauses once again
to worry about cowardice (IV.iv.43). Here it seems there is less danger
that Hamlet will lack the manly emotions that provoke violence. Yet
Shakespeare does not celebrate this resurgence of militarist and patriarchal ideology. Hamlet sees young Fortinbras as a sort of ideal. It is
difficult to imagine, however, that Shakespeare approves of Fortinbras's
boldness in taking away "Two thousand souls" in mere pride over a
worthless "straw" (IV.iv.25, 26) – or, as he puts it later (revising the esti-
mate of casualties), the "death of twenty thousand men ... for a fantasy"
(IV.iv.60–61).

Much of the remainder of the play involves following through the
deleterious consequences of such violence. We see this first in the piteous condition of Ophelia on the death of her father. In literature, loss
of a beloved is often represented as giving rise to madness. When the
loss is temporary, the madness may be cured by reunion, as in the case
of lovers. When the loss is permanent, it may be resolved only in death.
This is a literary enhancement of two salient properties of grief – the
mood-congruent processing of sorrow, which may foster a debilitating
depression; and the preoccupation of working memory with thoughts
of the deceased, which may lead to a sort of dissociation from the real,
surrounding world of perception and practical action.

One interesting aspect of Ophelia's speech is that there are repeated
suggestions that perhaps she has had more intimate relations with
Hamlet than we were earlier led to believe. Her songs express complaints of abandonment by a lover and a sense of regret over sexual
naïveté ("Before you tumbled me,/You promised me to wed" [IV.
v62–63]). In this respect, the eliciting conditions for her madness may
involve not only grief per se, but a sense of guilt and a feeling that she
has simultaneously lost her one possible attachment substitute.

Laertes enters with the violent bravado that Hamlet so desires. He is
ready to do in anyone he feels is responsible. As we would expect, he
attributes blame to any salient figure around – prominently Claudius.
But it is difficult to see such rash misattribution as admirable. Moreover,
despite the ideological association of manly anger with bravery,
Claudius and Laertes finally settle on a profoundly cowardly plan to
kill Hamlet. Laertes will not fight him fairly, but will secretly use an
unbated and poisoned rapier in an apparently safe fencing match with
Hamlet. Moreover, Claudius will offer Hamlet a poisoned cup of wine.
The only moment when Laertes is sympathetic is when he is not a man,

but a "woman" (IV.vii.189) who does, however briefly, feel grief over the death of his sister.

Subsequently, Shakespeare indicates that the cowardliness has to do with the act of murder itself, not the character of Laertes. Hamlet is no less deceitful when he has Rosencrantz and Guildenstern executed in England. Indeed, he makes a point of specifying that they should not even be allowed to confess their sins. Thus, Hamlet hopes to harm them eternally. His manly hatred does not allow them any recourse, any response. He rationalizes his action, dismissing ethical concerns simply because the two friends had "baser nature" yet still involved themselves with affairs of "mighty opposites" (V.ii.60, 62).

In part, Hamlet's anger enabled his murders. In part, the first murder (of Polonius) began to habituate him to the act. It was a sort of training in manliness. The play stresses such habituation, if for other feelings and gender ideologies. Thus, Hamlet urges his mother not to sleep with Claudius that night. He tells her that if she merely pretends to have the virtue of chastity, "custom" (III.iv.162) will eventually allow her to become virtuous, "For use almost can change the stamp of nature" (III.iv.169). The rub is that what works for virtue works for vice as well. The first murder makes the second and third possible. Hamlet becomes accustomed to killing, as the gravedigger becomes indifferent to death. As Horatio puts it, "Custom hath made it in him a property of easiness" (V.i.68–69).

The grave-digging scene opens the fifth act. It finally explains to us why King Hamlet appeared in the garb of his battle with Fortinbras, as we have already discussed. The scene also stresses the disgust inevitable in relation to the dead, and the ways in which this emotion may be modulated in the period of intense grief. It happens that the gravedigger throws up the skull of Yorick – an object of attachment for young Hamlet probably surpassed only by his own parents. But Yorick has been dead twenty-three years. Hamlet is not grieving for his loss. He does recall him with affection, dwelling in particular on the physical contact – "He hath borne me on his back a thousand times" (V.i.187–88); "Here hung those lips that I have kissed I know not how oft" (V.i.189–191). But now there is no need to suppress the spontaneous response of disgust. Now the physical remains are "abhorred" and his "gorge rises" at them (V.i.188, 189). Only a few pages later, we see attachment idealization and the disgust modulation of grief once more when Laertes jumps into Ophelia's grave to hold the corpse in his arms (V.i.252). But here, too, the genuine absence of disgust is not clear.

Ophelia is in a coffin, so perhaps the absence of disgust in this case is more show than substance. The feeling can be controlled because the eliciting conditions have been minimized.

By the final scene of the play, Hamlet is again heartsick ("how ill all's here about my heart" [V.ii.213–214]). However, this recurring grief is now modified by other emotion systems. Rather than accusing himself of unmanliness, he can casually dismiss the feeling as something that would only "trouble a woman" (V.ii.217). Yet here, too, the point is hardly celebrated. Hamlet does finally kill Claudius, but both he and Laertes die. The only victor is the rash Fortinbras who now is free to take back what King Hamlet had gained from Norway – and more.

The play is tragic, not only because it dwells on and reveals the workings of grief, but because it reveals the terrible consequences of a manly ethics of anger and hate. Those ethics have the ideological function of supporting patriarchal hierarchies and militarism. For our purposes, they are important because they are invoked against the more conciliatory and egalitarian feelings of attachment, highlighted in grief. Moreover, they have emotional appeal because they take up the anger that is already involved in mourning and allow some modulation of grief, and with it some relief from the terrible pain of separation that can make life itself abhorrent.[13]

Conclusion

In sum, by combining empirical research with the detailed and affecting depictions of grief in Issa and Shakespeare, we gain a greater sense of that emotion's complexity and a fuller comprehension of its eliciting conditions, its elaborative processes, its relation to mood repair, and so forth. Indeed, we gain insight into the nature of mood repair itself, particularly in the form of mood shift. Moreover, by integrating fragmentary knowledge about an emotion into a larger narrative structure, we gain a fuller understanding of a complex emotion as it develops. Thus, we gain a more complete and integrated – one might say, wholistic – understanding of grief.

One can speak of grief as a form of sadness, but perhaps the other elements of grief experience are more significant. First, grief derives

---

[13] Hamlet's situation is far from unique. For example, Lebel and Ronel discuss the ways in which "bereaved parents' anger" becomes "a motivating force for political and public activism" in Israel today (669). These parents face such Hamlet-like issues as the need to sustain anger and to deal with alienation from other attachment figures.

from the loss of an attachment relation. In connection with this, the bereaved person's imagination of the deceased loved one is guided by a prototype that relies heavily on memories of the beloved at the time when the attachment was initially fixed (e.g., in early childhood for parents). This also goes along with an idealization of the deceased person, including an idealization of the person's appearance. That idealization is often in direct contradiction with the decline and decay suffered by the beloved before death and, even more obviously, of the corpse after death. Thus, it may involve a modulation of disgust responses that may in turn lead to an enhancement of disgust for salient targets other than the deceased (e.g., relatives). A parallel process may affect anger directed at the deceased. Moreover, moments of disgust or anger aimed at the deceased may provoke feelings of guilt as well.

The loss of an attachment relation entails an increased sense of loneliness and anxiety. The anxiety relates to the loss of the loved one's care and the security that goes along with that care. It also fosters a sense that one's home (with the loved one) has been lost, and that what was home is now an alien place. More generally, it gives rise to a sense that one no longer has a partner with whom one can share emotional communications and emotional experiences. This loss is particularly important at a time of grief in that grief is a prime candidate for emotion sharing.

In connection with this, a grieving person may implicitly come to think of his or her interactions with others largely in terms of this loss. More exactly, he or she is likely to see all other interests – his or her own interests and those of others – as trivial in relation to the loss of the beloved. Moreover, he or she is likely to feel a sort of disgust at the activities of ordinary life, particularly on the part of those who were close to the deceased person. This results in part from the modulation of disgust aimed at the deceased. It also results from an enhanced sense of empathy with the deceased. Insofar as one (self-consciously or tacitly) imagines the lost beloved to be alive in another place, one may imaginatively empathize with his or her wish to be remembered and grieved. Deviation from that grief, then, becomes a sort of betrayal of the beloved.

In one's own case, such a betrayal only reinforces the sense that one had earlier failed to be fully involved with the beloved. Retrospectively, time apart from the beloved appears to be the result of terrible errors or even sins. Thus, a sense of one's own guilt, one's repeated failure in one's duties, is another component of grief, enhanced by unmodulated moments of disgust or anger, as already noted. As part of this, the bereaved person is likely to feel stabs of remorse for what he or she did in the past and pangs of regret for what he or she failed to do regarding the beloved.

This sense of guilt is complemented by a loss of pride. In grief, we see our own worth disproportionately through the eyes of the deceased person. The source of one's pride – the person whose praise one sought and whose blame one tried to avoid – is gone. It is therefore difficult to view oneself as having worth at all. It is difficult even to strive for worth. The criterion that set one's standards for such striving – the loved one's judgment – can no longer operate. This is true even in appearance. One may no longer take care of one's looks, for there is, so to speak, no one to see those looks, at least no one who matters.

These tendencies are only worsened by the effects of mood-congruent processing on one's perception and memory. The world and our past lives are always complex and ambivalent. In grief, we tend to see and recall only what is sorrowful (and disgusting), not what is joyful. We might put the point in a somewhat exaggerated way. Faced with a sewer on one side and roses on the other, the grief-stricken person will see and smell only the former. This bias in encoding is enhanced by the predominance of certain models for life in general and for one's own life in particular. These prominently include an inclination to charac- terize one's life in terms of darkness and cold. Darkness concretizes the bereaved person's sense of fear and disorientation; cold manifests his or her sense of physical isolation and homelessness.

Unsurprisingly, these patterns in processing often lead to a general devaluation of life, a sense that life is ugly and vile. More importantly, grief is deeply painful. The circuit of reward dependency is broken. The bereaved person is like an addict without a drug.[14] One's future seems hopeless and one's present is too painful to bear. It is unsurpris- ing that it is associated with thoughts of suicide.

Suicidal despair may be further enhanced by another aspect of grief – the sense of panic that results from the impossibility of any actional outcome. When experiencing an intense emotion, we acti- vate routines that allow us to respond appropriately to the eliciting conditions for that emotion. These routines may involve preserving

---

[14] Freed and colleagues note that the nucleus accumbens, part of the endogenous reward system, is involved in "yearning in unresolved grief" (33). They also note other links with "unattainable reward" in grief (37).

the condition if it is pleasurable, or changing it if it is painful. We experience panic when we have a heightened and immediate need to alter a painful or potentially painful situation, but have no means of doing so – in other words, when we experience action paralysis. That is always the case in grief. There is nothing we can do that will revive the loved one who is gone.

Of course, panic is not a continual condition, but it may be a recurring condition as one mourns. The same is true, in part, of sadness also. Though a grieving person may experience extended, mildly depressive mood states, he or she will also periodically feel intense moments of almost unbearable sorrow. These are often involved with expectation and working memory. Specifically, our minds spontaneously project various anticipations based on past experience. Those anticipations engage particular emotional responses, such as joyful hope. Such anticipations occur at various time scales. Most importantly, these include very proximate, unself-conscious expectations ("sensorimotor projections" and "working anticipations") – as when we expect to see a particular person through an open office door as we pass down the hallway. These spontaneous anticipations do not stop simply because someone has died. Rather, they continue. Moreover, when they occur, they deceive us, if only for a moment. We direct our attention, engage in action that betrays an expectation that the loved one will be there in the room, at the other end of a phone line, or wherever. But then we suddenly realize that the beloved will never again be in that room or on the phone. The pain of sorrow is intensified by contrast with the unself-consciously anticipated joy and the sharp gradient of change from that tacit expectation. This may revive our feeling that we must do something about the situation – thus producing once again the panic of action paralysis, the inability to produce plans (rather than mere fantasies).

Momentary anticipations typically occur when we are not concentrating on the deceased beloved. But a great deal of one's thought and imagination in grief is focused on him or her through recurring cycles of ruminative working memory. One result of this may be an almost hallucination-like sense of the deceased person's presence. The vividness of the imagination, the activation of emotional and perceptual memories, attract the bereaved person's attentional focus often far more than the real world of direct perception. Moreover, one's emotional responses – at least the ones that are enduring and consequential – may be confined almost entirely to circuits of imagination and memory, not the external world. Both the attentional focus and the emotional response can give the imagination a sense of reality while simultaneously "derealizing" the external world, making it seem unreal.

Like any painful emotion, grief involves not only mood-congruent processing, but also mechanisms of mood repair. (Indeed, the preceding analysis suggests that the mechanisms of mood-congruent processing and those of mood shift in particular are not necessarily contradictory and may be closely interrelated.) One of these mechanisms is an increased proneness toward attachment replacement. One qualification here seems to be that the attachment replacement should not take up the same social role as the lost love. Thus, Hamlet seeks a spouse, then a male friend. However, he rejects a substitute father.[15] On the other hand, perhaps this is a depictive idealization.

Another technique for emotion regulation involves the contradictory emotion system of anger. Anger is commonly activated by goal frustration. This is abundant in situations of grief. However, the frustration is diffuse and without a clear object or cause. In keeping with the usual, human practices of causal attribution, the bereaved are likely to attribute their anger, and thus assign blame, to whoever happens to be salient in the current environment – often relatives of the deceased.

Needless to say, like all other emotions, grief is not without ideological influences. In patriarchal and militaristic societies, grief and the attachment feelings that underlie it are associated with femininity. In contrast, anger may be fostered as an appropriately manly alternative to grief.

Issa's chronicle presents us with a fairly straightforward account of some prime features of mourning. *Hamlet* is, in a sense, more indirect. Despite appearances, much of the play involves a sort of mood repair, perhaps for Shakespeare himself. The second half of the play focuses on the patriarchal and militarist ideology of anger, exploring its often devastating consequences.

---

[15] Gertrude seeks a substitute husband, but there is no evidence that she is genuinely grieving.

5. Mirth

From Chinese Jokes to *The Comedy of Errors*

Mirth is our response of delight to something we find comic. It is what happens when a phrase, action, or idea "tickles our funny bone." The eliciting conditions of mirth include puns, pratfalls, silly costumes, goofy faces. The expressive outcomes include laughter,[1] smiling, and in some cases a kind of groan plus wince plus grimace. The valence of the feeling is positive. In consequence, any actional outcomes are likely to aim at preserving rather than altering the situation (e.g., by encouraging a comic performer to continue). As to characteristic cognitive operations, it tends to be associated with what might loosely be called right-hemisphere processing, at least in the case of language – thus sensitivity to multiple meanings rather than the suppression of multiple meanings in the service of univocal understanding.

Most of us can probably recognize that there is an emotional response with these characteristics. Initially, however, it seems difficult to say just what could define this as an emotion system. Commonly, we begin

---

[1] It is important to stress that laughter is an expressive outcome of mirth. Laughter is not an emotion system itself. Thus, it may surface as an outcome of emotions other than mirth or for other reasons. Much of the psychological research in this area fails to make this fundamental distinction. Thus, there is a great deal of attention to, for example, evolutionary precursors to laughter and correlates of laughter in other species. This is interesting and significant, but it does not directly tell us anything about mirth. Studying laughter rather than mirth is akin to studying screaming rather than anger (or fear); studying crying rather than sorrow (or joy); studying sighing rather than relief (or exasperation). Of course, laughter is not unrelated to mirth. Thus, Panksepp's arguments about the relation of laughter to play are clearly germane here (see 287–289). For example, this chapter argues for a deep connection between mirth and attachment. In keeping with this, Panksepp's analysis of laughter connects laughter with crying and thus with both "social-bonding" and "separation-distress mechanisms" (288). But at the same time Panksepp's research clearly shows that laughter is dissociable from any positive feeling (288) – which makes it clear, once again, that laughter is not mirth.

our account of a given emotion system by reference to eliciting conditions. For example, consider fear. We feel fear when faced with wolves, bears, rats, snakes, muggers, the prospect of losing a job, the prospect of a loved one passing away, among other things. In themselves, wolves, muggers, a pink slip from one's employer, and a diagnosis from a doctor do not have much in common, but it is easy to see what makes them eliciting conditions for this emotion system. Their presence greatly increases the likelihood that I will suffer pain in the future. But what could puns, pratfalls, and really big shoes possibly have in common?

Comic Evolution

To get an idea of this, it is worth turning to another case of emotion – sexual desire. Heterosexual men are likely to find various features of women's bodies (e.g., breasts and hips) sexually arousing. But they are much less likely to find other features (e.g., knuckles) sexually arousing. What could the relevant features possibly have in common that is not shared by the nonarousing features? There are two obvious properties. The first is that they tend to identify people as female; the second is that they tend to identify people as adult. Thus, breasts and hips are good markers of adult females. Moreover, the sorts of physical features heterosexual men tend to find arousing are also commonly associated with younger rather than older adult females. But what does this tell us? Primarily, it suggests that men tend to find attractive those features that signal a woman's fertility. This, however, is strange, relative to the case of fear. We generally do want to avoid being eaten by a wolf or to lose our job. But a man's primary sexual aim is quite often not one of producing offspring. So why would he find signals of fertility arousing? The answer is obvious in an evolutionary context. Individuals develop many sexual idiosyncrasies. However, across enough cases, there will be recurring features. These recurring features should be the ones that are more likely to be reproduced. If a particular inclination toward sexual arousal tends to lead to reproduction, there will be an enhanced likelihood that people with that inclination will have children, whatever their intention regarding children. In consequence, there is an increased likelihood of that inclination being passed on genetically, transmitted through upbringing via the particular child-rearing practices of this parent, or otherwise continued to the next generation.

Considering that most writers would stress only biological inheritance, I should perhaps explain further what I have in mind in suggesting that there are other possibilities. Suppose some features of sexual desire are fixed in a critical period largely through interaction with one's mother. This may result in someone finding particular features sexually appealing without a specific innate disposition to do so. In societies with free marriage, this will affect marriage choices and thus may result in offspring that end up acquiring similar preferences. If attraction to certain sorts of features makes it more likely that one will produce offspring, then that will operate whether the relevant inclinations are passed on genetically or developmentally. For example, a sexual preference for older women is less likely to produce offspring than a sexual preference for younger (but still adult) women. If, in a given case, a preference for older women is genetic, this should lead to diminished reproduction, thus fewer offspring with that genetic tendency. At the same time, if such a preference is produced through critical-period experiences, it will still lead to diminished reproduction, thus fewer offspring who might acquire this (nongenetic) tendency through upbringing.

Whether we are positing innate or critical-period propensities, it is valuable for us to consider reproductive advantage when trying to account for an apparently heterogeneous set of eliciting conditions for a particular emotion.[2] However, it is important not to consider reproductive advantage too narrowly. We tend to think of selective advantage largely in terms of likely impregnation. True, a propensity has adaptive advantages only if it leads to recurring reproduction. However, if I have lots of children but abandon them to die immediately after birth, I will not be passing on genetic or critical-period propensities. Thus, inclinations to attend to and aid children are equally crucial. Note that, here as elsewhere, there is a common tendency to say "attend to and aid *my* children," thus my own biological offspring. This is true for the purely genetic inheritance. However, it is not true for critical-period inheritance. Moreover, even with respect to one's own biological children, one's propensities in this regard are not a straightforward matter (as I will discuss further in this chapter, in connection with the difference between mechanisms and functions). In any case, the crucial point here is that a heterogeneous set of eliciting conditions may turn our attention not only to sexual inclinations, but to practices surrounding childrearing.

---

[2] I am leaving aside cases where the eliciting conditions have clear survival consequences, for their evolutionary function is obvious.

In connection with this, I have argued elsewhere ("Laughing"; see also *Understanding Indian Movies* 115–118) that mirth is best understood as a particular sort of adaptation bound up with childrearing (thus partially linked with attachment). Simply put, at least one set of elicitors for mirth comprises properties or events that occur when there is a discrepancy between a child's condition or activity on the one hand and his or her developmental level on the other. A mirthful response to children encourages adequate attention (rather than boredom) from caregivers but inhibits parental tendencies toward excessive worry (e.g., over toddlers' falls). This function is particularly obvious when children strive to achieve something within their "zone of proximal development" (as Vygotsky called it), though mirth is not confined to these cases.

This sort of striving and failure clearly includes many of the things we consider funny. Take, for example, pratfalls (as in the old routine of slipping on a banana peel) and other aspects of "physical comedy" – for example, a scene in a screwball comedy where Cary Grant has a terrible time sitting in a chair without falling off. This involves just the lack of coordination that we find in young children – falling on their backsides, trying unsuccessfully to climb up onto a chair, and so on. By this account, woozy drunks – a comic staple – are not funny because they are drunk, but because they are like toddlers. Other features of humor also fit with this view – such as our tendency to find ill-fitting clothes funny, or indeed to find humor in smallness. The point holds for certain sorts of imitation as well, due to the mimicry engaged in by children.

It may seem that puns and other forms of wordplay do not fit here. But, in fact, the cognitive processes that underlie punning are quite characteristic of children's linguistic usage. In both cases, the underlying operation is a matter of right-hemisphere overproduction of meanings with relatively little left-hemisphere inhibition of those meanings. As Chiarello and Beeman explain, the right hemisphere "is critical for the proper interpretation of ... jokes" (248). Thus, as Beeman points out, "patients with [right hemisphere damage] poorly comprehend jokes and humor" (272; see also Brownell and Martino 315). They have lost their right hemisphere-based "ability to access nondominant interpretations" (Fiore and Schooler 357). These nondominant interpretations are usually available because, as Chiarello explains, "a wider range of meanings is activated within the [right hemisphere] than within the [left hemisphere]." Moreover, "the [left hemisphere], but not the [right hemisphere], can supplement meaning activation with selection and integration processes that modulate and restrict the scope of available meanings to those that are closely related to current context." In contrast, the right hemisphere "maintains a broader range of related meanings" (145; see also Faust 180). As to children, Kane points out that in the first two years of life, a child's brain is like that of "an adult whose corpus callosum has been surgically severed, isolating its right and left hemispheres." In consequence, the left hemisphere does not "*suppress* a region in the other hemisphere by sending an *inhibitory* signal" (41). One result is that the speech of young children is "marked by ... 'poetic' (i.e., right-hemispheric) devices" (43), such as those to be found in jokes.

Of course, the process of punning is generally intentional in adults and unintentional in children. But differences of this sort are just what we would expect in a roughly evolutionary account. Again, an evolutionary account necessarily relies on a distinction between mechanisms and functions. This is true whether we are treating biologically (genetically) transmitted properties or properties transmitted through familial or social practices (sometimes referred to as "memes"[3]). To recapitulate the difference – the mechanism is the actual process by which certain behaviors are produced. The function is what such a mechanism tends to accomplish, always with some degree of indirectness. As emphasized earlier, mechanisms are never identical with functions. For example, a certain physical shape in a woman may cause sexual desire in a man. This is a mechanism. It approximates the function of fostering sexual relations between the man and a fertile woman, thus impregnation. But it is clearly not identical with that function. A woman may have that shape and not be fertile; conversely, a woman may not have that shape and be fertile. The same point holds for the mechanisms of mirth; they bear on certain sorts of things that children do. As such, they approximate a childrearing function, but they are not identical with that function. Indeed, with ingenuity, the mechanisms may be enhanced by adults in such a way as to intensify mirth in complete separation from that function. This may be precisely the way comedy operates.

The mechanism/function distinction has several consequences for our present concerns. First, humor is not at all confined to particular

---

[3] As Ritt explains, "Memes are information patterns that are culturally transmittable and undergo Darwinian evolution: variation among meme types is created when patterns are altered, recombined, or transmitted imperfectly, and selection takes place when more stable or more easily transmittable meme variants come to oust competitors that are less fit, i.e. less stable or transmittable."

things that children would be likely to do. It is only a matter of following the same general principles. A child may not be likely to make a pun that relies simultaneously on knowledge of Heideggerian Phenomenology and sexual perversion. But the general processes of production may nonetheless be the same. Second, this account does not imply that children's attempts at humor will necessarily be particularly funny. In fact, children are notoriously bad comics. The claim here is that children will do certain things spontaneously that we find (mildly) amusing and that the mechanisms producing amusement in these cases may be manipulated and intensified through wit. There is no reason to believe that children would in general be particularly good at such manipulation and intensification. Indeed, research on the children's development of humor indicates that the cognitive processing involved in self-consciously producing humor is not available to children (see, for example, McGhee's influential discussion).

The present account also suggests why laughter may be demeaning. First of all, it often puts the object of mirth in the position of a child. More exactly, there are two ways in which humor may operate – unintentionally, as with children, or intentionally. When humor is the result of intentional manipulation, then we are said to be laughing "with" the person. However, when the humor is unintentional – commonly, when it results from some sort of mismatch between intention or striving and accomplishment – then we are tacitly putting the person in the place of a child and laughing "at" him or her. This itself suggests why perhaps the two main comic character types are, in Northrop Frye's terminology, the "eiron" and "alazon." As Frye defines these terms, the eiron is a character who presents himself or herself as less than he or she is. The alazon, in contrast, is a character who presents himself or herself as more than he or she is (see Frye 39–40). In our terms, the alazon tries to act beyond capacity. When done in a way consistent with the strivings of children (e.g., in using vocabulary beyond his or her grasp), this becomes comic. In contrast, the eiron manipulates the mechanisms instantiated by the alazon. When the mechanisms are of the right sort, this too becomes comic.

Beyond putting someone in the place of a child, laughter may be demeaning in another way. Some mirth elicitors may involve pain to the object of our laughter. Insofar as we respond empathically to the person's suffering, that pain should, at some level of intensity, inhibit our mirth. If it does not, then we may be understood as lacking appropriate empathic response to the person. This general mechanism of empathic inhibition is one reason why it is funny to see baby plop down on his or her diapered backside, but not so funny to see him or her fall face forward – even though children do this with some regularity as well. The variable here, as in so much else, is bound up with attachment. We are more solicitous of the well-being of those to whom we are attached. In certain contexts, laughter suggests a lack of attachment, even out-grouping and dehumanization.

Life Under the Grandstand: More on Mechanisms

So, there is a crucial difference and a crucial relation between mech-anisms and functions in an evolutionary account. We have pointed toward some of the functional and mechanical properties of mirth. But we need to consider these, particularly the mechanisms, with more precision.

In an account of this sort, the main function seems relatively easy to identify. Children require attention. By our ordinary emotional cri-teria, however, they are pretty boring. Even attachment may not be adequate to train our focus on children with sufficient continuity and intensity. Children also require an appropriate degree of encourage-ment and correction. Ideally, a caregiver should have enough interest in a child to pay attention to what is happening with the child. However, the caregiver should not be so invested in the child's experience that he or she overreacts to the child's discomforts or responds too force-fully to errors. Put differently, we can imagine a situation in which a caregiver responds with panic every time a child falls down. We can also imagine a situation in which a caregiver responds with excessive corrective vehemence when the child makes an error. Alternatively, we can imagine a situation in which the caregiver simply ignores the child and thus does not notice when he or she is actually hurt or requires correction. A mirthful response to children's striving "solves" these problems. More exactly, there should be beneficial consequences for the child if the caregiver is likely to experience pleasure and reward in observing the child's foibles[4] – as long as that pleasure or reward is appropriately qualified through the activation of empathic pain sys-tems. In addition, the expressive outcome of laughter has the benefi-cial communicative result of reassuring the child in cases where actual harm is insignificant.

---

[4] In keeping with this, the "reward system ... is involved in humour appreciation" (Bell, Coulston, and Malhi 36).

But just what are the precise mechanisms? That question as always is more difficult. Since the mechanisms are multiple, we might begin with a specific type of trigger for mirth – verbal humor. As already noted, part of the mechanism involves right-hemisphere processing. In right-hemisphere language processing, we generate multiple meanings with relatively little constraint. That is an important condition for some forms of wit. But it is not a sufficient condition.

In order to get a better sense of how verbal humor operates, we might focus on the particular process of overgeneralizing categories. A child might readily point to a distant airplane passing overhead and say "bird." Most of us would not be inclined to find this funny. In contrast, suppose a child has an aquarium that sits on a shelf a foot above his or her head. He or she might point to an airplane and say "fish." At least some of us might find this mildly amusing. Finally, a child might point to an airplane and say "doggie." Most of us would probably find this confusing. Assuming this is correct, what is the difference in the three cases? The first and second cases are distinguished by the degree of the error. Most of us would say that birds and airplanes share many otherwise distinctive characteristics. In this way, "bird" is an appropriate, indeed banal metaphor for an airplane. "Dog," in contrast, appears to have no distinctive relation to airplanes. Anything that links a dog with an airplane (e.g., being visible) also links countless other things with airplanes (e.g., boots). "Fish," in contrast, has something distinctive in common with an airplane in the child's experience. We recognize that connection, thus the reason for the overgeneralization. At the same time, however, we recognize the discrepancy between the facts and the child's experience (an experience that motivates the extension).

This example suggests that there are at least two properties to comic utterances. First, they have to be somehow wrong by usual standards. Second, they have to be justifiable within some alternative framework. The general point has been taken up in many accounts of verbal humor. For example, Attardo's influential account posits the necessity of a "script opposition" (thus a conflict with a standard meaning, practice, etc.) and a "resolution." The point here is to further refine this widely acknowledged division and to give it explanatory force by relating it to frameworks that would operate in childhood.

One justification that could "resolve" a comic utterance involves multiple meanings. By the account presented here, puns should be funny to the extent that they do not communicate real relations, but do communicate comprehensible relations in a child-relevant framework – first of all, the framework of right-hemisphere language processing. In connection with this, consider a childhood joke that (I'm embarrassed to admit) I still find amusing. It is part of a series of fictional book title/ author pairs that rely on right-hemisphere processing. This one is "I just read a revealing autobiography – *Life Under the Grandstand* by Seymour Butts." To understand how this joke works, we may contrast it with two failed jokes: 1) "I just read a revealing autobiography – *Life Under the Grandstand* by Glimpse Arses" and 2) "I just read a revealing autobiography – *Life in Wyoming* by Seymour Butts." The problems with the second and third versions are obvious. "Glimpse Arses" does not work as a name. A child could be a bad enough joke teller to say something like this.[5] But that doesn't matter. A child is unlikely to spontaneously mistake "Glimpse" for a name. In other words, it is not the sort of mistake that fits the general principles of children's cognition. The difficulty with the third is that there is no clear relevance of Wyoming to backsides. It is like the case with dogs and airplanes. Note that in the case of this joke, more than one sort of comprehensibility is required. The name must be plausible as a name. It must also be relevant to the title.

Of course, the fact that this joke refers to a taboo area of the body is not irrelevant. *"Life as a Shoe Salesman* by Seymour Foot"* is, to me, funny – but not as funny.[6] On the other hand, I can imagine telling the latter joke to my mother, but not the former, suggesting that some people may be offended by this reference to tabooed body parts. This

[5] Again, children need not be particularly good at telling or even understanding jokes. This is because they generally lack the ability to recognize and reframe errors. As already noted, the point fits with accounts of children's development of humor (see, for example, McGhee). Moreover, it is just what we would expect from the preceding account. The sorts of errors children would make are precisely the sorts of errors we would expect children not to recognize. We might also expect them to have difficulty distinguishing justified from unjustified versions of mistakes they do not recognize as mistakes.

Of course, this is not to say that children should be mirthless. We would expect them to find certain simpler sorts of (childlike) triggers funny, such as parental imitation of children's behavior. We would also expect there to be emotion contagion in mirth. Finally, we might expect children to respond to simpler versions of some otherwise more complex mechanisms, as when they laugh at self-consciously applying the wrong name to an object (e.g., "noodles" for "chicken," to take an example from Pexman). This could be due to innate propensities that have not fully developed, or have not been modified by elaborative processing, or it may be due to the activation of emotional memories in which mirth was produced by emotional contagion due to parental laughter in roughly similar situations (similar, that is, from the child's point of view, if not from that of the parents).

[6] My favorite is actually *"Life as a Teacher* by I. Fillmore-Brain." But I suspect that involves an element of self-interest.

fits the preceding analysis particularly well. Some principles bearing on mirth relate to knowledge and verbal categorization. But if mirth really is a function of childhood development, it is unsurprising that some relate to propriety. After all, children learn how to observe rules of propriety, just as they learn how to walk or speak. Those rules too would be subject to the general mirth criterion of striving beyond one's capacity.

The issue, of course, is just how taboo topics arise in childhood, and thus how they produce mirth. In the case of sexual topics, they seem to arise through apparent naïveté, through an apparent incomprehension of the sexual nature of the topic. In these cases, the child has not yet learned to suppress certain unintended meanings or implications. The effect mimics the overgeneration of meanings, but in this case, it is not genuine overgeneration. Rather, it is an absence of certain meanings (the sexual ones) – again, an absence that suggests a discrepancy between the child's attempts to do something and his or her age-specific capacities. Though it is not specifically verbal humor, a case of this general sort may be found in Freud's anecdote about two children who play at being a married couple. The "husband" goes away on a journey for several years. When he returns, he tells the "wife" that he has been busy making money for their life together. The "wife" explains that she too has been busy, and proceeds to pull aside a curtain showing her many babies (*Jokes* 184).

I suspect that "bathroom humor" is slightly different and involves an extension of intrafamilial ways of speaking and talking to extrafamilial contexts. One reason why there would be some aversive response to jokes of either sort is that other systems of emotional response – prominently disgust – are more likely to be activated for taboo topics. The activation of the disgust system will tend to inhibit mirth responses.

Before going on, it is worth mentioning one area of humor that bears particularly on ethics – ethnic, religious, sexist, and related forms of humor based on in-group/out-group divisions. Humor of this sort relies on categorial overgeneralizations of the sort found in the bird/fish example. In these cases, however, the specific reference is to a social identity category of the sort children acquire in the course of national education, religious training, gender formation, and so forth. The same point applies to other in-group/out-group related jokes (e.g., jokes about feminists). Here, too, the connections have to both fail and be comprehensible, in this case as overextensions. When I was in high school, one popular sort of joke involved the frame, "How many x does it take to screw in a light bulb?" Here are some answers: For "Polack" (stereotypically dumb, but also stereotyped for state socialist inefficiency), "Five – one to hold the light bulb and four to turn the ladder"; for "Californian" (stereotypically hippy-ish), "Five – one to screw in the light bulb and four to share the experience"; for "Irishmen" – I don't actually remember, but it had something to do with whiskey; for "Feminist" (a gender-related identity group), "That's not funny!" Note that these are not interchangeable. For example, switching Californians with Poles or Irish with feminists just doesn't work (even though Poles and Californians are presumably comparably smart, and even though Irish are probably as sensitive to insult as feminists). With such switching, we end up with something like the dog/airplane connection. Conversely, it isn't funny to say, for example, "How many Poles does it take to screw in a light bulb? One." It's perfectly true. We know it is true. Thus, group-based humor operates on the presumption of stereotypes. Such humor typically applies to out-groups. As such, it also has an ideological function in helping solidify in-group identification.[7]

Mirth may also bear on individual identity. Most obviously, mimicry appears to be increasingly funny to the extent that it involves the imitation of individually distinctive traits – for example, in a comic's imitation of George W. Bush or vice-presidential candidate Sarah Palin.[8] This is consistent with our general model, for children often engage in excessive imitation – commonly of those who are older and often when striving to achieve something beyond their developmental level (e.g., in seeking to speak like an adult).

In the rest of this chapter, we will first look at some characteristics of humor in the Chinese tradition, then go on to Shakespeare's *Comedy of Errors*. Before that, however, we should briefly consider another aspect of humor – timing. We are all familiar with the importance of timing in joke telling or comic performance. A good joke can be ruined by the wrong sort of pause; a comic scene may fall flat because its pace is wrong.

We have seen that short-term expectations are often extremely important in emotion episodes. However, here a slightly larger set of temporal divisions may be valuable. Beyond perceptual projection and working anticipation, we might distinguish *primed sensitization*, *selective expectation*, and *priming dissipation*. These divisions fall into a sequence

---

[7] Ted Cohen has argued that jokes generally cultivate intimacy. In-group identity is, so to speak, the dark side of that intimacy.

[8] Holland has stressed individual identity (*Laughing*). However, he is referring to the "identity theme" of the laugher rather than isolating distinctive traits of some target.

of roughly the following sort. Anything we experience primes a range of possible understandings and related outcomes. We are more sensitive to those possible understandings and outcomes than to nonprimed alternatives. This is "primed sensitization." At some point, we may unselfconsciously select from among those alternatives and form a more particular expectation. This is "selective expectation." This may be either a perceptual projection or, what is perhaps more likely, a working anticipation. Alternatively, the priming may dissipate without selection. This is "priming dissipation." One possibility is that humor operates by priming possible outcomes of child-related mechanisms (e.g., right-hemisphere processing of polysemy) that will make sense of a failed action or utterance (e.g., a failed categorization). Because they are primed, they may be applied quickly once the punch-line arrives. But the priming may dissipate also, leaving incomprehension after the punch-line, at least initially. To be effective, then, the timing of a joke or comic scene must be slow enough that the priming occurs, but quick enough that it has not dissipated. Moreover, the effect of the comedy will be reduced insofar as we are able to anticipate the understanding, thus when we have shifted from primed sensitization to selective expectation. In general, anticipation reduces the impact of emotion elicitors – hence our attempts at "preparing ourselves" for bad news or imagining possible negative outcomes.

My mother had two expressions for jokes that did not work. One was, "You could see that one coming a mile off." This meant, of course, that she anticipated the humor before delivery; selective expectation had already occurred. The other – opposite, but equally ineffective – possibility was that the joke was hard to understand and had to be explained or took a while to figure out. In that case, she would sigh and say, "Well, if you have to draw pictures...." These jokes were lacking in primed sensitivity.

To illustrate, we might consider a joke modeled on *Life Under the Grandstand*. "At my university, girls with a sweet tooth decided to form their own sorority. They called it *Eta Pi*." This joke relies on priming, but not selecting, "ate" and "a" with "Eta" and saying "Pi" (with its dual priming) soon enough so that the priming of "ate" and "a" is not dissipated. It is ruined if one generates selective expectation by pausing in the middle of the first word – "Et-a Pi" – or if one dissipates the priming by separating the words, as in "Eta Sigma – I mean, Pi." (The coherence criterion is satisfied by the frame in which the members of the sorority are "girls with a sweet tooth.") Variants of this joke include the women's crew team forming a sorority called "Rho Rho Rho" or the future dairy farmers of America petitioning for their own fraternity to be called, simply, "Mu."

A Note on Chinese Humor

Humor sometimes seems to differ more across cultures than other emotion triggers do. We often just do not see what's funny in comedy from other societies. For this reason, it may be particularly important to consider mirth in another culture to test the generalizability of the preceding hypotheses. Moreover, it may be important to treat a wider range of humor, not simply a single work. A single work may be unusual in a culture, anomalous, or coincidentally consistent with western principles and practices.

Of course, there is insufficient space here for anything approaching a comprehensive survey of any tradition, western or other. Thus, the following discussion is necessarily preliminary, touching only on some of the most salient points of another comic tradition – in this case, perhaps the most highly developed tradition of non-Western comedy, that of China. I will base my discussion on Karin Myhre's concise but wide-ranging overview of "Wit and Humor" in China.

Myhre begins by stressing the conflict between "cultural orthodoxy" and "comic expression" (133). This is just what we would expect if indeed one part of humor relates to the period during which young children are being socialized into conventions of propriety. Myhre goes on to stress the multiplicity of meanings characteristic of Chinese humor (133, 135) – thus, in our terms, the centrality of right-hemisphere processing – and the function of humor in enhancing "social cohesion" (134), thus in-group categorization (and, by implication, out-group categorization). Myhre extends the point to issues of identity more generally, noting that Chinese humor often operates by "confusing things that are similar with things that are different" (135).

After these introductory comments, Myhre goes on to discuss Chinese joke collections, which extend back 1,800 years. In keeping with the preceding analysis, Myhre writes that the punch lines often "center on the failure of mental capacities, such as perception, memory, and reasoning," frequently bound up with "linguistic problems of double meaning" (137). The link with childhood becomes clearer when we consider the characters who suffer such failures. Like longer stories, jokes include character types. Myhre begins her list of these types with "doltish sons," continuing with "henpecked husbands, incompetent doctors, idiotic officials," and so on (136). Two things are striking about her list. The first is its broad similarity to parallel lists of western comic characters. There are some particular differences (e.g., western comedy may pay less attention to doltish *sons*, as opposed to, for example, doltish fathers in the New Comedy tradition). However, it is clear that the general orientation is the same. Moreover, much of the list is straightforwardly consistent with childhood striving beyond one's developmental stage. In addition, it is not difficult to discern parallels between the henpecked husband/wife pair and child/mother; indeed, such parallels rely in part on discrepancies in the husband's and wife's sense of the former's competence, which is just what we would expect. Myhre goes on to mention "braggarts ... flatterers, tricksters, and fools" (136), thus alazon and eiron characters, in Frye's terminology.

An interesting case is the gluttonous guest and the "stingy" hosts, stressed by Myhre (136). We find the gluttonous guest character in the parasite derived from Greek Middle Comedy (see Frye 175) and in the vidūṣaka character of classical Sanskrit drama (e.g., Maitreya in Śūdraka's *Little Clay Cart*, who complains, "What a mess I'm in. When Cārudatta had money in his pocket I could sit in his courtyard and eat scented sweetmeats day and night.... Now he's poor I have to go wherever I can get a meal" [27]). This is an intriguing case because it turns up in these distinct traditions. It also has an obvious bearing on infancy and childhood. Indeed, parents are always concerned about how much their children are eating. In societies where food is plentiful, we are perhaps not terribly worried about children eating too much. Indeed, quite the contrary, parents today may be more likely to be concerned that their children are eating too little. But this has not always been the case. When food is scarce, a new child may be genuinely resented as "another mouth to feed." The point is clear in such cultural traditions as that of the Fon, where the child who "eats one out of house and home" is elevated to mythological status in the figure of the tohosu (see Ellis 120; for a Yoruba example, see Tutuola 31–35). This is related to the discrepancy in norms that we have found to be a fundamental condition of humor. Children may eat relatively little in absolute terms. However, they eat with remarkable frequency (e.g., when normal people are supposed to be sleeping), and they eat a great deal relative to their body size. Indeed, there is a sense in which children's eating habits are a perfect case of striving beyond one's developmental level, for the apparently excess consumption is directly related to physical growth. (The point may suggest one source for fat jokes as well as the glutton/parasite/vidūṣaka character type, and the manner of childhood eating may point toward one source of the comic appeal of food fights.) Moreover, this is a case where evolutionary benefits seem clear. Particularly in times when food is scarce, there is a clear benefit to laughing at the spectacle of one's child shoveling in the mashed peas with two-fisted enthusiasm (e.g., it helps to inhibit a more resentful and covetous response). The Chinese glutton and related character types serve to manipulate and intensify these triggers.

The parent/child pattern arguably appears in the comic duos that extend back almost two millennia in China. These involve a comic "butt" and "a straight man" (143). Western readers will be familiar with the pattern from such comedy teams as Burns and Allen or Abbott and Costello. The Chinese pattern was extended to "more complex narrative dramas" as well (144).

Finally, Myhre notes the importance of "bawdy farce" (148). This brings us to the violation of sexual propriety. It is hardly necessary to note that this is an important aspect of western humor as well.

We need not rely on these general characterizations, however. Myhre gives specific examples. One of her first is directly parallel to *Life Under the Grandstand*. It is a joke collection, *Grove of Laughter*, compiled by "Fu-pai Chu-jen," which is to say "Master Bottoms' Up" (137). Here, once again, we find the prominence of right-hemisphere processing and the resolving frame linking the title and the author's name.

Other examples involve such issues as the relation between appearance and reality, particularly in connection with dreams. These extend our catalogue of epistemic errors from semantics – categorial overextension and multiple meanings – to inference from perception and spatial orientation. For example, one joke concerns a man dreaming about a play. His wife wakes him. He complains that he has now missed the play. The wife responds that he should go back to sleep because the play cannot yet be over. The success of the joke relies on a discrepancy with the standard understanding of dream/reality differences. The alternative frame (i.e., the set of assumptions that, though false, nonetheless make sense of the error) is foregrounded by the wife's assumption of precise temporal equivalence between the real world and an ongoing dream world. In this case, we find an instance of another overgeneralization. The wife is like a child who has acquired an understanding of the existence of unperceived objects, but has overgeneralized this to dreams (which, of course, do not exist when unperceived).

Many Chinese jokes concern out-groups as well, particularly bump-kins. A number of jokes concern the muddled agricultural understanding of certain ethnic farmers. For example, in one joke, a Sung farmer goes and pulls at the sprouts in his field to encourage their growth. The joke is that he has confused organic growth with the lengthening of some inanimate objects that occurs with stretching – again, a childlike overgeneralization.

Another ethnic joke concerns a fool from Ch'u "who marks the spot on his boat where he has dropped his sword overboard." He plans to look for the sword at that spot when the boat reaches the harbor (138). In this case, too, we have a violation of standard, adult inferences – that an object in motion continually changes its position relative to other objects. We also have an alternative frame that makes sense of the inference. This alternative frame can take two forms. One concerns inferences involving the sword. In this case, the fool (or child) makes false inferences about the constancy of spatial relations, in effect mis-applying an inference concerning the continued existence of unper-ceived objects. (When the ball went behind the screen, it stayed behind the screen – so, when the sword drops over the edge at this spot, it will stay at this spot.) The second possibility concerns perspective taking. In this version, the fool (or child) has failed to realize the need to shift perspective – prominently including spatial location – from current self to future self. The perspective of the future self will differ from that of the current self in a crucial way. This is parallel to young children's inability to project the perspective of others (e.g., with regard to knowledge[9]).

In sum, Chinese humor seems remarkably consistent with the pre-ceding account of mirth. It also helps us extend our understanding of the mechanisms involved in mirth. We can now explore some of these mechanisms in greater detail through Shakespeare's early comedy. In doing so, we will also be able to consider some political and ethical issues that arise in connection with mirth in that play.

The Comedy of Errors

This early play by Shakespeare,[10] based on Plautus's classic *Menaechmi*, focuses insistently on identity, both group identity and individual

---

[9] See, for example, the research discussed in Doherty 7–33 (though Doherty treats this in terms of belief rather than epistemic perspective, the point is the same).

[10] I will obviously be considering what the play tells us about mirth in the context of a perceptual, and in this case evolutionary, account of emotion. There has certainly

identity. It derives much of its mirth from the confusion of individual identities. At the same time, its dramatic tension and its ethical concerns are based primarily on in-group/out-group identification. The play begins with one such group conflict.

The towns of Ephesus and Syracuse have declared each other's citizens outlaws, condemned to death should they be found within the wrong town's boundaries. Thus Syracusans will be executed for visiting Ephesus and Ephesians for visiting Syracuse. Shakespeare shows a remarkable understanding of group dynamics when he counters this mutual hostility with the presence of twins. Two Antipholuses and two Dromios, the latter twins being servants to the former twins, were separated in a sea disaster many years earlier. The forlorn father of the Antipholuses, along with one son and one servant, made his way to Syracuse. The other Antipholus and Dromio ended up in Ephesus. The (apparently) bereaved mother of the Antipholuses also landed in Ephesus, but without knowing that one of her sons and one servant were there also.

Obviously, this division underlies the comic antics that follow. But it is important to note that it also has a thematic function.[11] Shakespeare

been discussion of the play as comedy. However, this has rarely involved an attempt to determine just what is funny in the play and why. When attempts have been made to explain humor in the play, they have been limited and have tended to rely on dubious psychoanalytic ideas. For example, Barbara Freedman views the "key to farce" as our inclination to "laugh at violence" (235). Of course, we do sometimes laugh at violence, but the crucial point is explaining when we do and when we do not. This is not to say that there have not been discussions of the play based on a better-supported cognitive architecture. Though she does not focus on mirth, Lalita Pandit ("Emotion") has discussed a wide range of emotional issues in this play, drawing on appraisal theory. Readers may wish to consult Pandit's essay for a different but related discussion.

  In keeping with the historicist orientation of much recent Shakespeare criticism, some critical work on humor in the play treats historical precedents. For example, David Galbraith discusses theories of comedy at Shakespeare's time. In keeping with the orientation of the present analysis, however, Galbraith points out that the humor in Shakespeare often "seems inconsistent with much of the comic theory" of the time. Moreover, this humor "throws more light on the limitations of that theory than on its own dramatic flaws" (14). Of course, here as elsewhere, there were historical issues at stake, historical inflections of universal patterns. These include changing norms surrounding politeness (e.g., regarding derision), gender (e.g., the appropriateness – or inappropriateness – of women laughing), the social functions of jest in different contexts, debates over the religious significance or valence of mirth, etc. For a valuable and learned discussion of these topics in relation to some of Shakespeare's other works, see Ghose.

[11] Much of the discussion on the play as comedy has concerned the issue of whether the play is thematically serious, thus how it should be categorized in terms of genre (see

has, in effect, recognized a fundamental principle of recent research in in-group/out-group formation. Group opposition has little, if anything, to do with actual differences between groups. It is solely a matter of naming. Research indicates that in-group/out-group effects are produced when people are arbitrarily divided into groups and do not even interact. The mere fact that we are placed in the same category as someone else leads us to evaluate that person more favorably and to evaluate those not included in the category less favorably (see Hirschfeld 1 and Duckitt 68–69). This propensity – and its ethical absurdity – could not be more evident than in a case where the antagonism is murderous, yet concerns groups that divide twins between them. Indeed, the point goes further, for it is precisely Egeon, the father of the twin Antipholuses, who is condemned as a Syracusan in Ephesus.[12]

But Shakespeare is not only concerned with arbitrary in-group/out-group divisions between people in different places. He is also concerned with the organization of groups in a single place, particularly the organization that sets some groups above others in terms of real social power. Put differently, he is concerned not only with national and related social categories, but also with economic classes. There is, after all, a way out for Egeon. He can, in principle, pay for his release (though currently he is without funds). In this way, the Syracuse/Ephesus group antagonism is not absolute. It is an antagonism that does not apply to the owning classes. The cruelty of class hierarchies is repeated in the treatment of the Dromios by the Antipholuses. For our purposes, one important aspect of such class hierarchies is that they repeat the hierarchy of the family, where the children are both physically and economically inferior to the parents. In this way, the comedy of the play derives primarily from the childhood-related confusions of identity while to a great extent the thematic concerns of the play

Miola "The Play" 17–20 for an overview of criticism treating this topic). Critics have generally recognized that the play has serious purposes. For example, Miola notes that, in comparison with its Plautine source, it "develops moral implications" ("Roman 24). Creaser makes the more specific point that, like a number of Shakespearean comedies, it involves "a conflict between law and justice" (84). Drawing on current theoretical idioms, Laroque states that the comedies generally exhibit a "desire to destabilize authority" (75) and to "transgress" (76). But these observations often remain fairly general. Edward Berry points in the direction of the present analysis in asserting that Shakespearean comedy "blurs the boundaries between 'self' and 'other'" ("Laughing" 134) and thus avoids full exclusion of the "other" (or out-group).

[12] The thematic point is intensified if we follow writers such as Anthony Miller in seeing the Syracuse/Ephesus conflict as parallel to that between England and Spain at Shakespeare's time.

bear on the parent-related class identities that organize society. The following discussion will, of course, focus on the former. However, the two are related.

Soon after our introduction to Egeon's plight, we learn his back story. Both the comic and thematic possibilities are suggested by Egeon's idea that his two sons "could not be distinguished but by names" (I.i.52) – which, of course, means that they cannot be distinguished in order to apply the right names initially. The comic point is pushed to true absurdity when we learn that they actually have the same name. This confusion of verbal and individual identity is an important aspect of the mix-ups that drive the comic plot, and are of course related to childhood acquisition of categories and names. But Egeon's claim has larger, ethical import as well. Specifically, it relates to the division in name between societies such as Syracuse and Ephesus, as well as the class divisions distinguishing Egeon with a hundred pounds (thus condemned to death) and Egeon with a thousand pounds (thus allowed to live). The class issue is particularly stressed when the twin Antipholuses are paired with twin Dromios, born at the same time and place ("That very hour, and in the selfsame inn" [I.i.53]), but purchased as slaves by Egeon.

Egeon goes on to explain how, some twenty-three years earlier, he and his family were divided by a shipwreck. Of course, the separation, the "unjust divorce" (I.i.103), did not end the feelings of attachment. The seeking that shapes the plot is driven by the desire for reunion with family. This stress on attachment, though not necessary for mirth, is apt to it. In this case, it helps give the play a sort of tolerant humanism that softens the impact of its ethical critique. Indeed, one could differentiate two sorts, or rather two orientations of comedy based on the degree to which they integrate humor with attachment. Humor becomes increasingly harsh and even demeaning to the extent that it lacks attachment, relying only on the pure mechanisms of child-related mirth; conversely, it becomes more compassionate and humane insofar as it is linked with attachment.

We next encounter the Syracusan Antipholus and Dromio. Antipholus introduces Dromio as someone who "Lightens my humor with his merry jests" (I.ii.21). This places Dromio in the position of a Shakespearean clown. As is well known, Shakespeare's clowns are prototypical eiron figures, commonly paired with some alazon figure who is socially superior to them. Alazon figures are, again, the characters that strive for accomplishments beyond their capacities. In this way, they are the characters who most directly manifest the comic discrepancies discussed earlier. For example, the alazon figure is more likely to misuse technical terminology. In contrast, the eiron figure often manipulates and intensifies such childhood mechanisms. Thus, he or she may use technical terms in ways that are typical of the alazon, but he or she does so more systematically, often elaborating discrepancies and coherences (thus both conditions for humor). The alazon is, of course, unaware of his or her failures. In contrast, the eiron manipulates wit self-consciously. In this way, the eiron is comparable to the author.

In the present context, one particularly interesting aspect of this is that the eiron/alazon relation – both in Shakespeare and in his New Comedy precursors – is parallel to the child/parent relation, not (as one might expect) the parent/child relation. In other words, it is the character situated in the position of the child who manipulates the mechanisms of wit, whereas the character in the position of the parent commits his or her errors obliviously. At one level, this is part of the commonly remarked "subversive" quality of humor, its tendency to make fun of the powerful. This is something we might expect. When group definition is held constant, we would expect people's spontaneous empathic response to be enhanced with respect to those who are less privileged or are exploited. For example, when a work treats members of the same society, one might expect readers to feel greater compassion for those who are dominated rather than for those who dominate. (In contrast, when treating in-group/out-group relations, humor does not appear to be particularly "subversive.") Perhaps more importantly, this situation does in some ways parallel that of parents and children. Children are often painfully aware of their failures, their errors in inference, recognition, action, and speech. In contrast, parents do not face the insistent corrections of familial supervisors and thus are in some ways much more likely to be genuine alazon figures (something children realize acutely as they move toward adolescence). In part for this reason, the familial parallels in comedy are often inverted, or at least mixed. In the case of *The Comedy of Errors*, the inverse parallel serves the political and ethical themes of the work as well.

Again, the theme of identity is prominent in the play. Syracusan Antipholus presents that theme in a way that simultaneously stresses the work's attachment concerns. Specifically, he compares himself and his brother to two drops in an ocean. He explains that, in failing to find his mother and brother, he loses himself (I.ii.35–40). The image is significant for at least two reasons. First, it suggests the quite reasonable point that one's personal identity is developed first of all in relation to the people with whom one has attachment relations, namely one's family. Of course, the odd thing here is that this would have happened in a critical period, some two decades earlier. Antipholus cannot now, in his twenties, form that childhood identity. This serves to give the play a sense of displaced time, a sort of parallelism with the relation of family members at that early period – just the period that is crucial for humor. The image of the two drops of water is also significant in that it continues the thematic concerns of the play. Specifically, the image does indicate that the two Antipholuses are the same as one another, but it also indicates that they are the same as everyone else (i.e., all the other drops making up the ocean). Again, the difference between an Ephesian and a Syracusan is not a matter of the people themselves, but of the categories applied to them.

Not long after this, the humor of the play begins when Dromio of Ephesus enters after Dromio of Syracuse has left. Antipholus of Syracuse of course thinks Dromio of Ephesus is Dromio of Syracuse and Dromio of Ephesus thinks Antipholus of Syracuse is Antipholus of Ephesus. They make a series of wild misattributions that we know are perfectly reasonable given their limited experience, a limited experience that happens to bear on the application of names – which, of course, they are overextending (in keeping with childhood mechanisms) – and to personal identity. The mirth is enhanced by right-hemisphere processing. Specifically, Antipholus of Syracuse has given his Dromio one-thousand marks in money. Dromio of Ephesus, of course, knows nothing of this. When asked about the "marks," he goes on to manipulate the ambiguity of the phrase, complaining about the bodily marks he has received from his master's beatings. He rather boldly suggests that perhaps his master would not appreciate the return of those marks, thus exploiting the related multiple meanings of "return." The confusion continues when Dromio of Ephesus mentions Antipholus's wife – a person unknown to Antipholus of Syracuse. Dromio is the sharper of the two, in keeping with his position as a Shakespearean "fool." Moreover, his physical mistreatment by Antipholus contributes significantly to the ethical concerns of the play. Nonetheless, both characters make the sort of comprehensible childlike errors described earlier.

Dromio of Ephesus reports back to his master's wife. His account is full of wordplay relying on the usual right-hemisphere processing. He then delivers a comic version of his dialogue with the Syracusan

Antipholus that is worth considering in more detail. Here is what
Dromio reports to his mistress, Adriana:

> When I desired him to come home to dinner,
> He asked me for a thousand marks in gold.
> "Tis dinner-time," quoth I. "My gold," quoth he.
> "Your meat doth burn," quoth I. "My gold," quoth he.
> "Will you come home?" quoth I. "My gold," quoth he;
> "Where is the thousand marks I gave thee, villain?"
> "The pig," quoth I, "is burned." (II.i.61–68)

Personally, I find the whole (reported) dialogue funny, with the last
line particularly delightful. Why is this? One of the sets of social
practices a child must acquire is proficiency in principles of conversation. In Gricean terms, children must learn to follow the cooperative principle. Neither participant is following conversation principles
in this case. But they are violating them in perfectly comprehensible
ways. Indeed, Antipholus is playing the role of the stubborn child for
most of this dialogue. We may not be so amused in real life, when
faced with the practical difficulty of child refusing to eat because he
has not been given a toy. But the complete obliviousness and fixity
of the attitude does at least partially follow the principles outlined
above. It is both socially anomalous and comprehensible for a given
developmental stage and certain limited experiences. Thus, Dromio
plays the parent trying to entice the naughty child to dinner. First,
he announces dinnertime; then he explains the possible ill consequences of delay; then he pleads. In each case, Antipholus simply
repeats his anomalous and incomprehensible, yet, in another frame,
perfectly reasonable demand. Then something happens in the final
lines. Antipholus steps into the parent role and demands obedience
from his inferior, putting Dromio in the position of the child. Dromio
replies with the apparently irrelevant repetition that previously
marked Antipholus's answers. Thus, part of the comic impact here
comes from childlike repetition. Moreover, in keeping with his role
as eiron, Dromio is a master of right-hemisphere processing – and
timing. He begins his reply by saying "The pig." This allows for at least
two interpretations. He may be addressing Adriana and referring to
his master unkindly (as in "The pig went on to slap me"). Or he may
be addressing Antipholus and elaborating on the situation of the dinner. We have just enough time to generate these alternatives when his
unexpected insertion of "quoth I" eliminates the former possibility.
This is followed by the repetition of "is burned." Here, as elsewhere,

Dromio proves himself a masterful manipulator of the mechanisms of mirth – not only in his final statement, but in the entire dialogue that he (mirroring Shakespeare) has fabricated.

It would be pointless to go through all instances of this sort in the play. However, it is worth remarking on one more. Again, both the degree of an anomaly and degree of secondary frame coherence enhance comic effect. Thus, in the case of a pun, the more the pun is extended, the more mirthful the discourse will be, generally speaking. Dromio is highly skilled at extending wordplay in just this way. Adriana threatens Dromio, saying, "Back, slave, or I will break thy pate across." Dromio relies on the right-hemisphere activation of both "across" and "a cross" for the final word. Taking up the second alternative, he replies that Antipholus "will bless that cross with other beating," punning on the dual senses of "bless" – "sanctify" and "wound." (Though now obsolete, the latter sense was current at the time, as indicated by the *Oxford English Dictionary*.) The repetition of "cross" here enhances the alternative semantics. He concludes that all this will give him a "holy head" (II.i.79–81). Thus we have across and cross, bless (sanctify) and bless (wound), and holy and holey. Dromio manipulates the ambiguity into an intense consistency, thus an enhanced comic effect.

Adriana quickly concludes that her husband's changed attitudes derive from sexual misbehavior. Thus, Shakespeare introduces the taboo topic of sexuality. Obviously, this would not be a humorous topic if empathic emotional responses entered to inhibit mirth responses. As a number of writers have noted, we may share someone's feelings in empathy or we may rely on our own knowledge to respond to another person's (or a character's) situation (cf. Gaut 207). In other words, we may simulate how a person feels or how he or she would feel, given our knowledge. Sometimes our knowledge is different from the other person's in ways that are important for emotional response. In this case, we know that Antipholus of Ephesus has not, in fact, changed. Rather, Dromio has confused one Antipholus with the other. Thus, Adriana's worry over sexual infidelity is unfounded – and thus we may continue to find the situation mirthful, despite her distress.

On the other hand, this does not fully explain our emotional response here. The point is clear when we consider a case such as *Othello*. There too we know that Othello's jealousy is pointless. We know that there is nothing that needs to be explained regarding Desdemona's behavior. But we experience something more like Aristotelian fear in that case, not mirth. What is the difference between these two cases?

The first reason we do not respond to Adriana with (mirth-inhibiting) fear or pity concerns what Noël Carroll refers to as "criterial prefocusing" ("Art" 202). This is our genre-based orientation to understand events in certain ways. Think of a scene in which a young woman is walking alone at night. In a horror movie, we have one expectation and one emotional response. In a romantic comedy, we have another. In the account of emotion we have been considering, this means that we recruit different memories, tacitly expect different outcomes, and so forth. In a play called *The Comedy of Errors*, we do not anticipate dire results from jealousy. Note that this is not simply an abstract confidence that things will turn out well. It is, rather, an imaginative propensity. We envision different results from jealousy in a romantic comedy – particularly one announcing from the start that errors will be comic. This is not primarily a matter of child-related eliciting conditions for mirth per se. Rather, it is primarily the result of general conditions on the relations among emotion systems, imagination, expectation, and memory.

On the other hand, children often have to learn just what counts as painful or dangerous – this is one function of emotion sharing – and they often modulate their emotional responses depending on audience and potential sympathy. Obviously, there are some pains that a child knows merit wailing. But a child will sometimes flop on his or her backside, look around (apparently to see who is looking), then begin the ear-piercing lament. Once assured of the child's well-being (due to the delay and the brief deliberation over audience), we often find such scenarios comic. There is an element of this in Adriana's complaint to her sister. Indeed, the reader more than suspects that Adriana is not wholly sincere in her implications. She asks, "Hath homely age th'alluring beauty took/From my poor cheek?" (II.i.90–91). It is difficult to imagine that she has not envisioned a strong reply in the negative (Lost thy beauty? Thou? That very Adriana who is the constant cause of soul-deflating sighs expired by the city's every youth? Fie! I would count it merry jest, if thou didst not speak so brainsickly of the matter!). In contrast, Othello's comments on his age and race are delivered in a soliloquy (III.iii.258–278). They cannot be aimed at sympathy and contradiction.

In keeping with this, the dangers threatened by Adriana, though severe, will be rather slow in developing, if they are possible at all. This leaves plenty of time for revelations to correct her misperception – or for her simply to change her mind. Specifically, she threatens that she will weep herself to death. This will obviously take a while. Moreover, it will serve as a clear signal that something is amiss, thus probably prompting action on the part of her husband or someone else. In contrast, Othello's idea that he will murder Desdemona suggests a potentially swift and unstoppable action.

A final contributing factor is, of course, the phrasing of the complaint. For example, Adriana relies on right hemisphere processing with her pun on deer/dear, when referring to Antipholus as an "unruly deer." There is also a pun in her claim that he "feeds from home" and she is only "his stale" (II.i.101–102). As such, she is, first, "A lover or mistress whose devotion is turned into ridicule for the amusement of a rival or rivals" (as the *Oxford English Dictionary* puts it). But in the context of feeding, there is also the suggestion of something that "has lost its freshness," often "straw" (to cite the *Oxford English Dictionary* once more). Comparing herself to old straw eaten – or left aside – by deer is already a comic pun. In addition, the eating metaphor suggests a sexual innuendo that may be "unintended" by the character, but is at the same time perfectly comprehensible and fitting.

As the play develops, we find that the techniques we have been considering are repeated, varied, and further developed. Thus, in the next scene, we again witness the class asymmetry between Antipholus and Dromio. This repeats the theme of the injustice done to servants, but also produces mirth, in part through Dromio's manipulation of the mechanisms for mirth. Moreover, taking up the issue of identity, Adriana draws on the same *drop of water* metaphor to affirm her identity with her husband (II.ii.122–132). This again suggests the relative arbitrariness of identity categories – in this case including gender categories – particularly where attachment is at issue.

There are, however, some new particular mechanisms. One error of childhood thinking involves overextending intentional or agentive causal explanations ("final causal" explanations, in Aristotelian terminology). Dromio of Syracuse manipulates this mechanism in arguing that men lose their hair due to their wit. Of course, this discrepancy with standard views would simply be puzzling, not funny, if it were not rendered comprehensible. Dromio does just this by explaining that a man goes bald to save the cost of haircuts and so that "at dinner [hairs] should not fall in his porridge" (II.ii.99–100). The line is perhaps funnier today than at Shakespeare's time, because we no longer use "porridge" to refer to soup. Thus "porridge" has a childlike sound to us, suggesting a further confusion of meals as well (breakfast for dinner).

Act two ends with reference to some other inferential discrimination problems that bear on both humor and childhood. The first is the
difference between dreams and reality ("What, was I married to her in
my dream?" [II.ii.185]); the second is the difference between illusion –
including "make-believe" or fiction – and reality ("This is fairy land .../
We talk with ... sprites" [II.ii.192–193]). As we saw earlier, the former
poses the problem of distinguishing different sorts of perception; the
second poses the problem of distinguishing different sorts of conception or imagination. Clearly, anomalous inferences drawn from a failure to discriminate between reality and dreams or make-believe are
not comic in themselves. They are comic only to the degree that they
are rendered comprehensible by reference to limited experiences and
inferential processes of the sort we find among children. That is precisely what occurs here.

Unsurprisingly, identity enters here as well. Specifically, Antipholus
of Syracuse wonders if he is "known" to everyone around him, but "to
myself disguised" (II.ii.217). One's sense of identity derives to a great
extent from others – usually, but not always, others with whom one
has attachment relations. Antipholus finds himself surrounded with
people who identify him, but he does not remember them or any relationship with them. His dilemma is a version of the situation of the
child who is continually confronted with strangers who nonetheless act
as if they are intimate familiars (e.g., unrecognized aunts and uncles).
Indeed, even self-identification can be a complex issue for children, as
when they puzzle over identifying themselves in photographs or when
they are asked about their location in a family or neighborhood by people who seem to know them better than they know themselves ("Are
you Sally Johnson's little boy?"; "Do you live on Elm Grove Lane?").

The opening scene of the third act involves the Syracusan pair being
entertained by Adriana while the Ephesian Antipholus and Dromio are
kept out of their own house. Once more, we witness the usual anomaly
and comprehensibility. The same point holds as we witness Antipholus
of Syracuse express his romantic longings not for his apparent wife,
Adriana, but for her sister, Luciana. The comprehensibility here also
fits with the general comic orientation or criterial prefocusing of the
play. Specifically, it averts the danger of problematic and worrisome
outcomes, as would occur if Antipholus of Syracuse were attracted to
Adriana. A parallel point occurs when the Syracusan Dromio reacts
with horror to the solicitations of his brother's fiancée. In both cases,
the comedy is bound up with identity definition. Thus Antipholus of

Syracuse tells Luciana, "if that I am I, then well I know/Your weeping sister is no wife of mine" (III.ii.41–42). Dromio, escaping the clutches of his soon-to-be sister-in-law, calls out to Antipholus, "Do you know me, sir? Am I Dromio? Am I your man? Am I myself?" (III.ii.73–74). This is followed by a series of fat jokes.

The fourth act works out some of the consequences of the preceding errors. The Syracusans come to the conclusion that they are bewitched and threatened by Satanic illusions. The people of Syracuse come to believe that Antipholus is possessed by the Fiend. Here we have another case of overextending intentionality in explanation. As we know, there are perfectly good natural explanations of all the characters' experiences. However, the characters themselves infer that the anomalies are the result of choice – in this case, the choice of supernatural agencies, specifically demonic ones. Once again, Shakespeare multiplies the coherence of anomalous inferences within the alternative frame. A courtesan approaches Antipholus of Syracuse asking for the chain his brother promised her. He responds by proclaiming "Satan, avoid! I charge thee, tempt me not!" (IV.iii.48). This is, of course, comprehensible given the limited knowledge and experience, the overextension of the names, the errors about individual identification, and so forth. But there is also a sense in which the courtesan is a temptation to be avoided – just as Adriana is.

An interesting feature of these developments is that particular statements seem to concentrate the humor of these situations. For example, Antipholus of Ephesus struggles against being bound and taken off for "treatment." Pinch, the alazon/healer determined to cure him of demonic influence, calls out for help, "More company! The fiend is strong within him" (IV.iv.108). In context, the line is, in my view, quite powerfully funny. Why is that? There is, of course, the parent/child-like situation of a disobedient youngster being removed to his room and putting up resistance to the punishment. But there is clearly more to it than that. Part of it comes from the utter obliviousness of the alazon to anything that does not fit his preconceptions. He has engaged in explanatory overgeneralization to such an extent that he fails to recognize even the natural explanations that are within his grasp. Indeed, he construes Antipholus's opposition to incarceration as further evidence for Satanic interference – even though anyone in Antipholus's position would react the same way. Of course, at the same time, this is also just the sort of reaction one might expect from someone possessed by demons – and, for Pinch, such possession seems to account for a wide range of other anomalies. In short, here, too, Shakespeare simultaneously increases the anomaly (by having the characters ignore natural explanations) and intensifies the comprehensibility in the alternative frame of category overgeneralization based on limited experience.

Another case of this sort occurs when the Ephesians have been bound and taken away, but now the Syracusans enter. Frightened by their experiences of the seemingly demonic Ephesus, they enter with their weapons drawn. Luciana, seeing them, cries out, "God, for thy mercy, they are loose again!" (IV.iv.145). Once more, the anomaly is enhanced. For example, there must be some clue as to the difference between the pairs or the audience would not be able to recognize them. If nothing else, the Syracusan Antipholus is wearing the chain mentioned earlier. But, of course, Luciana and the others do not notice any differentiating marks. Rather, they assume that it is the same pair they just saw bound. Presumably they take this new freedom also to be the work of the foul fiend. They flee in terror. Once again, we see the anomaly, and once again the alternative frame presents an intensified coherence – for the pair has drawn their swords, suggesting that they are indeed dangerous, and the speed with which they have apparently overcome their captors fits well with the demonic account of their behavior.

The final act of course resolves the confusions. First, the Ephesians do escape from Pinch. This leads to further errors of the same general sort we have been considering. But the characters initially maintain their erroneous framework of supernatural causes. Adriana exclaims "I see two husbands" (V.i.332) – a line that can be delivered to comic effect in different ways (e.g., with innocent bewilderment or sexual enthusiasm). The Duke states that "One of these men is *genius* to the other" (V.i.333; a "genius" is an "Attendant spirit" [Whitworth 175n.333]). He then asks, "so of these, which is the natural man,/And which the spirit?" (V.i.334–335). This in part recapitulates the processes we have seen already. However, it introduces a further discrepancy once again characteristic of childhood, a further kind of inference that the child must acquire – the discrimination between real objects, on the one hand, and reflections or shadows on the other. The connection is made explicit in the final dialogue of the play, where Dromio of Ephesus addresses his brother, saying, "Methinks you are my glass [or mirror] and not my brother" (V.i.419). Here, the Ephesian Dromio is suggesting an overextension of mirror recognition. He goes on to make a comment that is comic as it bears upon the child's fascination with his or her own body: "I see by you I am a sweet-faced youth" (V.i.420). If the preceding analysis is correct, we would expect vanity in such cases to be a source of mirth, as it is here.

Needless to say, in the end, Egeon is freed. Antipholus of Syracuse offers the thousand marks to free him. But the Duke says they are no longer needed – presumably because Egeon is related to Ephesian citizens. This brings the family together, Egeon's wife having already been found in the nearby abbey. Thus, the conclusion resolves the attachment/separation concerns of the play. The development and resolution of such concerns is not a necessary condition for mirth. But, given the preceding analysis, we would expect the conjunction to recur with some frequency and to be particularly effective in provoking a certain sort of mirth. Finally, the ending resolves the ethical concerns of the play, for the antagonism between Syracuse and Ephesus is tacitly recognized to be false.

On the other hand, the more sinister aspect of mirth remains. Shakespearean comedies are not without their out-groups and comic scapegoats. Here, Pinch is made the butt of derisive laughter as his former victims singe his beard, then douse the flames with muddy water, and cut his hair. A sanctimonious alazon is often the object of such derision in Shakespeare, and that derision is commonly a source of mirth. One's response to such scenes is, presumably, a function of the degree to which other emotion systems inhibit a mirth response. This is likely to vary with one's categorial identifications (e.g., if one is Catholic and sees Pinch's exorcism-like "therapy" as alluding to Roman Catholic practices[13]). It is also likely to vary with one's imaginative elaboration of the scene, based in part on one's sense of how serious the derision is – for instance, the degree to which it simply reduces Pinch to the status of a child groomed and washed by adults (or by rather incompetent children, who botch up the hair and use dirty water).

Thus, Shakespeare's play is largely a gentle romantic comedy, relying on attachment for its overall trajectory and developing just the sorts of mechanism we would expect from the preceding analysis. Thematically, it draws on mirthful identity confusions to develop a serious thematic criticism of national identity categories and class hierarchies. At the same time, it contains elements of a harsher satirical comedy that stress different, though no less expected, mechanisms, particularly in the context of in-group/out-group opposition.

---

[13] On this connection, see, for example, Anthony Miller 200. Miller indicates that a tacit criticism of Catholicism here is balanced by the positive portrayal of the Abbess.

Conclusion

Mirth appears to result from a particular configuration of properties or eliciting conditions. These eliciting conditions are exposed with particular clarity in literature, because so much literature – ranging from Chinese jokes to Shakespearean comedies – so powerfully produces mirthful responses in their audiences. These properties of mirth are all related to discrepancies between adult understanding and aspects of children's appearance, thought, or behavior. They appear to serve an evolutionary function of training parents' attention on children and modulating their response to children's errors. Mirth is inhibited by empathic pain. It may be derisive or perceived as derisive to the degree that such empathy is missing in particular cases, sometimes due to in-group/out-group oppositions.

Commonly, the eliciting conditions of mirth involve conflicts of the sort we would expect from children striving beyond their developmental level to achieve more adultlike thought, speech, or action. In each case, the discrepancy at issue is comprehensible by reference to an alternative framework that is characteristic of childhood. This is not to say that funny statements or actions are the sorts of things children would actually say or do. Rather, humor follows the same general principles, commonly with manipulation and intensification that are well beyond the capacities of even the most advanced children. (One of the few areas in which children are not funny when striving beyond developmental level is, precisely, humor.)

The simplest instances of such eliciting conditions are physical properties. Static physical properties would include physical size relative to clothes. Dynamic properties would include toddling gaits (repeated in comic drunkenness) and eating disproportionate to one's size (leading to the comic type of the parasite).

More complex instances are found in psychology and in children's epistemic errors. Some of these involve perception and general reasoning, as in the confusion of appearance and reality. Instances of this sort include dreams and fiction. Another, closely related case is children's misconstrual of the distinction between reflections and shadows on the one hand and reality on the other.

Other epistemic discrepancies occur with the overextension of the unperceived existence of objects or object constancy and the overextension of certain causal inferences. An important variety of overextension involves the expansion of intentional explanation to inanimate objects or supernatural agents. Discrepancies arise with respect to intentionality or subjective experience in other areas as well. Some of the most significant discrepancies derive from children's difficulties in projecting alternative perspectives, either for others or for themselves at another time or in another spatial location.

Further psychological discrepancies bear on language, categorization, and reference or identification. Some forms of humor rely on the overextension of categories in ways consistent with the limitations or biases of childhood experience. Others, such as puns, rely on right-hemisphere processing of polysemy. Among categorial overextensions, one important set involves in-group/out-group divisions. Instances of this prominently include ethnic jokes.

Category subsumption involves a sort of identity definition. But identity is not only general or collective. It is also individual. Some humor involves issues in individual identification. This is related to the child's mimicry of individual adults and to children's interest in themselves as objects of their own perception, as in mirrors.

Humor also often involves violations of social rules. Some of these bear on cooperative practices, such as rules of conversation. Others bear on propriety. These include proper ways of referring to oneself (e.g., inhibiting expressions of vanity), ways of addressing others higher in the social hierarchy, and avoidance of taboo topics in sexuality and bodily functions.

Finally, like other emotions, mirth has its own temporal characteristics. Specifically, we may distinguish primed sensitization, selective anticipation, and priming dissipation. Primed sensitization involves the priming of associations that will make sense of events that are anomalous relative to a normal or default case. Selective anticipation involves the expectation that a particular, nondefault explanation will apply. Humor is most successful when non-default, child-related associations are primed, but none has been selected for anticipation, and priming dissipation (i.e., the loss of primed associations) has not yet occurred. This allows ready understanding of the comic event (e.g., a pun) without the dulling effect of prior expectation.

6. Guilt, Shame, Jealousy

Macbeth, The Strong Breed, Kagekiyo,
and *Othello*

Macbeth and Emotions of Self-Blame

Feelings may be connected with any aspect of a literary work – most obviously events and characters, but also scenes or language. Often, a scene will prime associations that prepare the reader or audience for the event- and character-focused emotions that follow. For example, the dark, abandoned alley in a horror film may prepare us to fear for the heroine as she walks home late at night. The opening scene of *Macbeth* has such an emotionally orienting function.[1] Specifically, it begins to establish the background for the emotions of self-blame – guilt, shame, and regret – that will pervade the rest of the play.[2] By definition, all such emotions refer to some prior act or event that is, in retrospect, aversive. In each case, one feels some sort of emotional pain insofar as one connects oneself causally with that act or event. The following pages consider what properties differentiate these emotions and what the consequences of those properties might be.

The opening of the play is forbidding. First, there is the thunder and lightning – triggers for fright. Moreover, unnatural figures such as the witches are likely to provoke at least anxiety, if not actual fear.

---

[1] On the general idea of such emotional orientation, see Carroll "Art" and "Film."

[2] Though critics have, of course, recognized the importance of guilt in *Macbeth* (see, for example, Bradley), this has rarely been developed in relation to current emotion research. In fact, generally, there is relatively little criticism on *Macbeth* that draws on current emotion research. A significant exception is Pandit (*"Prophesying"*). Pandit offers a detailed exploration of the play in terms of appraisal theory, treating "prospect based emotions, attribution emotions and fortune of others emotions." In the course of this analysis, she at several points indicates the importance of attachment for the emotion structure of the play. Readers interested in an alternative approach to the play that draws on recent cognitive work in emotion may wish to consult her essay.

More importantly, the scene – including the physical appearance of the witches – prepares us for disgust. What we in the audience see from the first moment must be consistent with their unpalatable androgyny, as later explained by Banquo – "You should be women,/And yet your beards forbid me to interpret/That you are so" (I.iii.45–47). The witches conclude their colloquy with the well-known lines, "Fair is foul, and foul is fair./Hover through the fog and filthy air" (I.i.11–12). Their references to what is "foul" and to the "filthy air" further associate the scene with disgust. Moreover, what is crucial for our present concerns, these images introduce one of the most common cognitive models activated in shame – being soiled.[3] As will become clear, it is no accident that Lady Macbeth later characterizes the blood of murder specifically as a *"filthy* witness" that one must "wash" (II.iii.51, emphasis added).

The second scene takes up both blame and disgust when the Captain refers to the rebel, Macdonwald, explaining that "The multiplying villainies of nature/Do swarm upon him" (I.ii.11–12). The reference to villainies clearly points toward aversive acts. Through its suggestions of vermin, "swarm" serves to link these villainies with feelings of repulsion.

An obvious point about "villainies" is that it implies a moral evaluation. The actions of Macdonwald are not merely aversive to the speaker, but morally blameworthy. This sort of moral evaluation is commonly seen as a central feature of guilt particularly. However, it will play only a minor role in my account. As should be clear by this point, in my view, one's moral *judgment* is not fundamental in generating one's emotional response. Rather, that judgment is part of the working memory-based processes that serve to modulate emotion system activations through perception, concrete imagination, and emotional memory. Judgments of an act as moral or immoral have motivational consequences only insofar as those judgments recruit such emotion triggers in elaborative processing.[4]

---

[3] Needless to say, the word "shame" can be used to refer to a range of feelings, including feelings of disappointment in task failure that do not involve disgust. I am obviously focusing on a more intense form of shame than mere disappointment – a form highlighted in *Macbeth* and *Othello*. One difficulty with research on shame is that it does not always clearly distinguish these different uses of the term. For example, de Hooge, Zeelenberg, and Breugelmans have done valuable research on responses that people call "shame." However, I suspect that the "approach behaviours" they discover (122) bear on the nondisgust variety. The same points apply to "guilt." Thus, for example, Parkinson and Illingworth rightly explain that their research treats "one form of what people describe as 'guilt'" (1612). For other senses of "guilt" and "shame," see, for example, Sheikh and Janoff-Bulman and Xuereb, Ireland, and Davies.

[4] In connection with this, it is worth noting that the moral judgments themselves are not a result of pure logic. Rather, they are at least in part the result of standard emotional

One of the most socially consequential modulatory functions of moral judgment is to inhibit spontaneous empathy.[5] As we saw in Chapter 2, a particularly important form of such empathy inhibition involves in-group/out-group divisions. Insofar as someone character-izes another person as part of an out-group, he or she will feel less empathic identification with that other person. This is in some degree the result of a broad emotional tendency relating to parallel versus com-plementary emotions, as discussed in Chapter 1. Part of what it means to characterize someone as an in- or out-group member is that one sets a default value for one's emotional response to that person's emotion expressions – parallel for an in-group member, complementary for an out-group member.

Returning to *Macbeth*, we find a manifestation of this fundamental organizing principle of social emotions – that is, their partial contin-gency on group division. The Captain moves from vilifying the rebel Macdonwald to eulogizing the in-group exemplar, Macbeth, celebrat-ing his bravery in battle (I.ii.16). The following account of Macbeth's behavior serves to clarify the relation of moral judgment to empathy. Macbeth "ne'er shook hands nor bade farewell to" Macdonwald, but "unseamed him from the nave to th' chops,/And fixed his head upon our battlements" (I.ii. 21–23). The image stresses precisely Macbeth's lack of empathic response to Macdonwald. The statement is, of course, phrased ironically – who would shake hands or bid farewell in battle? But, at the same time, it stresses the difference between seeing someone as a thing – a physical container to be "unseamed," an animal carcass to be sliced to the "chops" – and a conscious being who would have a sub-jective and painful experience of that slicing and unseaming. Moreover, such an experience would be manifest most directly and obviously on

mechanisms, including mood-congruent processing and mood repair. Thus, depend-ing on the intensity of his feelings and the precise nature of his circumstances, Smith's spontaneous feelings of guilt may lead him to judge himself guilty through processes of mood-congruent processing, even if more objective criteria would exonerate him. Conversely, those same feelings may prompt rationalizing self-exculpation through mood repair.

[5] There is a delightful example of this in *Adventures of Huckleberry Finn*. Huck has coop-erated with Jim, a runaway slave. When he thinks of Jim's ingratitude to his owner (221) and the town's response to Huck's own betrayal (222), then, he explains, "my conscience went to grinding me." As he reflects on the moral issue, he feels increas-ingly "wicked, and low-down and ornery." He finds that (like Macbeth after Duncan's murder) he cannot pray (222). So he determines to turn Jim in. Fortunately, empathy overcomes his moral good sense. He recall's Jim's affectionate behavior, tacitly realiz-ing what will result for Jim if he is returned to slavery. He decides that he will not turn Jim in, announcing "All right, then I'll *go* to hell" (223).

Macdonwald's face. There is no more blatant indication of empathy inhibition than the placing of Macdonwald's head on the battlements. Rather than mirroring Macdonwald's pain (in a parallel emotion), the victors celebrate that pain (in a complementary emotion). Macdonwald is clearly and saliently an out-group member here. Moreover, his putative immorality guides additional elaborative processes that further inhibit empathic response. As such, the complementary response to his pain is just what we would expect. (Of course, for anyone who is likely to experience a parallel emotion, this exhibition of the head should have a fear-inducing rather than celebratory function.)

This inhibition of empathy is further indicated by a peculiar aspect of the Captain's speech. He goes on to describe Macbeth's passage through the enemy ranks with "doubly redoubled strokes upon the foe" (I.ii.38) as memorializing "another Golgotha" (I.ii.40). The reference is almost shocking. Macbeth is killing the rebels. The place of the killing is represented as a latter-day Golgotha. Golgotha is most famous as a place where an important historical figure was killed for being a rebel, for (supposedly) representing himself as a "king" – specifically, "King of the Jews," as the legend on his cross had it. Moreover, his execution culminated his "passion," the extended period of suffering that led to his death. That passion has been the focal point of Christian meditation for centuries, meditation that constitutes the single exemplary act of empathy enhancement in Christian tradition. It cannot be accidental that Shakespeare has his Captain compare Macbeth to the executioners at Golgotha – thus, implicitly, paralleling the dead soldiers with Jesus. This image in part prepares for the much later connection of the orphaned Malcolm with "a weak, poor, innocent lamb" (IV.iii.16).

There is a hint of some more direct empathy at the end of the Captain's report. He cannot speak further after his reference to Golgotha. He ends with his own weakness, perhaps anticipating death. "I am faint," he says. "My gashes cry for help" (I.ii.42). The words themselves do not determine the empathic impact of the scene. It is up to the director to decide how much we feel for the Captain, how much we feel that Duncan is heartless (or, more properly, mirror neuron-less) in his response. In any case, the words point us to possibilities for empathic engagement.

The emotional orientations of these opening scenes – with their suggestions of fear, disgust, and empathic response to the suffering of others – begin to suggest some of what might go into an account of guilt and shame, as well as regret. Specifically, we may distinguish three types of self-blaming emotion. In one type, we are concerned primarily with prudential consequences of the act, such as being caught by the police and punished. We may refer to this as "regret."[6] Clearly, it involves fear. A second type of aversion relates to our sense of our qualities or achievements relative to others or relative to our own self-expectations – thus our comparative sense of ourselves along some value axis, as defined by prior expectations (cf. Oatley, Keltner, and Jenkins 185). For example, suppose I lose a foot race. I may evaluate my performance negatively, recalling my loss with aversion. If I anticipated winning, then I will feel disappointment. If I placed a wager on winning, then I may feel regret. I might, in some circumstances, even feel *self-disgust* and therefore *shame*.[7] Of course, we would not ordinarily feel disgust at ourselves simply for losing a race. But it is easy to elaborate on the case to make such a response more plausible. For example, suppose I lost the race – even to the one-legged octogenarian – due to a slothful training regimen of drooling naps followed by meals of corn-dogs and milk duds. Then the disgust response may be fitting. In combination with the self-blame for losing the race, this would produce shame.

---

[6] I should stress that, here as elsewhere, I am not claiming to discover the "true meaning" of "regret," "shame," and "guilt." Rather, I am claiming to isolate and differentiate emotions. These will only partially correspond to our ordinary-language uses of particular terms. Those uses are almost always variable and to some degree inconsistent. As Oatley, Keltner, and Jenkins point out, "Some of our most influential emotions do not even have very specific names in English" (53).

[7] Note that, by this account, disgust felt by other people is certainly relevant to one's experience of shame, but that is because it tends to foster or intensify self-disgust. In other words, the disgust of others alone is not sufficient to produce shame, as the term is used here. Moreover, by this account, shame is not necessarily connected with our sense of "neediness," as in Nussbaum's usage (see, for example, *Hiding* 15). Of course, Nussbaum is speaking of "primitive shame," not all shame. However, there are two differences here. First, Nussbaum's is perhaps the paradigm of an appraisal approach to emotion. Thus, her account of shame includes much more abstract (appraisal-based) eliciting conditions – or, rather, the account presented here necessarily involves something fundamental and perceptual, thus a sort of "primitive shame," at every level. Second, this is never a response to neediness. It is, again, a response to concrete disgust triggers (perceptual, imagined, or remembered). These are not even functionally approximated by "neediness." Indeed, Nussbaum's account does not seem well designed to explain one's shame at losing the race due to excessive naps and milkduds, and one's lack of shame at losing the race due to spraining one's ankle (which leads to neediness, but not self-disgust). On the other hand, none of this matters for Nussbaum's compelling argument that "a liberal society has particular reasons to inhibit shame and to protect its citizens from shaming" (15). Moreover, either treatment of shame is compatible with her ideal of "a society that acknowledges its own humanity, and neither hides us from it nor it from us" (17).

This leaves us with one remaining set of triggers for aversion at one's past acts – the empathic feeling one has with regard to victims of these acts. This is "guilt"[8] (or, equivalently, "remorse"[9]). In this usage, then, guilt is bound up with compassion. This fits with research connecting "proneness to guilt" with "enhanced empathic responsiveness" (Tangney 603). Parker and Thomas cite Tangney's work indicating that guilt "hinged on (a) an empathic awareness of and response to someone's distress and (b) an awareness of being the cause of that distress" (216). The point is also linked with the fact that "the goal [or actional outcome] of guilt is generally thought to be reparative" (Branscombe and Doosje "International" 9), as well as the common view that "guilt reflects an acceptance of responsibility for a moral violation that results in harm to another," responsibility that "should create a willingness to take corrective action" (Branscombe, Slugoski, and Kappen 17).[10]

Needless to say, in real human acts, guilt, shame, and regret are likely to be combined. We will see this combination in the rest of the play. But we can also at least begin to discern the differentiae of each.

Returning to the play, we find that fear becomes more prominent in the subsequent scene, when Macbeth begins to imagine the murder of Duncan. This does not mean, however, that Macbeth's primary emotion will be regret. In anticipation, any aversive outcome – including guilt or shame – will elicit fear. The differences come in precisely what

---

[8] Note that, by this account, guilt will not commonly involve anger at oneself or shame (as posited by Scheff and Retzinger 13). I suspect that anger at oneself is connected primarily with regret and results from some negative consequence to oneself. That negative consequence may involve, for example, harm to a loved one, thus it may be conjoined with guilt. I doubt, however, that the two feelings are strictly simultaneous even in that case. Rather, I suspect that they alternate, with (perhaps rapid and subtle) shifts in attentional focus, elaborative processing, etc.

[9] There are problems with any ordinary language term here, as already indicated. Here and further on, both terms ("guilt" and "remorse") are confined to a narrow, technical sense.

[10] On the other hand, guilt is commonly "self-focused." As Iyer, Leach, and Pedersen explain, "self-focused negative emotions, such as guilt, provide only limited motivation to help the disadvantaged." In contrast, "emotions that focus on the plight of the disadvantaged themselves provide bases of more general support for helping behavior" (275). Similarly, Branscombe and Miron note that "empathy appears to be primarily affected by the perceived severity of the victim's need." In contrast, "distress-based guilt" will lead to ameliorative action only when "the costs of restoring justice" are "perceived as lower than the identity costs involved in not restoring justice" (331) – in other words, with guilt, helping is motivated by calculations based on self-interest. We will address this self-focused/other-focused division in Chapter 8 through the discussion of beneficence and meretricious charity.

kind of outcome one envisions (i.e., punishment, failure and revulsion, or empathy with a victim in pain). We cannot yet be sure about this, but we can begin to guess that, in this case, it involves concern for the victim. Macbeth makes it clear that his aversive emotion results from the concrete envisioning of the act. It is a "horrid image" that causes his "seated heart" to "knock at [his] ribs" (I.iii.137). It seems clear that the image is not one of punishment. This is not to say that Macbeth does not feel any worry over such possibilities. He does. This is suggested in a later scene when he frets over "the consequence" (I.vii.3). But that is not what is at issue in the "horrid image."

"Horrid" is ambiguous between empathy and disgust. However, the larger passage suggests that it is more a matter of the former than the latter. Research indicates that the physiological description is inappropriate for disgust regarding bloodshed (see Rohrmann and Hopp) – though Shakespeare may simply have gotten the heart rate response wrong here. More significantly, Macbeth characterizes his "horrible imaginings" as "Against the use of nature" (I.iii.139, 138). "Nature" here may be understood as referring specifically to the natural mirroring response we all have to other people's suffering. There is some support for this in the use of "nature" elsewhere in the play. When Lady Macbeth calls for her unsexing, she links "remorse" with the "visitings of nature" and opposes both to "direst cruelty" (I.v.39–41). In her speech, it seems clear that "nature" is linked with "human kindness" (I.V.13), specifically with the nurturing qualities of mother's milk, as we will see when we consider her speech.

In any case, Macbeth's response to the temptation of murder is not a calculation of likely consequences, nor is it an abstract moral evaluation. It is almost a sensory experience. Indeed, the power of this imagination is indicated by the usurpation of working memory that Macbeth describes. His emotion systems are largely unaffected by current perceptions and are aroused, rather, by imagination. In consequence, his working memory is cyclically occupied with the horrid images of the possible murder. The final result is that "nothing is but what is not" (I.iii.143). Thus, he experiences the sort of derealization of the perceptual world that we witnessed already in grief, when working memory is controlled by thoughts of the lost beloved. We will see that this recurs with the experience of guilt after the murder.

At the end of the fourth scene, Macbeth recurs to his ambivalence about the regicide – his strong motivation for the act paired with his strong anxiety regarding it. Again, there is a hint that empathy may have a particularly important place. Specifically, Macbeth wishes that the night will be so dark that even "Stars" will "hide [their] fires," that there will be no "light" to "see," that "The eye [will] wink at the hand; yet let that be/Which the eye fears, when it is done, to see" (I.iv.51–53). The point of these lines is that Macbeth envisions a single aversive outcome of the murder – his own seeing of Duncan's death. Seeing this death would not involve seeing his own failure, at least not in this particular task. Moreover, in itself, it would not involve seeing his own possible or actual punishment. Thus, we would not expect that seeing Duncan's death would elicit regret or even shame. Rather, seeing the death would most clearly provoke an empathic response and consequently guilt. This is suggested later when Macbeth returns to the image of night, calling on it to "Scarf up the tender eye of pitiful day" (III.iii.50), which is to say, wrap a scarf over the sensitive eyes of day that is full of pity. In short, he is calling on night to block compassion. Because Macbeth simultaneously desires the kingship, he hopes that he can somehow do the deed without seeing the death itself, thus without exposing himself to the remorse-provoking sight.

In scene five, Lady Macbeth's comments suggest the same thing. She worries that Macbeth will not murder the king. However, she does not reason that he will be defeated in his attempt, nor that he will make imprudent decisions. Rather, she worries that his "nature" is "too full o' the milk of human kindness" (I.v.12–13). In other words, her worry is that Macbeth will feel empathic impulses that are too strong to allow him to murder.

An interesting aspect of Lady Macbeth's worry here is that she sees Macbeth as *dispositionally* prone to empathy. Her criticism is, then, a criticism of his character, not simply of a possible act (or, in this case, non-act). This division between global character disposition and response in a particular case relates not only to guilt, but perhaps even more significantly to shame. If Macbeth has a particular propensity toward empathy, thus guilt, Lady Macbeth may have a particular propensity toward disgust and shame. Indeed, as we will see, Lady Macbeth's emotional response to the murder involves a strong sense of disgust, though it does combine this with empathic sensitivity, thus guilt.

Lady Macbeth's famous "unsex me here" speech prepares us for that complex response. She rejects the "compunctious visitings of nature" (I.v.41), which is to say, the natural experience of "remorse" (I.v.40) based on mirroring and empathy.[11] But she recognizes her own susceptibility to such natural emotions and herself hopes for a version of Macbeth's blindness to the deed. In her phrasing, she calls for the murder to take place in "dunnest smoke" so that "my keen knife see not the wound it makes" (I.v.46–48). Thus, like Macbeth, she wishes to avoid seeing the death she inflicts, a death that would inspire an empathic response through concrete perceptual experience. On the other hand, she focuses on the wound, thus on the blood that will later cover her hands. In this way, she suggests a form of disgust, perhaps more than empathy.

Both the empathy and the disgust, thus guilt and shame, are emphasized elsewhere in the speech. Alluding to the "milk of human kindness" (I.v.13) that makes Macbeth prone to compassion, she calls for the milk of her breasts to be replaced by "gall" (I.v.43). This image further connects the idea of empathic "human kindness" to the paradigmatic case of maternal nurturance. It indicates that this exemplary case of empathic care stands as the precise opposite of the ability to act cruelly, presumably because it carries with it the likelihood of the most intense guilt. This parent/child image also hints at an attachment relation with Duncan. That attachment relation should enhance her feeling of empathy toward Duncan. By the same token, it should increase her feeling of guilt about any cruelty toward him. These ideas are developed when she subsequently speaks of nursing a child and feeling "How tender 'tis to love the babe" (I.7.56). In contrast with her husband, however, she explains that, had she the motivation of Macbeth, she would have "plucked [her] nipple from his boneless gums/And dashed the brains out" (I.7.58–59). Here, too, the indication is that empathy – particularly empathy enhanced by attachment feelings – serves to prevent such cruelty. Of course, she is saying that she *would* commit this violent act. But the rhetorical point of choosing this act is precisely that it is almost impossible, due to the attachment and related empathy of the mother. That empathy is precisely what becomes guilt after the act is committed.

---

[11] The lines are "Make thick my blood;/Stop up th'access and passage to remorse" (I.v.39–40). I find it impossible to follow William Carroll and others in seeing this as a call to "halt her monthly menstrual flow" (348). It may be that the reference to her sex and blood call up associations with menstruation. These may, in turn, further associate compassion with femininity. In this way, critics may be right to note some sort of link here. But the call to the spirits is not a call for menopause or, alternatively, pregnancy. It is a call to stop remorse.

At the same time, Lady Macbeth's speech develops imagery that is rich in disgust. To say that her breasts should be filled with gall is to say that her body should be repulsive and emetic. Similarly, dashing out the child's brains is an act that would produce not only dread, but disgust. Here the play suggests even more clearly that Lady Macbeth has a distinct proneness to – or at least concern with – disgust, particularly with respect to matters involving self-blame.

In sum, Lady Macbeth's speech manifests a struggle to rid herself of both empathy and disgust – thus, after the act, both guilt and shame. In the end, as we will see, she fails on both counts.

A peculiar aspect of Lady Macbeth's response here is that she does not seem concerned about failure, which, by the preceding analysis, should be part of shame. But the problem disappears when we recognize that Lady Macbeth's sense of failure need not concern the killing of Duncan as such. Self-blame may be specific or global, bearing on a single act or a larger condition or quality, as Lewis stresses.[12] Indeed, this speech itself suggests a concealed sense of broader failure. Moreover, it is a sense of failure that is profoundly connected with the imagery of motherhood. Specifically, Lady Macbeth refers to a child that she herself nursed. But Macduff explicitly tells us that Macbeth "has no children" (IV.iii.217).[13] The apparent contradiction has been

---

[12] See Lewis's extremely valuable discussion of global and specific attributions in shame and guilt (as well as pride and "hubris"). As should be clear, the present account does not follow Lewis in confining shame to global judgments (see also Lickel, Schmader and Barquissau 41). However, the two accounts of shame and guilt are related. One is probably more likely to feel disgust at an uncontrollable character property (on shame as an uncontrollable character property, see Branscombe, Slugoski, and Kappen 28–31). It does not seem, however, that the crucial issue here is character (for shame) versus (free or controllable) action (for guilt) per se. Rather, the crucial issue seems to be disgust versus empathy. For example, I may feel ashamed for having lost a race because I was intoxicated even if I am not a drunkard – thus even if my inebriation was a controllable act, not an uncontrollable character property or the result of such a property. Indeed, the opposite may be the case. I may feel ashamed if I am particularly proud of my (normally) abstemious character. Note that here again we have a difference from appraisal theories. "Controllability" is primarily something one evaluates abstractly, whereas disgust is more clearly perceptual.

[13] In addition, Macbeth says that the witches "put a barren scepter in my grip" (III.i.63). It is perhaps worth noting that some critics have taken this to indicate that Macbeth is incapable of having children (due to "sterility" [William Carroll 348]). This idea appears to rely on a psychoanalytic identification of the scepter as a phallus. It also unnecessarily complicates the issue of Lady Macbeth's children. In fact, the statement seems to indicate more simply that Macbeth does not have a successor, thus someone to whom he could pass on the scepter, and that the witches implied he would not have one.

given different solutions. One obvious possibility is that we are to understand that the child has died (see Levin 274). This gives a sort of pathos to Lady Macbeth's call for her milk to be taken and replaced with gall. If we are to understand that any children she bore have died in infancy, then we may infer a sense of her own failure, including her failure as a nurse to her own child. The image of killing her child thus begins to take on a different resonance – a sort of desperate attempt at mood repair, directed against her own global shame.[14] More generally, both images may suggest that she sees herself as having failed as a mother, and, still more broadly, as a woman. Her call to be unsexed is one possible response to this failure.

Not long after this speech, at the beginning of the second act, Lady Macbeth finds that she cannot kill Duncan. There is a particular reason – a reason having to do with attachment, thus with empathic sensitivity. Specifically, he "resembled/My father as he slept" (II.ii.12–13). Despite her bravado about dashing out the brains of her child, she is not free from attachment and empathy. Moreover, she does not exculpate herself simply because she does not actually plunge the dagger into Duncan's flesh. She still sees herself as responsible for the act – which grows no less aversive with time, no less like killing her own father as he slept, no less a sign that she is, in effect, a failed daughter, just as she is perhaps a failed mother.

Lady Macbeth's views of herself as a mother, a woman, a daughter are obviously bound up with the gender ideology treated in the play. Indeed, when Lady Macbeth boasts that she could have dashed

---

[14] The preceding analysis obviously gives a different emotional valence and a different interpretation than is perhaps standard in Shakespeare criticism. For example, Janet Adelman has stressed maternal threat in her psychoanalytic reading of the play. Clearly, Adelman has a point. But that threat is emotionally complex and, it seems, already bound up with a sense of shame. More generally, critical analyses of the representations of women in the play are very important for understanding the play's gender ideology. But critics often seem to underestimate the complexity and nuance of such representations, particularly in relation to representations of men in the play. A good example occurs in William Carroll's summary of one aspect of the play – "In *Macbeth*, the female body is represented in two primary ways: as demonic, and as maternal" (345). Although such observations do point us toward important issues, they also tend to occlude the complex feelings of attachment, compassion, guilt, shame, and so on, that motivate such representations. Indeed, it is not simply that women are good if they are maternal and bad if they are not. Men too are good if they are maternal. The admirable version of Macbeth is precisely the one filled with the "milk of human kindness" (I.v.13). Goodness is generally linked with attachment and enhanced empathy.

out her own child's brains, she is chiding Macbeth with being unmanly. She is, in other words, aiming to provoke action (by Macbeth) as a response to a form of category-based self-blame bound up with a sense of self-disgust (at being feminine). Macbeth is stirred by her ideological appeals and calls for her to "Bring forth men-children only!" (I.vii.73). The statement is superficially laudatory, linking Lady Macbeth with manly virtues. But it simultaneously reminds us and her of her failure as a (child-bearing) woman. Moreover, it gestures toward a deep problem with the gender ideology that celebrates those manly virtues – the very violence that makes her fit to bear male children also suggests a maternal incapacity that leads to the death of those children. This problem, generalized beyond child-bearing, will become increasingly clear in the course of the play.

It is important to mention that Macbeth himself takes up the image of the "naked newborn babe" – in this case, caught in a storm. He links that image with "Pity" (I.vii.21 – which is to say, roughly, compassion, in the sense given in Chapter 8). He thereby tacitly invokes the enhanced empathy of attachment. The point is particularly relevant in that he stresses his "trust" with Duncan, not only as "his subject," but as "his kinsman" (I.vii.12–13). In keeping with this, when contemplating the murder a few lines later, Macbeth imagines how "the horrid deed" made visible to the "eye" will produce "tears" that "drown the wind" (I.vii.24–25) – precisely the sort of grief that derives from empathy-enhancing attachment.

In the beginning of the second act, Macbeth and Lady Macbeth do kill Duncan. We therefore witness the transformation from anxiety over possible guilt, shame, and regret to actual guilt, shame, and regret. Immediately after the murder, Macbeth introduces five common characteristics of self-blaming emotions. First, he reports that he heard Duncan's sons say "God bless us!" but could not respond "Amen" (II.ii.32–33). In connection with this, he frets over his spiritual alienation and its consequences. "I had most need of blessing" (II.ii.36), he explains. Here Macbeth begins to suffer from the regret that goes along with *anticipations of punishment* – in this case, eternal punishment.[15]

Shortly after this, Macbeth turns to a more mundane punishment that he anticipates. Now, he fears, he will no longer be able to sleep.

---

[15] In ordinary speech, this would be referred to as "guilt," primarily because of its moral gravity. In the technical sense used here, however, this is a case of regret because it concerns possible punishment.

This not only stresses the immediate regret he feels; it also points toward the *working memory preoccupation* with the aversive act, a preoccupation that marks many intense emotions and that may literally lead to sleeplessness,[16] as well as a more general inability to feel at peace. As we will see, this is related to the derealization of the present material world that Macbeth had already begun to experience in anticipation of the murder.

Third, *issues of disgust, thus shame*, are introduced as Macbeth begins to worry over the bloodstains on his hands. He fears that no amount of water will "wash this blood/Clean from my hand" (II.ii.65–66). In keeping with what we have already noted, however, it is Lady Macbeth who will be most tormented by shame.

Macbeth ends the scene with the following lines: "To know my deed, 'twere best not know myself./Wake Duncan with they knocking! I would thou couldst!" (II.ii.77–78). The first line offers a summary of self-blaming emotions. Previously, Macbeth had wished that he would not perceive the (aversive) action. Now, he cannot turn his mind away from it; it fills all the space of his working memory. But he would not suffer if he did not at the same time "know himself," which is to say, *spontaneously feel himself causally responsible*.

Finally, as indicated in the preceding quote, Macbeth responds to a knocking at the gate. The knocking will wake those who are sleeping within. He recalls Duncan's corpse and feels the fundamental actional impulse of guilt – *changing the situation by making reparation for it*. The most obvious way of changing the situation involves reversing the action and compensating for the victim's pain. In the case of murder, such reversal and compensation are impossible. But reversal is precisely what Macbeth calls for – the resurrection of Duncan as if he had merely slept and not died. In retrospect, the preceding line ("'twere best not know myself") now takes on a different sense, suggesting a second possibility for changing the situation. This is punishment, specifically punishment that inflicts at least the same degree of suffering on oneself as the initial act inflicted on the victim. In this case, that degree of suffering is, of course, death – the most extreme form of not knowing oneself.

---

[16] See Schmidt and Van der Linden (should empirical documentation be required). Interestingly, Schmidt and Van der Linden note that, for subjects feeling guilt, sleep may be restored by "reparative action" (553). This is impossible for Macbeth, since the act of murder is irreparable – hence the idea that he has "murdered" sleep.

The culmination of Macbeth's manliness is the slaughter of Macduff's family. This murder of mother and child is designed by Shakespeare to present the most intense instance of an empathy-provoking act. It combines our sensitivity to helpless childhood with our sensitivity to attachment relations. In the end, we will see that, despite his habituation and his apparent hypermasculinity at this point, even Macbeth is not impervious to such empathy. His death at Macduff's hands is, in part, the outcome of his lingering guilt over this massacre.

It is worth noting that the same concerns of gender ideology affect Macduff's very brief mourning over his wife and children.[18] This ideology, along with the social position of men in the society of the play, underlie Macduff's ability to engage in mood repair by "Let[ting] grief/ Convert to anger" (IV.iii.230–231), as Malcolm puts it (anger being an emotion system that inhibits sorrow, as we saw in Chapter 4). As with Macbeth, this modulation is inseparable from his ability to engage in action rather than being immobilized.

Again, the condition of Lady Macbeth is strikingly different. It is taken up at the beginning of the final act. As we have seen, she has been unable to divert her attention from the murder toward issues of practical consequence. Almost the only actional outcome available to her is to try to overcome the feeling of disgust that underlies her shame. This feeling of disgust is represented in the play by her sense of being physically unclean. In the famous scene of her sleepwalking, we see her scrub her hand, trying to remove the stain of blood.[19] That stain is, of course, a memory of the murder. But it is not a random memory. It is a memory linked with her physical revulsion at the act and at herself. In keeping with this, she stresses "the smell of the blood," which cannot be concealed by "All the perfumes of Arabia" (V.i.40–41). Noxious smells are, of course, particularly key in disgust.

---

[18] The point is noted, perhaps in different language, by a number of critics of the play – see, for example, Orgel. However, sometimes critics miss the emotional complexity of the passage when they focus on the gender ideology – and thus they tend to miss the complexity of the play's response to gender ideology as well. When Macduff hears of his family's murder, Malcolm tells him to "Dispute it like a man." Macduff responds, "I shall do so;/But I must also feel it as a man" (IV.3.221–223). Orgel concludes that this passage "says that murder is what makes you feel like a man" (346). It seems clear, however, that there is a contrast between *grieving the loss* as a *human person* ("feel it as a man") and *overcoming the attack* as a *male* ("dispute it like a man").

[19] Unsurprisingly, the scene is the topic of extensive critical commentary. See, for example, Levin for an influential analysis.

Though shame is predominant in Lady Macbeth's behavior, her words also express empathy, thus guilt. The clearest indication comes in her recollection and question, "The Thane of Fife had a wife. Where is she now?" (V.i.34). The statement suggests compassion both for Lady Macduff and for the bereaved Macduff himself. It is undoubtedly no accident that Lady Macbeth's moment of empathy is connected with the slaughter of a family – the death of a wife and (though unmentioned) a child. It is bound up with her recognition of the attachment relations that are part of familial bonds – the very relations she sought to deny in her earlier speech about nursing.

The physician attending her recognizes that Lady Macbeth has few options. Her working memory sustains hardly any thought but the murders, thus feelings of self-blame. As he puts it later, "she is troubled with thick-coming fancies" (V.iii.40). Reality has become less real than memory. There is no way to "Pluck from the memory a rooted sorrow," as Macbeth puts it (V.iii.43). Moreover, it is not merely sorrow, but a withering shame of self-disgust. No amount of nightly hand washing can remove the recollected stain or its stench. One way – perhaps the only way – of ending the pain from this unalterable fact is suicide. When he leaves Lady Macbeth's side, the physician tells the waiting gentlewoman, "Remove from her the means of all annoyance" (V.i.63). Nonetheless, later, "by self and violent hands," she takes her life (V.viii.71).

Though he has the practical distractions already mentioned, Macbeth is, in the end, little better. He becomes so "familiar" with "horrors" (V.vi.14, 13) – so habituated to cruelty – that he has no reaction even to Lady Macbeth's death. But this dulling of negative emotion is not a positive development. It is part of a generalized loss of feeling, more akin to severe depression than to peace. Indeed, his sense of guilt and shame build toward an almost suicidal propensity on his part as well. He finds himself "aweary of the sun" and "wish[ing] th'estate o' the world were now undone" (V.vi.49–50).

Like his wife, Macbeth seems, in the end, more concerned with the massacre of innocents at Fife than with the regicide. He tries to avoid fighting with Macduff. Convinced that he is invulnerable in battle, he does not wish to harm Macduff any further than he has already. "My soul is too much charged/With blood of thine already" (V.viii.5–6), he explains. It is an exemplary moment of empathic ethical constraint. It is as if Macbeth recognizes at last the pain he has caused by his murders.

He recognizes it, not in the dead, but in the bereaved, the man who – like Macbeth himself – has lost his wife and child. When Macbeth first learns that Macduff can kill him, he retreats in fright, announcing, "I'll not fight with thee" (V.viii.22). However real his feeling of guilt, it is, in the end, not so strong as to stifle his will to live. Macduff taunts him with social humiliation – "We'll have thee …/Painted upon a pole, and underwrit,/'Here may you see the tyrant'" (V.viii.25–27). The prospect is infuriating, but it would also be reparative. Ultimately, Macbeth does fight Macduff. But rage may not be the only motivating factor. Guilt remains, and the need for reparation or punishment. Faced in the end with only two options – irreparable remorse or death with punitive disgrace – Macbeth may not wish to die so fervently as his shame-afflicted wife. But surely he does not want to live.

The Strong Breed

Here, as elsewhere, one might worry that Shakespeare's treatment of emotion – in this case, guilt – may be personally or culturally idiosyncratic. To address this, we might briefly consider an African treatment of the topic – Wole Soyinka's short tragedy, *The Strong Breed*.

The play takes place in a Nigerian village. Eman has left his home and set up a small clinic with the help of Sunma, the daughter of a local leader named Jaguna. The new year celebrations are approaching. These involve the selection of a "carrier" or scapegoat who will take on the sins of the preceding year and "carry" them out into the bush, cleansing the village for the new year.[20] In Eman's village, the position of carrier was hereditary. In keeping with this, the carrier returned to the village after removing its sins. In the new village, however, some stranger is chosen to serve as carrier and he is forbidden from returning. At the start of the play, Eman is unaware of these differences.

As the play begins, Sunma is anxious to have Eman leave the village during the new year's celebrations. This is presumably because

---

[20] Much of the criticism on the play has stressed its sacrificial orientation, particularly in relation to myth and religion (see, for example, Egberike, Gopalakrishnan, and Lyonga). Some criticism has taken up sacrifice in relation to tradition more broadly. For example, Msiska argues that *The Strong Breed* offers "a notion of Self as Agency that is a critique of African tradition," but also involves a "reclamation" of "Selfhood … as a site of responsibility and transformation" (187). These are clearly important topics. However, the focus of the following analysis is, of course, on guilt, which may be linked with sacrifice but is not a matter of mythological patterns or the nature of tradition.

he would be a candidate for carrier. There is, however, another, more likely candidate – Ifada, a boy who is suffering from cognitive and physical disabilities. Sunma shows contempt for Ifada, demeaning him as "some horrible insect" (116) and sending him away. Eman is baffled by this, but it becomes clear that Sunma is undertaking a self-conscious strategy of inhibiting her empathy for Ifada. Indeed, she goes on to insist that she does not have "any pity left for him" (117). This inhibition of empathy – thus the guilt it would be likely to entail – is crucial if she wishes to facilitate Ifada's choice as carrier and thereby to avoid losing Eman.

Eman is, again, unaware of the circumstances. In opposition to Sunma, he stresses three empathy-enhancing conditions. First, Ifada is "helpless." The inability to help oneself is one condition for enhanced compassion. Second, he is "alone." This disallows empathy inhibition by reference to other people having responsibility for him. For example, we commonly – and, in most cases, rightly – inhibit our practical empathic responsiveness to children who are hungry or ill when their parents are around; the responsibility for the child's well-being falls on the parents. Finally, Eman explains that he and Sunma "are the only friends he has" (117), noting the (empathy-enhancing) attachment relation.

Following this, a sick girl enters. She brings an effigy, her version of a carrier, that she hopes will take away her sickness. She asks Eman for some clothing for her carrier. When Eman gives her the clothing, Sunma reacts with alarm. Clearly, Sunma does not wish to see a carrier effigy in Eman's clothing, since that might encourage Eman's selection as the real, living carrier. In addition, Sunma may have some concern that, due to contact with Ifada and the girl, Eman will be seen as "polluted," thus putting him at greater risk of being taken as the carrier. Here we see another form of empathy inhibition, in this case one practiced by entire societies. The idea that certain groups are polluted fosters a sense of disgust in their regard. The idea that their pollution may be communicated through contact or perhaps even proximity discourages the sorts of human interaction that would overcome disgust and foster empathy.

Having failed thus far in her efforts to protect Eman, Sunma next tries to undermine Eman's empathy with the villagers he serves through the clinic. Specifically, she insists that the village is hostile to him and she claims that, as an outsider, "nobody wants you" (120). Such an in-group/out-group division is, again, a powerful means of undermining the parallel emotional responses that are involved in compassion.

When this too fails, Sunma finally resorts to gender ideology, berating Eman for being unmanly.[21]

Finally, Sunma gives up. But just as she gives up, she hits on something in Eman's character that indicates why he won't leave, why there is more to his insistence than ordinary fellow-feeling. Specifically, Sunma says that Eman seems always to be closing himself off from her, from anything she wants, as if "doing anything for me makes you unfaithful to some part of your life." She continues, "If it was a woman then I pity her for what she must have suffered" (122). This is our first hint that what drives Eman is, ultimately, a sense of guilt and a desire to engage in some sort of reparation, even though he can never undo the past events for which he blames himself. In light of what we have seen in *Macbeth* – along with the general operation of literary idealization or intensification – we may already begin to wonder if this guilt and inadequate sense of reparation may not lead to Eman's death. Subsequently, Eman explains to Sunma that he is "very much [his] father's son" (126) and that he "find[s] consummation only when" he has "spent" himself "for a total stranger" (125). Though the references are still unclear, we may begin to suspect that Eman is in this alien village precisely so that he can "find consummation" through spending himself. What this involves becomes clearer when we learn that his father was the carrier for his village.

In the interim, we see two men capture Ifada and drag him off. He has clearly been chosen as the carrier. Not long after, he runs to Eman's door, terrified, seeking help. He has escaped from the village leaders. When Jaguna and the others find him, Eman intervenes. Eman too is not averse to invoking gender ideology. In this case, he insists that "A village which cannot produce its own carrier contains no men" (129), because the carrier's act must be voluntary. Here, he learns that the carrier cannot return to the village or he will be killed.

There is a blackout, after which we learn that Eman has taken the place of Ifada. This is, then, his act of reparation, and perhaps his self-sacrifice. But we do not yet know why he is acting in this way. It could simply be empathy with Ifada – and it is in part that. But we are presented with a series of memories and imaginations, the thoughts of Eman as he now runs from the village leaders. Through these, we learn that there is more to Eman's self-sacrifice. There is a foundation in guilt.

---

[21] There has been some attention to gender ideology in the play, though in a different way from that discussed here (see, for example, Ndiaye on gender stereotypes).

But why is he running? Jaguna claims that he is "A woman, that is all." His colleague, Oroge, however, replies that he "took the beating well enough" (112). There is some other reason. We may suspect that it is almost a sort of suicide, a provocation to the village leaders. Eventually, the provocation succeeds.

Once the flashbacks begin, we can piece together Eman's history. He was the only son of the village carrier. As a youth, he became disgusted with the corruption of the village leaders and left home. He was away for twelve years. That entire time, his young love, Omae, lived with his father and waited for him. When he returned, she conceived his child but died giving birth. His suffering is a combination of grief for his own loss and a profound sense of guilt. He feels that he has killed Omae – or, more technically, in thinking of this terrible event, he spontaneously attributes a necessary causal role to his own actions. The guilt he experiences is the result of this spontaneous feeling of causal responsibility combined with empathy, both for Omae's pain and death, and for his father's loss of the girl who had come to be his daughter. (Once again, we see empathy intensified by attachment.) Then there is the further guilt over abandoning his father, who dies in a final act of carrying.

It is important to understand just how Eman makes his causal attribution here. He blames himself, but not for some narrowly causal act, such as having sex with his wife. What choice did he have about that? Could he have refused her, after she had waited for him? In blaming himself, he fixes on the necessary condition for everything that followed. "I wish I had stayed away," he explains; "I wish I never came back to meet her" (133). Here, no less than in *Macbeth*, what is done cannot be undone.[22] But the first step in responding to the tragic error is doing the opposite of what caused the blameworthy events initially. In this case, for Eman, that means leaving the village and going among strangers.

---

[22] It is perhaps worth noting here that this complexity of causal attribution is lost in the artificial and narratively limited scenarios presented in moral judgment tests, as commonly used in empirical research on morality. We no doubt learn something when asking people about pushing someone on a railroad track versus pulling a switch for the train (see, for example, Hauser). But these forced-choice scenarios are also misleading in certain ways. Yes, it probably is true that, everything else being equal, we see a greater moral responsibility in the former case than in the latter. But in real life, our attributions of blame are much more complex and variable. Once again, this suggests the value of literature as both a source of hypotheses and a source of evidence. The complex literary cases may indicate how our intuitions on the simple cases are inadequate.

It means refusing Sunma for fear that she too will die in childbirth.[23] It means sacrificing himself rather than his father and his wife.

In a later recollection, he reflects on Omae. He repudiates his own manly quest for virtue in those twelve years of exile. He affirms that she had just the strength of will and moral knowledge that he had sought. But, alluding to his own part in causing her death, he says bitterly that this "truth ... was killed in the cruelty of her brief happiness" (144). He walks to her grave and pours sand from the mound onto his head. The suggestion is that he will bury himself, that indeed the only reparative action he can take is to join her in death.

Shortly following this act at Omae's gravesite, Eman sees his father in the role of carrier. As his father runs off, Eman calls after him, "Wait father. I am coming with you" (145). We can infer that Eman's father is now dead. He has gone on his last journey as carrier. Eman is following him, not only in being a carrier, thus taking on his father's social role, but also in dying. In both ways, he is doing whatever little he can to rid himself of his own sins – first, against his wife; second, against his father.

Just after this, we see the final scene. The girl's effigy has been hung. Jaguna's words suggest that this is precisely what has been done to Eman as well. Thus, Eman's virtual suicide has ended the pain of his own guilt, a pain against which he could do very little else. But the villagers look up at Eman's corpse and can say nothing. Silent, "they crept off" (146). They have not succeeded in suppressing their own empathic responses. At the end of the play, their own deep sense of guilt is palpable. It will have consequences, just as Eman's guilt did.

Kagekiyo

Of course, Soyinka's play is written in English by a modern author thoroughly familiar with Shakespeare. The fifteenth-century Japanese drama, *Kagekiyo*, provides us with a work from a genuinely unrelated tradition. It is also respected as both "realistic" and "psychological" (Shimazaki 252). Finally, it allows us to focus more on shame to which the play refers repeatedly.

This well-known play of the Noh repertoire concerns a warrior named Kagekiyo and his daughter, Hitomaru, from whom he has

---

[23] The children in Eman's line are reputed to cause the death of their mothers in childbirth – "No woman survives the bearing of the strong ones" (133).

long been separated. The opening lines of the play explain Kagekiyo's situation. He fought for the Tairas against the Minamotos. His side was defeated and he was exiled. This clearly constitutes a loss, the sort of loss that would underlie shame.[24] Moreover, the fact of exile begins to build the sense of social isolation that pervades the play and is a central feature of shame. Indeed, he is exiled to a place named "remote" (260n.8). The contrast to his former place of pride is striking. He was "the one most sought-after" with great "fame" such that "everyone looked at him with envy" (280). Of course, shame involves self-concealment and self-isolation, not only isolation by others. As Lickel, Schmader, and Barquissau put it, "the motivation elicited by" shame is a "desire to hide, disappear" (47). As Fearon notes, shame leads to a series of "'hiding' behaviors" (67). In keeping with this, Kagikiyo seeks to "hide" himself (276) when his daughter comes to see him. Indeed, more generally, he is "too ashamed ... to settle down" (278n.25). As this suggests, Kagekiyo is engaged in one of the few actional outcomes that allow any possible reduction in shame – removal of oneself from others, thus removal from their expectations and their disgust. In this particular case, Kagekiyo would be even more sensitive to any disapproval or disgust, because the source would be his own daughter.

What, then, is the source of Kagikiyo's shame? One obvious factor is the loss of the war. The play suggests, however, that Kagikiyo's most profound sense of failure comes not so much from the loss itself as from the accumulating uselessness of his everyday existence. It is the shift from fighting to begging that pains him most deeply. In sharp contrast with what one might expect from a warrior, he "idly ... sleep[s]" (262). This is a sort of constant failure, and one opposed directly to his former success. His life is *"asamashi"* or "shameful" (263 and 262n.12). He is "Ashamed of his present state, so changed from the past" (270; "shame" here is *"haji"* [271]). The point is repeated by Kagekiyo himself (272). In keeping with this, he explains that he "helplessly cast away – the catalpa bow" (272); that is, he had to "give up being a samurai" (273n.20). Thus his name (*"na"*) is lost (272, 273). (Ikegami notes that name, na, was part of a "constellation" of ideas relating to honor and shame in samurai culture [1352].) It fits with his loss of name that he initially denies being Kagekiyo.

---

[24] This is perhaps particularly true in the context of Japanese warrior culture, as Ikegami discusses.

Again, the person to whom he denies being Kagekiyo is his own daughter. This suggests another possible source of his sense of failure. After meeting Hitomaru, he recalls that her mother was a courtesan and that he "placed [his daughter] in the care of a landlady." "Since it was a girl," he explains, "I thought her to be useless" (266). This may foster guilt, from empathy with the girl and perhaps her mother. Indeed, the following lines mention her "sorrow over the estrangement of father and child"[25] (266). At the same time, it may foster shame, as it indicates that he has had no more success as a father (or husband) than as a warrior.

Indeed, shame is far more prevalent here. By the preceding analysis, we would expect something beyond a sense of failure. Specifically, we would expect disgust. It is not absent. Kagekiyo is so "wasted and emaciated" that he is "Repugnant even to my own self" (262)[26]. He feels that he is beyond pity (262), presumably because he sees himself as necessarily and even rightly an object of disgust from others.

In the end, he agrees to tell his daughter a story of his actions as a warrior, a story, we might assume, that represents a past he can be proud of. He begins the tale of an expedition. On his own part, this involves the sort of "swift independent action" that, according to Ikegami, was necessary for a warrior "not to incur shame" (1358). But there are two problems. First, when reenacting the battle, Kagekiyo is forced to rely on "his walking stick as a weapon," at least in some performances (as Shifuma Shimazaki explains [256]). This not only makes salient his blindness, thus decline. It also recalls his own reference to his walking stick in explaining that he can no longer afford to be angry, since he is so dependent on others (274). The second problem is that the heroic episode trails off into an uncertain conclusion. Kagekiyo does not defeat his opponent – and now he is "weakened and feeble"; "even his mind" is "Distracted" (286). He concludes with hope that he will soon escape this pain, that his "cruelly long life will soon come to an end" (286). He and his daughter part. His hope is that at least she will not have to share his shame.

---

[25] The French translation of Godel and Kano makes the point more forcefully, suggesting such an interpretation of the lines: "Quelle tristesse pour l'enfant/qui n'a pu s'épanouir dans la proximité de ses parents" (463; "What sadness for the child/who could not flower near her parents").

[26] Godel and Kano render this "L'image que de moi j'offre/aux bords extrêmes de la décrépitude/me remplit de dégoût" (461; "The image I offer of myself/at the extreme edge of decrepitude/fills me with disgust").

Thus, *Kagekiyo* presents a concise treatment of some key elements of shame. As we would expect, these centrally include failure and self-disgust. The play also relates shame to public exposure and brings in such associated feelings as despair. But the play's brevity makes its treatment of all these issues somewhat elliptical. For a fuller treatment of shame, as well as the public exposure of humiliation and other related topics, we may return to Shakespeare.

Othello: Jealousy, Humiliation, and Shame

Othello begins with loathing. Roderigo is speaking to Iago. He asks if Iago still holds Othello "in his hate" (I.i.6). Iago affirms that he does, as if it is a virtue. In turn, he urges Roderigo, "Despise me/If I do not" (I.i.6–7). Hate is closely allied with shame. Again, shame combines a sense of failure or loss and self-blame with self-disgust. Similarly, hate often (perhaps always) combines a sense of failure or loss with blame of someone else (thus anger) and disgust with that other person. The play begins with Iago insisting that he feels anger and disgust toward Othello. Moreover, if he does not have those feelings, then Roderigo should feel anger and disgust toward Iago.

This gives rise to some questions. First, what provoked Iago's anger? Specifically, what is his failure? Iago explains it in the immediately following lines. He was passed over for promotion and his place was given instead to Cassio. This entails that he is stalled in the progress of his career (I.i.27). Iago insists that he himself deserved the promotion far more than Cassio – thus he does not blame himself for the failure.

What about Roderigo? He is seeking the love of Desdemona. Since Desdemona has just married Othello, he has failed in this, and Othello would be the salient person to blame. At the same time, Iago has agreed to aid Roderigo in his pursuit of Desdemona. If Iago does not hate Othello, he may be less vigorous in his aid, thus partially blameworthy for Roderigo's failure to win Desdemona. Clearly, Iago can be loyal only to one or the other, Roderigo or Othello, in this conflict.

This all indicates what failure is at issue in each case. But what about the disgust? How does disgust enter at all? Why are we not dealing simply with anger?

We begin to get some hint that the disgust is related to the out-group categorization of Othello when we notice that they refer to him, not by his name, but by his category – "his Moorship" and "the Moor" (I.i.29, 54). The subsequent course of the act makes this connection clearer.

Roderigo first indicates this when he refers to Othello as "the thick-lips" (I.i.63). Subsequently, Iago speaks of Othello's sexual relations with Desdemona in animalistic terms. Othello is "an old black ram ... tupping" a "white ewe" (I.i.85–86), "the devil" engaged in siring children (I.i.87), a "horse" (I.i.109). His union with Desdemona is "the beast with two backs" (I.i.114). Roderigo joins in, stating that Othello is "a lascivious Moor" whose "gross clasps" are soiling the "fair" Desdemona (I.i.123, 119). Iago concludes by restating his "hate" (I.i.131).

Here one might ask whether the disgust is simply that of Iago and Roderigo or if it is Shakespeare's as well. In other words, one might wonder if Shakespeare is merely showing us characters filled with hate or is being hateful himself. The obvious way of deciding on this is by considering the character of Othello himself. As we will see in our further discussion of the play, Othello is not represented in either hateful or stereotypical terms. Iago himself says that the Venetians have no military leader of comparable skills – "Another of his fathom they have none" (I.i.150) – and points out that Othello is necessary for the military interests of the state ("the State ... Cannot with safety cast him" [I.i.144, 146]). Moreover, despite some claims by critics that Othello is rash and overly emotional, he in fact shows himself to be calm and reasonable in the difficult situations with which he is faced.

Yet, as is well known, Othello eventually comes to believe the accusations Iago makes against his wife, Desdemona. Ultimately, he kills her in a rage of jealousy. How does this happen if Othello is indeed calm and reasonable? Does some sort of racist ideology arise here? Has Shakespeare made him cruel and irrational due to his ancestry?

In fact, it seems that almost the exact opposite is the case. Rather than presenting us with a racist portrait, Shakespeare presents us with an account of the corrosive effects of racial hatred and humiliation, the relation of shame to the experience of hatred and humiliation, and the further relation of jealousy to shame.[27] Othello's apparent gullibility

---

[27] This is hardly the first analysis to address the issue of racism in the play. Some critics have seen the play as at least complicit with racist ideas (see, for example, Gillies 25–27). Others have maintained that the play is, in effect, opposed to racism (see particularly Orkin and citations; see also Bartels). With few exceptions (see the following notes), neither set of critics has explored the emotional structure of the play in relation to racism. Indeed, systematic treatments of the play drawing on emotion research are, in general, rare. It is important to note in this context that some critics have maintained that it is anachronistic to discuss the play in terms of racism (see Neill). However, others have offered compelling evidence that there was racial categorization at the time that constitutes racial out-grouping (see Orkin, Barthelmy,

and proneness to jealousy and rashness are not general but limited to particular circumstances. Moreover, they are inseparable from his sense of being always marginal to Venetian society as a Moor, his sense that he is constantly at risk of being targeted by hatred, disdain, and disgust, and that this risk comes even from his own wife.

A number of years ago, I published an argument along these lines ("Othello").[28] It has given rise to a certain amount of misunderstanding.[29] Perhaps some of this derives from a lack of clarity on my part regarding

Crewe [especially 28n.25], and O'Toole [especially 63–64]). Bovilsky offers a particularly lucid and systematic treatment of race and racialism in the Renaissance. She nicely outlines some of the recurring patterns in racialist discourse (see 11–12) and clarifies some of the historical variety in beliefs about and attitudes toward race. It is worth noting that both the recurring features and the variations are just what one would expect from an understanding of racialism in terms of (highly malleable, but also highly emotionally consequential) identity categories and in-group/out-group relations.

[28] The year after my earlier essay appeared, Fernie drew on many of the same passages to make a closely related argument. Fernie particularly stresses shame. The following analysis will obviously also stress shame. Thus, our accounts converge and support one another to some extent. On the other hand, the present account of shame is different from Fernie's. For example, Fernie seems to see shame as contagious ("Othello has simply caught the disease of shame which we have seen is spreading through the play" [35]). This does not seem to fit either the play or the operation of shame. (Shame is, loosely speaking, contagious in circumstances where everyone has the same thing to be ashamed of – say, some group misbehavior. But that does not apply here.) Drawing on a sort of commonsense version of psychoanalytic thought, Fernie goes on to see Othello as "latently ashamed" throughout the play (35). A more fine-grained analysis of the operation of shame suggests that Othello cannot entirely avoid the awareness that many people think ill of him due to his race. Given esteem in other areas and a secure attachment relation, however, this need not give rise to episodes of shame and is not appropriately thought of as chronic, unconscious shame. More generally, Fernie does not locate his analysis in the context of a neurocognitive architecture. Again, his presuppositions are more a combination of commonsense with some psychoanalysis. This leads not only to a different understanding of shame (not Fernie's main concern, of course), but also to differences with regard to the interpretation of the play – as the example of Othello and chronic unconscious shame suggests.

[29] Marcus Nordlund contends that I am one of several critics who claim that "Othello's jealousy derives from the color of his skin" (176). The equivocal phrasing is undoubtedly intended to tar all such critics with the brush of racism. Indeed, Nordlund goes on to say that such critics "deny [Othello] a substantial part of what makes him human" (178). In fact, one main point of my original article was to oppose the view that Othello's jealousy derives from his racial background. This reading is commonly put forth as a critique of Shakespeare, suggesting that the play is racist, as just indicated. There do not seem to be any cases where it is put forth in order to conclude anything about Africans. In any case, my point in that essay was that Othello faced a situation where virtually everyone around him at some points saw him as an outsider and thus – in keeping with usual in-group/out-group divisions – as inferior in a range of ways. He has direct evidence of this at many points, including from his own

the place of jealousy in the play. Before going on, therefore, it may be worth saying a few words about jealousy, specifically sexual jealousy, explicitly previewing some of ideas we will be considering in *Othello*.

First, sexual jealousy begins with an attachment relation.[30] Purely sexual relationships may be "possessive," but jealousy is not a matter of possession. Simple possessiveness over access to sex – of the sort writers point to among some primates – seems comparable to a child's not wanting other children to play with his or her toys. It does not seem comparable to a child wanting mom not to turn her attention to anyone else (e.g., a new sibling). The latter, but not the former, is a matter of jealousy – or, at least, a proto-form of jealousy. Indeed, it is not even clear that human males exhibit that much sexual possessiveness in nonattachment relations. There does not seem to be much research on the topic. Studies of sexual jealousy tend to focus on couples, where there is presumably some degree of attachment. But (to judge from literature and film) sexual relations not involving couples – casual, one-time affairs and prostitution – seem to suggest a degree of nonpossessiveness in purely sexual relations.

Of course, this is not to say that sexuality has no role in jealousy. It is in fact very important. However, it is important as a marker of a particular sort of attachment reciprocity. Here is the way that it seems to work. Attachment involves a strong desire for reciprocity. When attachment is combined with reward dependency, that desire for reciprocity is intensified greatly. When attachment is combined with sexual desire, the need for reciprocity extends to sexual desire. More precisely, a very strong feeling of attachment tends to be highly individuating, as we have seen, and highly exclusive. When combined with reward dependency, it commonly involves an addiction-like craving for a reciprocated attachment that is individuating and exclusive. When a strong, reward-dependent attachment is combined with sexual desire in romantic love, it leads to an extension of these preferences to sexual desire. The result is an intense longing for reciprocated sexual desire that is individuating and exclusive.

---

wife, as we will see. This bias need not have been constant, and it certainly would not have been continuously expressed. But it was present, in very obvious ways. That presence makes Othello's sense of trust fragile – his sense of trust in the community generally, and in Desdemona particularly. It contributes to jealousy by making Iago's arguments plausible.

30 This is not an idiosyncratic view. See, for example, Levy, Kelly, and Jack, who argue that the data on jealousy are best accounted for in terms of attachment.

The problem is, of course, that, unlike attachment, sexual desire is not individuating and exclusive. Sexual behavior may be, but it is unlikely that sexual feelings will be. On the other hand, in at least the initial phases of romantic love, we may feel enhanced disgust at the thought of sexual contact with anyone other than the beloved (as noted in Chapter 3). In connection with this, we are also likely to feel an intensified disgust at any thought of the beloved's sexual contact with someone else – often along with anger at this breach of reciprocity.

Sexual jealousy, then, combines any anger at a breach in attachment reciprocity (prominently its individuating and exclusive orientation) with disgust at the imagination of the beloved engaging in sexual contact with someone else. This is, obviously, different from shame. But it is not unrelated to shame. Specifically, betrayal by one's beloved is always a failure. Furthermore, one is always oneself salient in such cases, thus always a possible target for causal attribution. Finally, jealousy is, again, bound up with a sense of disgust. Insofar as that disgust can come to affect one's understanding of oneself as well as the beloved, jealousy can always verge on, or even overlap with, shame. It may seem that this sort of shifting between self-disgust and disgust with someone else is highly unlikely. However, it is not. Disgust focuses on the same bodily products and acts and activates many of the same emotional memories in both cases. Their target is largely a matter of just who is salient at any given moment. As long as the other person is salient, then the disgust will be connected with him or her. But as soon as the jealous person becomes salient for himself or herself, then the activation of the disgust system can easily be reoriented toward the self.[31] Indeed, such changes in salience are likely, as are cycles of jealousy shifting into shame shifting back into jealousy. One obvious cause of a shift toward salience of oneself, thus toward shame, involves other people's attitudes. For example, suppose Jones is jealous of his wife, who he believes is having an affair. He may initially focus his attention on his wife and her lover. However, suppose people make unflattering comments on his appearance. This may draw his attention toward himself and for a time shift his predominant feeling from jealous disgust at his wife to self-disgust, thus shame. Note that such comments could be individual (e.g., referring to his baldness or his weight). But they could equally refer to some group property, such as his race.

---

[31] On the general operation of misattribution in emotion and its relation to salience, see Oatley, Keltner, and Jenkins 123.

Finally, we have just noted that there are cases where social hate – prominently disgust – may foster shame. But shame may also be hidden – again, it is a matter of self-disgust. Even when self-disgust is provoked by the responses of others – indeed, even if that is the usual case – that provocation may be hypothetical. One may feel ashamed about something that others would despise if they were aware of it. As Lickel, Schmader, and Barquissau put it, "Even though shame does not need to occur in a truly public situation, shame does bring with it a feeling of exposure" (41). When such hidden shame is actually exposed, this gives rise to another feeling – humiliation. Thus Rustomji writes that, "When the shame experienced is high in intensity it is experienced with feelings of intense humiliation following discovery" (144). As Nussbaum puts it, humiliation is the "public face of shame" (*Hiding* 203). Note that humiliation is likely to be blamed on someone else (e.g., the agent who exposes one's shame). As such, it is a likely source of rage.

The preceding analysis is supported by the empirically based observations of a number of writers. For example, DeSteno, Valdesolo, and Bartlett explain that "threatened self-esteem functions as a principal mediator of jealousy" (626; see also Harris 119). Moreover, "a primary and pancultural determinant of self-esteem is the perception and evaluation provided by others" (628). Finally, "threatening an individual's self-esteem has the potential to produce an aggressive response" (628).[32] This aggressive response may often be bound up with rage at the exposure of one's shame, thus at humiliation.[33] The general idea goes back at least to the important work of Scheff and Retzinger.[34] It is consistent

---

[32] Various "literary Darwinists" should take note of another point made by these authors – "the previously prevailing view that jealousy stems from sex-specific, evolved modules sensitive to reproductive threats ... has encountered formidable theoretical and empirical difficulties" (627). Harris's work has uncovered some of those difficulties, as has work by Russell and Harton.

[33] Given this account, we would expect there to be differences in the way people respond to spousal infidelity, depending on different social attitudes. Some societies would foster feelings of shame and humiliation, whereas others would not. I take that to be at least one crucial reason for the sorts of cultural differences reported in the literature on jealousy (for examples, see Oatley, Keltner, and Jenkins 66).

[34] Scheff and Retzinger seem to be to overstate their case in making shame "the *master emotion*" (xix), though it may have a special place in some aspect of emotional response or social relations (just as attachment appears to have a sort of "master" role in emotional development). Their generalization about "protracted violence" and shame (xviii) is also questionable. It seems likely that protracted violence often results from governmental decisions, complex ideological responses of fear and anger, military routines, spirals of collective blame, and other factors. Finally, it seems unlikely that shame must always "go unacknowledged" (xviii) in order to produce violence. On

with more recent research in areas such as terrorism. For example, Lord Alderdice points to the connections among "humiliation, shame and rage," explaining that, in political conflicts, humiliation and shame "provoked deep anger and fear and created a capacity for responses at least as violent as those that had been experienced" (205). The same point undoubtedly holds for more personal conflicts, both real and imagined. Lickel, Schmader, and Barquissau make the point generally that "shame is ... often associated with corrosive anger" (52). Indeed, there is evidence that domestic violence – a behavior obviously relevant to *Othello* – is bound up with shame. As Jennings and Murphy put it, "Abusive men use anger and *violence* to counteract and repress their shame by 'turning the table' on the shame-eliciting person or event." Moreover, the great "fear" of such men is "abandonment by their mates" (22). In short, the rage of jealousy is not a simple matter of sexual possessiveness.

Returning to the play, we may now see that the disgust expressed by Iago and Roderigo suggests that race is the point of insecurity where Othello may be vulnerable to both jealousy and shame. But before entering into this, it is important to stress again that the problem is not to be found in some quirk of Othello's nature, particularly not some putative racial defect.[35] The second scene of the play begins with Iago trying to provoke Othello's rage by speaking of a third party's slander against him. But Othello remains unmoved. Not succumbing to a sense of humiliation, he comments only, "Let him do his spite" (I.ii.16). Moreover, Othello speaks proudly of his ancestry, suggesting that he is not inclined to be ashamed – technically, he does not have a high degree of trait shame (i.e., shame as a personality inclination). Thus, he explains, "I fetch my life and being/From men of royal siege" (I.ii.20–21).

Now, Desdemona's father enters and regales Othello with racial abuse. It is possible that Othello had not encountered these attitudes

the other hand, Scheff and Retzinger are undoubtedly correct that unacknowledged shame is quite common, that it is one important part of both initiating and sustaining many protracted conflicts, and that it has a much more central role in our emotional lives than we admit. (One very important consequence of this last point is an undermining of the simplistic but widespread division of the world into shame cultures and guilt cultures [see 5–6].) If they have overstated their case, that is only what one would expect from a path-breaking work of this sort.

[35] The stereotype of Moors as impulsive and vengeful was clear in the source of the play (see Cinthio 175; see also Davison 63). On the differences between Shakespeare and Cinthio in this respect, see Berry ("Othello's" 316).

before. As a successful military leader, he may have been treated well, addressed respectfully. But now he has chosen to have sexual relations with a Venetian. This one act would be likely to enhance and disinhibit any disgust Venetians might feel for a member of an out-group. We see this in Brabantio. He enters with armed men. They draw their swords. But in keeping with his rational calmness, Othello refuses to fight. Then Brabantio assaults him with words. He begins by characterizing Othello as "foul" (I.ii.61). He goes on to accuse him of using "foul charms" and "drugs" (I.ii.72, 73) to deprive Desdemona of her senses. In effect, he is accusing Othello of what we would today characterize as rape. His reason for assuming this is that Desdemona could have married someone from "our nation" (I.ii.66), thus not a member of a racial out-group. He makes reference to the "curlèd" hair of the Venetians, as opposed, presumably, to the rougher, African hair of Othello. More significantly, he characterizes Othello as "a thing ... to fear, not to delight" (I.ii.70). The fear is inseparable from his race, for the property that makes him such an (inhuman) thing is his "sooty bosom" (I.ii.69). Subsequently, Brabantio repeats the accusations and insists that love between Desdemona and Othello is "Against all rules of nature" (I.iii.101), as if it were a case of bestiality.

Brabantio's speech is suffused with hate – anger and disgust – directed to an identity category imposed on Othello, that of "Moor." I say "imposed on Othello" because Othello has a more fine-grained view of ethnicity and of individual identity. In speaking of his adventures, he separates a range of peoples – not simply Moors and Venetians, black and white.

On the other hand, even if he was previously not subjected to racial abuse, and even if he himself does not divide the world into Moors and Venetians, it is clear that he has always been subjected to racial categorization in Venice. People undoubtedly always referred to him as "the Moor," not by his name.[36] They undoubtedly showed that they saw him primarily as an instance of his racial group. They almost certainly referred casually to his unappealing skin color as well. What he has just witnessed is the sharp change from respect, combined with racial categorization, to racial anger and disgust. Seeing this in Brabantio, he may well be sensitized to the possibility of seeing it in Desdemona as well. After all, as Othello himself explains, once Brabantio "loved me" too (I.iii.127).

---

[36] The use of "the Moor" instead of "Othello" has been noted by several critics (see, for example, Derek Cohen).

When Desdemona is finally introduced, she does not refer to Othello by his name, but by his ethnic category, "the Moor" (I.iii.187). Subsequently, she explains her love, tacitly admitting that a black complexion – including Othello's black face – is ugly. She states, "My heart's subdued/Even to the very quality of my lord" (I.iii.245–246). Thus, due to her love, she has accepted even his "quality." The term is ambiguous, but it includes distinctive traits or features (see the meanings listed at "Quality" in *Oxford*); his visual appearance is the obvious interpretation. The racial implication becomes clearer when she begins the next sentence with the statement, "I saw Othello's visage in his mind" (I.iii.247). It is obvious here that she must be saying his face is not something that would attract her. She can love it because she sees past its appearance to the noble soul behind it. Such a statement about Othello's face need not refer specifically to his racial category, but again, her references to him as "the Moor" seem to make this the obvious interpretation. This view is further indicated by the Duke's subsequent comment on Othello's appearance. In effect repeating Desdemona's comment, with a clearer racial reference, he explains that Othello is beautiful due to his moral value. "If virtue no delighted beauty lack," he explains, Othello "is far more fair than black" (I.iii.284–285). In this case, it is evident that Othello's ugliness is precisely his blackness. Such statements, particularly those by Desdemona, are likely to introduce some degree of insecurity – and a potential for shame – in a lover who longs for unique, exclusive reciprocity in sexual desire. Indeed, as the entire play suggests, this has general consequences for Othello's security of pride or self-esteem.

The scene ends with Iago and Roderigo. Much of what they say concerns shame and hate. Roderigo says that it is his "shame" to dote so much on Desdemona (I.iii.312). Subsequently, Iago, now alone, reflects upon his "hate" for "the Moor." He explains, "it is thought ... that 'twixt my sheets/H'as done my office" (I.iii.377–379). This is not only an instance of disgust and anger directed at Othello. It also suggests the possibility of both shame and humiliation. Iago says not only that Othello may have seduced his wife, but that other people believe this. Thus, his shame has been exposed.

In Iago's next conversation with Roderigo, the racist disgust is clear again. Iago insists, indeed, that eventually Desdemona will "disrelish and abhor the Moor," going so far as to "heave the gorge" or vomit (II.i.231–232). He partially convinces Roderigo that Desdemona's desires are turning toward Cassio. I take it that this further shows that Othello's subsequent jealousy is not a racist stereotype, for Roderigo is similarly gullible.[37] But it also suggests that the reason for Othello's gullibility is his sense of the hypocrisy and potential racial hatred in those around him. It is precisely that racial hatred that works on Roderigo's mind when he considers that Desdemona may already be turning from Othello to Cassio.

From here, Iago begins to work out his plan to harm those who have caused him to fail and who have humiliated him – Cassio and, above all, Othello. First, Iago and Roderigo make Cassio drunk and lure him into a brawl. Here, too, the calm and reasonable Othello ends the conflict. But he must punish Cassio. Cassio's response fits the present analysis perfectly. He suffers a deep sense of failure for his unbecoming behavior and self-disgust for his inebriation. As he explains, "It hath pleased the devil drunkenness to give place to the devil wrath. One unperfectness shows me another, to make me frankly despise myself" (II.iii.295–297). He further connects this with social humiliation, wailing, "I have lost my reputation!" (II.iii.261–262).

Cassio ultimately goes to Desdemona for help. Desdemona approaches Othello and pleads his case, explaining that "so many a time,/When I have spoke of you dispraisingly," Cassio "Hath ta'en your part" (III.iii.71–73). The lines are astonishing, not for what they tell Othello about Cassio, but for what they tell him about Desdemona. Desdemona has just said that she frequently spoke ill of Othello, confiding her antagonism to Cassio. Though Othello does not respond badly at this point, it is difficult to see how this would not introduce doubts about Desdemona's feelings. These doubts would stem most obviously from the fact that she was "dispraising" him. But they stem even more profoundly from the fact that she is telling him about this, oblivious to the fact that this is likely to be hurtful to him. Rather than the enhanced empathy one expects with attachment, Desdemona seems to suffer from a reduction in empathy – presumably due to in-group/out-group divisions.

Later in the same scene, Iago begins to work on Othello. He first stresses how the thoughts and actions, even of one's beloved, are unknowable – a point consistent with the deception Desdemona

---

[37] Like so much else in this and other plays, the topic of suspicion and related issues, such as probability, have been treated by scholars in an historical context. Needless to say, in addition to the transhistorical and cross-cultural features of emotional response, associated causal attribution, and so forth, there are historically particular influences bearing on the use of evidence, probability judgments, and so on. For a discussion of some of these topics in *Othello*, see Altman and Hutson. (Hutson also treats these topics in *The Comedy of Errors* and *Hamlet*.)

practiced on her father. Othello still affirms that "Desdemona's honest" (III.iii.225). But a worry has entered his mind, and he begins, "And yet, how nature erring from itself – " (III.iii.227). The suggestion of this utterance is that Desdemona's nature is honest, but she, or anyone, may drift from their nature due to temptation. Iago cleverly takes up the idea of drifting from nature to give it a racial meaning. He pretends to agree with Othello, saying that "in all things nature tends" to unite people of their "own clime, complexion, and degree." Thus Desdemona's "erring" from "nature" was her initial marriage with Othello. Iago quickly links this error with disgust, stating that "one may smell" something "rank,/ Foul," and "unnatural" (III.iii.230–233) in this.

Iago's speech has the desired effect. But it does not have that effect on its own. It has that effect because it is combined with Desdemona's statement about dispraise, her implicit admission that she is repulsed by his color, the broader racial rejection Othello experiences when he enters into a sexual relation with Desdemona, the casual reduction of his personal identity to an identity category (prominently through the substitution of "the Moor" for his name) and the linking of that category with ugliness, and so on.

More exactly, Othello is convinced that he has lost Desdemona – "She's gone" (III.iii.266). Of course, he feels jealousy. He wishes for the same singular and exclusive feeling from her as he has for her, saying that he would not for anything "keep a corner in the thing I love/For others' uses" (III.iii.271–272). (The sexual implications of "corner" here are, of course, not irrelevant.) But what is important is just why he is prone to accept Iago's claims. He lists several possible reasons. One, his age, he dismisses, saying, "yet that's not much" (III.iii.265). Another, is implausible – lack of skill at conversation. After all, it was precisely his conversational skills that won her love initially (as Othello well knows [see I.iii.148–149 and 163–165]). The remaining reason seems to be the one that is convincing to him – "I am black" (III.iii.262).

To a great extent, Othello blames Desdemona for her (supposed) infidelity. But Othello's reflections also include self-blame,[38] that is, causal attribution to his own salient properties, specifically his blackness. There is a hint of self-disgust as well. We see this when Othello declares that "I had rather be a toad/And live upon the vapor of a dungeon"

---

[38] This is not surprising, for "Romantic rejection is … a symbolic evaluation of one's deficient worth – in other words, a humiliating blow to one's self-esteem" (Baumeister, Wotman, and Stillwell 379).

(III.iii.269–270). There could be little that is more loathsome than a toad in a vaporous dungeon. But Othello considers himself in a worse – presumably more repulsive – state still. For much of the rest of the play, Othello moves among jealousy, shame, and humiliation. His actions are rarely the result of only one of these emotions. We see this clearly in his next discussion with Iago. There he complains that "My name, that was as fresh/as Dian's visage, is now begrimed and black/As mine own face" (III.iii.383–385). He begins with the humiliation of other people's disparagement and disgust ("My name ... is now begrimed and black"), but turns quickly to an apparent self-disgust, aimed at the same racial category that provokes disgust in others ("begrimed and black/As mine own face").

What actional outcome is there for Othello's feelings here? He opts for the deaths of Cassio and Desdemona. As already indicated, humiliation gives rise to murderous rage. The rival is the primary cause of one's humiliation, for he or she is the "victor," the person who has taken one's expected place. But the beloved is the one whose disdain and disgust began the entire sequence of events. More importantly, he or she is the one whose disdain and disgust are most painful – overwhelmingly so, in fact. The intensity of this pain is due to the fact that these feelings contrast so strikingly with the attachment and sexual desire for which one longs. It also derives from one's intensified sensitivity to the beloved's feelings. Both factors mean that the beloved's aversion is likely to prove almost unbearably hurtful for the lover – thus a potentially powerful source of anger.

The next scene opens with Desdemona searching for the handkerchief that Othello gave her. Desdemona cannot find it. (The audience knows that it has been taken by Emilia.) She thinks that Othello is particularly "noble" and "true of mind," so he will not blame her. But, she explains, "it were enough to put" at least some other, "jealous" men "to ill thinking" (III.iv.26–29). What she does not realize is that it is more than an ordinary love token. It was given to Othello by his mother and is therefore a symbol of both his love – particularly his attachment bonding – and his heritage. Her careless disregard of this gift would, it seems, be of a piece with the racial disdain and disgust he already suspects. Later, he sees Cassio with the very handkerchief. The cause seems obvious: Desdemona not only does not love him, but, along with Cassio, mocks him.

Subsequently, Desdemona pleads again for the restoration of Cassio to his former position. The plea is doubly unfortunate. First, it suggests again the lack of exclusive reciprocity in Desdemona's love – even without a sexual relation, she does seem to have an attachment bond with Cassio. This in itself may have harmful consequences for Othello's sense of himself, particularly insofar as it suggests a racially based exclusion of Othello from this bond. The point is in keeping with research on self-esteem. As Tesser points out, following Leary and Downs, "self-esteem is rooted in concerns with being excluded by others" (196). As Leary puts it, "self-esteem is strongly tied to how valued and accepted the individual feels at a given moment" (210); it is bound up with "the perceived security of one's interpersonal relationships" (213). Tesser adds that "the social consequences to self-esteem are amplified in the context of psychologically close others" (196).

Leary's stress on the social aspect of self-esteem leads to the issue of humiliation and the second problem with Desdemona's action here. Desdemona's plea makes a show of her feelings for Cassio to others. Though Emilia is the only other person present, she is perhaps the worst witness, for her knowledge of the scene is likely to make its way back to Iago, who will take it as further evidence of Desdemona's infidelity – a response Othello can all too easily infer. In Othello's current frame of mind, this semipublic exposure is humiliating. This is particularly significant here for, as Jennings and Murphy contend, "battering men are ... afraid of rejection and humiliation by other males" (24) and "pathological jealousy" may result from "both the shame of losing the female love object and the humiliation of being exposed ... in the eyes of men" (27). On the other hand, in keeping with the preceding discussion, Othello could have had this reaction without the near certainty of public exposure. All that was needed was his counterfactual imagination of public reaction. Fearon explains that shame may bear on "ones immediate or imagined relationships" (65), thus the response of "a hidden chorus of invisible males," as Jennings and Murphy put it (28).

In the fourth act, Othello berates Desdemona in terms that show clearly his complex emotional state. He first complains that he has been made "The fixèd figure for the time of scorn" (IV.ii.53) – again, an object of disdain, and perhaps disgust. He moves from this sense of humiliation to jealousy, the feeling that his singular and exclusive love for Desdemona is not reciprocated. He speaks of the place "where I have garnered up my heart,/Where either I must live or bear no life," lamenting that he has been "discarded thence" (IV.ii.56–57, 59). It is worth noting that, at this point, Othello neither speaks of nor suggests murder. He rather hints at a suicidal despondency in this loss of an attachment relation. Desdemona, or her love or soul, is the place where he has set his own life (here, heart). He has only two options – to live in her love or, if she "discards" him, to die. Finally, he turns more directly to disgust. He may be discarded from that beloved place, he explains, or, adding a third possibility, "keep it as a cistern for foul toads/To knot and gender in" (IV.ii.60–61). Here, he shifts from Desdemona's soul or love to her body, where other men (here, toads) may produce offspring.[39] This clearly returns us to jealousy. However, self-disgust, shame, and humiliation are not absent. Specifically, there is some ambiguity as to which person is the proper object of disgust. Desdemona is most obviously identified with the cistern, and Cassio with the toad – but Othello has already connected himself with toads ("I had rather be a toad/And live upon the vapor of a dungeon/Than keep a corner in the thing I love/For others' uses" [III.iii.269–272]). In any case, it seems clear at this point that Othello's feelings involve a strong component of disgust, presumably involved with both shame and jealousy.

The murder of Desdemona culminates the dramatic tension and audience emotion. However, it adds little to our understanding of Othello. Perhaps the major change from the preceding scenes is the addition of rationalization. Othello's Christian belief might lead him to have a prospective regret of the act, a sense that the murder could lead to subsequent punishment. In addition, and perhaps more significantly, his attachment to Desdemona might inspire prospective guilt over her suffering. Rationalization is a process of emotion modulation leading to mood repair. Specifically, it involves effortful elaborative processes

[39] Readers familiar with Paster's discussion of the passage (*Humoring* 69–76) will recognize that she interprets it very differently. It is difficult to follow Paster's contention that the cistern is inside Othello. It seems clear that he is "discarded thence" through Desdemona's rejection and that, as the (imagined) adulteress, Desdemona is the one whose "cistern" is a place for "foul toads/To knot and gender in." Moreover, it seems clear that the cistern is not a historically specific reference to the way drinking water produces toads in one's stomach. It is, rather, a transhistorical sexual reference. Finally, the passage appears primarily to involve disgust, not "fear" (72). It is difficult to see toads and cisterns as fear-provoking rather than disgust-provoking.

Despite these points, Paster's analyses generally provide a suggestive complement to those presented here – and in the discussion of *Macbeth*, which she also treats. Specifically, Paster is interested in exploring Shakespeare's use of ideas about emotions that were current at his time. This is precisely the aspect of emotion that the present analyses pass over. Again, these analyses concern the nature of emotion as revealed by the plays, rather than the theoretical ideas about emotion that are expressed more or less explicitly in the plays (e.g., through references to "smoky vapors ascending from heart to brain" [Paster *Humoring* 26]) and that, in light of recent research, have no validity.

that alter some property of the emotion experience (e.g., causal attribution or projected outcomes). Othello's rationalization sounds as if it was taken from the Inquisition. He will kill Desdemona because, if he does not, "she'll betray more men" (V.ii.6). That, of course, would harm the men. But it would also harm Desdemona's soul. Thus he is preventing her from committing further sins. That makes a difference, because he insists that she should pray for forgiveness – "heavens forfend! I would not kill thy soul" (V.ii.32), he explains. Thus what he does will be a "sacrifice," not a "murder" (V.ii.65), because it will simultaneously serve to protect society and to save Desdemona. As such, it will entail no punishment (thus regret). Nor will it entail empathy and guilt, since it is for her supposed benefit. It is widely recognized that "extreme ... violence" may be rationalized by "[m]oral justifications" such as the view that "it is for the person's own good" (Anderson and Huesmann 272). This scene suggests that one mechanism of this rationalization may involve an inhibition of empathy through a concrete imagination of subsequent events or acts – here, Desdemona's further adulteries or, alternatively, her postconfession salvation – just as we would expect from the perceptual account of emotion. In this case, there is presumably a dissipation of punitive imaginations (e.g., regarding Hell) and emotional memories bearing on regret as well.

As it turns out, however, Othello is overcome with rage. He kills her before she can confess. By now, he has so fully inhibited spontaneous inclinations to empathy that her weeping does not inspire any compassion. Rather, it provokes further anger and, it seems, disgust – manifest, for example, in his order, "Down, strumpet!" (V.ii.79).

In the end, Othello learns the truth about Desdemona's fidelity and Iago's plotting. In his final speech, Othello expresses a profound sense of shame. He recounts a story of how, once, "a malignant and a turbaned Turk/Beat a Venetian." In response, Othello "took by th' throat the circumcisèd dog" and killed him (V.ii.349–352).[40] Through this

[40] Work by Lickel, Schmader, and Barquissau suggests that this earlier action itself may have involved a sense of group difference and opposition, specifically Othello's sense that he would be categorized with this "turbaned Turk" and blamed for his act. As they explain, "People who are targets of collective blame may also try to manage blame by publicly punishing the group member who committed the wrongdoing" (50). They go on to point out that a further strategy of "Distancing ... is particularly linked to shame." Moreover, this may be combined with punishment, leading to the "death" of the "offending group member" (51). In this way, the anecdote may suggest a history to Othello's sense of racial out-grouping, a sense of being the object of collective blame. It may also suggest the specific circumstances in which he would be likely

anecdote, it is obvious that he fully blames himself for the murder of Desdemona. But there is little suggesting empathy with Desdemona and a remorseful feeling of guilt over her suffering. He alludes to her twice in the speech, in both cases by analogy. In one case, she is "a pearl" (V.ii.343), thus a feelingless – and, presumably, white – thing; in the other case, she is a faceless, nameless "Venetian" (V.ii.350). Rather, he feels a deep disgust, signaled indirectly by his identification of the Turk – his own counterpart in the anecdote – with a "circumcisèd dog." What is perhaps most striking about this, however, is that his disgust in the anecdote – and thus presumably in his own self-reproach – is not aimed primarily at the action, but at out-group properties. Othello kills himself just as he killed "a malignant ... Turk," not a "malignant criminal."[41] Moreover, this Turk was a "dog," thus not a human, at least in part because he was "circumcisèd" due to his (out-group) religion. Moreover, the crime of the Turk – and thus presumably the crime of Othello – was harming "a Venetian," not so much an individual as an instance of a particular social category. This construal of his act goes against everything in attachment relations, for these are (once more) particularizing. The fact that Othello himself adopts this social construal suggests again that the crucial motivations, both in this final action and elsewhere, are more a matter of shame and humiliation than of jealousy proper (though, of course, the jealousy is important as well).

In certain respects, Othello exhibits a case of what is called "stigma endorsement," in which people from stigmatized groups "share to some extent the negative views about their condition" (Dijker and Koomen 286). But, crucially, his behavior follows from emotional aspects of this endorsement – or, more precisely, the intertwining of a concrete self-imagination with such emotional aspects, prominently including shame.[42] The final result of this shame is unsurprising. There is no actional outcome he can engage in that will ameliorate his condition

---

to act murderously – when threatened by group-based shame. On the other hand, the incident took place in Aleppo, which would not seem to be a place where Othello would experience these feelings with respect to Europeans.

[41] Cf. Leslie Fiedler 195.

[42] It is worth noting here that some writers have criticized social identity theory for "fail[ing] to capture the more pernicious forms of prejudice" (Spears and Leach 337). Spears and Leach suggest that this may result from a lack of "attention to the emotional bases of malice toward outgroups" (337).

of self-blame and disgust – perhaps because the disgust particularly is aimed as much at a property as at an action. Or, rather, there is no such actional outcome, except suicide, the destruction of that property and the person who manifests it.

In many ways, Othello's final actions conform to recent accounts of the relation between self-esteem and aggression. Specifically, Sedikides and Gregg point out that instability or fragility of self-esteem seems to be bound up with "proneness to anger and hostility" (106). But *Othello* also complicates this idea. Specifically, it suggests that self-esteem may not only be fragile or unstable; it may be vulnerable at specific points even when generally strong. Again, Othello does not appear to be prone to anger or hostility in general – quite the opposite. He becomes violent only – and readily – in particular circumstances. Those circumstances involve a confluence of attachment rejection and social denigration, with a general loss of trust. Moreover, Othello does not evidence the standard tendency of people with "unstable self-esteem ... to use excuses" for "self-enhancement" (Sedikides and Gregg 108). Indeed, his final speech stresses that no one should "extenuate" anything he has done (V.ii.338). This seems to be bound up with two things. First, there is his recognition that he misplaced his trust in Iago. Second, and more importantly, there is the recognition that he misplaced his distrust in Desdemona. This partial reestablishment of attachment reciprocity with Desdemona may be crucial to the absence of self-justification.[43] At the same time, however, this recognition of his own responsibility for the violation of an attachment relation rapidly intensifies his self-disgust. Given the impossibility of undoing his shame (due to the death of Desdemona and due to the association of this shame with his racial category), this also leads to the peculiar violence of his suicide – an act that is both a complete self-abnegation (thus the opposite of self-justification) and a sort of racial attack on a dehumanized outgroup (as Othello himself now becomes the "malignant ... Turk" and "circumcisèd dog"). Rustomjee notes that "a shamed person is at high suicidal and/or homicidal risk" (145). Due to the complex, enduring nature of his shame, and its relation to his attachment bonds, Othello's death is, in effect, both a suicide and a homicide.

---

[43] The point is consistent with the idea of Parker and Thomas that "a safe, nonretaliating ... relationship can provide a foundation for ... development of empathy and guilt" for "those experiencing shame" (223).

Conclusion

The value of literature in the study of emotion may be particularly highlighted in relation to such emotions as guilt, shame, and jealousy. This is because these emotions involve complex interactions of emotion systems that occur in the context of complex interactions among people. These interactions are obviously important. Yet approaches drawn from experimental psychology and neuroscience tend to be particularly weak in these areas. Moreover, here as elsewhere, our comprehension of these emotions is further enhanced by the wholistic integration of partial insights that is enabled by literary narrative.

The eliciting conditions for guilt, shame, and regret first involve a past action that is aversive and a spontaneous attribution of causality to oneself. Thus, we may refer to all three as "self-blame emotions." One can experience self-blame emotions for future actions. However, these occur in simulations where one imaginatively places oneself after the act. This "future anterior" imagination is what gives the feelings of guilt, shame, and regret their deterrent function. If I refrain from doing something due to guilt, it is because, through simulation, I know (imaginatively) that I will experience guilt after the fact.

It is important to stress here that the causal attribution must be part of the unfolding emotion episode itself. I may reason that I had a causal role in some event, but still not experience guilt, if the attribution is purely inferential. Conversely, I may not bear any responsibility for a particular act, but I may feel guilty, insofar as my emotional experience incorporates me as a causal factor.[44]

Guilt is a response to an aversive event in which there is a victim with whom one feels empathy. This suggests that guilt should be intensified in cases where empathy is intensified – most obviously when one has an attachment bond with the victim or when the victim is helpless. By the same token, we would expect guilt to be decreased in cases where

---

[44] Here and elsewhere, that incorporation is not, for example, a matter of subsuming events under causal laws or even necessarily believing in one's causal responsibility. It is often simply a matter of saliency in emotional response. Such causal incorporation may also result from innate or acquired routines that turn one's attention to one's own actions in the development of the emotion-eliciting events. Group identifications are another source for such attributions. This is why it is possible to feel "collective guilt" for activities by members of an in-group. In keeping with the preceding analysis, collective guilt occurs "when the individual's collective identity or association with a group whose actions are perceived as immoral is salient" (Branscombe and Doosje "International" 3).

one's causal role is not salient (e.g., when voting for a candidate who supports a war killing hundreds of thousands of people we do not see). We would also expect guilt to be reduced when there is some opposition in identity categories – thus an in-group/out-group division – between oneself and the victim. We would expect this to affect guilt because identity category opposition tends to inhibit empathy.

Shame, in contrast, involves a sense that one has failed relative to prior expectations. One's sense of failure is likely to vary in intensity with the degree to which the expectation is bound up with one's sense of identity. For example, one's failure in physical combat is likely to be more painful if one is a samurai than if one is a literature professor. This may be particularly true insofar as that identity is connected with communal perceptions and expectations in addition to one's own self-expectations. But the intensity of the sense of failure is probably not as important as the activation of a further emotion system – disgust. In order to find an act truly shameful, we should not only be disappointed in our performance (relative to our expectations for ourselves) or embarrassed about our public showing; we need to experience disgust. Most obviously, we may experience disgust at the act itself, as when this is an act of bloodshed or sexual depravity. But we may also experience disgust at any salient causal precedent to the failure, as when some act of sensual indulgence gave rise to the failure. I may feel disappointed with myself if I miss the final exam because I spent the night studying in the library. But I am unlikely to feel disgusted with myself – unlike a case where I spent the night in, say, a brothel.

Of course, if I do miss the final exam for whatever reason, I am likely to regret my actions because they are likely to have harmful consequences. Regret is distinct from guilt and shame in involving fear or anxiety about possible results, rather than empathic pain/compassion (as in guilt) or self-disgust and a sense of failure (as in shame). Needless to say, it is routinely combined with both guilt and shame in real life.

All three self-blame emotions may orient one's attentional focus toward memories of the act itself. The memories may, in turn, dominate working memory processes. This may lead to an experience of the derealization of the current, material world. This derealization is particularly likely when no actional outcomes are available that would change the situation in a productive way.

Ideally, actional outcomes for aversive emotions involve behaviors that alter the aversive situation. This is particularly difficult in the cases of guilt and shame. There are greater possibilities for regret. The aversive quality of regret is focused primarily on consequences of the act, thus things that have not yet happened. There may be at least some leeway in fending off those consequences. In contrast, both guilt and shame are focused on the past act itself. The most obvious actional outcome for guilt is reparation, some sort of compensation delivered to the victim. The second is subjecting oneself to the same pain as the victim. If the act involves a death, then the former is not possible. On the other hand, the guilt-induced desire for punishment seems generally to be weaker than the desire to live. This is expected, given that our empathic response to other people's suffering is typically less than our response to our own suffering. In consequence, guilt seems less likely to provoke suicidal action than shame, even when reparation is not a possibility.

As this suggests, the situation of shame is related, but different. It too may be focused on an unalterable act in the past. But there is no real issue of compensation, except perhaps to oneself. One way of overcoming shame is by addressing the failure, thus achieving some parallel excellence, some compensatory success. It is more difficult to address the disgust. Ordinarily, we respond to disgust by avoiding the disgusting object. But that is clearly not an option if one is the disgusting object oneself. On the other hand, disgust may bear on different aspects of oneself. It may target a changeable propensity, such as a bad habit. Alternatively, it may encompass a more seemingly "essential" and unalterable identity category, as seems to be the case with Othello. In the case of a changeable propensity, it would seem that shame may be overcome by reform, by changing one's habits, or whatever. In the case of an identity category, however, there may be no opportunity for avoiding the disgust, other than death.

Shame is closely related to social contempt and humiliation. In social contempt, other people respond to one as disgusting and a failure. This can lead easily to shame. Such a transition seems particularly likely when some attachment figure feels contempt for us. Our enhanced empathic sensitivity to such a person's feelings and our expectations regarding their emotional responses make their contempt more salient and more emotionally consequential. Shame leads us to desire concealment. Humiliation results from the exposure of one's shame, leading to a combination of shame with social contempt. In some cases, that contempt may not be real, but only imagined. This is not necessarily any less likely to provoke a feeling of humiliation. When one blames oneself for the exposure of one's shame, then the result is a redoubled sense of shame. When one blames others, it may lead to destructive rage.

Hate is also relevant to this set of complex emotions. In hate, one feels both anger and disgust at another person. The anger results from a personal failure that is causally attributed to the other person. This deflecting of blame from oneself is likely to be rationalized as disapproval of the other person's action as "objectively" immoral, mistaken, or whatever. Here, as elsewhere, the disgust at the other person may focus on the act itself or more enduring identities.

Rationalization involves elaborative thought that serves to modulate emotion through processes of mood repair. In other words, it helps reduce aversive qualities of emotion experience. It does this through the usual mechanisms of emotional modulation, such as attentional reorientation (e.g., toward more positive possible outcomes), recategorization of acts (e.g., "sacrifice" versus "murder," in the case of Othello), and so on. In terms of the account of emotion outlined at the beginning of the book, these forms of elaboration do not change the emotion directly, but they alter precisely what memories are activated, what concrete images are produced in anticipations, what aspects of the current situation are observed, and so on. In other words, they affect what emotion elicitors we experience, thus what emotion systems are activated and in what degree.

Finally, jealousy may be understood as a desire for particularized, exclusive reciprocity in an attachment relation. The intensity of the longing varies with the intensity of the attachment. Thus, jealousy does not result from sexual desire per se. There is sexual possessiveness, but that is continuous with possessiveness regarding territory or objects. On the other hand, as sexual desire and reward dependency become connected with attachment, one's longing for the other person's presence, contact, attention, and so on is intensified. In keeping with this, one's desire for particularized, exclusive reciprocity is intensified and extended. Given that we necessarily have a range of human social interactions, the exclusive particularity of attachment relations cannot be generalized to all aspects of interaction. (For example, only pathological cases of jealousy involve the demand that one's beloved not converse with anyone else.) One would therefore expect distinctive aspects of one's relationship with the beloved to become particularly important for exclusivity. This should be especially true for aspects of the relationship that rely on proximity, physical contact, and other features of the relationship that are related to attachment. One result of this is that we would expect sexuality to become a particularly important feature of exclusive reciprocity in romantic relationships.[45] Beyond this, the sexual aspect of an attachment relation may increase the sense of disgust that one feels at the thought (or perception) of sexual contact between the beloved and someone else. Thus, sexuality may come to have a particularly important place in jealousy. Nonetheless, jealousy is still primarily a function of attachment.

By this account, one probably would not expect rage to be a primary outcome of jealousy. It is possible that jealousy could lead to rage against the rival. However, it seems more likely that the focus of jealousy would be on the beloved and that a feeling of rejection would give rise to something like panic. This analysis suggests, then, that the murders and brutality often associated with jealousy are not, primarily, the result of jealousy. Rather, they are more likely the result of humiliation, which is often associated with jealousy.[46] Again, humiliation is particularly painful when one feels demeaned and despised by an attachment figure. This will occur regularly in cases of sexual infidelity. On the other hand, jealousy as understood here can give rise to a feeling of helpless despondency that could lead to suicide.

Macbeth presents us with a complex treatment of guilt and shame in the persons of Macbeth and his wife. Wole Soyinka's *The Strong Breed* explores the relation between guilt and reparation, whereas *Kagekiyo* examines shame and its relation to social esteem and attachment. Finally, *Othello* develops a subtle depictive representation of the interactions among shame, humiliation, jealousy, and hate, all in relation to the operation of social identity categories.

---

[45] This helps explain such data as those of Penke and Asendorpf, who found "No evidence for a sex difference in sexual jealousy" (3).

[46] The idea goes against common accounts of male jealousy in Evolutionary Psychology, because it has little to do with having "a chance to reproduce" or the risk of "spending resources on another man's progeny" (Christine Harris 102). Indeed, it does not suggest that there should be a great difference between men and women in this regard, since either might feel humiliated. This fits with Christine Harris's finding that a "meta-analysis of jealousy-inspired homicides, taking into account base rates for murder, found no evidence that jealousy disproportionately motivates men to kill" (102).

7. From Attachment to Ethical Feeling

Rabindranath Tagore and *Measure for Measure*

The Morality of Leaving Home

In his 1894 collection, *Sonar Tari*, Rabindranath Tagore has a poem about leaving home. The speaker – whom I take to be roughly equivalent to the poet – is working at a distance from his family and has returned for religious holidays. Now it is time to leave. There is great frenzy in the home. Servants rush about bearing great loads for the journey. The poet's wife seems to pack everything in sight until the stack of goods towers over the helpless writer who pleads for some restraint. Just outside this bustling throng is a four-year-old girl, the poet's daughter, who sits teary-eyed, guarding the door. When, at last, he approaches to leave, she announces, "I won't let you go." But, of course, he goes anyway; the separation is inevitable. As he passes along the road toward his destination, everything he sees reminds him of his daughter; in every sound, he hears the words of the little girl, heartbroken by the door. "From all directions today," he reports, "that sad heart-rending wail reaches my ears,/ringing without pause, and in my daughter's voice" (85).

There are many ways we could approach this poem. The most obvious is metaphysical, the Vedāntic interpretation according to which all the material world is change, and change is the source of suffering. That suffering, then, pervades the human condition, for every joy results in longing – like the girl for her father and the father for the girl – and we can never hold on; everything passes; everyone leaves; we must always let go. But it is no less possible to consider the poem in relation to another set of concerns that recur throughout Tagore's writings – ethical concerns. For it is not simple churning of the guṇas, the causally definitive components of prakṛti or matter, that lead the poet and his daughter to this mutual loss. It is also choice.

Considering the poem in relation to such ethical concerns is in part a matter of interpretation. But it is also in part a matter of another sort of hermeneutic inquiry, one in which the reader uses the poem to guide and test ethical reflections. Such reflections take the poem as their starting point and as an ongoing source for development and challenge. However, the primary aim of such "hermeneutic elaboration," as we might call it, is not revealing unrecognized meanings in the text, though that is certainly a subsidiary goal. Rather, the primary aim is understanding the moral topics themselves. In keeping with this, then, the main preoccupation of the following reflections will be with exploring the ethical issues suggested by Tagore's text. We will be concerned with explicating the poem itself only insofar as this contributes to our exploration of these ethical issues.

The complex of moral concerns bearing on this poem is neatly encapsulated in the title of Tagore's 1915 novel – *The Home and the World*. This title is open to a number of interpretations. It refers, for instance, to the fact that changing social practices, shifting governmental policies, and political events (the world) may affect domestic routines, familial customs, personal relations (the home) in both liberating and destructive ways. But it also refers to a tension – between one's life within the family and one's life as it is lived in relation to larger units of village, district, state, nation, and even the global community. This tension has many aspects. One is ethical. It concerns what one should choose to do – in the home, in the world, and, perhaps most crucially, in the relation between the two, particularly when our duties in one conflict or seem to conflict with our duties in the other.

One such conflict occurs as the poet makes a choice about leaving his daughter. He has obligations in the home. He has obligations in the world. How can he reconcile the one with the other, when the former tells him to stay at home while the latter calls on him to leave?

But here one might ask if leaving is an ethical issue at all. What guides the poet to his work in the world? Is it only self-interest, the ahaṃkāra or egoism that, as the *Upaniṣads* stress, leads us to pain? If so, it is, of course, the same ahaṃkāra that drives the daughter, and we are back in the metaphysical interpretation. In that case, there is no real ethical issue at all, but merely a prudential one.

The question, then, is this: When the "importunate" (85) world bewails its state to the poet, is there any reason to believe that the poet has a moral relation to that plea and to the pain it expresses? If so, is there any way of thinking about that in connection with the moral relation the poet has to the heartache expressed by his tiny daughter, sitting forlorn by the door? The question is particularly pressing because the poet tells us nothing about his occupation or about the people who live and suffer in this importunate world, speaking only of "mother earth" (84) as he passes along the road, moving further away from home, deeper into the world.

But there is a clue. All these events occur in the context established by the opening lines of the poem. There is another still point amidst the fuss of leave-taking, a figure parallel to the girl, and to the earth that speaks with the girl's voice. It is an "ancient ... beggar-woman" lying on "a tattered cloth" (82). She is the beginning of all this, the point of reference, constantly present throughout what follows, though never again mentioned. Her lack of all things contrasts painfully with the poet's excess of food and clothing, the great mounds of stuff weighing down his carriage. As she is a beggar, we know that she is importunate, more than the child. We know that as an old woman she should be respected by her family, a family she lacks even more profoundly than the girl. Her thin arms, easily imagined, seem no more capable than the girl's "two little hands" (84) of holding back all that leaves. In entering the world, can we say that the poet takes up a set of moral obligations that in some way include this woman? Can we even speak of the poet as having such obligations?

The issue is, of course, not unique to Tagore's poem, nor to his situation, nor to nineteenth-century Bengal, nor to India. It is a universal dilemma. We have duties toward those who are near to us, those we love. We also have duties toward those who are not near to us, even those we despise. Are those duties equal in force or do they differ? (These are sometimes referred to as the "equal pull" and "differential pull" hypotheses.[1]) Does one have a greater obligation to one's own children than to children anywhere else? Does the poet have a greater obligation toward his daughter than toward the beggar woman with the tattered cloth? Does he have any obligations at all toward that woman and those like her whose pain is expressed in the "heart-rending wail" of the earth, a wail that reaches the poet's ears in the voice of his daughter? Finally, the issue is not purely personal. It has consequences at every level of social and political life. We know, of course, that the

[1] See, for example, Sommers.

war in Iraq increases the likelihood of a terrorist attack on the United States.[2] In that way, there is not much of a moral dilemma there. But suppose for a moment that President Bush was correct. Suppose that a war killing tens of thousands of Iraqi children would decrease the likelihood of a terrorist attack on the United States. This decrease would, in some tiny measure, affect our children. Would our obligation to protect our children in that case – however slight the protection – outweigh our obligation to prevent (or not to be complicit in) the deaths of other people's children in such great numbers? If not, would it make a difference if the protection of our children were greater and the number of Iraqi dead were smaller? Is there some point at which a balance is reached – so much security for my children equals a pile of dead Iraqis just this high, but not higher?

What Morality Is Not

Even to consider these issues, we need to begin with some notion of just what morality – ethics, obligation – is. That's easy, one might say. Morality is what one should do. But, obviously, this merely rephrases the dilemma. What constitutes this "should"? What defines it, and how do we know about it? One way of filling in the statement is to say that it is what one should do as opposed to something else. But as opposed to what? What one would like to do, perhaps. So, the idea of ethics stands in contrast with the idea of self-interest. That is fine. But here another question arises – just what is self-interest, insofar as it is opposed to ethics? Suppose the poet really wants to do something that will improve the life of the aged beggar woman. It's not that he wants to impress someone or get a tax break. He really wants to do something beneficial. He'll feel good after doing so, and he knows that – specifically, he knows that he will feel relief, due to his empathic sense of the deprivations in her life, which are made worse by the difficulties of her advanced age.[3] The anticipation of feeling relief provides the primary motivation for him to help her, whether he thinks of it that way or not. Does that mean that acting to benefit this woman falls outside the

---

[2] See, for example, Cole and Lobel.

[3] Note that, a feeling of pride in his action would be different. Specifically, pride may be problematic in establishing a moral hierarchy in which he views himself as superior to the beggar woman. This is likely to be obvious in his behavior and may, in turn, cause the woman emotional harm, perhaps even overbalancing the material benefits of the aid. We will turn to some issues of this sort in the following chapter.

realm of ethics because it partakes of self-interest? Perhaps some people would say so. But, I suspect, most of us would not. Doing something to genuinely improve an old, homeless, destitute woman's condition remains a moral act even if one feels empathic relief after doing so.

On the other hand, there is something to the contrast with self-interest. We all know that moral dilemmas commonly arise when we strongly want to do something for ourselves, but also feel that we should do something else. The problem, perhaps, is that the idea of self-interest is too vague. Alternatively, it may be ambiguous, comprising discernible sorts of self-interest, some of which contrast with morality whereas others do not. One possible response here is to isolate a semantic field, a set of related but distinct concepts or ideas that will help us delimit the proper extent of ethics.

Within the Indic tradition, such a semantic field has already been isolated in the *puruṣārthas*, the goals of life. Ancient Indic writers isolated four broad motivating forces for human action: *kāma*, *artha*, *mokṣa*, and *dharma*. Kāma is pleasure, more exactly sensory pleasure, and prototypically sexual pleasure. Artha is wealth and power. More generally, we might say that kāma is physical enjoyment whereas artha is social enjoyment – enjoyment of position, authority, means. Mokṣa is "release," specifically freedom from rebirth, but more generally the liberation given through inner peace, through being undisturbed by the changing world. Dharma is, of course, duty, ethics, morality. Its subtypes and details are developed with great rigor and precision in the Indian tradition. But what does it mean broadly – duty, ethics? Contrastively, it means a motive force that is not kāma, not artha, and not mokṣa.

There are two ways in which the contrasts in this semantic field are commonly, if tacitly, understood. The first is through strict negation. Dharma, in this construal, excludes kāma and/or artha, and/or even mokṣa. Different approaches to ethics tend to emphasize one or another contrast, but all have a similar effect. In each case, the primary content of ethics is (emphatically) *not* following some particular, alternative goal. Cross-culturally, the most common contrastive definition bears on kāma – first of all, in its prototypical sense of sexual pleasure. In this view, the peak of moral achievement is chastity; the nadir of moral depravity is promiscuity. Kāma may also be understood in its broader sense of pleasure. In this case, morality becomes renunciation of pleasure; its opposite is hedonism. The ethical paradigm is, then, the ascetic.

Artha may be understood primarily as wealth or primarily as power. In either case, the resulting ethics is a matter of self-denial and obedience. When morality is understood as the negation of artha, it is understood as an embrace of poverty and of lowliness, of deference, of accepting one's place in society, renouncing ambition, insolence, pride.

Even mokṣa may be seen as an opposite of ethics, when one pursues one's own spiritual advancement rather than attending to the world and its demands. A striking case of this is the early Hindu prohibition on Śūdras, members of the servant caste, from studying the sacred texts or engaging in certain religious practices – as in the famous story from the *Rāmāyaṇa*: Rumor spread that a Śūdra boy was pursuing spiritual discipline; Rāma, learning of this, went and faced the boy with the accusation; when he confessed the crime, Rāma beheaded him, thus preserving the moral order.[4]

These three approaches might be called "ethics of negation." They take the semantic field of goals – a field explicit in the Indic tradition but implicit in other traditions as well – then define ethics as the opposite of one or more nonethical goals. There is another approach, however. We may call this alternative the ethics of complementarity. In this case, the content of ethics is not the denial of kāma, artha, and mokṣa. Rather, the ethics of complementarity involves a shift in viewpoint. It is a change from concern about one's own achievement of goals to a concern about others' achievement of those goals. It is a genuine turn away from egocentrism toward what might be called "allocentrism," a sort of systematic empathy.

Of course, here too the mere opposition to egocentrism is vacuous without a more specific sense of the semantic field, the alternative goals that might animate our moral action. In this case, also, the puruṣārthas neatly represent ethical practices. The most common complementary ethics concerns artha, first of all with respect to wealth. The moral ideal of complementary artha is the person who feeds the hungry and houses the homeless. In other versions, that ideal is an entire society that provides for those who are least able, a society that protects its members against impoverishment. This form of ethics may also address artha in the sense of social authority. In that case, the highest practices of ethics are those that empower others. Obviously, these moralities may be manifest in various ways. In their more narrowly personal versions,

---

[4] See cantos 73–76 of the "Uttara Kāṇḍa."

they involve charity and respect. In more social versions, they may manifest themselves in movements for socialism and democracy.

The complementary ethics of artha are related to the complementary ethics of kāma, but only to a very limited degree. The experience of pleasure is commonly built on the absence of pain (for example, enjoyment of food is a pleasure that includes the overcoming of hunger). The complementary ethics of artha tends to focus on the extinction of need or suffering rather than the provision of enjoyment. But there is an ethics of enjoyment as well, a complementary ethics of kāma. When we seek to free people to pursue their sexual desires (e.g., in opposing restrictions on gay or lesbian relations) or even to cultivate their capacities in art, sports, or elsewhere, we are concerning ourselves with their pleasure. Due to its direct contradiction of the policing tendencies of most negative ethics, the complementary ethics of kāma is viewed by many people as scandalously unethical. In keeping with this, in the West, it has been associated with countercultural trends. Indeed, the complementary ethics of kāma is nicely summarized in the 1960s slogan, "Make love, not war."

The complementary view appears also with respect to mokṣa. In this case, the ethical ideal is not someone who pursues his/her own peace, but someone who pursues the peace of others. A paradigmatic case of this is the bodhisattva in Mahāyāna Buddhism. The bodhisattva renounces his or her own release from the world of suffering so that he or she can aid all other creatures in achieving liberation.

Tagore probably never formulated an account of ethics along these lines. Nonetheless, it seems reasonable to characterize his implicit moral view as complementarist – indeed, complementarist on all three axes – and as opposed to the morality of negation. Indeed, many features of his work could be illuminated by an analysis in these terms. However, the crucial task in the present context is not explicating Tagore per se, but rather exploring some of the moral (and emotional) issues raised by his poem. We have made a start in distinguishing negative and complementarist ethics. But this is far from resolving any moral issue. Suppose we opt for complementarist ethics. There remain complications and contradictions in this approach. In the case of mokṣa, for example, we may be inclined to admire the ethical ideal of the bodhisattva; but we may have less benevolent feelings for the proselytizing zealot, who also follows a complementary ethics of spiritual salvation.

More exactly, there are two issues that arise once one has chosen a complementary ethics. First, there are different ways in which the

228 What Literature Teaches Us about Emotion

complementarity may be articulated, with different results. How, then, should we formulate our ethical commitments? Second, for any given formulation, we are likely to encounter conflicting interests and obligations. How do we resolve these? We should briefly consider these two problems in turn.

The Development of Ethics

There are three obvious components to an action, thus three obvious ways of evaluating an action, whether the evaluation is ethical or not. These components are the intention of the actor, the form of the action itself, and the effects of the action. Suppose I see someone leaving behind her purse at a riverside café. I pick up the purse, then run after her. Unfortunately, I crash into the waiter who is hurrying out the door from the kitchen. The collision causes me to inadvertently toss the purse out into the river. For a moment, I am crestfallen – but then there is a great explosion in the water. My intention was to return the purse. My action was throwing the purse in the river. The effect was saving everyone at the café from a terrorist attack. Obviously, each component is relevant to certain sorts of ethical and nonethical evaluation. However, different ethical systems have tended to stress one component or another. It may seem at first that intention is the most crucial component no matter what. After all, in this case, I can presumably be credited with intending to return the purse. But I cannot be blamed for throwing the purse in the river or praised for saving the lives of the café patrons. This apportionment of merit derives from the fact that I only intended to return the purse. However, this is not quite right. The value of my intention is parasitic on the value of something that I envision as resulting from the intention – either the act itself or the consequences of the act. My intention to return the purse is a morally right intention only if the envisioned action or the envisioned result is morally good.[5] Put differently, when I am determining what would be the right thing to do, I do not ask, "What would be a good intention?"; rather, I ask, "What would be a morally good act?" or, alternatively, "What would have morally valuable consequences?"

For these reasons, ethical theories have tended to stress the act itself or consequences of the act. Some systems articulate broad principles

---

[5] There are complications here regarding what we might reasonably expect the action or outcome to be, but we can leave those aside.

that determine the intrinsic moral quality of actions (Kantian ethics is one paradigm of this kind). Others emphasize the calculus of morally relevant effects (Utilitarian ethics is the best known case of this sort).

We cannot go into the arguments for these positions. However, the crucial point here is that, in coming to ethical decisions, most of us rely on both intrinsic evaluations and calculations of effect. We judge the intrinsic morality or immorality of different possible actions (e.g., telling the truth versus lying in a tenure evaluation). We judge what we can reasonably infer about the likely outcomes of these actions (e.g., "If I truthfully tell the tenure committee what I think his scholarship, Jones may lose his job"). We then judge what force the intrinsic value of the actions should have relative to their likely outcomes in the case at hand. In short, our everyday approach to ethical decisions is pragmatic. It is not a matter of following a consistent philosophical line.[6]

Of course, even the complex interaction of intrinsic principles and consequentialist calculations is not all there is to our quotidian ethical pragmatism. If we treat morality in purely Kantian and Utilitarian terms, we leave out something that is central to our moral evaluations in real life. Indeed, we leave out what is almost certainly the most important part of everyday moral decision. That is, of course, emotion. We decide on what is right or wrong by looking at acts and at consequences and feeling something about them. Suppose I am presented with evidence that corporal punishment in schools does, on the whole, produce better behavior in school children, thus a better atmosphere for learning. (As far as I know, this is not true. But suppose for the moment it is.) I might nonetheless imagine the practice and feel that it is "not worth the price." Phrasing it in terms of "price" may seem to suggest that I arrived at my decision by abstract calculation, separating out ethical costs and ethical benefits. However, in all likelihood, my response was not a result of ethical calculation. It was rather the result of my feelings about a complex of conditions and events – including the intended outcome and the stated means.[7] Moreover, this response was based not on

---

[6] For example, this pragmatic approach seems to characterize Hauser's respondents. Faced with questions about saving some people by harming others, they apparently consider both the overall outcome and the intrinsic morality or immorality of the actions.

[7] As the model of Chapter 2 would lead us to expect, our moral response is also a function of prior, "incidental" emotional arousal, that is, arousal caused by irrelevant factors (see Horberg and colleagues 972 on disgust). Presumably one function of moral reflection is to inhibit the consequences of such incidental arousals.

abstract inferences, but on concrete imagination (brief and spontaneous or sustained and effortful) and on links with emotional memory.

It is worth noting here that by the perceptual account of emotion, the role of our emotion systems should extend to many aspects of moral decision, such as spontaneous causal attribution or blame. This is, it seems, precisely what we find. The point is suggested by some of Hauser's research, though Hauser's interpretation of his data is different. For example, when faced with a moral dilemma of sacrificing one person to save five others, people tend to say that pushing Jones in front of a tram (to keep the tram from hitting five other people) is more morally blameworthy than switching the tracks of a tram so that it hits Jones (see 128). One plausible account of these data would suggest that this difference is a matter of emotion-guided causal attribution and related emotional tendencies toward self-blame (not Hauser's innate morality module). These tendencies bear on such emotion variables as degree of physical contact, temporal proximity, and salience. Thus, we are more likely to engage in ethical/emotional self-blame if our action involves close physical contact with the victim, his or her suffering follows in near proximity, and his or her suffering is highly salient – as in pushing someone to death rather than shifting the tracks of a tram. (The point is suggested by Oatley, Keltner, and Jenkins when they explain that, in one option, "the participant must imagine using his or her own hands to push the stranger to his gruesome death" [285].)

Similar points apply to the perceptual projection and working anticipation aspects of emotional response. Again, Hauser's data are relevant, and here too an emotion-based analysis suggests alternatives to Hauser's account. Specifically, it seems extremely unlikely that respondents fully adhere to the premises of Hauser's examples. For Hauser's cases to work, we need everyone to believe with complete emotional certainty that, for example, pushing Jones in front of the tram will prevent the tram from killing other people. Respondents almost certainly imagine possible outcomes of this chain of events and tacitly include the possibility of failure, despite the certainty expressed in the formulation of the cases. Thus, they are judging a case where it is possible for us to sacrifice Jones while not managing to save the others. (In contrast, a failure in switching the tracks seems less likely and it does not worsen the initial situation.) This once again suggests that our moral evaluations derive from our emotional responses to concretely experienced and/or imagined situations.

Hauser's studies are certainly valuable. They suggest important points about the nature of moral response. Of course, like all research data, they are ambiguous, as the alternative interpretations suggest. It would take us too far away from the topic of emotion and literature to explore the possibilities and problems of this research, but one further point is relevant here. Perhaps the greatest limitations of Hauser's research are the same as the problems with all research based on such brief, imaginary, forced-choice scenarios – "trolleyology," as a colleague of my calls it. They simply have no ecological validity. They require people to imagine scenarios that they would never experience – or, if they did experience, would do so in much more detailed and extended contexts. These problems particularly highlight the richly developed detail of literary stories. Again, literary stories have problems too. The point is not to reject philosophers' anecdotes, but to make room for a variety of approaches and data.

Returning to ethical theory, we find that, of course, Kant and Utilitarianism have not been the only options. An affective approach to ethics may be found as well. Adam Smith's treatment of moral sentiments is probably the most famous instance of this approach; it also figures in the work of some contemporary neuro-ethicists, who emphasize the importance of empathic response in the origins and development of moral agency.[8] Moreover, attention to emotion is not incompatible with principled or calculative approaches. Indeed, a model incorporating all three seems to make the most sense. Emotional response provides the fundamental, motivational force for our action. However, that emotional response takes as its objects the action in question and the consequences of that action. Our concern with the intrinsic value of actions, crystallized in moral principles, and with the calculation of consequences may lead us to expand and systematize our otherwise limited imagination of those actions and consequences. In any case, it is likely to alter our elaborations in some ways. As a result, it is likely to change our emotional response.

Conflicts of Feeling

Unfortunately, this does not yet solve our problem. Indeed, in some ways, it intensifies it. Perhaps many different types of feeling can have

[8] See, for example, Prinz.

a moral function. Moreover, any given situation may give rise to many different sorts of feeling – and their consequences for action may be mutually exclusive. Thus, we are brought back to ethical contradiction, or rather a particular form of ethical contradiction – the conflict of emotion. For example, we may feel disgusted at cowardly collaboration with cruelty, but we may also feel compassion for those same collaborationists when their complicity is due to fear. Moreover, this conflict is not a simple and unalterable fact of our spontaneous response. We may cultivate certain emotional responses (e.g., disgust and anger) and inhibit others (e.g., empathy or compassion). In the long run, we may develop our moral sensibility toward greater indignation, disdain, pride, sympathy. But which should we choose in cases of incompatibility? How should we direct or seek to form our moral sensibility?

To discuss this more fruitfully, it may be worth considering for a moment precisely which feelings do, or should, enter into moral judgment. Here, we might return to our initial idea of the moral as the nonegocentric, an idea that we developed into the notion of ethical complementarity. If the morally relevant emotions are not egocentric, then just what are they? To understand goals, we turned to ancient Indic tradition (with its delimitation of the puruṣārthas). To understand nonegocentric emotions, we may do the same. The Indic tradition has a large body of theory that deals with such emotions. It is not ethical theory, but aesthetic theory. Specifically, what the Indian aesthetic tradition calls *rasa* is precisely this nonegocentric emotion. It is emotion that we feel, not on our own behalf, but on behalf of others.

The original rasa theorists gave a list of eight primary rasas: erotic, comic, pathetic, furious, terrible, odious, marvelous, and heroic. We can easily imagine ethical functions for most of these. We have already noted the odious (a feeling of disgust) and the pathetic (a feeling of compassion). We may be angry (thus experience the furious) at cruelty; fearful (experiencing the terrible) at the prospect of devastating moral outcomes, and so forth. Whereas any rasa may have an ethical function, it seems to be the case that most practical ethical systems – systems that seek to train people's moral sensibilities in particular ways – stress one or two. Indeed, this is almost invariably the case. It is unsurprising, given the fact that emotional responses often contradict one another. A hierarchy of emotions resolves that problem. Historically, two or three rasas tend to have dominated practical ethical systems. Specifically, militaristic ethics – unsurprisingly, a prominent feature of every dominant society – value the heroic sentiment; they may also cultivate anger and disgust for the enemy. In direct opposition to militaristic ethics, we have what might be called "humanitarian ethics," which cultivates the pathetic rasa, sensitivity to other people's suffering.[9]

Tagore made ethical use of a wide range of rasas in his works. For example, there are scenes that provoke indignation, thus the furious, as when ordinary Indians are humiliated in *Gora*. But this anger is, I believe, always muted. It is rarely, if ever, sustained. It is rarely, if ever, the focal point that would serve as a central ethical emotion. There are characters – for example, Indians who mimic the British and disdain other Indians – who inspire the odious sentiment or disgust. However, this disgust is mitigated by other factors – sometimes mirth, sometimes compassion. There is heroism, but it is of an unusual sort. For example, in *The Home and the World*, it is the very nonmilitaristic Nikhil who exhibits heroism, whereas the militant Sandip behaves in a cowardly way.

One might think that Tagore's central ethical emotion is compassion, that he tacitly adopts one of the two main theoretical approaches to emotion and morality – liberal humanitarianism. Of course, there is an element of that in Tagore. But there is something that is fundamentally not very pathetic about most of Tagore's suffering characters (one may think, for example, of the defiant widow, Binodini, in *Chokher Bali*). They are not, generally, objects of simple pity on our part, and Tagore does not encourage the sense of superiority that often seems to go along with humanitarian ethics.[10]

Let us return for a moment to the poem with which we began. What do we feel for the daughter? Compassion, yes. But there is something more that I suspect most readers feel. We want Tagore to pick her up and hold her or, barring that, we want to pick her up and hold ourselves. We do not simply want to do something nice, something good. I at least feel something for this imagined child that is both empathy and

---

[9] It is important to stress that rasa theory is not fundamentally a matter of ethics. This is important because it suggests that Indian tradition may be somewhat less moralistic than much Western tradition, following Plato. On the other hand, there are aspects of the tradition of rasa analysis that lend themselves to ethical, and even political, use. For example, there is an egalitarian impulse at the foundation of Indian aesthetic theory. The lowest caste was traditionally excluded from the Vedas or sacred texts. Thus the Veda of drama – Bharatamuni's *Nāṭya Śāstra* – was divinely created to be "common to all the . . . castes" (2). Aesthetic value is in this way the one universal value in this tradition, the one value that is not shared out unequally, based on social hierarchy. Moreover, as such, "it will serve as a guide in all (human) activities" (2).

[10] We will consider pity and compassion more fully in the final chapter.

deeply ego-relevant. I want her to be happy because, incomprehensibly, I care about her. Indeed, temporarily, I care about her in the way that the poet himself cares about her. In other words, I care about her in the way a parent cares about a child. This feeling was not present in the initial list of rasas – but it was added later. It is *"vātsalya,"* parent/child affection, or what we have been discussing under the name of "attachment." This rasa was a prominent one in Indian literature. It is arguably the emotional center of Tagore's tacit ethics.[11]

However, this immediately returns us to the issue of just who is the proper object of our ethical obligations. Think again of the beggar woman with her tattered cloth. Why should the world of such a woman have any ethical claim on the poet? If attachment is at the core of one's ethical system, shouldn't one's obligations be only to those with whom one shares attachment relations – children, parents, siblings, friends? But doesn't that, then, risk reducing all ethics to an extended form of self-interest? This is not, I believe, what Tagore implies. In Tagore's work, it seems clear that we have obligations in the home and obligations in the world. To consider this, we need to return to the issue of equal ethical pull versus differential ethical pull.

Conflicts of Obligation

Conflicts between types of dharma have been of deep concern in Indic tradition. For example, the *Bhagavad Gītā* begins with Arjuna taking up a specific ethical issue – what does one do when one's familial dharma (i.e., one's duty to kin), conflicts with one's caste dharma (i.e., roughly, one's duty as a member of a particular occupational group). Such a conflict arises here, for the *Gītā* concerns a war between Kṣatriyas (i.e., members of the ruling/warrior caste) who are also from the same family. Western tradition has paid attention to this issue as well. One key aspect of such conflict is whether our ethical obligations are shared out equally among all people or are stronger for some people than for others. Here we might consider the following hypothetical situation, a version of which has been discussed by a number of writers. You are on a field trip to the beach with your daughter's grade school. The children have been warned to stay out of the water. Despite constant supervision, two naughty children – one of whom is your daughter – make

---

[11] For further discussion of ethics and attachment in Tagore, touching on a broader range of works, see Hogan "Reading Tagore Today."

it out into the water. You hear cries for help. You look up and realize that both children are drowning. There is time to save only one.
Whom do you choose? Many people respond that they will save their
own child, and many people believe that this is not only the natural
response, but the morally right response. This is sometimes called the
"common-sense" view,[12] and examples of this sort are often taken to
count against the "equal pull hypothesis." In this common-sense view,
our moral obligations are not the same for everyone. They are stronger for our own children than for other people's children.[13] The issue
obviously has bearing on ethical judgment in general; it has particular
bearing on an ethics of attachment.

Despite common views, however, it may be that this example does
not, in fact, get us very far in determining what ethical obligations
really are. First, we may share intuitions about this case. But what is to
say that our intuitions should determine our ethical evaluations? After
all, our spontaneous decisions – uninflected by moral deliberation –
are based on, precisely, our intuitive/emotional response to situations.
Faced with the two drowning children, many people might never even
think of this as an ethical dilemma. Emotionally, they would be driven
to save their own daughter – while perhaps shouting for someone else
to save the other child. The purpose of ethical theory is to help us think
through the relevant issues to determine if we should perhaps inhibit
our spontaneous intuitive/emotional response in particular cases.
One key way of doing this is by cultivating other sorts of emotional
sensitivity – thus, in effect, changing our intuitions (through effortful
elaborative processing).[14] In this way, it seems wrong-headed to rely
too heavily on spontaneous intuition in making theoretical judgments
about ethical issues.

---

[12] See Bok 40.

[13] Some writers argue, not only that the differential pull hypothesis is wrong, but even
that it misrepresents common intuitions (see Nussbaum "Patriotism" 13). Nussbaum
presents what is, in my view, a compelling case for the equal-pull hypothesis.

[14] Note that this is not a matter of choosing reason over emotion or of otherwise putting
emotion and reason in opposition with one another. Theoretical reflection leads us to
consider the ways we should understand and imagine the ethical situation – for example, the degree to which we should envision other people's pain – before making our
decision. But that decision nonetheless remains based on emotional response. In other
words, our elaboration changes in specific instances, but this altered elaboration has
effects only insofar as it changes our developing emotional response in those instances.
Far from being opposed to emotion, reason or elaborative inference must be integrated
with emotion if it is to have any consequences.

On the other hand, few of us would be prepared to say that there really is equal pull, that it doesn't matter which drowning child one saves, or that, to return to our poem, the poet's obligation to the old beggar-woman is the same as his obligation to his daughter.[15] The preceding analyses point us in the direction of at least a partial solution. Complementarist ethics leads us to be concerned with the goals of others. A focus on attachment as a – perhaps the – key ethical emotion tells us not simply that we should give parent/child feelings a prominent place in our own ethical decisions; it tells us specifically that we should (empathically) recognize and value the attachment relations of others. This valuing of someone else's attachment necessarily changes my precise obligation in particular cases. When my daughter and someone else, both drowning, see me on the shore, both hope to be saved. But if I were to choose the other child, my daughter would not only drown; her final moments would be further embittered by a sense of betrayal. My own recognition of her attachment changes the ethical situation.[16] The point applies not only to children.

How, then, does attachment bear on people to whom we are not related? For example, how does it bear on the old woman with the tattered cloth in Tagore's poem? The preceding analysis suggests that our moral self-cultivation should, perhaps, focus first and foremost on vātsalya, attachment or affection – not pity, not heroism, not disgust. Yet this is not a matter of our own personal attachment. Moral training here is complementarist. Our moral focus, then, should be on others. In keeping with this, our complementarist response operates in two ways, parallel to being the object or subject of an attachment bond. First, we are concerned about others in the way that we are concerned about our own personal objects of attachment – our children, parents, spouses, siblings, friends. Thus we are concerned about their well-being in the

---

[15] In part, this is just a matter of socially assigned responsibility. I have far more socially assigned responsibility for my children than for other people's children. There is a parallel situation if I am assigned responsibility for children in group A and not group B. When one child from each group is drowning, I presumably have greater obligation to the former. But this does not fully resolve the problem: What happens if one child from group A is drowning, but the other child is my daughter?

[16] This idea may have some intuitive appeal as well. We might imagine this variation on the situation. We have the same outing. My daughter is not one of the drowning children. However, I am wearing the same swimming trunks as the father of one of the girls. I am also roughly his height and build. That girl is shouting, "Daddy, help!" clearly mistaking me for her father. The other girl is simply shouting "Help!" realizing that I am not her father. My guess is that most people would incline toward my saving the first girl rather than the second.

same way. Second, we are concerned about their attachment bonds. This is important because it recognizes their fuller humanity as subjects, not reducing them to children as mere objects of attachment. In both ways, our response is a function of our concrete imagination of other people's condition. Our own personal attachments – stored as emotional memories – add empathic urgency and depth of feeling to that moral imagination.

In this way, the poem we have been considering may be seen as an exercise in training our ethical sentiments. The old woman is parallel with the child; she is also parallel with the world, filled as it is with suffering, and identified by Tagore as our mother (84). We should understand her and respond to her, not with patronizing pity, but with the affection we have for a mother or a child and with the concern we have for the affections of a mother or a child. In short, the poet's emotional interests rightly lead him to the deep love he feels for this particular girl, his own daughter. But at the same time, they take him beyond the child to the larger world, to other children in the world, and to mothers, sisters, fathers, brothers in that world. The daughter and the beggar woman, the home and the world, are not fully the same, but their analogy is so close that one cannot reasonably feel for or respond ethically to one without feeling for and responding ethically to the other.

This point is, of course, not limited to our own society – national, religious, ethnic, or whatever. It has profound consequences for our relation to the larger world as well. In a time of war, with its celebration of militaristic ethics, this is perhaps particularly obvious and pressing. We might conclude this part of our analysis with a brief quotation from another poem, a poem also about ethics and vātsalya. The poem begins, "When I heard pigeons cooing in the trees,/Hot tears covered my face.//When the lark chirped, my thoughts composed/A message for my son.... Mohammad, do not forget me." The poem is by Sami al Haj – at the time of writing, a prisoner in the U.S. government detention facility at Guantanamo Bay.

Attachment, Disgust, and the Dynamics of Moral Emotions

We have been considering moral orientations in relation to a small number of distinct emotions – anger, attachment, and so forth. But, of course, emotion systems do not operate in isolation from one another. They interact. Before going on to Shakespeare, it is important to say a few words about the interaction among moral emotions.

Leaving aside a few pathological cases, we all have all these emotions. Individually, we may be more inclined to one emotion than another. Thus, we may be more inclined to one form of ethical response. However, it is unlikely that we are entirely consistent and univocal either in emotional responses or in associated ethical responses. Jones may be more inclined to respond with compassion and attachment, whereas Smith is more inclined toward anger and heroic energy. But it is unlikely that Jones is entirely lacking in anger or Smith in compassion. The interactions among emotion systems are important both for understanding the relatively stable propensities of our individual emotional and ethical responses and our individual variability in reaction to particular experiences. The emotion systems that bear on our ethical reactions tend to differ due to different response propensities (e.g., moods) and different eliciting conditions, with the eliciting conditions sometimes differentiated further by biases in subjective construal.

Here we might consider, for example, anger and fear. When anger operates as the dominant moral emotion, it is centrally a response to perceived harm. (For ease of exposition, I will speak here in functional terms. Again, the emotional force of an "appraisal" derives from its perceptual, imaginative, and mnemonic incidentals, not from its inferential or probabilistic logic.[17]) Instances range from the experience of physical hurt to the belief that one has unfairly lost a job. Its actional response is commonly aggression against the object, though it may involve confrontation that falls short of aggression. It is most obviously associated with reciprocity-based moral systems, such as the *lex talionis* (e.g., "an eye for an eye"), which help guide reflective elaboration.

Anger-based moral orientations tend to be highly punitive and oriented toward violence. These tendencies are enhanced when the fear system is activated as well. Fear involves the anticipation of future harm or frustration and thus necessarily goes beyond reciprocity for past actions. It involves the need for prevention of possible hurts. The most certain prevention comes from the elimination of the threatening

---

[17] One reader of this manuscript felt that my speaking in terms of appraisal shows that there is not really a difference between appraisal and perceptual accounts of emotion. This is not true. However, it is almost always easier to speak in terms of a functional approximation than to speak in terms of precise mechanisms. The situation is somewhat parallel to gravitation. Unless it is necessary to a particular point at issue, no Newtonian or Einsteinian would avoid saying "the apple falls to the ground" or "the sun rises" in order to give more theoretically accurate statements. This does not mean that Aristotelian, Newtonian, and Einsteinian (and common-sense) accounts are all the same.

object. The degree and kind of violence promoted by a given moral orientation is in part a function of the extent to which the fear and anger systems are activated in that case.

Needless to say, inhibition plays a role here also. In the case of anger and fear, the most obvious inhibitions come from empathy. Empathy is not an emotion system per se, but rather a sort of meta-system. It alters the dynamics of our emotion systems by aligning them with the emotions of someone else, at least for the time when we are mirroring the emotional expressions of that other person or effortfully simulating his or her experiences. As such, it tends to inhibit our tendencies toward punitive or preventive violence, while also diminishing our sense of hurt at the actions of others. For example, if someone insults me, empathy may lead me to realize that I had said something earlier that could be taken as a slight to him, thus provoking the insult.

Again, leaving aside sociopaths, we all have anger, fear, and empathy. The proportion of these in any given case will vary with circumstances and with our own enduring propensities. We all have more empathy and less anger with the hungry man who stole a loaf of bread than with the armed robber who shot the poor fellow at the convenience store. However, individually, we may be more or less inclined toward generalized empathy or toward anger and/or fear. Thus, if our propensity is toward greater generalized empathy, we may be more inclined toward forgiveness of the perpetrator, limitation of punishment, alteration of harm-provoking conditions (such as poverty), help of the victim, and so forth. If our propensity is toward greater anger and/or fear, we may be more inclined toward greater blame of the perpetrator, and so forth.[18]

Anger, fear, and empathy form one "cluster" of morally relevant feelings that affect our general predispositions and help guide our judgment in individual cases. There are other clusters as well. A second important cluster has more bearing on our current concerns – that involving attachment and disgust.[19] As just noted, the opposition between anger

---

[18] It seems likely that people vary incrementally across a continuum of such predispositions. In contrast, the moral ideas we use to elaborate these tend to be dichotomous (e.g., fear-or-anger-prone vs. empathy-prone), as the preceding description suggests.

[19] One reader of this discussion suggested similarities with Shweder's tripartite division of moral codes. Shweder and colleagues isolate "three thematic clusters" as "culturally coexisting discourses of morality" (141). The present account is consistent with Shweder's analysis on some points. For example, both accounts claim that moral attitudes tend to cluster together and that the various clusters turn up cross-culturally. Shweder's analysis stresses differences in the degrees to which different cultures stress or downplay different clusters. The present account is broadly compatible with that

and fear on the one hand and empathy on the other has both situational and enduring consequences for moral orientation. The same is true of the opposition between attachment and disgust. Both attachment and disgust focus particularly on the bodies of other people. An ethics of attachment – that is, generalized attachment in the sense suggested by Tagore's poem – focuses, first of all, on others' requirements for life, such as food and shelter, though it is readily extended to desires as well (as in care for sexual minorities). It emphasizes such virtues as nurturance, kindness, corporal works of mercy, and so forth. Put differently, an ethics of attachment tends to be a complementary ethics of both artha and kāma. It is attentive particularly to bodily needs, but it crucially includes needs for human contact, love, and esteem as well. In contrast, an ethics of disgust often focuses on bodily functions, particularly the ejection of substances from the body – feces, semen – or the ingestion of substances into the body. It tends to be concerned with the limitation and/or concealment of these processes in order to limit aversive feelings in others. Thus, as a moral emotion, disgust leads us to emphasize cleanliness and shame. In the case of cleanliness, the physical virtue is extended to a moral virtue, but with a continued reliance on bodily cases. For example, chastity in both deed and thought is a prime case of moral "cleanliness."[20] Put differently, an ethics of disgust

idea. However, Shweder is isolating "discourses," whereas the present account focuses on emotional responses; discourses may represent only part of emotional elaboration – or even mere rationalization. Moreover, there is no clear relation between the clusters presented here and those in Shweder's list. Shweder's first cluster "relies on regulative concepts such as harm, rights, and justice"; his second "relies on regulative concepts such as duty, hierarchy, interdependency, and souls"; his third "relies on regulative concepts such as sacred order, natural order, tradition, sanctity, sin, and pollution" (138). Empathy would probably enter into harm, but also into certain sorts of duty. Anger could enter into justice or hierarchy or sacred order. Fear too could bear on the sacred or hierarchy or justice. In short, there does not seem to be much similarity in the two accounts.

[20] Of course, our moral use of the word "disgust" includes much more than the cases I am considering. As Rozin, Haidt, and McCauley discuss, there is reason to connect a number of these cases with activation of components of the disgust system (762–763). This is important and is something that should be taken into account in a full discussion of disgust. On the other hand, there has been some controversy over whether or not the different types of disgust should all be considered one emotion (see, for example, Simpson and colleagues and Borg, Lieberman, and Kiehl). Moreover, even if we connect them, it is not clear that all cases of "moral disgust" involve the robust activation of the disgust system in the way that we find with cases of bodily "uncleanliness." Alternatively, if they do involve such robust activation, they presumably also involve the activation of emotional memories, the generation of perceptual imaginations, and so forth – all bearing on perceptual cases of disgust. The present discussion is confined to these more central cases.

commonly entails an ethics of negation focused particularly on bodily pleasure, primarily sexual pleasure. However, it may also be extended to needs, such as food, particularly insofar as these needs are associated with pleasure.[21]

Here, too, we all have both tendencies. Few people feel ethically unmoved by images of isolated and hungry infants, and few are ethically unaffected by old men dropping their pants in front of schoolchildren. But just how strongly we react to these and other cases depends on where our usual balance of emotion systems stands. Some of us are much more likely to respond to disgust-provoking components of situations or actions; others are more likely to respond to attachment-based needs.

It is also important to note that the present account differs from the appraisal-based accounts of writers such as Nussbaum. There is certainly an overlap between triggers of disgust and our "animality," as Nussbaum stresses (*Hiding* 89, following Angyal, Rozin, and William Miller). However, the alignment is imperfect (e.g., we do not seem to find hair disgusting in general, nor do we find most aspects of eating disgusting). Moreover, in the present account, our emotional responses are much more fragmentary and inconsistent than any "policing of the boundary between ourselves and nonhuman animals" (89) suggests. Of course, here as elsewhere, the mechanisms involve functional approximations. But the function, in this case, is the avoidance of contaminants (as Nussbaum herself indicates [see 74]), not being animal-like.

[21] One reader pointed out that there are some parallels here with Lakoff's division of moral orientations into the "strict father" and the "nurturant parent." It is true that Lakoff's "strict father" does share some features with anger-related morality and perhaps disgust-related morality. In addition, the "nurturant parent" does share some features with empathic moral response and with attachment-based response. This is unsurprising. We are looking at some of the same phenomena. Thus, the patterns we isolate in the phenomena should have some similarities. However, it should be obvious that the present organization of the data is quite different from Lakoff's. First, there is no one-to-one correspondence between Lakoff's categories and those given here. Some anger-based morality is included in Lakoff's strict-father morality; some disgust-based morality may be included as well. There are also aspects of both categories that fall outside strict-father morality – for example, aspects of disgust over the enjoyment of food (or even sexuality), except insofar as this is added more or less arbitrarily. In connection with this last point, it is not clear that Lakoff's organization of politics into these two tendencies is theoretically well-supported; it seems to be a division into tendencies Lakoff likes and tendencies he dislikes. Personally speaking, I largely agree with Lakoff's preferences. This does not mean, however, that they form theoretically rigorous categories. More importantly, the present account seeks to explain moral divisions motivationally by reference to emotion systems. Indeed, these motivation systems guide the organization of the data. In contrast, Lakoff bases his division on metaphorical structures. He is probably correct that these particular familial metaphors do play a role in our thought about morality and politics at certain times. However, it is far from clear that these metaphors are as ubiquitous and dominant as Lakoff indicates. In contrast, it does seem clear that our emotion systems are ubiquitous and dominant in ethical and political motivation.

Given the nature of disgust, there are only a few categories of objects that may serve as paradigms for disgust. These are often bodily products, such as feces and sperm, or related actions, such as defecation and sexual intercourse. They also include anything that is decayed. Any of these can give rise to moral dispute. For example, the precise treatment of corpses (e.g., whether it is proper to bury or cremate them) can be disputed on moral grounds. However, given the nature of human interests and actions, these are less likely to be matters of moral concern than matters of prudential concern or cultural convention. Among objects of disgust, it appears that those related to sex are the most intensively regulated and those that give rise to the most intense moral revulsion. In keeping with the intensity of disgust-based moral revulsion relating to sex, Nussbaum notes the importance of disgust to homophobia and misogyny (see, for example, 205, 347).[22] At the same time, sexuality and attachment are mutually enhancing systems. Thus an attachment orientation is likely to produce a morally benevolent view of sexuality – in direct opposition to a disgust orientation.

An interesting aspect of this opposition regarding sexual morality is that it is rarely provoked by direct perceptual experience. People who oppose homosexuality – or, for that matter, premarital or other forms

---

[22] Indeed, disgust is connected with nonsexual prejudices as well. As Rozin, Haidt, and McCauley point out, "disgust sensitivity is positively correlated with negative attitudes" to a wide range of out-groups (770). These prejudices operate in part by way of associations between despised groups and filth, vermin, and so on. Thus Kathleen Taylor reports research suggesting that "extreme prejudice ... may be distinguished by high levels of disgust" (597). This leads her to predict that "minority groups who transgress (or who are believed to transgress) majority social codes in disgust-sensitive domains – for example, food, sex, waste disposal – are more likely to be targets of extreme hostility, atrocities and genocide than those who do not" (613). Conversely, people who have particularly strong disgust sensitivity, particularly interpersonal contamination, "are predisposed to prejudice" (Hodson and Costello 696).

It is worth noting that Hodson and Costello distinguish between core disgust and interpersonal disgust. In support of this division, they point out that "people are disgusted even by sterilized objects associated with undesirable others" (693). From an appraisal point of view, that is an argument for a division. However, given the framework presented in Chapter 2, this is just what we would expect. The evaluation of the objects as contaminating is not rational in the sense that we will not get any disease from such objects. But our disgust does not result from such rational calculations; it results from images and emotional memories. Moreover, in the case of someone such as Hitler (a standard example in this context), we would not expect any modulation of this disgust response through elaborative processing. Finally, the perceptual account seems to fit the more complex profile of "moral disgust" as incorporating a number of different emotions in "appraisal" – or, in our terms, elaboration processes – as discussed in work by Simpson and colleagues.

of non-normative sexuality – do not typically do so because they are seeing or have seen anyone engaging in these sorts of sex. Their disgust is not the direct disgust of smelling something rotten. In this way, the initiation and extension of their disgust response must be largely or even entirely the product of their own imaginative elaboration. Thus, those who reject sexuality on the basis of disgust are probably the ones who imaginatively dwell on sex most fully. This is in keeping with the well-known finding that homophobia is connected with an inclination toward "significant sexual arousal to male homosexual erotic stimuli" (Adams, Wright, and Lohr, 443).

Thus, we might expect to find that sexual tolerance is associated with attachment-based attitudes whereas sexual intolerance is founded on disgust responses. Moreover, we might expect the latter to be bound up with an attentional and imaginative focus on and elaboration of sexuality. Finally, we might suspect that, in many cases, a person's morally damning attentional and imaginative focus is driven in part by his or her own sexual desires. Of course, in these cases, the disgust should inhibit the desire – and it presumably does most of the time. But in some contexts, the inhibition may go in the opposite direction (with desire inhibiting disgust). This may lead to apparently hypocritical self-indulgence on the part of moral rigorists.

To understand these points more fully, we might now turn to *Measure for Measure*.

Love and Contempt in a Time of Syphilis: Shakespeare's *Measure for Measure*

Shakespeare's *Measure for Measure* begins with the Duke of Vienna turning over his authority to his deputy, Angelo. Specifically, the Duke grants Angelo control over "Mortality and mercy in Vienna" (I.i.44) and the power "to enforce or qualify the laws" (I.i.65). We learn subsequently that the Duke had, for some years, not enforced laws restricting sexuality. It is Angelo's job to rectify this situation. But the Duke's phrases – "Mortality and mercy," "enforce or qualify" – suggest that the point is to arrive at some sort of reasonable equilibrium between tolerance and rigor.

Since the play is apparently going to advocate a shift toward chastity and away from license, it makes sense that the next scene should activate disgust with respect to sexuality. On the one hand, the scene is comic. But much of the comedy is based on suggestions of venereal

244 What Literature Teaches Us about Emotion

disease. Referring to Mistress Overdone, Lucio, with the help of a bystander, explains that he has "purchased as many diseases under her roof as come to ... three thousand dolors" (I.ii.46–47, 50), thus three thousand dollars or three thousand sorrows. The pun makes the line comic, but the idea is hardly comic at all. This and other references in the course of the play suggest a concern about the spread of venereal disease, fostered by prostitution and other nonmarital sexual relations. This reflects worries of many people in Shakespeare's London. Indeed, there were attempts to put an end to prostitution as a means of curbing the spread of venereal disease (see Siena 559). Moreover, as Kevin Siena shows, at the time, writings on venereal disease often operated to raise alarm about sexual practices. For our purposes, the key importance of these writings is that they served to foster disgust. Of course, any imagination of sexuality would become more repugnant by the association of sex with symptoms of syphilis, such as rashes, "mucous membrane lesions," and "patchy hair loss,"[23] not to mention gonorrhea and "other urethral and genital complaints," that were at issue during the period (Siena 556). This response was enhanced by the ways in which writers characterized sexuality. For example, Siena quotes one late-sixteenth-century work that warns the reader about the dangers of contact with "the Pocky Streams of the diseased woman" (559).

In this way, the initial setting of the play may increase audience sympathy with characters who follow a disgust-based morality. But this enhanced sympathy is quickly undermined. Claudio has been imprisoned and will be killed in three days. His crime was "getting Madam Julietta with child" (I.ii.74). Now, audience members may be shocked by the severity of the judgment – death as a punishment for sex. Clearly, this is not a morality of anger based on some sort of parallel between the crime and the punishment. It is an annihilation of something repugnant, just what one would expect from a disgust-based morality.[24]

---

[23] U.S. Department of Health and Human Services, Centers for Disease Control and Prevention; http://www.cdc.gov/std/syphilis/STDFact-Syphilis.htm#symptoms (accessed March 18, 2009).

[24] In keeping with this, Taylor notes, "Disgust may prompt ... attempts to remove the disgusting stimulus" (598). Moreover, Wheatley and Haidt note that feelings of disgust lead test subjects "to rate transgressions as more morally wrong" (781). They then go on to rationalize these judgments (783). Jones and Fitness report research showing that disgust sensitivity led to an increased sense of the frequency of crime in the community, an increased inclination to "attribute evilness" to suspects, and an increased tendency to recommend harsh punishments (613; for the properties tested, an inclination to anger did not produce these results [619], indicating again that this is not a case of anger, but of disgust). Moreover, Jones and Fitness conjecture that this inclination may

Moreover, the act of killing Claudio is an act of depriving a wife of her husband and a child of its father. The morality enacted by Angelo is, then, a morality that is sharply and directly opposed to attachment relations. Indeed, in this case, its effects are the precise opposite of a morality of attachment of the sort we discussed in relation to Tagore.

Somewhat surprisingly, when Claudio is introduced, he explains his condemnation with imagery saturated in disgust. He confesses that he has acted too freely and parallels himself with a rat devouring poison (I.ii.132). The metaphor compares the sexually active Claudio to a rat – a highly disgust-inducing creature – and the act of sex itself to ingesting something that should be disgusting to us, poison. It is as if Claudio has here given us, not his own analogy for sex, but that of Angelo or anyone who advocates a rigid, disgust-based sexual morality. Claudio goes on to explain that, in fact, he and Juliet were as good as wed, only they had kept their relation secret due to concerns over the dowry. Finally, Claudio speaks of his sister, Isabella, who is about to enter the nunnery, thus renouncing sex forever. As an exemplar of chastity, she is a sort of ideal for a disgust-based morality. Thus, she seems particularly well placed to plead with Angelo for Claudio's life. Claudio asks Lucio to appeal to her for aid.

The Duke soon begins to pose as a Friar in order to covertly observe the development of his plan. His first statement about this disguise is that he is unaffected by "the dribbling dart of love" (I.iii.2). Thus, the suggestion is that, like Isabella, the Duke may be an exemplar of chastity. Moreover, the *"dribbling* dart" (emphasis added) suggests venereal infection, thus disgust. The Duke then speaks of Angelo as a "man of ... firm abstinence" (I.iii.12). The division of characters seems set, then. There are the promiscuous and disease-ridden prostitutes, pimps, and libertines on the one hand and the holy and chaste men and women on the other. But things are not that simple. The Duke explains his dilemma. There is sexual liberty because he has followed the practices of "fond fathers" who have "bound up the threat'ning twigs of birch,/Only to stick it in their children's sight/For terror, not to use" (I.iii.43–46). In short, he has followed an ethics of attachment and empathy, but he has done so too unreservedly. He feels that he must provide a corrective balance by invoking the alternatives. The choice of

be generalized in the case of crimes that are widely viewed as intrinsically disgusting (623). Angelo's dehumanization of Claudio, evident in the lack of empathy, also fits with research suggesting a connection between disgust and dehumanization (see Hodson and Costello 696).

Angelo as his replacement guarantees that the primary alternative will be disgust. In short, the play seems perfectly designed as a study in the contrast between our two moralities.

The fourth scene takes us into the life of Isabella's nunnery with its strict and – Shakespeare suggests – absurd rules of sexual isolation. Obviously, the nuns do not have sexual contact with men, but other sorts of interaction are severely limited as well. They can interact with a man only "in the presence of the prioress" and, more extreme still, "if you speak, you must not show your face,/Or, if you show your face, you must not speak" (I.iv.11–13). The point, it seems, is not to suggest the admirable rigor of chastity, but the unnaturalness of the practice.

The second act begins with Escalus pleading for Claudio. He first alludes to attachment relations, referring to Claudio's father. He then turns to empathy – again, an emotional meta-system enhanced by attachment. He spells out the (empathic) relation between Angelo or anyone and Claudio: "Had time cohered with place or place with wishing,/Or that the resolute acting of your blood/Could have attained th' effect" perhaps Angelo too would have "Erred in this point" (II.i.11–13, 15). Escalus's contention is particularly plausible, given the common link between desire and disgust at desire (e.g., in homophobia, as already noted). Angelo responds with perfect consistency in his opposition to empathic qualification of rigoristic judgment, urging that, should he commit such a sin, then he too should be killed. In fact, Angelo has a reasonable point concerning law. The fact that a judge may have committed the same crime in the same circumstances does not mean that the law should not be applied. Of course, the irrelevance of the judge's own propensities also does not mean that the law should be applied, since that law may be unjust.

In any case, it may seem at this point that Angelo is merely a mechanical servant of the letter of the law. But the second scene begins to suggest that he is emotionally motivated to enforce the antifornication laws. Juliet is soon to give birth. Unmoved by any feelings of empathy or any sense of the attachment relations involved in motherhood, Angelo expresses nothing but contempt – fundamentally, a form of disgust. He reacts even to the mention of Juliet's name as if she is some bit of excrement, the very thought of which exudes a disagreeable odor – "Dispose of her ... with speed" (I.ii.16–17), he orders. Subsequently, he cannot characterize her as a woman or a mother, but only as "the fornicatress," repeating the order that she "be removed" (II.ii.23).

Isabella enters and her language too suggests that disgust may underlie her choice of lifelong chastity. Specifically, she explains that fornication is "a vice that most I do abhor,/And most desire should meet the blow of justice" (II.ii.29–30). But she is softened by attachment to her brother. Hearing Isabella's appeal on behalf of her brother, Angelo recognizes the flaw in Isabella's argument. He replies that he would condemn Claudio in the same way even if he were "my kinsman, brother, or my son" (II.ii.81). When Isabella appeals to "pity," Angelo rightly replies that he must equally have pity for "those I do not know,/Which a dismissed offense would after gall" (II.ii.101–102). For our purposes, the crucial point is that Isabella's appeal has not moved beyond the level of egocentric attachment, the seeking of her own private satisfaction. It is not properly moral until it is generalized beyond self-interest.

Isabella also appeals to empathy. That appeal is more properly moral (even if it is not, in itself, legally compelling). Like Escalus, she stresses a particular sort of empathy. This is not the empathy of simulating how one would feel if one were the other person, with his or her personality, background, and so forth. Rather, it is the empathy of simulating how one would feel *oneself* if one found oneself in the same circumstances as the other person. In this form of empathy, one does not try to imagine having a different personality or history. Rather, one imagines having altered circumstances. Angelo rejects these appeals.

Despite this, Angelo immediately begins to contemplate – not merely fantasize, but plan – his own act of fornication. Unsurprisingly, Angelo immediately thinks of his own sexual desire in terms of disgust objects – "carrion" that is physically "corrupt" in warming weather (II.ii.166–167). He refers to women generally as "waste ground" – opposing them to the "sanctuary" represented by Isabella. Yet, he still desires her "foully" (II.ii.169, 173). Angelo's extensive meditation on the vileness of his own cravings for Isabella indicates once again that disgust-based sexual morality may be marked by a propensity toward imaginative sexual elaboration.[25]

[25] The point has been noted in a very general way. For example, Legatt points out that the play "sees a perverse sexuality in the law that regulates sex" ("Comedy" 146). It is worth emphasizing that this combination of sexual disgust, violent punitive orientation, and prurience is not a thing of the Puritan past, or some merely peripheral phenomenon today. It can be found in many current legal practices surrounding sexuality. Wypijewski notes that teenagers are being prosecuted for sex crimes, such as

Soon Juliet is introduced – near delivery, but in prison. The Duke interviews her about her relations with Claudio, establishing that they were based on mutual love and consent. This operates to eliminate ethical considerations of violence that would tell against Claudio. In terms of the present analysis, they largely eliminate concerns of ethical anger and retribution, leaving the ethics of disgust as the clear source of the condemnation. A bit of standard patriarchal ideology enters when the Duke and Juliet concur that she was more at fault than Claudio. However, this does not seem to be borne out by the rest of the play, where in fact the men are portrayed as far more culpable with regard to women than the reverse.

The following scene has a sort of parallel interview, this one between Angelo and Isabella. Here, the disgust/attachment opposition is fully on display. Angelo takes up the common image of moral cleanliness in his exclamation against fornication, "Fie, these filthy vices!" (II.iv.42). He goes on to make the bizarre argument that conceiving a child illegitimately is directly comparable to murdering someone. This allows Angelo to suggest that the murder of Claudio is in fact a direct and equal recompense for Claudio's begetting of a child. The occlusion of the attachment relations here is complete. In Angelo's account, no part of state execution seems to involve a violation of a person's attachment relations (through, for example, the bereavement of Juliet or the partial orphaning of her child, in Claudio's case), and no part of the new child's life calls out for the care implied in such relations (e.g., the presence of a father).

Isabella again pleads for compassion. Angelo replies cleverly. Recurring to the imagery of sex as filth along with imagery of taste that is appropriate for disgust, he asks her about the "sweet uncleanness" (II.iv.54) of extramarital sex. If it does not merit death, then surely it is a lesser crime than killing. But if it is a lesser crime than killing, shouldn't Isabella be willing to engage in it to prevent a killing? The question is clearly unfair. It fails to distinguish between the nearly marital and consensual relations of Claudio and Juliet and any possible relations between Angelo and Isabella; it ignores the difference between having mercy for someone else's transgression in the past and planning one's

child pornography, when they pose "provocative[ly]" in a bathing suit for their boyfriend (8). She notes that school officials have been assiduous in searching through cell phone files to find illegal naked photos that students have taken of themselves. The punishments do not go so far as execution, but the legal system does actually allow for a life sentence (8).

own transgression in the future; and, most significantly, it sets aside the issue of consequences for the society as a whole (e.g., the propagation of bribery and abuse of power) and the different social roles and moral responsibilities at play in the two cases.

On the other hand, many audience members are likely to feel that there is a point here. If yielding to Angelo will save her brother's life, then Isabella might do it, choosing the lesser of two evils. But, of course, this is not the lesser of two evils from the perspective of a disgust-based morality. Isabella suggests this when she explains that she would never "yield/My body up to shame" (II.iv.103–104). The phrasing is exact. Again, shame is bound up with a sense of oneself as disgusting. In keeping with this, Isabella denounces such a "foul redemption" (II.iv.113), going on to reject "the thing I hate" (II.iv.119; hatred combining anger with disgust), along with Angelo's "fouler" "license" (II.iv.146, 145) and "abhorred pollution" (II.iv.183). Her disgust with sexuality here is quite extreme. This is in part contextual, associated with the specific image of Angelo. But the reference to "*the* thing I hate" (emphasis added) seems to suggest a more encompassing rejection of sex.

This imagery continues when Isabella explains the situation to Claudio. Thus, she describes Angelo's expression of sexual desire as "His filth within being cast" (III.i.93 – "cast" appropriately meaning "vomited up," as the editor explains [80n.93]). Unsurprisingly, Claudio does not see things in quite the same light. This is in part because he lacks his sister's sensitivity to disgust triggers, but it is also because his fear of death has inhibited his own empathic capacities. Isabella recurs to her sense of shame. This serves in part to inhibit her usual feelings of empathy with her brother and thus facilitates anger. This in turn leads her to call for her brother's swift death (III.i.131). It is worth noting that her reference to shame is followed by a conjecture that her mother may have been unfaithful – thus foul, filthy, polluted – for how otherwise could she produce such a son as Claudio (III.i.141–143)? This is another case where someone who is particularly disgusted by sex also appears to elaborate on it in imagination.

In his monastic disguise, the Duke counsels Isabella that she can save her brother without sacrificing her chastity. Angelo had been contracted to wed Mariana. However, when her dowry was lost, he abandoned her, fabricating accusations against her honor (III.i.230–231). The story has at least two functions. It challenges the patriarchal ideology expressed by the Duke in his interview with Juliet. At least here, the real fault in the male/female relationship lies with the man. Subsequently, we learn of a still worse case. Lucio first impregnated Kate Keepdown, then abandoned her despite promises of marriage (III.ii.201–206). More exactly, in both cases, the real faults lie with men *from the perspective of attachment*, for an attachment-based ethics should foster an enhanced commitment to the attachment feelings of one's partner. Second, the story of Angelo and Mariana establishes a situation parallel with that of Claudio and Juliet. A key difference – beyond the sexual consummation – is that Claudio remained faithful to Juliet, expressing his attachment to her, whereas Angelo abandoned and slandered Mariana. Angelo's lack of empathy is particularly salient, as he "Left [Mariana] in her tears, and dried not one of them with his comfort," being, rather, "a marble to her tears" (III.i.229–30, 233). Certainly from an attachment perspective, the greater crime by far is that of Angelo.

Now the Duke contrives to have Isabella arrange to meet with Angelo in darkness. They will substitute Mariana for Isabella and, as a result, Angelo will consummate his relation with Mariana – thus committing only the crime committed by Claudio. However, thinking that he has slept with Isabella, he will (the Duke assumes) pardon Claudio. Once the mistake comes to light, Claudio will be free and Mariana will have received back the man she loves.

Given the Duke's rather liberal attitude in this scene and in the preceding years, one might wonder why he has initiated the reform led by Angelo. The reason is suggested in the next scene, when the Duke expresses his own disgust at sex work. He denounces the "filthy vice," the participants' "abominable and beastly touches," all of which proceed "stinkingly" (III.ii.24, 25, 29). Shortly after this, Pompey the bawd says of his mistress that "she hath eaten up all her beef" (III.ii.56), meaning her prostitutes, perhaps suggesting that she has ruined them all through sex work. As a result, "she is herself in the tub" (III.ii.57), thus suffering from venereal disease (see 88n.56 and 88n.57). Again, the suggestion is that social circumstances – not just those in the play, but those in Shakespeare's London – have intensified disgust responses, particularly with regard to sex, thereby enhancing disgust-based ethics for a range of people, including even the Duke (and perhaps Shakespeare himself). This is presumably part of Shakespeare's attempt to present a moderate or balanced ethics that includes a version of (in our terms) both disgust- and attachment-based alternatives.

The fourth act takes us to the issue of a morality bearing on violence and a morality bearing on sexuality. We saw earlier that Angelo viewed conception out of wedlock as a moral violation no less serious than murder. Now we are faced with Pompey switching from his illegal profession as a bawd, facilitating sex, to the legal profession of an executioner's helper, facilitating death. The executioner worries that a bawd will discredit the profession of state killing. The irony of the scene is clear. Shakespeare contrasts the two sorts of moral focus. First, there is the focus on attachment and empathy, which promotes an opposition to violence and a general tolerance toward sex. Second, there is the focus on disgust, which promotes an opposition to sex and a greater tolerance toward violence (at least insofar as it is an outcome of and response to disgust). The contrast is further elaborated when the Provost contrasts Barnardine and Claudio, both condemned to death. Claudio, he explains, has his "pity." Barnardine, however, does not, "Being a murderer" (IV.ii.62, 63). Yet, from the point of view represented by the state, with Angelo's great orientation toward disgust, the two are equal – and the violence of the state is not only innocent, but positively laudable in eliminating someone who has participated in unclean sexuality.

Despite the Duke's strategy, Angelo proves untrustworthy and sends orders for Claudio's execution. This plot twist has several consequences. Most importantly, it makes the morality of the play clear. The attitude of sexual disgust is not only problematic from an attachment perspective; it is associated with hypocrisy. It does not subordinate egocentrism, but furthers it in Angelo's case. In that way, it does not really count as a moral response at all, for, at least here, the moral judge's own actions fall entirely outside the purview of his moral judgments. It may seem that this is simply accidental, a quirk of Angelo, a biased characterization penned by the anti-Puritanical Shakespeare. In other words, it may seem to be a bit of Shakespeare's own ideological orientation. But one would actually expect a pattern along these lines. In general, our disgust responses diminish with respect to ourselves – products, smells, and activities of our own bodies are less repugnant than parallel products, smells, and activities of other bodies. Insofar as we base ethical response on disgust, we would expect an inverse correlation between the stringency of our (disgust-based) moral responses and the degree to which our own bodies are the object of those judgments. However logically inconsistent, it is not emotionally inconsistent for Angelo to be tolerant of his own (apparent) fornication, but to respond with revulsion to the similar acts of others.

Of course, in this case, Angelo's motivation is not simply disgust; it is also a matter of fear that conduces toward violence. Thus, Angelo reflects that Claudio "should have lived" except that he "Might in the times to come have ta'en revenge" (IV.v.30, 32). This fusion of disgust-based ethics with a response derived from fear is unsurprising and suggests some of the moral problems with fear (e.g., its tendency to overwhelm all other elaborative considerations and lead to rash and excessive decisions). On the other hand, the fear component of this decision is not moral, but prudential. This may inhibit Angelo's ability to rationalize his act. In any case, he begins to feel guilt, as suggested by his exclamation, "Would yet [Claudio] had lived!" (IV.v.34) and his subsequent lament that he forgot his "grace" (IV.v.35). Grace is an interesting concept in this context, for it is, in effect, anything that contributes to one's moral self-worth but for which one is not oneself responsible. In the end, the comedy of the play relies on multiple acts of "grace," particularly with respect to Angelo – most obviously in the fact that he is saved from actually committing the murder of Claudio.

The final act culminates and resolves these events. For our purposes, the first important revelation occurs when Mariana explains that Angelo "thinks he knows that he ne'er knew my body,/But knows he thinks that he knows Isabel's" (V.i.203–204). The statement has many purposes in the plot. In the context of emotion – prominently desire and disgust – it suggests the importance of imaginative elaboration. Angelo was filled with desire for Isabella and something like disgust for Mariana (suggested by his denunciations of her supposed dishonor). But the body he actually experienced in satisfying his desire was Mariana's. What Angelo enjoyed, then, was not sensation per se, but sensation embedded in a fantasy elaboration. The point is made salient later, when Mariana explains "this is the body/That took away the match from Isabel,/And did supply thee at thy garden house/In her imagined person" (V.i.210–213). The suggestion of the play is that Angelo will be satisfied with Mariana as readily as he was with "Isabella," because "Isabella" was, in fact, Mariana. But this is an idealization. It seems more likely that Angelo will not be able to subdue his desire to his conditions and experience the same enjoyment in sex with Mariana. Rather, he will imagine Mariana differently from the way he imagined Isabella. The point has consequences not only for Angelo (for whom most readers probably do not have much sympathy). They bear crucially on Mariana as well. It seems highly unlikely that she will receive anything approximating the individual attachment and desire she longs for (due to her own attachment to Angelo). This is part of the reason that, as a romantic comedy, the play is problematic. There is, in addition, the difficulty that, though Angelo is not, by "grace," guilty of actual murder, he is a man who proved himself capable of profound cruelty. His feeble sense of empathy and intense sense of disgust are hardly promising traits in a husband.

The ending of the play develops the issue of mercy and the biblical theme of doing unto others as you would have them do unto you. To his credit, Angelo now follows his ideas consistently and affirms the need for his own execution. At this point in the play, Isabella believes that her brother has indeed been killed by Angelo's orders. She nonetheless pleads for Angelo's life on the grounds that killing Claudio was only following the law and that he did not commit the sexual crime he intended. The play stresses that this is an act of mercy. From the present perspective, however, it is most importantly a generalization of attachment ethics. We see this particularly by attending to the context in which Isabella makes her appeal. Mariana first pleads that the Duke not marry her to Angelo simply to make her a widow. When her prayers have no effect on the Duke, Mariana in desperation turns to Isabella, begging her aid. Isabella is clearly moved by Mariana's attachment and the pain that will be caused her by Angelo's death. In taking up Mariana's case, then, she adopts a genuine ethics of attachment. Unlike her plea for Claudio earlier in the play, she is not motivated by her own private or egocentric attachments. Rather, she is acting in accordance with a generalized and complementary attachment concern, in this case particularized with respect to Mariana.

The story ends with the Duke asking for Isabella's hand in marriage. Thus, rather than returning her to the nunnery and a life of chastity, it introduces her – along with the other previously celibate characters – into a life of sexuality and, presumably, attachment. In the context of the play, the conclusion is neither entirely plausible nor even necessarily the most desirable outcome.[26] However, its importance lies in its tacit rejection of a politics of disgust along with the associated celebration of chastity, and its embrace of a politics of attachment. It is clear that a politics of attachment has its limitations. Its liberality is open to abuse, and can lead to ethical violations, even violations of attachment obligations, for that reason. But it is a humane politics, and its flaws cannot be repaired by a politics of disgust.[27] As recent empirical research shows,

---

[26] Indeed, some critics have seen it as no less inhibiting than a return to the nunnery (see Magnusson 173).
[27] For an extended and illuminating analysis of problems with the invocation of disgust in law particularly, see chapter 3 of Nussbaum *Hiding*.

a politics of disgust is bound up with dehumanization (Hodson and Costello), racism (Taylor), right-wing authoritarianism (Hodson and Costello), the assumption of guilt (rather than innocence), and the rationalization of irrational condemnation (Wheatley and Haidt; Jones and Fitness).[28] Shakespeare's play suggests some of these problems with an ethics of disgust and points toward a partial, if perhaps necessarily imperfect, response to them.

Conclusion

The realm of ethics appears to have something to do with making choices that oppose our egocentric inclinations. These egocentric inclinations may be isolated in several ways. One way is by reference to large nonethical categories of human goal pursuit – prominently, social well-being (including wealth), pleasure (prominently sexual pleasure), and spiritual realization. The contrast between these goals and those of morality may be understood as a matter of "pure negation." In this case, ethical principles are viewed as requiring the repudiation of the nonethical category. For example, ethics may be seen primarily in terms of rejecting sexuality, or giving up autonomy or wealth, or even setting aside one's own individual spiritual interests. The ethics of pure negation tend to stress one or another of these tendencies, particularly the first or second.

However, negation is not the only option. One might also adopt a "complementarist" approach to defining ethics. In this view, it is ethical to concern oneself with other people's social well-being, other people's pleasure, or other people's spiritual achievement. Tagore's work suggests that one valuable approach to ethical evaluation may focus on attachment. This would involve generalizing our attachment orientation toward the well-being of other people and increasing our empathic sensitivity to other people's own attachment relations.

The reference to attachment reminds us of the mutual relevance of ethics and emotion. We act in ways that are ethical (or unethical) only if we have a motivation to do so. In other words, ethical action is no more separable from emotion than is any other sort of action. At the same time, emotional response is itself bound up with ethical or, more generally, normative thought. Again, our responses to events and our

---

[28] I should note that the research is not entirely consistent on these results; see, for example, Horberg and colleagues.

choices of actions are the result of two things – our spontaneous emotional reactions to changing conditions and our imaginative elaboration of those conditions (thus our causal attributions, our anticipations, and so forth). The latter may involve ethical schemas as well as ethically relevant anticipations of one's own empathy and guilt.

Any emotion system may be recruited to ethical ends. However, only a few recur prominently. Since emotion systems have excitatory and inhibitory relations with other emotion systems, they tend to cluster together into sets of emotional/moral alternatives. One such set involves the interweaving of anger and fear on the one hand and the intensification of compassion on the other. Anger and fear respond to perceived or imagined hurts from others – both individuals and outgroups considered collectively. They also tend to foster responsive violence and inhibit empathy. Compassion, in contrast, responds to the perceived or imagined hurts experienced by others. It tends to inhibit responsive violence.

Another important cluster concerns disgust and attachment. Disgust – which may be conjoined with fear and/or anger – responds to decay and to body products, primarily those of other people. In ethical terms, it is often focused on sexuality. It fosters a desire to eliminate the object of disgust and inhibits empathy. Disgust tends to diminish with respect to oneself. This may give rise to an apparent double standard in disgust-based ethics, such that one seems to hold oneself to a lower standard than others. In one sense, this is true, but, in another sense, there may be only one standard, a standard whereby moral condemnation decreases with decreasing disgust. In contrast with disgust, attachment tends to be tolerant or even supportive of sexuality. It serves to enhance empathy and inhibit disgust. (As Shaver and Mikulincer point out, the attachment system is "apparently dominant … in many cases of intersystem conflict" [54].)

Tagore's poem is a fruitful source for "hermeneutic reflection" on these topics. In hermeneutic reflection, one takes a literary text as the basis for one's examination of a particular ethical issue. However, one's aim is not, first of all, to explicate the text. One takes up the text somewhat more freely to address the ethical issue.

In a more interpretive vein, we find that Shakespeare's play forcefully develops the conflicts between an ethics of attachment and an ethics of disgust. Indeed, it does so with such systematic rigor that one might almost imagine that Shakespeare formulated ethical alternatives in these terms. At the outset, it includes some suggestions that a moderate version of the ethics of disgust may be important for social well-being. Indeed, attachment may, in certain cases, apparently overvalue others, potentially extending leniency beyond what might be consistent with social prudence. Nonetheless, the play ends with events that heavily favor an ethics of attachment with all that this entails – for compassion, for forgiveness, and for at least a degree of liberality in sexual relations. Indeed, by the end of the play, it is no longer clear that disgust should have any moral role.

8. Compassion and Pity

The Tempest and Une Tempête

Ethics against Adaptation

Feeling for others is ubiquitous in everyday life. We cringe when we see someone mildly injured, become teary when we hear of someone's joy or suffering, experience a sort of terror when we read about barbarous events that occurred in the distant past. As many writers have noted, it is not intuitively obvious why this should be the case. The straightforward evolutionary function of emotion is egoistic. Fear, for example, leads me to flee situations (e.g., being eaten by a predator) that would threaten my ability to reproduce. My feelings for others, however, sometimes actually work against this function. For example, I may become so concerned about someone else being eaten by a predator that I do not flee, but stay and help him or her – perhaps getting myself eaten in the process. The "selfish gene" idea helps explain this for kin. If I save relatives, then I am preserving some shared genetic material. But what about when someone risks their life for strangers?

The fact of feeling for strangers is perhaps not as difficult to account for in evolutionary terms as it might initially seem. In order to understand why, we need to return to a point stressed earlier: The biological mechanisms produced by evolution merely approximate functions; they are not identical with functions. In some ways, the point is obvious within evolutionary theory. But evolutionary theorists often talk as if functions have a direct causal role in adaptation, and this leads to conceptual confusion and mistaken inferences. The problem is exacerbated by misconstrual of the distinction at the theoretical level.

Here, we might consider some relevant comments by Stephen Jay Gould, one of the most important recent theorists of evolution. In his *The Structure of Evolutionary Theory*, he draws on Aristotle to contrast

257

efficient and final causes in evolution. Final causes are goals or purposes and are part of our ordinary way of explaining human action (see, for example, 85). Gould is presumably drawing on Aristotle to make the operation of evolution more readily comprehensible to readers. However, it is crucial to remember that there are in fact no final causes in evolution. There are only mechanisms that, in the proper circumstances, may have the same consequences as goal pursuit. When writers do not maintain this distinction strictly, they begin to speak as if nature really had goals. Thus, we find Gould writing that "As functionalist theories, both Lamarckian soft inheritance and Darwinian natural selection share a defining premise that environmental information about adaptive design somehow passes to organisms, and that organisms then respond by fashioning traits to enhance their competitive ability" (1179). In fact, this is backwards. Organisms do not first encounter nature, then respond by fashioning something. That is what happens in goal pursuit. Rather, organisms spontaneously produce mutations that subsequently encounter nature and, in consequence, lead to enhanced reproduction – if they happen, by chance, to be adaptive.

This problem affected even Darwin himself. Indeed, it is perhaps the primary source of his difficulty in accounting for ethics. As Gould explains, when treating "human morality ... Darwin did throw in the towel after long struggle – for he could not render altruism towards non-relatives by organismal selection" (133). Subsequently, Gould summarizes Darwin's view that "altruistic behavior" runs "against our deeper biological drive for seeking personal advantage" (134). The fact is, there is no such drive – which, if it existed, would be final causal, a matter of goal seeking. Rather, there are mechanisms that, in specific circumstances, roughly approximate seeking personal advantage. More generally, there are mechanisms that, in concert with one another and with the environment, generally promote the passing on of one's genes. Given this, there is not any necessary, obvious, a priori opposition between evolution and altruism. Altruism need only result from the mechanisms in some conditions. Those may or may not be conditions where the mechanisms approximate functions.

It seems clear that fellow feeling has selective advantages for people living in groups for the simple reason that everyone in the group is more likely to survive and pass on their genes if the group functions well together. This is most obvious in cases of conflict with other groups (e.g., when warfare leads to the deaths of many members from the losing group).[1] Given that empathic response can be disrupted by in-group/out-group divisions, empathy – and, presumably, altruism – would favor in-group members.

On the other hand, this presupposes that a genetic predisposition toward altruism-fostering empathy had already spread within the group. How might that have happened? We may suppose that, initially, feelings for others had selective benefits only for kin relations (thus people with whom one shares the distinctive genetic material that will be passed on). It is overwhelmingly unlikely that genetic mutation would produce such fine-grained sensitivity that one would feel strong empathy only for kin. For this to be the case, we would have to have perceptual sensitivities that somehow give the information yielded today by genetic testing (e.g., a doubting father would only have to look at the child to know whether it is his biological offspring). Moreover, our empathic response would have to be sensitive to this information – turning on for kin and turning off for non-kin. Moreover, if this were the case, it would be difficult to explain how large-group altruism (e.g., in national armies) would occur at all, even after the spread of the genetic propensity.

However, most of the same genetic benefits would accrue to a much simpler mechanism by which one shared the feelings of other people generally, with intensity of response resulting from a few simple variables. These variables include perceptibility, trust, and attachment. In other words, the basic, simple complex of mechanisms would be something like universal empathy (based, for example, in mirror neuron systems) modulated by the degree to which one actually perceives the other person's emotion (e.g., sees his or her weeping face), along with the degree to which one has a relation of trust and/or attachment with that person. In societies where cohabitation is at least partially a function of kinship, perceptibility alone would already incline one to provide greater aid to kin – for the simple reason that one would see and hear their pain more often and more readily. Trust itself seems to be a function of familiarity (or at least apprehension, indicating distrust, results from lack of familiarity [see Oatley *Emotions* 73]). This yields a similar result – that is, people in most societies tend to be more familiar with

---

[1] Note that this is not selection operating at a supraorganismal level, as Gould discusses. It is simply organism-level selection operating in an environmental context that includes groups.

kin than with others; conversely, non-kin are more likely to be unfamiliar. Finally, attachment is overwhelmingly more likely to arise among kin. Other variables might enter as well – for example, sensitization to detailed expressive features of in-group members, category-defined orientations toward parallel or complementary emotional response for in-group/out-group divisions, and so on. Collectively, these (simple) mechanistic variables would make fellow feeling very likely to contribute to the function of passing on of one's genes. But, again, they would not constitute that function; they would only approximate it.

For our purposes, a couple of things are important about this function/mechanism division. First, "the" mechanism of feeling for others is not governed by a single property, as the kin-selection function might suggest. Rather, it is the result of many factors. Those factors, moreover, are open to change. We can inform ourselves more concretely and more precisely about the sufferings of other people, making them more perceptible. We can familiarize ourselves with members of out-groups and, through elaborative processing (e.g., imagination), we can moderate our spontaneous tendencies to distrust them. We can develop sensitivities to the expressive properties of faces that are different from our own and those of our family. In other words, if we wish, we can make our fellow feeling *less* kin-based (something that would presumably not be possible if the mechanism itself were directly a matter of kin selection).

Within cognitive science today, one popular view of ethics is that our ethical principles are innate and evolved. For example, Marc Hauser has made an influential argument of this sort, drawing on Chomskyan ideas about innate principles with predetermined parametric options that are set by culture or upbringing. It would take us beyond the scope of the present book to consider Hauser's and related arguments. However, it is worth mentioning these evolutionary approaches to clarify the "nonadaptationist" features of the account advocated here. According to our nonadaptationist account, the nature of ethics is directly opposed to the selfishness of genes. Of course, the emotional and other responses that bear on ethics must have evolved, just as all our physical and mental capacities evolved. (At least, that is what we have to assume, given current theories.) But it does not follow from this that every aspect and every consequence of every evolved property must have an adaptive function. Again, a capacity is selected in evolution because, in the environment of evolutionary adaptedness, it has more selective benefits than existing alternatives – not because all

its results in all environments are fitness enhancing. In the non-adapta-
tionist view, it is precisely this discrepancy that allows for ethics.

More exactly, there are two crucial disagreements between the nonadaptationist view proposed here and much mainstream evolutionary
ethical theory. First, the former does not include anything that may reasonably be referred to as an evolved ethical system. This is, in effect,
a consequence of the other disagreement. Clearly, we do make use
of human cognitive and affective architecture when we make ethical
decisions or respond to situations ethically. It does not seem, however,
that our ethical propensities are congruent with the adaptive functions
of those architectural features, at least not in any way that bears on
the specificity of ethics. The account we have been developing accepts
the view of writers such as Martin Hoffman and William Rottschaefer
that empathy has a "central role ... in moral agency" (Rottschaefer 84).
Moreover, it agrees with Rottschaefer that empathy is "an evolutionarily
based ... capacity" that has a "motivational" function in "the exercise
of moral agency" (97). However, as a nonadaptationist account, it goes
on to view empathy as ethical precisely to the degree that, in specific
cases, it does not serve an adaptive function (although empathic capacity certainly evolved due to being adaptive on the whole).[2]

Here we might consider three simple cases. First, I see that my trek-
king companion is suddenly afraid. I share his feeling and in consequence join him in fleeing from the danger. We would usually not
consider this ethical (though one could make a case that there is a
very small ethical component related to obligations to my future self).

[2] Keith Oatley has pointed out that a contention such as this raises a series of philosophical
issues surrounding just "who or what is in charge" in making ethical decisions. He rightly
noted that readers interested in this topic might wish to consult Stanovich. Stanovich
addresses such issues as whether we are always at the mercy of our "selfish genes."
He argues that "The lumbering robots that are humans *can* escape the clutches of the
selfish replicators" (10). His argument is stimulating and consequential. Nonetheless,
if the preceding account is at all accurate, this may not really be much of an issue for
the present discussion. Again, there is a difference between evolved mechanisms and
evolutionary functions. Evolved mechanisms *often* fail to serve evolutionary functions.
Thus, they are clearly not at the mercy of selfish genes. It is more apt to say that selfish genes are at the mercy of the (only partially effective) evolved mechanisms. Given
the nature of the mechanism of empathy, there will be cases where it operates against
adaptive functionality, thus against reproducing the (selfish) genes of the empathiz-
ing person. The point is almost trivial, given the difference between mechanisms and
functions. On the other hand, the long-standing problem of free will does remain. For
(yet another) discussion of that in relation to contemporary cognitive neuroscience, see
Hogan "Imagining."

Second, there is the more complex case of saving one's own child from drowning. Clearly, there is an ethical component there (and a much stronger one than saving oneself). But the act is not solely ethical. We like parents to love their children, so we respond warmly to such acts by parents. But, arguably, such acts are ethically admirable only to the degree that they are not driven by specifically parental feelings – of, say, reward dependency.[3] Finally, consider the case where one saves a stranger from drowning. This seems almost paradigmatic of ethical action. In short, everything else being equal, it seems that my saving someone else's child is more of a purely ethical act than saving my own child,[4] which is, in turn, more purely ethical than saving myself.

In contrast with Hauser, then, this account denies that ethics is innate and evolved. Moreover, it locates the very possibility of ethics in the gaps between our empathic or other mechanisms on the one hand and their evolutionary functions on the other hand. Put differently, if mechanism and function coincided, then there would be no such thing as ethics. There would only be the things that evolution has led us to do – things that it would not make any sense to judge ethically, just as it does not make any sense to judge the pumping of one's heart ethically.

The Tempest

One important conclusion of the preceding section is that the mechanisms of empathy diverge from the adaptive functions of empathy. Again, consequences of that divergence include the possibility of cultivating different sorts of empathic attitude. Thus, we may enhance or inhibit our responsive sensitivity to others' emotions,[5] imaginatively elaborate on our initial responses in different ways, engage in or refrain from certain sorts of actions that reply to other people's emotions, and so on.

---

[3] Note that I am speaking of the *act* as ethically admirable, not the character of the parent. We often feel that a parent is not ethically admirable if he or she does not feel attachment for his or her child. This is a complex issue, related in part to an entire history of practices on the parent's part. A discussion of that topic is beyond the scope of the present chapter.

[4] This does not refer to the forced choice scenario when the two are drowning at the same time. As discussed in chapter seven, other things are not equal in that case.

[5] For example, research by Immordino-Yang and colleagues suggests that the neural substrates for different sorts of compassion are the same, but that relative to compassion for physical pain, compassion for social pain requires "more substantial cognitive processing related to cultural factors" (8021).

The Tempest is in many ways a play about empathy – or, more properly, about the inhibition of empathy. Such a view fits with standard interpretations of the play, though the latter are rarely, if ever, developed in these terms. Specifically, Shakespeare's play is widely read as dealing with racial out-groups – commonly, native Caribbeans, Africans, or Irish – in the context of European colonialism.[6] Many elements of standard postcolonial interpretations (e.g., the supposed location of the events in the Caribbean) are implausible, as David Kastan has argued (see 272–273). Moreover, it is not clear that Ariel and Caliban should be understood as representing historically specific groups of people.[7] Nonetheless, the play is pervaded by suggestions of colonialism and slavery, as well as class hierarchies. These all involve social group divisions (even if we cannot link them unequivocally and consistently with particular group identities from the real social world at Shakespeare's time). Such group divisions – by class, nationality, ethnicity, and race – are precisely what inhibit empathy in the play and, along with empathy, ethical thought and action.

The play begins with a literal tempest, a storm created by Prospero to strand his usurping brother on the island where Prospero is himself exiled. In the opening scene, the Boatswain works to save the ship. In doing so, he comes into some conflict with the aristocrats on board. They, in turn, condemn his rough manner and even go so far as to suggest that he should be hanged for showing inadequate deference to his betters. This scene introduces a sharp inhibition of empathy by categorial identity – in this case, class identity. The Boatswain clearly has appropriate fear for the safety of the crew. He is appropriately modulating that fear by reference to his duties as Boatswain. Finally, he has the skills required to save the ship. This should make him the object of admiring compassion. But even Gonzalo, the best of the aristocrats, can see only his insubordination.

The second scene begins with Prospero's daughter, raised on the island since infancy. She has witnessed the shipwreck and experienced emotional contagion, followed by empathy. She pleads with her father

---

[6] Influential postcolonial treatments of the play include work by Takaki, Paul Brown, Barker and Hulme, and Skura.

[7] The often-cited fact that "Caliban" is an anagram of "canibal" seems to be remarkably slim evidence for anything. Prospero, after all, is Italian. Ariel's name comes from Hebrew. One can make a reasonable case that Caliban's mother's name is derived from Greek (sy/su + corax/korax). But no one seems to have concluded that the play is about Italians colonizing Greeks who had colonized Jews.

to do anything he can to calm the sea, explaining, "O, I have suffered/ With those that I saw suffer!" (I.ii.5–6). Prospero explains that, in fact, no harm has been done. All the sailors are safe. He then commends the "virtue of compassion" in his daughter (I.ii.33).[8] By chance, he uses the word "compassion" in almost precisely the sense we will be using it in the following pages. Specifically, Miranda's response involves a sense of identification that neither idealizes nor undervalues the victims of the tempest. (Both under- and overestimation may inhibit empathy, as we will discuss in the penultimate section.) Her only sense of superiority is simply a pragmatic matter of her ability to appeal to Prospero. Moreover, this appeal itself shows that her compassion is combined with practical goodwill – a combination that is far from invariable (a point to which we will return).

Here we learn the background of Prospero's exile. Prospero was the Duke of Milan. His brother, Antonio, conspired with the Duke of Naples, Alonso, to dispossess Prospero, exiling him to an island inhabited only by the sorceress, Sycorax. The heartlessness of this usurpation is stressed by the fact that they abandoned both Prospero and his weeping infant daughter (I.ii.157). Clearly, this indicates a great inhibition in empathy, though not an inhibition based on group difference. It is most obviously based on a conflict in self-interest, but it is more complicated than that. It is true that Antonio wanted the title and authority of being Duke. Yet, in a sense, he already had those. Prospero had delegated his authority to Antonio, and Antonio enjoyed the benefits of that position. The difficulty in this case was that the position was insecure. Being a mere surrogate, Antonio could at any point find himself deprived of the position to which he had grown accustomed – for Prospero could always decide to resume his position as duke. In this way, the inhibition of his empathy is, in effect, a form a fear – fear for the loss of what had become normal life. But that too is not all there is to it. The well-being to which he accustomed himself was the well-being of an authoritative position, dominance in a hierarchy. In other words, it was a position

---

[8] Criticism on *The Tempest* includes little treatment of empathy or related feelings – though Kirsch views compassion as central, "a tonic chord in the whole of the action" (345). (Kirsch approaches the play historically, relating its treatment of compassion to contemporary ideas, specifically those of Montaigne.) However, those critics who have addressed compassion have tended to note Miranda's sympathetic inclinations (see Kirsch 345), perhaps because of Prospero's comment. Heather James gives the point particular weight, arguing that her "compassionate response to the shipwreck" results in a challenge to Prospero's authority and thus "sets the precedent for" others in the play (368).

where he had no ordinary obligation to empathize with others. Indeed, since he was duke, others had to be sensitive to his feelings. But a reciprocal sensitivity was not needed. It is precisely this asymmetry in empathic sensitivity that marks class differences more generally, the sort of asymmetry that we saw in the opening scene between the aristocrats and the Boatswain. The point fits with empirical research (see Anderson and Keltner 153).

After narrating their initial exile, Prospero gives a surprising account of the effects of empathy, or at least emotional contagion. He explains that he would have sunk into complete despair had it not been for the spontaneous smiles of his tiny daughter (I.ii.183ff.). This suggests the beneficial effects of emotion sharing. Indeed, it extends these. Here, emotion sharing is beneficial not only for the person who feels the emotion initially (in this case, the baby Miranda), but also for the "recipient" of the emotion (Prospero). The emotions of others may, so to speak, interrupt the sequence of our own mood-congruent processing, breaking a self-sustaining cycle. When that cycle is one of sorrow, the effect is ameliorative, which is undoubtedly one of the reasons why social interaction can be emotionally beneficial (as, for example, Caccioppo and Patrick stress). With respect to Prospero and Miranda, the point is undoubtedly given further force by the general mirth-provoking features of children.

Shakespeare goes on to introduce the other inhabitants of the island – Ariel and Caliban. Both are servants of Prospero. Prior to Prospero's arrival, the island was ruled by Sycorax. She had "painfully" imprisoned Ariel (I.ii.336), then died without releasing him. Prospero freed Ariel, then took him as a bondslave. The sequence relates narrowly to empathy. Prospero might have released Ariel as an act of beneficence based on compassion. But he did not. Indeed, he threatens Ariel with returning him to misery if he even murmurs with dissatisfaction (I.ii.355). Here again we have an apparent instance of self-interest inhibiting empathy. However, this case too is more complex. Prospero does not merely have an interest in keeping Ariel as his slave; he also views Ariel as a class subordinate. His demand for deference from Ariel is directly parallel to the demand of the aristocrats from the Boatswain in the opening scene.

The situation with Caliban is somewhat different. He is the child of Sycorax, the former ruler of the island. In that respect, he could be considered a member of the same aristocratic class as Prospero. In keeping with this, Prospero initially treated him well. However, he sought "to violate the honor" of Miranda (I.ii.426–427). It is difficult to say precisely what this involved. This may be understood as a violent attempt at forcing Miranda to have sex with him. In that case, readers today would count this as a crime deserving punishment, thus justifying Prospero's control. But it could just as easily be interpreted as an attempt by Caliban to woo Miranda, perhaps along the same lines as Romeo tries to woo Rosaline (who, he explains, will not "ope her lap to saint-seducing gold" [I.i.217]). In either case, Prospero responded to Caliban's intensity of feeling with disgust and viewed his pursuit of that feeling (thus his failure to modulate it appropriately) as a grievous moral fault. Prospero's response was undoubtedly intensified by some ethnic or racial identity-group difference, in keeping with standard interpretations of the play. The result was the loss of whatever empathy he had for Caliban. That loss, in turn, intensified the opposition in identity categories. Indeed, this opposition is stressed by Prospero right at the introduction of Caliban. Specifically, he draws on one of the standard metaphors that serve to inhibit empathy with out-groups, swearing that Caliban is the child of "the Devil himself" (I.ii.391–392).

The scene continues with the introduction of Ferdinand, the son of Alonso. Miranda and Ferdinand meet. In good Shakespearean fashion, they immediately fall in love. Miranda already has high trait empathy (thus a character-based inclination toward empathy, and specifically toward compassion). This is intensified by her attachment to Ferdinand.[9] Prospero insists that he will imprison Ferdinand. Miranda, anticipating Ferdinand's suffering, urges compassion. But Prospero rejects this appeal. The rejection is based in part on social hierarchy. When Ferdinand resists Prospero's domination, Prospero controls him with magic and uses a body metaphor to affirm either patriarchal or class hierarchy. Specifically, he says that will not allow his "foot" to be his "tutor" (I.ii.574). This may mean that he will not allow Miranda to teach him compassion. Alternatively, it may indicate that he will not submit to the authority of Ferdinand, who has just drawn his sword. (The second reading is perhaps more likely, since the following sentence is "Put up thy sword, traitor" [I.ii.574].) In either case, it suggests that

---

[9] Hatfield, Cacioppo, and Rapson note that imagining someone else's feelings is likely to be "an especially potent determinant" of empathy "when individuals love" (9). In keeping with this, they report that "Some researchers have contended that we are especially likely to mimic the facial expressions of those for whom we care" (22; see also 38). Neurological research on "the mother's comparative response to her own baby and another baby" indicates this as well (Iacoboni 127).

empathy – whether empathy for Ferdinand's imprisonment or empathy for Miranda's attachment-enhanced compassion – is inhibited by social hierarchy. Of course, Ferdinand is in fact an aristocrat. Moreover, they are members of the same national/ethnic identity group. Presumably for these reasons, he is not subjected to serious pain in the following acts.

The second act turns to the rest of the shipwrecked party. When most of the party sleeps, Antonio tries to convince Alonso's brother, Sebastian, to murder Alonso and usurp his position as King of Naples. Sebastian agrees, obviously driven by self-interest. However, he hesitates – perhaps because neither social hierarchy/class difference, nor identity opposition, nor fear enters into Sebastian's motivation and therefore his spontaneous empathy is less constrained. Indeed, it may even be enhanced by attachment.

Here, the play introduces another emotional factor that inhibits empathy – anger. Caliban begins the second scene by cursing Prospero with excruciating tortures. We have no reason to believe that Caliban would refrain from enacting these curses if it were within his capacities to do so. They straightforwardly imply a lack of empathy with their target. Caliban is clear about his own anger. Moreover, he not only expresses his feeling, but gives the reasons for it – Prospero's mistreatment. In this way, he moves to the level of moral modulation. His considers the cruelty of Prospero's actions and his own relative innocence, punished as he is "For every trifle" (II.ii.8). (Of course, to whatever degree Caliban's representation of Prospero's cruelty or his own innocence is false, we have a case of rationalization.) The act ends with Caliban joining with a jester (Trinculo) and a butler (Stephano) from the shipwreck. Ultimately, they plot the overthrow of Prospero.

The third act begins with Miranda's compassion for Ferdinand's labors and her attempts to take over his work for him. This instance of beneficence is noteworthy because it does not rely on a sense of superiority (e.g., greater competence). Indeed, it seems likely that Miranda would suffer more in the labor than Ferdinand. This is noteworthy because it suggests that Miranda's empathic suffering is actually more intense than the pain experienced by Ferdinand. This is the opposite of the effect we would ordinarily expect. We tend to experience our own pains as more intense and those of others as less intense, even when all objective criteria lead us to expect them to be comparable. The enhancement experienced by Miranda is, again, the result of attachment. This suggests that attachment has even more powerful effects on empathy, compassion, and beneficence than we might have anticipated.

Soon the play turns to Caliban, Trinculo, and Stephano, as they plot to take the island from Prospero. Stephano has been established as the king of this little band. This allows for comic variations on inhibition of empathy through class. Specifically, as soon as his control of the liquor supply makes Stephano into the presumptive ruler of the island, he begins to treat Trinculo with the same haughty disdain that we have seen in the "legitimate" aristocrats. For example, he threatens Trinculo with hanging, should he prove a "mutineer" (III.ii.36), in this case by speaking ill of Caliban despite Stephano's prohibition. It seems that Shakespeare does this in part to develop a criticism of class hierarchies without giving direct offense to actual aristocrats in his audience. In any case, Stephano's rough handling of Trinculo illustrates once more the inhibition of empathy due to social stratification – this time, parodically.

In the fourth act, Prospero responds to the plot. Needless to say, he does not acknowledge Caliban's claim that he should have inherited the island from his mother. Rather, he rationalizes Caliban's rebellion as the result of his demonic nature – "a born devil" (IV.i.215), thus a devil due to his ancestry, his ethnic, racial, or related identity category. This is particularly striking because it is Prospero who deals in magic and thus might seem to be associated with the devil. As Caliban puts it, "I am subject to a tyrant,/A sorcerer, that by his cunning hath/Cheated me of the island" (III.ii.42–44). In any case, this identity-based inhibition of Prospero's empathy is combined with a degree of fear, for Prospero temporarily "forgot that foul conspiracy" (IV.i.156), thus allowing it to proceed. In combination, these emotional conditions lead to a response that goes beyond indifference. Indeed, Prospero seems to relish the pain of his victims. In other words, he seems to experience an enhanced complementary (antiempathic) response, thus the opposite of Miranda's enhanced parallel (empathic) response to Ferdinand. Prospero thinks that he will "plague" Caliban and the others "even to roaring" (IV.i.219–220). This point of intense emotional expression (roaring) would ordinarily be one that arouses a hearer's empathic pain. The suggestion here is that it will do the opposite in Prospero's case. At the end of the act, Prospero has his "goblins ... grind" the mutineers' "joints/With dry convulsions, shorten up their sinews" and engage in further tortures (IV.i.289ff.).

The fifth act resolves the various plot sequences. Antonio, Alonso, and the others have suffered much anguish – in part from their sense of guilt over the usurpation and exile of Prospero. Now they are "Brimful of sorrow and dismay" (V.i.16), as Ariel puts it. They are so wretched, he explains to Prospero, "That if you now beheld them, your affections/Would become tender" (V.i.20–21). In saying this, Ariel recalls the perceptual basis of empathy. He further suggests that there is always some point where the pain of another person will affect us empathically; there is always some degree of intensity that will overbear anger or other inhibitors. It is not entirely clear, however, whether or not this is true. Prospero does release the group, but it is not evident that he is ever genuinely "kindlier moved" (V.I.28), as he puts it. Moreover, if he is, this may be because he shares central identity categories with them – he is, in his words, "One of their kind" (V.i.27).

It seems, in the end, that Prospero has genuine empathy with only one, or perhaps two, of his antagonists. First, there is Gonzalo – "Holy Gonzalo, honorable man,/Mine eyes, ev'n sociable to the show of thine,/Fall fellowly drops" (V.i.69–71). We know from the initial recounting of his history that Prospero exempted Gonzalo from his anger and indeed felt gratitude toward him. Like enduring attachment, gratitude enhances empathic sensitivity. Indeed, there is a hint that he feels something like a familial bond with Gonzalo.

The other link is more surprising, and less certain. There is something almost paternal in Prospero's statement about Caliban – "this thing of darkness I/Acknowledge mine" (V.i.324–325). There is a clear suggestion that he will pardon Caliban (V.i.325). Will the pardon extend all the way back to the attempted violation of Miranda? From his side, Caliban promises, "I'll be wise hereafter,/And seek for grace" (V.i.326–327). Each seems almost to recognize the pain of the other and to promise a small bit of beneficence.[10] Despite the play's pervasive stress on the inhibition of empathy, then, perhaps here at the end it hints that even the divisions of identity are not entirely impermeable to compassion.

Une Tempête

Though there is this slight hint of resolution in the end, there is not really anything in Shakespeare's play that suggests a concrete, practical way of establishing empathy and thus ethical thought and action. The conclusion of Césaire's play is far less hopeful than the ending of Shakespeare's play. Nonetheless, Césaire does suggest that there are

[10] This is consistent with a broad tendency in the romances, which, as Michael O'Connell points out, tend to involve self-criticism and forgiveness.

possibilities for pursuing not only an ethics, but a larger-scale politics based on empathy. In this way, despite the ending, it is a more hopeful play than Shakespeare's. It may also be a play that shows us more about empathy and ethics, for it is not so confined to their inhibition.

Césaire transposes the action of *The Tempest* to an island in the Caribbean and famously presents Prospero as a slaveholder, with his two slaves – the apparently loyal Ariel and the rebellious Caliban. By shifting the context of the play in this way, Césaire foregrounds conflicts of group identity and renders the related political issues far more salient. He does not, however, leave aside the topics of compassion and pity. Indeed, the play is more insistent – and more positive – in its treatment of compassion than is Shakespeare's original.

The opening parallels that of Shakespeare's play. Interestingly, Césaire has Gonzalo spell out part of what lies behind the inhibition of empathy shown by the aristocrats in Shakespeare's play. Specifically, he tells the Boatswain, "My dear fellow, I can quite understand your being nervous, but a man should be able to control himself [*se dominer*] in any situation, even the most upsetting" (10; 15[11]). Given the circumstances, it seems extremely unlikely that the aristocrats would show anything approaching the Boatswain's self-control. However, the suggestion is that they envision themselves as proceeding with far more equanimity. Such a sense of superiority is both emotionally and ethically consequential, as we will discuss in the next section. In response, the Boatswain makes direct reference to the class difference – and also to genuine competence in coping with a crisis at sea – by telling the aristocrats, "If you want to save your skins, you'd better get yourselves back down below to those first-class cabins of yours [*vos cabines de luxe*]" (10; 15). Césaire also rather attenuates the hostility of the aristocrats, and puts the most damning lines (about the Boatswain "end[ing] up on the gallows" [11]) in the mouth of Antonio rather than Gonzalo. Indeed, Gonzalo actually defends the Boatswain, suggesting a degree of admiring empathy (11).[12] In this case, then, Césaire enhances the characters' empathic response (a response that was apparently absent in Shakespeare's opening scene). In connection with this, he makes the class antagonism less absolute.

---

[11] Here and in subsequent citations, two page numbers or page spans separated by a semicolon refer to the English and French texts respectively. When only one number or span is given – or a series, separated by commas – it refers to the English text, unless otherwise noted.

[12] In the next section, we will return to the combination of empathy and admiration.

The second scene gives us the compassionate Miranda, who exclaims that "A person would have to have a heart of stone not to be moved" or, more literally, "the heart would have to be harder than a rock not to be torn" (12; 19). The image of tearing parallels the shredding of the ship in the storm. Indeed, just as the ship would have to be more solid than a rock not to split, so too would a person's heart have to be harder than a rock not to be rent. The image therefore directly suggests the mirroring operation of compassion.

The play turns to Césaire's variation on the usurpation of Milan. Prospero had been planning an imperial venture. Alonso and Antonio usurped his position to take charge of that venture. This alters the motivation of the usurpers, tying it more narrowly to greed. This simplifies the initial motivation of Antonio particularly. However, this simplification is compensated for with complication elsewhere. Antonio initially accomplishes his usurpation by denouncing Prospero to the Inquisition. For our purposes, this is relevant in two ways. First, it provides a "moral" pretext by which Antonio could rationalize his greed. In this context, he may see it, not as greed, but as a properly moral rejection of a heretical leader. Second, he does this precisely by associating Prospero with the devil, a standard model for undermining empathy – and one that has had particular importance in interracial relations.

One striking thing about Prospero's tale in both Shakespeare and Césaire is that it serves to undermine compassion – and, indeed, is told by Prospero in response to Miranda's expression of empathy. This is, again, one possible function of stories. In this case, the function is brought out particularly by the introduction of Ariel, who immediately expresses "pity" ("pitié," thus pity or compassion) that the ship so "full of life" has been wrecked (16; 22).

As indicated earlier, it initially seems that the fundamental difference between Ariel and Caliban is the difference between a loyal slave and a rebellious one. Along these lines, readers often view the distinction as that between the house slave and the field slave (on that distinction, see Malcolm X 243). But this introduction of Ariel suggests something else entirely. Both Ariel and Caliban want their freedom. Neither supports the slave system. The division, then, is not as simple as it first seems. At the same time, there is still a real difference. Ariel's politics are based on empathy from the start. His first appearance is a protest against violence. Prospero complains that "intellectuals" are always like that (16). Ariel responds by asking Prospero to relieve him from that *type* of work – presumably violent work, work that requires an absence of empathy. When Prospero will not agree to this, Ariel presses his demand for freedom. If one wants a parallel for Ariel, it is not to be found in the house slave, but in the parliamentary parties working for independence through legal channels – most obviously, a party such as the Indian National Congress as oriented by Gandhian principles and practices.

Césaire does not draw out the exchange between Prospero and Ariel, but rather introduces Caliban almost immediately. He enters saying "Uhuru!" (17), Swahili for "freedom." This associates him with a number of African national liberation movements, perhaps most obviously the Kenyan Mau Mau rebels – a very violent group who serve well as a contrary to such nonviolent political movements as Gandhi's Indian National Congress.

Prospero immediately assimilates Caliban to a monkey or ape, drawing on an animal model that operates to inhibit empathy. Caliban replies by connecting Prospero with a vulture (17). This too tends to inhibit empathy – though, of course, there is a difference. The metaphor of an ape, as commonly used, suggests intellectual and cultural inferiority that is racially based. It puts Caliban outside the realm of empathic identification for reasons of social group identity. In contrast, the metaphor of the vulture, as commonly used, suggests moral disgust. It may be understood as particular to Propsero.

Césaire goes on to develop some elementary empathy for Caliban on the part of the audience by stressing his attachment bond with his mother and his loyalty to his mother. When Prospero denounces her as "a ghoul," Caliban responds, "Dead or alive, she was my mother, and I won't deny her!" (18). This tends to foster our empathic sense that he has appropriate feelings. Moreover, he has moral control over any inappropriate feelings. Thus, he refuses to denounce his mother, even if he is tempted by the material gain that may follow from agreeing with Prospero. Césaire turns from this to an explicitly moral issue. Specifically, Prospero accuses Caliban of trying to rape Miranda – an accusation that, if true, would clearly inhibit most audience members' empathy with Caliban. Caliban responds, "old goat, you attribute to me your libidinous ideas" (my translation, from *Une Tempête* 27).[13] The

---

[13] The original is "tu me prêtes tes idées libidineuses" (27). The verb "prêter" means "to lend." Thus, Propsero "lent" his libidinous ideas to Caliban. Miller interprets that as meaning that Prospero "put those dirty thoughts in my [Caliban's] head" (19). But a standard usage of "prêter" for intentions is to *attribute* intentions, and often to do

point is crucial, for it makes Caliban more rather than less sympathetic. Far from being a potential rapist, he is – or, at least, claims to be – the victim of Prospero's own sick sexual fantasies.

Prior to this, Caliban has accused Prospero of confining him in "The ghetto" ("Le ghetto" [19; 26]). This may serve to suggest the United States and the struggles of New World Africans. Here many readers are likely to wonder if there is a connection between Ariel and Martin Luther King, Jr. on the one hand and Caliban and Malcolm X on the other. Two pages later, this link is confirmed when Caliban tells Prospero not to call him "Caliban," but to call him "X." This follows Prospero's identification of Caliban with the Devil ("Diable!" [*Une Tempête* 28][14]) – again, a model with consequences for empathy.

Caliban now departs and Ariel enters again. His first sentence appeals to "mercy" ("miséricorde" [21; 29]). Mercy may be considered a form of beneficence in which the target is in fact guilty of some moral fault and deserves punishment. In the case of mercy, the beneficence consists in mitigating the punishment, perhaps eliminating it entirely. Ariel is referring to the people who have been shipwrecked. Prospero responds that they need only repent to be granted his pardon. This is mercy in one sense, but – as is usually the case with Prospero – it is not clear that this act is based on compassion rather than self-interested calculation. In any case, if it is based on compassion, the reason for Prospero's unexpected fellow feeling is that there are fewer inhibitions on empathy in this particular case. Césaire has Prospero explain this explicitly – "They are men of my race, and of high rank" (21). Thus they are not separated by social stratification or other identity category.

Now Miranda and Ferdinand meet. Once again, we find Miranda associated with "pity" or compassion ("pitié" [22; 31]). As in Shakespeare, this feeling is enhanced by the attachment bonds now formed between the two. Here, too, Prospero makes Ferdinand his slave.

The second act begins with a meeting between Caliban and Ariel. Ariel asserts their brotherhood, their shared suffering and shared hopes (26). At first, this may seem surprising. It is not what one would expect from the "house slave" meeting the "field slave." However, it is what one would expect from someone whose politics are based on empathy. Affirming their shared suffering and hope is precisely affirming a

so falsely (see Petit and Savage 506). I therefore take it that Miller has translated the passage as meaning almost the precise opposite of what it actually does mean.

[14] This is missing from the English translation.

mutual compassion. Unsurprisingly, Caliban does not agree. He characterizes Ariel as an "Uncle Tom" ("oncle Tom" [26; 36]). At first, the dialogue works rather strongly against Caliban. He shows an apparent unwillingness to treat Ariel with the same compassion as Ariel shows for him. But Ariel also comes across as naïve. He insists "one thing" has been genuinely "achieved," for Prospero "promised" his "freedom" (26). The vision offered by Ariel is humane and hopeful, but Caliban's response is forceful as well. For Caliban, Ariel's ideals and expectations are all mere fancy, a pipe dream that in the end keeps Prospero in power. Ariel denounces violence and, pushing his politics of compassion to the limit, says that he is not merely trying to liberate the oppressed, but the oppressor as well. He wishes to free Prospero from moral depravity. Specifically, he wishes to provoke recognition in Prospero; he wishes "to trouble [or perturb][15] his serenity" (*Une Tempête* 37), presumably by fostering, in Prospero, compassion for those he brutalizes. Caliban replies that Prospero has no conscience (27). Worse still, he only feels himself when he crushes someone else (27; 38). In other words, Prospero's entire relation to Africans is the opposite of compassion. It is an emotionally complementary response to their suffering, not an emotionally parallel one. Ariel explains that he sustains himself with a vision of the future in which all three will be brothers, sharing their skills in a better world – thus a world in which each engages in beneficence for the others. Caliban, once again, views this as deeply naïve. But he has nothing to offer in its place. Indeed, he explains that, if he cannot free himself from Prospero's yoke, he will dynamite the entire island, sacrificing his own life if it will mean destroying Prospero as well. This is the extreme of empathy inhibition through anger, for it excludes compassion even for his future self.

Césaire subsequently takes us to the shipwrecked nobles. The scene shows these men tantalized by food that is magically brought to them, then removed, then brought again. When the food is returned, Gonzalo observes that perhaps the "Powers" behind the magic took "pity" ("pitié" [31; 43]) on them. Here, the sense seems closer to the derogatory use of "pity." But, in fact, there is something more sinister going on here. Alonso observes that this transportation of the food serves to make them aware of their "dependent status" ("dépendance" [31; 42]).

---

[15] For some reason, Miller translates "troubler" as "destroy" (27). This makes Ariel's aims vindictive by suggesting that he will not merely lead Prosper to change, but will leave him in a continual state of suffering. This is not the implication of the original.

Prospero explains that if they eat the food when it is returned, that is "a sign of submission" (31). Giving food in this case is a form of beneficial action that serves to affirm and enhance the superiority of the giver (i.e., Prospero). The point has only limited application to Alonso and his companions, but it has clearer application to colonized countries (e.g., when colonizers provide some form of food aid during famines that have been created by colonial policies). Ariel comments, "It is evil to play with their hunger as you do with their anxieties and hopes" (32). Césaire obviously intends the point to be generalized.

The plot of Sebastian and Antonio follows. Here again Césaire fills in the empathic concerns that are only suggested in Shakespeare. Specifically, Shakespeare has Sebastian halt the killing and take Antonio aside. It seems that this is because attachment concerns enhance his empathic response and thus inhibit the cruelty of murder. But, if so, this is not explicit. In contrast, Césaire has Sebastian exclaim "He's my brother!" (34) before the pause and consultation that allow Alonso to live.

Césaire introduces the plot of Caliban, Stephano, and Trinculo in act three. In this version, Stephano proclaims republican ideals. Caliban, once again, surrenders all claims to the island simply to procure the help of Stephano. This recalls those national liberation movements that ally themselves with outside powers, in effect surrendering their independence to the allies whose function is, supposedly, to help them achieve independence. There are some hints in this passage that Césaire could have the Soviet Union in mind. But any rival to the dominant colonial power would operate in much the same way.

After this, we see Prospero planning his punishment of Caliban. Again manifesting his politics of empathy, Ariel intercedes, asking for Prospero's indulgence and understanding (50). But Prospero refuses. He characterizes Caliban as evil, thereby rationalizing his inhibition of empathy through moral categorization and associated elaborative thought. The next scene opens with Caliban's parallel refusal of empathy with Prospero, in this case through an identity category, by which he identifies Prospero as a "hereditary" enemy (52; 74). Here Césaire suggests that both "enemies" employ the same techniques of empathy inhibition.

Astonishingly, however, when faced with the opportunity of killing Prospero, Caliban cannot act. Despite everything, he sees Prospero as another person, with feelings parallel to his own. In the next scene, Prospero frees Ariel. Thus, Césaire expresses a sort of faith in the ultimate triumph of an empathic politics. But Caliban does not thereby lose our compassion or our admiration. He delivers a stinging condemnation of Prospero's colonialism. It is stirring and fosters an admiring shared anger. But there is something wrong. Caliban and Prospero express their mutual hatred (63). They will stay, to fight one another, to respond to violence with violence (65). In the end, Prospero is aged and alone on the island. Caliban is nowhere to be seen. It seems clear that the empathy-inhibiting politics of identity and moral superiority – practiced by both Prospero and Caliban – have been destructive for both. Only Ariel's politics of compassion and beneficence would have helped either of them.

Literary Empathy, Pity, and Compassion

Empathy is always fundamental to literature.[16] Our emotional response to stories is inseparable from our empathic response to the characters, their situations, actions, capacities, and so forth. Of course, this is, first of all, "aesthetic empathy," not the sort of practical empathy we might experience in the real world. After all, literary characters are not real. Thus, beneficence would be misplaced – arguably pathological – in their case. At the same time, however, literary works are connected with our empathic relations to real people outside the fictional stories. If nothing else, our relations to social identity groups (races, nations, classes) in stories are likely to be continuous with those relations outside stories.

The two plays we have just considered bring out this aspect of literary empathy with particular force. At the same time, however, they suggest a kind of relativity about the empathic effects of literary works. After all, not everyone is a member of the same in-groups, and these plays are clearly aimed at different audiences, with different group compositions. This, in turn, points toward a complication. The literary enhancement or inhibition of empathy will operate differently for

---

[16] Some aspects of common views about empathy and literature have been challenged in important work by Suzanne Keen. Keen is right to caution against exaggerated claims for the moral efficacy of literature. However, she seems to hold literature to rather too high a standard. Specifically, she often seems to view literature as morally beneficial only if it inspires moral heroism. In fact, empathic effects of literature seem quite real, as empirical studies indicate (see Oatley "Communications"), even if they rarely lead to heroism. For further discussion of Keen's ideas, see the afterword of my *Affective*.

different audiences, given the different affiliations and empathic incli-nations of various audiences – some black, some white, some neither. It is worth considering this point in slightly more detail.

When there is a social division between two groups, perhaps the best way of blocking intergroup empathy is by representing the out-group as hostile toward the in-group. This is because such a representation is most likely to give rise, not to parallel feelings (in this case, anger against the in-group), but complementary feelings – either fear for the in-group or reciprocal anger against the out-group. For example, a film stressing black anger against whites is unlikely to foster white empa-thy with blacks. However, the same film may appeal to black audience members, fostering their empathy, depending on how the anger is por-trayed (e.g., if it shows defiance of racial injustice and noncowering indignation by blacks against white oppressors).

Conversely, perhaps the best way to inspire intergroup empathy is to portray the out-group as nonthreatening and as suffering in ways that could be alleviated by the in-group. At the same time, mute suffering on the part of fellow group members may give rise to a sense of moral disgust and thus inhibit empathic response within a group. To take a famous example, Harriet Beecher Stowe's *Uncle Tom's Cabin* may have been enormously effective in inspiring white pity for black slaves. But at the same time it may have filled many black readers with disgust for the (apparent) subservience of the black characters.[17]

We may formulate this issue in a preliminary way by reference to the distinction between compassion and pity, if we use the word "pity" in its more pejorative sense. Specifically, a work that appeals to a white audience by presenting a passive, suffering black community may be offensive to blacks even if it produces apparently benevolent action on the part of whites. Part of the reason for this is that such action is likely to be viewed as belittling, thus as pity, rather than as respectful, thus as compassion. To understand this difference more fully, however, we need to engage in a more fine-grained analysis of empathy.

The basic form of empathy involves imagining the actual responses of the other person. There are other possibilities as well, however.

---

[17] In fact, Uncle Tom is far from subservient. Most obviously, he refuses to give up the location of two escaped slaves even as he is tortured to death. However, he does often seem to be viewed as subservient, perhaps because of his gentle and benevolent manner.

Two are particularly important. The first is imagining oneself in the position of the other person. The second involves imagining some normatively standard person in that position. Complicated as it may seem, we commonly do all three. We may refer to these as "allocentric empathy," for empathy focusing on the actual responses of the target; "projective empathy," for empathy focusing on our own hypothetical responses (some authors refer to this as "sympathy"); and "normative empathy," for empathy focusing on some evaluative standard. The division is important and is, indeed, central to our judgments about individuals' character and virtues – even though it is almost always implicit.

The following scenario may serve to illustrate these points. Jones has to go into battle. Because he has fairly steely nerves, I may imagine his condition the night before battle with relatively little apprehension. In contrast, I may imagine myself in his place and feel a great deal of fear for him. This is fear for Jones, and not for myself, because I have no possibility of going into the battle and I have no particular relation to Jones that makes my interests depend on his well-being. I also have some idea of how fearful an ordinary soldier should be and I might imagine that condition. This gives me a standard against which I evaluate my projective and allocentric responses. Through these simulations, I may come to understand that Jones has less fear than I would have or than what I imagine a "good" soldier would have. In consequence, my allocentric fear for Jones is less than my normative or projective empathy. One result of this is that I am less inclined to "feel sorry" for Jones – but I am more inclined to *admire* him.

Now we are in a position to say something more systematic about the difference between compassion and pity. Given the different types of empathic response, we may distinguish those in which allocentric and projective empathy are roughly equivalent, those in which allocentric empathy differs from egocentric empathy in the direction of an ideal (itself defined by reference to normative empathy), and those in which allocentric empathy differs from egocentric empathy away from the ideal. To take the preceding case, we may distinguish between cases where Jones is just about as fearful of battle as I would be (the equality condition), where he is less fearful (the superiority condition – since the difference is toward the ideal), and where he is more fearful (the inferiority condition – since the difference is away from the ideal). Compassion is a form of empathy in which the equality condition holds.[18] Pity, in contrast, is a form of empathy in which the inferiority condition holds. Obviously, there is a third possibility as well. We might refer to it simply as "admiration." Pity is clearly problematic in certain ways. It is perhaps less obvious that admiration is often no less problematic. Idealization – the extreme of admiration – is not only likely to be false; it is also likely to greatly diminish our empathy with the aversive feelings of the target. For example, it is likely to lead us to imagine his or her sorrow or fear as less than it really is. This will limit our feelings for that other person, and our helping behavior.

Of course, the equality, superiority, and inferiority conditions are not entirely uniform because emotions are not entirely uniform. Again, emotion episodes involve different components. These components may imply different criteria for relative empathic evaluation. For example, focusing on phenomenological tone, we might consider someone superior who feels attachment love more strongly or fear more weakly. This is the case with Jones's steely-nerved entrance into battle. He is superior to me simply in the force of his feeling. Perhaps even more importantly, we may evaluate ourselves and others by reference to our capacities for inhibiting or modifying emotional impulses, particularly with respect to moral precepts. For example, I may imagine Jones as no less fearful than I would be when going into battle, but I may imagine him as more successful in controlling his fear. Finally, there are actional outcomes. I may imagine Jones as quite brave but hopelessly unprepared to actually fight a battle – not fully understanding the operation of his weapon, proper safety procedures during combat, and so forth. There are, of course, other ways in which we can imagine evaluative gradations. However, these three – phenomenological tone, ethical modulation, and actional outcomes – appear to be the most consequential for empathy generally and for its ethical relevance in particular.

Our admiration for a target increases to the extent that he or she is superior to us in these three areas. Jones is fully idealized to the extent that his feeling of fear is relatively weak; his ability to modulate that feeling by reference to ethical principles is high; and his competence in relevant action is great. Note again that this evaluation significantly

---

[18] In keeping with this, Oveis and colleagues note that "trait compassion significantly predicted perceived self-other similarity" (621). As we would expect, the causality here is not unidirectional. On the one hand, "Perceived self-other similarity ... appears to amplify compassion-related responses to others" (619). On the other, "induced compassion produced a globally heightened tendency to view oneself as similar to others" (624).

diminishes our empathic response to Jones. Indeed, there is a point at which idealization becomes so thoroughgoing that we can no longer be said to feel any empathy at all.

Our inclination toward pity initially increases with the inferiority of the other person in each area. We pity someone who is more fearful than we are. We pity them more if we feel that they do not have the capacity to inhibit that fear by reference to moral principles. We may have still greater pity if we imagine them to lack the capacities to act appropriately in response to the fear and the principles.

At the same time, our empathy in such cases is not limitless. At a certain point, it begins to decrease and eventually dissipates. Specifically, our empathy for "excessive" feeling reaches a limit at disgust. We may no longer feel pity for Jones once we find his greater fear so excessive as to be despicable. This is probably related to our sense that the emotions in question do or do not fall within some sort of acceptable human range, whatever we may (tacitly) take that to be. Our empathy for moral weakness begins to diminish significantly as that weakness produces empathy-inducing harm to others (e.g., as Jones's inability to moderate his fear leads to the wounding or death of fellow soldiers). It reaches an end-point when we can imagine no way of overcoming the weakness – for example, through support and aid. In other words, we tend to lose empathy for Jones when we feel that he will never inhibit his excessive emotions. Finally, our empathy for lack of ability diminishes to the extent that we view the other person as responsible for his or her incompetence.

In short, we are most likely to pity someone if we imagine him or her to have inferior, but not grossly excessive, emotional sensitivities, corrigible limitations on moral autonomy, and an excusable lack of behavioral competence. Put differently, we have greater pity for someone to the extent that we infantilize them, to the extent that we view them as experiencing the emotional intensities, inhibitory limitations, and behavioral incapacities of children, along with the child's possibility of developing out of those intensities, limitations, and incapacities. In connection with this, it is unsurprising that paternalistic racism, paternalistic colonialism, and the like tend to be associated with childhood and adolescent models for the subject peoples.[19] The limited empathic response of pity for an individual or group is perfectly congruent with a cognitive model of the target as a child.

---

[19] See Nandy 11–18; see also Hogan *Culture* 134–140.

As the final point suggests, evaluations may bear on individuals or on groups. Both sorts of evaluation may be problematic. Generally, however, we should be particularly skeptical of group judgments, because the likelihood of some group being morally superior or inferior, even for a particular property, is very slight. As such, group evaluation is likely to be false for a large number of individuals. The exceptions to this are probably all tied to very limited aspects of distinctive practices of the groups (e.g., on the whole, firefighters probably are superior to the average person in their bravery when faced with fires). Thus, it is often valuable to distinguish between identity-group pity (e.g., pity based on racial categorization) and individual pity.

On the other hand, ultimately, the crucial issue for both individuals and groups is simply the accuracy of the value judgment and, to some extent, its justification. Pity is generally not objectionable if it is based on a reasonable assessment of the target's propensities and capacities – for example, when the target actually is a child. The point applies to group pity and individual pity – though, again, group judgments are much more likely to be both inaccurate and unjustified. Indeed, it applies to compassion as well. Though rarely objectionable, compassion is rather pointless if it is inaccurate (e.g., if I feel compassion for someone's bereavement when he or she has not actually lost a loved one).

Of course, accuracy alone does not make either pity or compassion morally valuable. These feelings are morally consequential only by way of behavior in the world. The fundamental distinction here is obviously between empathic responses that give rise to action and those that do not. We may refer to the former as "actional empathy" or "kindness" and the latter as "benevolence" ("well wishing") or, in literary and related contexts, "aesthetic empathy." It may seem that empathy should always give rise to action. That is not true. For example, empathy is obviously fundamental to audience response in a theater. However, it is no less obviously inappropriate for audience members to engage in action that responds to the condition of the characters on stage. Moreover, there are situations in which we are not authorized to take action. Suppose I see a parent trying to comfort a hurt child. Unless I have some special expertise that would substantially change the child's (or the parent's) well-being, I generally should not act on my empathic feelings. This point brings us back to pity. Pity, again, presupposes that I am in some way superior to the person with whom I empathize. In this way, I am more likely to feel authorized to act when feeling pity than when feeling compassion or admiration.

In connection with this, we may distinguish different motives for empathy-based action. In each case, our motives are ultimately ego-based, but there are differences in the precise nature of that basis. Typically, there are three motives that figure in empathy-based action. One has to do with receiving some reward, such as gratitude. Another has to do with self-esteem. A third has to do with altering the condition of the target in order to alter one's own empathic feeling (e.g., I may try to relieve the other person's suffering because my empathic response makes his or her suffering painful for me).[20] All three motives enter in most cases of empathic action, but the relative importance of each is clearly consequential. It is particularly evident that there are cases of kindness genuinely aimed toward improving the condition of the target. We may refer to these as *beneficence*. (We saw an example of this at the start of Shakespeare's play, when Miranda tries to aid the victims of the tempest.) In other cases, however, our primary motivation is a matter of self-esteem or reward. Sometimes, kindness of this sort has almost no chance of producing improvement in the condition of the target. This is *meretricious charity*. It is obviously most common in cases of pity.[21]

A final axis of difference concerns the duration or extent of our empathic interest in others. There is obviously a range of interest extending from a narrow moment of immediate empathy (barely beyond emotional contagion) to an entire life trajectory. When I see a non-English-speaking stranger struggling to communicate his need for information, I experience a momentary empathic interest in the betterment of his condition. If I happen to speak his native language, I may step in and translate, but I am unlikely to involve myself in his well-being after that brief intervention. We might refer to this as "concern." In contrast, I am likely to have a large, ongoing interest in the well-being of my spouse or child. We might refer to this as *care*.

[20] Note that the first and second are self-focused whereas the last is other-focused, in the sense discussed by Iyer, Leach, and Pedersen. As noted in Chapter 6, research by this group indicates that "self-focused" emotions "provide only limited motivation to help the disadvantaged," whereas other-focused emotions "provide bases of more general support for helping behavior" (275).

[21] The likelihood of meretricious charity is increased by the fact that the endogenous reward system appears to be activated by an attitude of compassion or pity and related behavior (see Kim and colleagues). Thus, one may experience internal neurochemical reward even in the absence of external compensation.

Put very simply, then, we now have a sense of what is wrong with pity and what is right with compassion.[22] Specifically, we see that, other things being equal, meretricious charitable pity, particularly that based on group evaluations, is the most problematic. In order to refer to this tendency concisely, we might use the term "paternalism." This is what Césaire's Caliban opposes. In contrast, when accurate, the most desirable and admirable sort of empathy is beneficent, compassionate care. Unsurprisingly, it is often associated with attachment. This is what Césaire's Ariel embodies and advocates. What makes Césaire's play poignant, however, is that this feeling is not absent from Caliban, as suggested by his attachment to his mother. Nor is it absent from Prospero. But even Ariel's best efforts cannot reconcile them to one another in this feeling.

Conclusion

One current view of ethics is that it is a distinct and evolved cognitive system. This chapter began by arguing that ethics is not an evolved system per se. Rather, there are mechanisms that have evolved because they approximated adaptive functions (outside of ethics). In certain contexts, those mechanisms may come to have ethical consequences. Moreover, those ethical consequences occur (most often) at just those points where the mechanism diverges from its adaptive function. The fundamental instance of this is empathy. It evolved because it tends to reproduce one's genes or those of one's relatives. However, its mechanism continues to operate in contexts where the consequences actually harm such reproduction, as in non-kin altruism.

---

[22] One reader objected to the discussion of pity and compassion, writing that "I am less concerned about whether my attitude might be called pity or compassion than with whether I am able to treat any mentally competent adult human being on terms of equality and respect." It is important to stress that the goal of this discussion is not to isolate some putative "real meaning" of the words. Rather, the goal is to present an analysis of just what sorts of emotional responses are ethically relevant, how those responses relate to one another and to ethical judgment and behavior (or actional outcomes), and how they bear on different audiences for literary works. In short, the point is not that a particular sort of emotion or behavior should be given a certain name. The point is that there are certain emotional and behavioral tendencies, which we may for convenience refer to as "pity," "compassion," and so forth. The isolation of those tendencies has both descriptive and explanatory consequences. Put differently, it is not linguistic analysis, but part of a theoretical account of ethics and emotion. It should therefore help us understand more fully our own behavior and that of others. As a result, it should help us treat others "on terms of equality and respect."

Empathy may involve imagining some other person's experience as such (allocentric empathy), imagining oneself in his or her situation (projective empathy), or imagining some relevantly standard person in that situation (normative empathy). We commonly engage in and compare the outcomes of these three forms of empathic simulation. If the other person is superior to us, we experience admiration; if he or she is roughly equal to us, we experience compassion; if he or she is inferior to us, we experience pity. After a certain point, our pity for someone else will decrease as we come to see his or her feeling, moral inhibition, and competence as falling increasingly below the norm. This decrease is qualified by the degree to which we imagine the person's deficiencies to be corrigible and the degree to which we view him or her as blameworthy for those deficiencies. Both idealization (the extreme of admiration going beyond the norm) and pity tend to be problematic because they may lead us to underempathize with the other person and to behave inappropriately.

Clearly, the ethical point of empathy is to produce action. We may distinguish between action-producing empathy or kindness and inactive empathy or benevolence. (In the context of literary response, we may refer to inactive empathy as "aesthetic empathy.") An agent's motives for empathic action may be to ameliorate the condition of the other person ("beneficence"), but they may also be to obtain some reward or to enhance his or her own self-esteem ("meretricious charity"). Finally, our empathic interest in someone else may be confined to immediate circumstances ("concern") or it may extend to longer periods – ultimately the person's entire life trajectory ("care").

Literature relies on empathic response for our engagement with characters and stories. But it may also enhance or inhibit our empathy with real people outside the story – most obviously, with people in certain groups (e.g., the poor). Enhancing empathy commonly operates somewhat differently depending on a work's goals and target audience. Some strategies are valuable if our goal is to produce beneficent compassion across group lines – that is, in-group/out-group compassion (e.g., from European Americans to African Americans). Other strategies may be required if our goal is to produce beneficent in-group/in-group compassion, which is to say, solidarity (e.g., from African Americans to other African Americans). For example, to enhance Europeans' beneficent compassion for Africans, an author may be well advised to reduce the anger of African characters, at least insofar as it is aimed at Europeans, and to enhance depictions of suffering on the part of Africans. (Again, suffering tends to trigger parallel, rather than complementary, emotional responses. It therefore works against the complementary orientation of in-group/out-group divisions.) On the other hand, this is likely to foster pity, perhaps along with meretricious charity. Moreover, this might produce precisely the wrong result for African audience members. It might lead to a sense of shame or at least wounded pride (e.g., if Africans seem to be presented as lacking skills or other means for independent achievement). In contrast, African solidarity may be enhanced by an affirmation of the pride and dignity of Africans, including their anger. This, in turn, may provoke empathy-inhibiting responses of fear or reciprocal anger on the part of Europeans.

These points are nicely illustrated by certain aspects of Shakespeare's *The Tempest* and Aimé Césaire's *Une Tempête*, which construct their in-groups and out-groups in somewhat different but not at all unrelated ways. Césaire's play is particularly noteworthy in this respect because Césaire seeks to balance the portrayal of in-groups and out-groups in such a way as to develop beneficent compassion on all sides, as well as solidarity and pride among the oppressed.

Shakespeare's *The Tempest* implicitly stresses the inhibiting force of both fear and anger with respect to empathy. In some ways more importantly, the play also foregrounds the inhibiting force of class hierarchies. In a sense, upper classes are imaginatively impoverished with respect to those below them. In this play, they seem almost incapable of entering into empathic relations with subordinates. Moreover, when there is a violation of the hierarchy, they experience anger. Combined with the general lack of empathy, this gives rise to a response in which they feel complementary rather than parallel emotions – even to the point of relishing the pain of a punished subordinate. At the same time, the play hints that empathy can cross even the most antagonistic group divisions – though it does not indicate how this might be encouraged or productively developed.

Césaire's *Une Tempête* is no less focused on empathy than is Shakespeare's play. Indeed, Césaire renders more explicit some of Shakespeare's suggestions about empathy and the inhibition of empathy – for example, those relating to class and to ethnic identity categories. Césaire, then, integrates this into a political framework. In the end, he suggests that a politics of (empathy-blocking) anger – though often justified by the cruelty of oppressors – is ultimately self-destructive. The superior option is a politics of empathy, which begins with compassionate, caring beneficence toward the (oppressed) in-group but seeks to generalize that compassionate care and beneficence to all sides – including even the (oppressive) out-group.

Afterword: Studying Literature Shaping Emotion

Madame Bovary and the Sublime

In the preceding chapters, we stressed the ways literature depicts "real life" emotions and fosters empathic versions of those emotions in readers. But stories not only elicit short-term emotion events in readers; they affect our long-term emotional responsiveness – a point depicted by authors themselves since at least *Don Quixote*. Indeed, there would hardly be any point in treating moral or political issues in literature if the emotional effects of a work lasted merely a few minutes beyond the reading itself.

Literature can have moral consequences only insofar as it alters what we feel about situations and people, what we are motivated to do in our personal and social lives. As the example of *Don Quixote* suggests, this may occur through our precise imagination of goals, our construal of conditions in which we find ourselves, or other aspects of elaborative processing. Guided by stories, such processing may, in our imagination, transform windmills into threatening adversaries – or, what is more likely, an innocuous dark-skinned fellow passenger on a plane into a sinister terrorist.

Literary works also create emotional memories that may inflect our responses to the world long after reading. For example, consider Kamala Markandaya's treatment of rural poverty and hunger in *Nectar in a Sieve*. Many readers (including myself) are deeply moved by the events of this novel. This experience forms emotional memories that should have consequences when those readers hear reports of hunger or witness rural poverty. The importance of stories for young children, and their emotional engagement with such stories, may suggest that plots and characters affect critical period developments as well.

In short, literature not only depicts and provokes emotional experiences; it contributes to the formation and operation of our emotion systems in a range of ways. The example of *Don Quixote* also indicates that literature itself is a valuable source of information about that contribution. Of course, it would take another book to treat this topic adequately. However, it is worth briefly sketching some of the principal ways in which literature impacts our emotional lives, in order to gain a basic understanding of how this impact fits with the analysis of emotion set forth in the preceding chapters. In pursuing that task, this chapter will follow the general methodology of the book, focusing on a literary depiction of literature's long-term emotional effects.

A Life Ruined by Stories: *Madame Bovary* and Her Literary Emotions

Madame Bovary is one of the most important novels in the history of literature. Along with *Don Quixote*, it is one of two works that is particularly famous for its analysis – and criticism – of literature as a source of romantic misunderstandings of the world. Thus, Jonathan Culler stresses (and criticizes) "the seriousness with which Emma's corruption is attributed to novels and romances" (146). Henry James sees Emma as "a victim of the imaginative habit" (195). Peter Gay states that "If she had read less, she would have suffered less" (87). Some interpretations qualify the blame, dividing it between literature and personality. For instance, Bernard Paris notes that "her reading" has led to "unrealistic expectations" and "destructive 'ideals.'" However, he goes on to stress that this reading could only have its effect through *"interaction"* with her "individual psychology" (194). Nabokov goes a step further and sees the main problem in Emma. She is "a bad reader" who "reads books emotionally, in a shallow juvenile manner" (136). Similarly, Schehr writes that Emma does not "appreciate the literary value of a novel," but "retains clichéd images ... onto which she can graft her desires" (215).[1] Even in these final cases, however, it is clear that the texts themselves are far from irrelevant.

In fact, the following analysis will only partially agree with these critics, whether they primarily blame literature for Emma's misery or

---

[1] Ultimately, Schehr generalizes this beyond Emma, claiming that it is not only Emma who "fails to learn from her reading," for, in general, "reading does not matter" (215).

focus instead on Emma's own flaws. It is clear that Emma's imagination of romantic love has been affected by both the idealizations and ideologies of literary works. However, it is also clear that she has developed a certain fineness of emotional discrimination and a sensitivity to emotional relations that seem largely lacking in those around her. Put differently, it is not at all clear that Emma suffers from a narcissistic personality (as Paris argues[2]), an unusual degree of emotional or other "foolishness" (as Culler indicates[3] [140]), or even that she is a superficial reader of literature (as Nabokov claims), or a character who "is not the least little bit complicated" (in Henry James's words [211]). Moreover, I am unconvinced that her suffering is primarily the result of her reading. She is indisputably flawed, and some of her flaws derive from the books she read or the way she interpreted those books. Those "literary" flaws are connected with idealization and ideology, as we would expect. At the same time, however, the literature Emma encounters has also allowed her to understand that her husband's affection and devotion are inseparable from an almost pathological insensitivity to her feelings and interests. Stories have allowed her to imagine forms of passion and attachment that involve enhanced empathic understanding and care. In some ways, she is unfair to Charles, who is a decent and well-meaning man. Moreover, literary idealizations lead her to overestimate Rodolphe tragically. But there is something right about her desire for a greater bond of love. Her imagination has been formed to hold out such a possibility, and that is one source of her suffering. But in that respect, she is like a worker or peasant who has learned through stories to imagine a life not defined by grinding poverty. Such imagination may lead the worker or peasant to feel the pain of that poverty more acutely and perhaps even engage in acts of rebellion that ultimately only make things worse. But such an imagination is perhaps the only way of beginning to foster resistance to a situation that should be changed.

Critics have not entirely missed these points. Some have touched on it briefly. Culler acknowledges that, in some cases, there is "a measure of truth" in her "dissatisfaction" (140) and even an "exhilaration" in certain "modes of escape" – though, he adds, these "easily" become

---

[2] I should say, however, that Paris does rightly point to a number of problems with her aspirations and fantasies, which a full interpretation of the novel would have to take into account.

[3] Culler too presents an illuminating discussion of the novel, with many insights that a fuller treatment would need to incorporate.

"trivial, vulgar, insubstantial"[4] (141). Gay maintains that Flaubert is not an opponent, but a defender of "pure" Romanticism – though, as it turns out, this is a form of Romanticism of which his "characters" are "incapable" (see 79–80).

Though his focus is very different from that presented here, Stephen Heath is one of the few critics to have fully developed an approach that stresses the positive value of Emma's literary feelings (i.e., her emotions as transformed by literature). Heath first outlines "Emma's constant passion for things" (60), her "fetishism of objects" (63). This is the fault that is ultimately her downfall, for it drives her into ruinous debt. It does not seem to derive from novels or even from her own personality. Heath points out that, in this respect, "her aspirations mirror her class" (64) and are found in a range of other characters, from Charles's mother to Homais who ends the novel receiving the cross of honor. In fact, what elevates Emma above these other characters is reading – for example, education through which her "aspiration runs beyond situation which is then *known* as mediocre" (70). In connection with this, and in opposition to standard views of Emma, Heath asks, "Should we not, on the contrary, assent to her revolt against the mediocre world around her and recognize the value of her reading as the refusal of her oppressive life as Madame Bovary?" (77).[5]

The basic plot of *Madame Bovary* concerns Charles and Emma Bovary (née Rouault). Charles is a generally kindly but somewhat unself-consciously egocentric man of, at best, mediocre intellect. He becomes a health officer and marries the daughter of one of his patients. Nurtured by romantic stories, Emma finds herself disappointed in life with Charles, whom she does not love. She engages in two failed extramarital affairs – one with the Lothario, Rodolphe; the other with the more sincere but ultimately fickle and pusillanimous Léon. In the course of these affairs, she runs up huge debts. In the end, abandoned by both lovers, facing the financial ruin of her family, she poisons herself. Charles, deeply grieving, is plunged into poverty. He eventually dies, after learning of her infidelity. Their young daughter is sent off to a series of relatives. The last of her foster parents puts her out to work in a cotton mill.

---

[4] Culler is probably right about this, but it is also probably less significant than other problems in Emma's life.

[5] Readers interested in exploring aspects of *Madame Bovary* beyond the impact of literature on the formation of emotion may wish to consult Heath's valuable book.

Needless to say, the novel is not without its own ideologies and idealizations (though, in each case, the text is complex and nuanced; moments of apparently patriarchal or class ideology are contradicted by other moments that are inconsistent with such ideologies). But our concern is the way it represents Emma's emotional propensities as formed by literature. Clearly, this formation will operate differently in the case of different emotions. Here, we are dealing primarily with romantic love. We will concentrate on the early parts of the novel because this is where the literary effects are established. Their consequences follow a fairly predictable path thereafter.

Emma marries Charles believing that she feels love for him. This is perhaps her one crucial mistake, for she simply does not love him. On the other hand, we need not interpret this as a personal mistake. To a great extent, it seems to be a problem with the way marriages are contracted in Emma's society. They do not allow the partners adequate means of learning what their feelings are or will be.

In any case, Emma's lack of love immediately introduces us to her reading. She explains that "the words *felicity, passion,* and *inebriation* ... seemed so beautiful in books" (69, here and below, my translation). The point, of course, is that love is represented in books as producing felicity, passion, and inebriation. She feels none of these. But is this the fault of her reading? That is the obvious interpretation. She has been misled into maintaining an impossible ideal. But, in fact, Flaubert shows remarkable insight here in isolating the three component systems of romantic love. "Passion" clearly refers to sexual desire. "Inebriation" or "drunkenness" ("*ivresse*") is an apt characterization of the endogenous reward system response, recalling its relation to addiction. Finally, "felicity" is a generalized feeling of well-being of precisely the sort one experiences in a secure attachment relation.[6] Thus, Emma's reading has led her to understand romantic love quite well. This understanding has guided her elaborative anticipation of what married life will involve. The contrast with her actual experience produces

---

[6] This passage is frequently quoted by critics, but it appears they often misunderstand it. Culler sees the reference to felicity, passion, and intoxication as "evidence" that "Emma's desires are created by a language of romance" (166). Similarly, Elissa Marder sees this passage as indicating that "any and all words could potentially become meaningless in the language of life" (137). But it seems, rather, that Emma seeks experiential understanding of the words "felicity," etc., precisely because they are not meaningless – precisely because they represent a desire that is not created by language, but derives from the way our emotion systems are integrated in romantic love.

recurrent experiences of disappointment, leading to a more enduring mood of dissatisfaction.

Perhaps without the reading, Emma would simply have accepted her lot, not realizing that she could be experiencing passion, intoxication, and attachment. Perhaps she would not have imagined alternatives. But her current ability to imagine romantic love is only a problem due to the constraints that prevent her from pursuing such love in any socially approved way.

Moreover, it becomes clear that Emma actually feels disgust for Charles. The point is suggested right before the passage we have been considering. Charles, who clearly does feel all three components of romantic love, simply cannot keep from touching Emma. But Emma pushes him away. This is what one would expect. Intimate relations with the secretions and smells of another person's body provoke disgust. That disgust would be inhibited by desire, reward dependency, and attachment. But Emma does not have any of these positive feelings, thus her disgust system is likely to be aroused without inhibition. This arousal may be still further enhanced by her dissatisfaction. Indeed, dissatisfaction might be understood as involving mild anger and disgust responses to a person or situation (in relation to imagined alternatives). In keeping with this, her dissatisfaction is directly opposed to beauty in the passage we have been considering – for felicity, passion, and inebriation appeared "beautiful in books." As we saw in earlier chapters, our sense of a beloved person's beauty derives significantly from the individuating orientation of attachment. It is directly opposed to the grossly common elicitors of disgust that characterize the bodies of people to whom we are not attached, especially those for whom we do not feel desire and in whose presence we do not experience reward satisfaction.

The reference to books, beauty, and romantic love ends one chapter (chapter 5 of part 1). The next chapter begins with a brief history of Emma's literary reading. Flaubert notes that she read *Paul et Virginie* as a young girl, evidently around the age of twelve. (In the next sentence, Flaubert mentions that Emma was sent to the convent at the age of thirteen [70], presumably indicating that she had read Saint-Pierre's novel just before this.) This novel represents an idealized love ultimately made tragic by social interference in the natural development of the lovers' relationship. The basic story is a fairly standard romantic plot, developed in connection with concerns of the period (such as colonialism and intercultural relations). The story clearly served to provide Emma with early, crucial exemplars for romantic love. These highly salient instances would subsequently guide her expectations about the intensity of romantic longing, and the depth of feeling shared by lovers. In part, they would do this directly – as models and as emotional memories – and in part they would do this indirectly, through their effects on the formation of prototypes.

As to the last point, stories such as *Paul et Virginie* would have led Emma to form both character and narrative prototypes. The character prototypes would subsequently affect her expectations of and thus response to real people, such as Charles. This need not be problematic. Romantic longing can be very intense and can intensify shared feeling, empathy, willingness to sacrifice oneself for the beloved, and so on. Emma has every reason and right to desire this. At the same time, however, these prototypes may lead to elaborative processes that result in false expectations or that guide behavior in harmful ways. Before marriage, character prototypes may have led Emma to imagine life with Charles in a way that was really not possible, given Charles's personality. Moreover, the literary idealization of romantic love typically leaves out triggers of disgust, anger, and other emotions that would have inhibitory effects on the passion and inebriation for which Emma longs. Insofar as her elaborative imagination excludes these feelings, moments of disgust or anger in real life could become particularly intense by contrast with expectation.

The imagination of sequences of events, or "scripts," for romantic love would also have effects. Expanding beyond *Paul et Virginie*, we might expect such scripts to include the sorts of heroic anticipations that Emma has with respect to Rodolphe and Léon later in the novel. Perhaps the most important aspect of these scripts, however, is not the heroism per se, but rather the self-destructive quality of that heroism.

As discussed in the opening chapter, our enjoyment of tragic stories suggests that we experience some pleasure in simulation, even when this simulation concerns intrinsically aversive events. Certain sorts of tragedy can systematically intensify this pleasure by multiplying relevant emotion triggers and guiding elaborative processing around such events. For example, a primary aesthetic and ideological purpose of heroic literature is to elevate the pleasure surrounding a tragic imagination of death in battle. Authors accomplish this by a number of means. First, they often make the pain itself less salient (e.g., we are rarely given the sense of how excruciating a wound can be). Second, they give the hero some intense, salient emotion that is empathically pleasurable – prominently, what the Sanskrit theorists refer to as "energy" or "energetic enthusiasm" (see Bharatamuni 91), a form of single-minded engagement with forceful physical pursuit of some goal. This may be highlighted by a momentary hesitation, a brief, fearful "pause" (as the Sanskrit theorists would say [see Dhanaṃjaya 24]) that enhances our response to the heroic energy through contrast. Note that this is a form of idealization because it tends to remove ambivalence from the heroic action itself (e.g., the actual battle with the enemy), thereby reducing its aversive quality. A third technique is making the heroic pursuit unequivocally moral. This serves to guide the reader's elaborative processing and associated recruitment of memories, minimizing at least certain sorts of unpleasant associations. Finally, authors commonly represent the heroic act as glorious in the sense of producing fame and awe among people generally.

By enhancing emotionally pleasurable aspects of the hero's suffering and death, and by reducing painful aspects, authors may produce a powerful emotion. The emotion is not lacking in sorrow, fear, and anger. However, the aversive quality of those emotions is overwhelmed by the pleasure of the larger experience – in part due to the tendency of our emotion systems to take emotionally ambivalent inputs and produce emotional valence – that is, an overall positive or negative response (see Ito and Cacioppo 69 on this tendency). This emotion, developed systematically in tragedies, is clearly not something we would ordinarily refer to as a sense of *beauty*. However, it no less clearly has an aesthetic quality. Specifically, this simulation of a strongly aversive event with intense pleasure-enhancing associations appears to be precisely what literary theorists since Longinus have been trying to understand under the name of the *sublime*.

Clearly, sublimity is not confined to heroic plots. It occurs in all the major genres. There is a sublimity to sacrifice in sacrificial plots and – our main concern here – there is a sublimity to romantic tragedy. The techniques for developing the sublime are the same in all three cases. In the case of romantic love, the tragic lovers evidence the same single-minded, almost oblivious engagement in pursuing their dangerous goals. There may be a moment of hesitation, a pause (as when Juliet questions whether she should take the sleeping potion). But this is followed by full commitment. The goal of union is unquestionably good, because the lovers in some sense belong together. Finally, there is glory in their self-sacrifice as they achieve renown for their love (again, *Romeo and Juliet* provides a good example).

The heroic sublime often has practical consequences. Indeed, it is commonly designed to have such consequences. It is a tool of propaganda to encourage young men to sacrifice themselves for king and country. But, if the heroic (or sacrificial) version can have an impact in real life, so too can the romantic version. The greatest effect of Emma's readings may not have been in her affairs with Rodolphe and Léon, but in her suicide; it may not have been in her life, but in her death. Literary simulations made such a death appear sublime; Flaubert is at pains to show that it is, in fact, pathetic and brutal.

In keeping with this analysis, Flaubert presents Emma as having what we might refer to as "high trait sublimity" – a strong, personality-based inclination toward responding pleasurably to the glorification of pain. At the convent, she focuses on images of "the sacred heart pierced with sharp arrows" and "the poor Jesus who falls when walking with his cross"; she subjects herself to acts of "mortification" (70). Flaubert stresses that she does not find mere beauty appealing, but turns continually to the sublime (e.g., "She did not love the sea except because of its storms" [71]).

At the age of fifteen, she reads continually about romantic love. Here too she focuses on "persecuted ladies," fainting, "sobs, tears," death (72). Her heroines are "unfortunate" women, such as Joan of Arc (72). It is all pleasurable pain – suffering bound up with felicity, passion, and intoxication; attachment, desire, and reward. One might even begin to suspect here that Emma's later misery may be almost self-willed, almost planned, as she continually makes choices that push her toward the sort of exquisite agony that characterizes the Romantic sublime.

At that point, however, it is all still simulation. It is difficult to say just what the real consequences of such fantasies might be. Certainly there would be some, but they might be limited and relatively inconsequential. However, at this point, a crucial event occurs: Emma's mother dies. Flaubert explains that "she wept a great deal the first days." But then she managed to modulate her grief by drawing on the literary sublime. The transitional work here was Lamartine's "Le Lac," which treats the poet's loss of his beloved (73). The link is appropriate, for it connects her attachment to her mother with the attachments of romantic love. This integration of personal grief into literary sublimity brings her fantastical world of sweet suffering into relation with her lived world of human attachment. From now on, it will be difficult for her to consider or respond to any attachment object without these emotional memories affecting her spontaneous response, without these prototypes guiding her elaborative imagination.

These passages suggest something that we would expect from the preceding chapters – that stories figure not only in the formation of emotional memories and in the development of prototypes that guide elaborative processing; they also figure in the shaping of emotional sensitivity and response as these occur during a critical period. Here, it seems crucial that Emma began to read romantic stories just before the onset of puberty, then through the early period of puberty. Attachment and reward clearly develop before puberty. However, one might expect that puberty would have at least some critical period effects on the development of sexual desire. After all, this is the period when sexual desire grows into its full physical form, with possible actions and pleasures. Thus, one would expect experiences, real or imagined, to have more fundamental and enduring consequences during this period.[7] Moreover, one would expect some significant changes in the attachment system at this time. This is, after all, the period during which children systematically separate from parents. Generally, this separation is gradual and partial. Attachment to parents remains, as well as the reciprocal relations that are part of this attachment. In Emma's case, however, the separation was more sudden and complete. This adds a traumatic element to Emma's attachment relations. In context, this was likely to enhance her inclination to modulate painful feelings through sublime imaginations.

Soon Emma returns home, still a young girl, now motherless. She is clearly in need of a substitute attachment relation. In this way, she is like Hamlet at the time of his father's death. However, her relative youth makes the need far more intense. Also like Hamlet, her options are limited. She sees Charles, but only briefly, and at his best. What she does not see is necessarily filled in by imagination – and, in her case, that imagination is guided by the sublime prototypes of romantic tragedy. She comes to believe that she possesses "that marvelous passion" that she glimpsed before only "in the splendor of poetic skies" (74). Flaubert's language seems to mock Emma, and perhaps that is what Flaubert intended. If so, it was unfair of him. Emma's emotional needs and limited knowledge brought her into error here. Her sense of sublimity – suggested by the word "splendor" – has misled her.

---

[7] The idea is at least compatible with the view that there may be "several critical periods" of brain development related to "hormonally dependent sex differences" (Gorski 1131), and that "during puberty, it is likely that structural changes [occur] in the central nervous system" (1141).

She has misunderstood Charles. But, again, the aspiration is not itself objectionable – far from it.

Indeed, however much Emma may frame her dissatisfaction in terms of Charles's mediocrity, the faults in Charles go deeper than mere averageness. The faults in their relationship are real – and, again, Emma's exposure to literature helps reveal those faults, even if it is not adequate to give her a full understanding of them. Despite Charles's obvious attachment to Emma, it is clear that he is no less operating under illusions than she was. The main difference is that Emma has been open to contravening evidence. She recognizes that Charles is not the man she imagined. Charles cannot achieve this realization about Emma. The problem is that his intellectual deficits are not only a matter of reasoning and knowledge. He is also enfeebled in emotional sensitivity and understanding – just the traits that Emma has been cultivating through her reading of literature (as one might expect from empirical studies of literature and emotional intelligence [see Oatley "Communications"]).

Specifically, Emma's dissatisfaction with Charles is not simply that he is slow, dull, unaccomplished. It is, most importantly, that she cannot share her emotions with him. She feels an "ungraspable malaise" that she needs to express. If only "Charles had wished," if "his gaze, just once, had met her thought," that would have been something, an opening, a possibility. But he is entirely oblivious, insensible to what she feels. The absence of emotion sharing is fundamental to her growing "detachment" (75) from him. Flaubert explains that Charles's conversation is filled up with commonplace ideas, what "everyone" thinks, "without arousing emotion" (76) – the opposite of the particular individuality of emotion sharing. This feelingless talk is bound up with his lack of literary interest or experience. As Flaubert explains, "When living in Rouen, [Charles] was never curious to go to the theater" (76). The point is not some sort of an aside. It is, in part, an explanation. Charles returns home in the evening, sits at dinner, and tells "one after the other all the people he met, the villages he visited, the prescriptions he wrote and, satisfied with himself," finishes his meal (77). Emma is reduced to reciting poetry alone in the garden at night (78). This may seem an exemplary instance of her foolishness. But I take it to be a profound instance of her loneliness, a loneliness produced by the impossibility of sharing emotions with her husband – an impossibility that crucially includes the sharing of literature that she finds moving.

In light of such daily experiences, Emma realizes that she has made a terrible mistake. She asks herself why she married (79) and tortures herself with imaginations of what relationships she could have had. She imagines a different man, "beautiful, spiritual, distinguished, attractive" (79), a man that she could desire ("attractive") and admire ("distinguished"), but perhaps above all a man with whom she could share her sense of beauty and sublimity – for the sense of sublimity is precisely what characterizes Emma's ideas about and feelings of the "spiritual."

Later, she tries to find "imaginary satisfactions" (92) for her needs in literature. She brings a book to dinner, reading while Charles chews and talks. This is not simply a foolish preference for fantasy over reality. It is an indication that, indeed, she can achieve as great a sense of sharing with an unresponsive book as with Charles – that, indeed, Charles's talk runs on with such imperviousness to Emma that she may as well be reading a book. She dreams of other dinners – "people of letters" in "restaurants ... after midnight ... full of ideal ambitions" marked by "something sublime" (92–93).

As time passes, lacking even basic emotion sharing, Emma's loneliness only increases. She buys "blotting paper, stationery, a penholder, and envelopes," but finds she has no one to write to (94). She stops playing the piano for there is no one who listens, no one with whom she can share this art (96). Sometimes she tries talking to Charles about "things she has read, such as a passage from a novel." But, in the end, this is hardly different from sharing "confidences with her greyhound" (96). Drawing on images from *Paul et Virginie*, she sees herself as on a ship "in distress" (96). Here, in a pattern we have seen elsewhere, her despair in intensified by the apparent impossibility of doing anything to alter her situation. "The future" for Emma "was a completely black corridor" with "its door well shut at the end" (96). This is no longer sublime. It is simply painful, with no redeeming elevation.

Here, we might contrast Emma's first relationship with Léon. Her affair with Rodolphe is misguided and self-destructive. Her later affair with Léon is little better. But for a brief time, early in the novel, her connection with Léon seems both real and significant – not the product of almost willful misunderstanding, not a confused longing for the sublimity of pain. From the start, it is clear that he has at least something of her taste for the sublime. He values the same "grandeur," the "torrents" and "precipices" of nature (116). More importantly, they have their love of literature in common, their immersion in stories – "adventures ...

characters" (117). Their romantic involvement is not a matter of sexual opportunism prettified by romantic imaginations, only half believed (or, in the case of Rodolphe, not believed at all). This relation is founded on emotion sharing, "a common sympathy" (119). Indeed, it is both more profound and, at once, more literary than Emma's sexual relations – for "a sort of association established itself between [Emma and Léon], a continual commerce of books and romances" (132), an ongoing exchange of physical texts, of the stories those texts contain, and of the feelings that the two people share through those stories and their discussions about the stories.[8] Later, in the "funereal" day after Léon departs, Emma remembers their joys – the two of them deep in the garden, Léon reading aloud and "the fresh wind from the prairie fluttering the pages of the book" (155). It is the precise opposite of her despondent recitation of poetry, also in the garden, but alone, after her marriage.

Ironically, this is the one relationship about which Emma is uncertain, the one where she hesitates to affix the label "love" – though it is the only one of her relationships to which the term clearly applies. It is the only relationship that genuinely involves mutual attachment, desire, and reward dependency. Moreover, it is the only relationship in which those mutual feelings can interact and enhance one another due to emotion sharing. However, this gentle feeling is unrecognizable as love. It does not sear her with pain. It is not sublime. Love, she thought, would be a "hurricane" that would "throw her over" and "carry her entire heart into the abyss" (133).

Unfortunately, the social situation in which Emma finds herself does not permit this relation to continue. Léon must leave. When he returns, things are not the same. It seems that she has only two choices – the terrible loneliness of life with Charles or the pretence of love with Rodolphe, then later with the altered Léon. Her literary reading helps her realize what she is missing with Charles. It probably does lead her to brood on that loss, thus to intensify the feelings of disappointment and longing. But it does not create those feelings. They are part of the social condition. Her readings undoubtedly facilitate her misapprehension of

---

[8] Laurence Porter maintains that there is an "incompatibility" between Emma and Léon. For example, "Léon's tastes are closer to the Romantics under Napoleon I, to Chateaubriand or Senancour; Emma's are closer to the frenetic and Gothic literature of the following generation" (140). He may be right about the difference, but that hardly suggests an incompatibility. On the contrary, it suggests the value and even sincerity of their dialogue, their sharing of literature and feeling across different points of view. Attachment, passion, and reward dependency are not mere narcissism, after all.

Rodolphe and, later, of Léon as well. But they do not force that misunderstanding. Even here, the problem is her social conditions. She has too few possibilities for action. She chooses what seems best and tries to imagine that it is better than it is, drawing on the images, memories, and prototypes of romantic stories. Even her suicide is not only the result of imagining love as tragic and tragedy as sublime; it is also the result of having exhausted all options for action. All that remains in her imagination of the future is that final, terrible, and yet, in fancy, magnificent death.

Conclusion

In short, *Madame Bovary* suggests that literature is far from being the only element in the formation of emotion. There are fundamental human needs – for attachment, for reward, for sexual engagement, for the sharing of emotions. Moreover, there are social conditions that either constrain or facilitate the fulfillment of those needs. On the other hand, literature is also far from being inconsequential. Throughout our lives, stories can alter the way we respond to situations spontaneously or the way we elaborate on them imaginatively. Stories encountered during a critical period may have even more profound and pervasive consequences. Indeed, it seems that literature may broadly affect the way we engage in simulation, including the degree to which we associate certain types of suffering with exaltation.

More exactly, literature not only depicts emotion; it contributes to the formation of emotion. It contributes to this formation in three ways, through its effects on 1) spontaneous response, 2) elaborative processes, and 3) actional outcomes. In addition, it bears on the social and interactive modulation of emotion, primarily through both experiential and communicative emotion sharing.

As to spontaneous response, literature most obviously produces emotional memories. This occurs throughout our lives. However, it may be that stories have more enduring formative effects when encountered during a critical period. Early adolescence may be such a period for sexual desire. In connection with this, it seems at least possible that stories encountered during that period, stories that produce emotional effects, may inflect the development of sexual desire in much the way that real experiences do. Moreover, stories may affect the integration of distinct emotion systems during periods when they first become connected. This may be the case with the integration of sexual desire, attachment, and reward in romantic love. This is made particularly likely by the fact that adolescence is a period when one component (sexual desire) matures and another (attachment) alters significantly.[9]

Of course, if literature does have these effects, it is unlikely that they apply uniquely to sexual desire and romantic love. A wide range of emotions may be affected through the formation of emotional memories and through critical period experiences. One difference, however, is that the works we conceive of as "verbal art" are likely to have their effects only after childhood. Thus, they are more likely to affect emotion systems that undergo critical developments in adolescence or later. For emotions with critical periods in early childhood, simpler narratives (e.g., children's stories) are likely to take on this role.

The effects of literature on elaborative processing are perhaps even more obvious. Stories contribute to our prototypes for persons, events, actions, and conditions. These prototypes guide our imagination of what is likely to happen in the future, our construal of what happened in the past, even our encoding sensitivities, thus our ongoing perception of what is happening in the present. This can have a wide range of enhancing and/or inhibiting effects. For example, some prototypes will lead us to pay greater attention to particular individuals as possible romantic partners or possible sources of danger, while discounting others. That enhanced attention will be accompanied by fuller elaboration, thus more vivid emotion-producing images, greater recruitment of emotional memories, and so on. Indeed, our emotion-inducing expectations derive not only from prototypes and other generalized structures, but also from particular memories, presumably including those that derive from literature. As Schacter, Addis, and Buckner explain, "thoughts of past and future events" seem "to draw on similar information stored in episodic memory and rely on similar underlying processes, and episodic memory is proposed to support the

---

[9] Keith Oatley, perhaps wearing his novelist hat rather than his psychologist hat, pointed out to me that literature is able to produce these effects in part through techniques of narration. Indeed, the effects of *Madame Bovary* itself are not solely a matter of the story, but also of the way it is narrated. As Percy Lubbock noted, like many other novelists, Flaubert sometimes presents his story events as they would be "perceived" externally, whereas at other times, he gives us access to "unexpressed thought" (65). Undoubtedly, the ways in which authors create narrators and limit or extend their knowledge about characters is an important – and, to some extent, distinctive – part of the emotional effects of literature generally. Indeed, an analysis of narrational features and their effects could provide one future task for an ongoing research program in literature and emotion.

construction of future events by extracting and recombining stored information into a simulation of a novel event" (659–660).

The effects of literature on emotion can involve particularly complex organizations of ambivalence as well. The experience of sublimity presents a striking case of this sort. Again, in order to be adaptive, simulation must have some intrinsic appeal for both pleasurable and aversive contents. If imagining painful outcomes is only painful, then I am unlikely to imagine those outcomes, thus realizing that I should avoid them in real life. Literature enhances this pleasure – thereby limiting the deterrent effect of aversive imagination – by several means. First, it often makes the pain less salient. Second, it often stresses some associated but pleasurable emotion, such as a single-minded engagement in action. Third, it marks the action as fully moral, thereby guiding our elaborative processing and recruitment of emotional memories. Finally, literary works often develop portrayals of ancillary benefits, such as admiration from others. As a result, many tragic sequences in literature produce the pleasurable pain of sublimity. The sublime appears in all the main literary genres, potentially encouraging practical actions in the real world – heroism, self-sacrifice, and the sort of suicidal romanticism found in *Madame Bovary*.

This reference to practical consequences leads us to our final topic. In the opening chapter, we considered how the sharing of literature manifests a fundamental emotional propensity. Flaubert's novel seems to suggest that literature helps shape our emotion sharing as well. Emma feels despair over her relation to Charles and joy in her relationship with Léon. In each case, the respective feeling is inseparable from her desire to share emotion-laden stories. Emma's concern here is not just with the anecdotes of her daily routines; it is not just with personal histories. Indeed, these personal histories seem far less important than the literary works that absorb her interest and provoke her affections. These are, again, detailed depictive representations, separate from her, from Charles, from Léon. They are detailed depictive representations to which each person can respond and which can serve as a touchstone for their emotional similarities and differences.

Of course, here, the effects of literature are not a simple result of the literature itself, in combination with the prior affective and cognitive condition of the reader. The effects in this case are equally a product of the dialogue that occurs between the readers who are sharing their thoughts and feelings. This reminds us of the importance, not only of literature, but of literary study as well. This book began with an argument for the value of literary study in contributing to our understanding of emotion. The importance of dialogic sharing of emotion suggests that literary study is also consequential because it contributes to our elaborative processing of individual literary works, thus our recalibration of our own responses in interaction with the responses of others – even, one hopes, the enrichment of our sensitivities and empathies. In other words, literature and literary study are important not only for our scientific knowledge of emotion, but for our emotional lives as well.

For Nabokov, Emma Bovary's tragedy was bound up with her being a superficial reader (136). The preceding analysis suggests that her problems were primarily a matter of the circumstances in which she found herself. Indeed, her reading would have had a salutary effect of enhancing her recognition of emotional possibilities, had her life options been less dismally limited. Nonetheless, that analysis also indicated that Emma's problems were compounded by a perhaps excessive propensity toward an imagination of and delight in the sublime, which drew her to the tragic almost as much as it drew her to a lover. But perhaps both Nabokov and I are wrong in faulting Emma's relation to literature in any way. Perhaps the ultimate tragedy of Emma's life was not that she read wrongly. Rather, the tragedy was that she never had the chance to fully integrate that reading in a dialogue that would value but also limit the sublime; a dialogue that would affirm but also qualify the ideality of felicity, passion, and intoxication; a dialogue that would itself sustain a less turbulent but more fulfilling mutuality of shared emotion. The point does not apply to Emma Bovary alone. It speaks to the fundamental purposes of literature and criticism, which realize themselves not only in reading, but in emotion-sharing dialogue about that reading.

Works Cited

Adams, Henry, Lester Wright, and Bethany Lohr. "Is Homophobia Associated with Homosexual Arousal?" *Journal of Abnormal Psychology* 105 (1996): 440–445.

Adelman, Janet. *Suffocating Mothers: Fantasies of Maternal Origin in Shakespeare's Plays*, Hamlet *to* The Tempest. New York: Routledge, 1992.

Alderdice, Lord. "The Individual, the Group and the Psychology of Terrorism." *International Review of Psychiatry* 19.3 (2007): 201–209.

al Haj, Sami. "Humiliated in the Shackles." *Amnesty International* (Fall 2007): 19.

Altman, Joel. *The Improbability of Othello: Rhetorical Anthropology and Shakespearean Selfhood*. Chicago, IL: University of Chicago Press, 2010.

Amaral, David. "The Functional Organization of Perception and Movement." In Kandel, Schwartz, and Jessell, 337–348.

Anderson, Craig and L. Rowell Huesmann. "Human Aggression: A Social-Cognitive View." In Hogg and Cooper, 259–287.

Anderson, Cameron and Dacher Keltner. "The Emotional Convergence Hypothesis: Implications for Individuals, Relationships, and Cultures." In Tiedens and Leach, 144–163.

Angyal, Andras. "Disgust and Related Aversions." *Journal of Abnormal and Social Psychology* 36 (1941): 393–412.

Archer, John. *The Nature of Grief: The Evolution and Psychology of Reactions to Loss*. London: Routledge, 1999.

Aristotle. "Poetics." In *Aristotle's Theory of Poetry and Fine Art with a Critical Text and Translation of the Poetics*. Ed. and trans. S. H. Butcher. 4th ed. New York: Dover, 1951.

Attardo, S. *Humorous Texts: A Semantic and Pragmatic Analysis*. Berlin: Mouton de Gruyter, 2001.

Bachorowski, Jo-Anne and Michael Owren. "Vocal Expressions of Emotion." In Lewis, Haviland-Jones, and Barrett, 196–210.

Baddeley, Alan, Michael Eysenck, and Michael Anderson. *Memory*. New York: Psychology Press, 2009.

Bair, Deirdre. *Samuel Beckett: A Biography*. New York: Harcourt, Brace, Jovanovich, 1978.

Barker, Francis and Peter Hulme "Nymphs and Reapers Heavily Vanish: The Discursive Con-texts of *The Tempest.*" In *Alternative Shakespeares.* Ed. John Drakakis. London: Methuen, 1985.

Barnard, Mary, ed. and trans. *Sappho: A New Translation.* Berkeley, CA: University of California Press, 1958.

Bartels, Emily. "Making More of the Moor: Aaron, Othello, and Renaissance Refashionings of Race." *Shakespeare Quarterly* 41.4 (1990): 433–454.

Barthelemy, Anthony. *Black Face Maligned Race: The Representation of Blacks in English Drama from Shakespeare to Southerne.* Baton Rouge, LA: Louisiana State University Press, 1987.

Batson, C. Daniel and Laura Shaw. "Evidence for Altruism: Toward a Pluralism of Prosocial Motives." *Psychological Inquiry* 2.2 (1991): 107–122.

Batson, C. Daniel, Paul van Lange, Nadia Ahmad, and David Lishner. "Altruism and Helping Behavior." In Hogg and Cooper, 241–258.

Baumeister, Roy, Sara Wotman, and Arlene Stillwell. "Unrequited Love: On Heartbreak, Anger, Guilt, Scriptlessness, and Humiliation." *Journal of Personality and Social Psychology* 64.3 (1993): 377–394.

Beeman, Mark. "Coarse Semantic Coding and Discourse Comprehension." In Beeman and Chiarello *Right,* 255–284.

Beeman, Mark and Christine Chiarello, eds. *Right Hemisphere Language Comprehension: Perspectives from Cognitive Neuroscience.* Mahwah, NJ: Lawrence Erlbaum, 1998.

Bell, David, Carissa Coulston, and Gin Malhi. "Mentalizing, Mental Illness and Mirth: Linking the Psychology of Theory of Mind and Humour in Psychotic Illness Disorders." *Acta Neuropsychiatrica* 22.1 (2010): 35–37.

Belsey, Catherine. "The Name of the Rose in *Romeo and Juliet.*" In White, 47–67.

Berry, Edward. "Laughing at 'Others'." In Leggatt *Cambridge,* 123–138.

"Othello's Alienation." *Studies in English Literature 1500–1900* 30.3 (1990): 315–333.

Bharatamuni. *The Nāṭya Śāstra.* Delhi, India: Sri Satguru Publications, n.d.

Bok, Sissela. "From Part to Whole." In *For Love of Country.* Ed. Joshua Cohen. Boston, MA: Beacon Press, 2002, 38–44.

Bolitho, Harold. *Bereavement and Consolation: Testimonies from Tokugawa Japan.* New Haven, CT: Yale University Press, 2003.

Bonanno, George, Laura Goorin, and Karin Coifman. "Sadness and Grief." In Lewis, Haviland-Jones, and Barrett, 797–810.

Borg, Jana, Debra Lieberman, and Kent Kiehl. "Infection, Incest, and Iniquity: Investigating the Neural Correlates of Disgust and Morality." *Journal of Cognitive Neuroscience* 20.9 (2008): 1529–1546.

Bovilsky, Lara. *Barbarous Play: Race on the English Renaissance Stage.* Minneapolis, MN: University of Minnesota Press, 2008.

Bower, G. H. "Affect and Cognition." *Philosophical Transactions of the Royal Society of London, Series B* 302 (1983): 387–402.

Boyd, Brian. *On the Origin of Stories: Evolution, Cognition, and Fiction.* Cambridge, MA: Harvard University Press, 2009.

Bradley, A. C. *Shakespearean Tragedy: Lectures on* Hamlet, Othello, King Lear, Macbeth. London: Macmillan, 1904.

Branscombe, Nyla and Bertjan Doosje, eds. *Collective Guilt: International Perspectives*. Cambridge: Cambridge University Press, 2004.
"International Perspectives on the Experience of Collective Guilt." In Branscombe and Doosje *Collective*, 3–15.
Branscombe, Nyla and Anca Miron "Interpreting the Ingroup's Negative Actions Toward Another Group: Emotional Reactions to Appraised Harm." In Tiedens and Leach, 314–335.
Branscombe, Nyla, Ben Slugoski, and Diane Kappen. "The Measurement of Collective Guilt: What It Is and What It Is Not." In Branscombe and Doosje *Collective*, 16–34.
Brewer, Marilynn and Miles Hewstone, eds. *Emotion and Motivation*. Malden, MA: Blackwell, 2004.
Brown, Carolyn. "Juliet's Training of Romeo." *Studies in English Literature* 36 (1996): 333–355.
Brown, Paul. "'This Thing of Darkness I Acknowledge Mine': *The Tempest* and the Discourse of Colonialism." In *Political Shakespeare: New Essays in Cultural Materialism*. Ed. Jonathan Dollimore and Alan Sinfield. Manchester, UK: Manchester University Press, 1985, 48–71.
Brownell, Hiram and Gail Martino. "Deficits in Inference and Social Cognition: The Effects of Right Hemisphere Brain Damage on Discourse." In Beeman and Chiarello *Right*, 309–328.
Butler, Emily, Boris Egloff, Frank Wilhelm, Nancy Smith, Elizabeth Erickson, and James Gross. "The Social Consequences of Expressive Suppression." *Emotion* 3.1 (2003): 48–67.
Butler, Judith. *Gender Trouble: Feminism and the Subversion of Identity*. New York: Routledge, 1999.
Cacioppo, John and William Patrick. *Loneliness: Human Nature and the Need for Social Connection*. New York: W. W. Norton, 2008.
Cacioppo, John, Penny Visser, and Cynthia Pickett, eds. *Social Neuroscience: People Thinking about Thinking People*. Cambridge, MA: MIT Press, 2006.
Cai, Zong-qi, ed. *How to Read Chinese Poetry: A Guided Anthology*. New York: Columbia University Press, 2008.
Callaghan, Dympna. "The Ideology of Romantic Love: The Case of *Romeo and Juliet*." In White, 85–115.
Carroll, Noël. "Art, Narrative, and Emotion." In *Emotion and the Arts*. Ed. Mette Hjort and Sue Laver. New York: Oxford University Press, 1997, 190–211.
"Film, Emotion, and Genre." In Plantinga and Smith, 21–47.
Carroll, William. "Discourses of the Feminine." In *William Shakespeare, Macbeth: Texts and Contexts*. Ed. William Carroll. Boston, MA: Bedford, 1999, 344–352.
Carson, Anne, trans. *If Not, Winter: Fragments of Sappho*. New York: Knopf, 2002.
Césaire, Aimé. *A Tempest*. Trans. R. Miller. New York: TGC Translations, 2002.
Une Tempête, d'après "La Tempête" de Shakespeare: Adaptation pour un Théâtre Nègre. Paris: Éditions du Seuil, 1969.
Chari, V. K. *Sanskrit Criticism*. Honolulu: University of Hawaii Press, 1990.
Chen, Lei, Shuhua Zhou, and Jennings Bryant. "Temporal Changes in Mood Repair Through Music Consumption: Effects of Mood, Mood Salience, and Individual Differences." *Media Psychology* 9 (2007): 695–713.

Chiarello, Christine. "On Codes of Meaning and the Meaning of Codes: Semantic Access and Retrieval Within and Between Hemispheres." In Beeman and Chiarello *Right*, 141–160.

Chiarello, Christine and Mark Beeman. "Commentary: Getting the Right Meaning From Words and Sentences." In Beeman and Chiarello *Right*, 245–251.

Chomsky, Noam. *Knowledge of Language: Its Nature, Origin, and Use*. New York: Praeger, 1986.

Cinthio, Giraldi. "Selection from Giraldi Cinthio *Hecatommithi*." In *The Tragedy of Othello, The Moor of Venice*. Ed. Alvin Kernan. New York: New American Library, 1986, 171–184.

Clark, David, Nashaat Boutros, and Mario Mendez. *The Brain and Behavior: An Introduction to Behavioral Neuroanatomy*. 2nd ed. Cambridge: Cambridge University Press, 2005.

Clark, Margaret S. and Joan K. Monin. "Giving and Receiving Communal Responsiveness as Love." In Sternberg and Weis, 200–224.

Clore, Gerald L. and Andrew Ortony. "Cognition in Emotion: Always, Sometimes, or Never?" *Cognitive Neuroscience of Emotion*. Ed. Richard D. Land and Lynn Nadel with Geoffrey L. Ahern, John J. B. Allen, Alfred W. Kaszniak, Steven Z. Rapcsak, and Gary E. Schwartz. Oxford: Oxford University Press, 2000, 24–61.

Coddon, Karin. "'Suche Strange Desygns': Madness, Subjectivity, and Treason in *Hamlet* and Elizabethan Culture." In *Hamlet*. By William Shakespeare. Ed. Susanne Wofford. Boston, MA: Bedford Books, 1994, 380–402.

Cohen, Derek. "Othello's Suicide." *University of Toronto Quarterly* 62.3 (1993): 323–333.

Cohen, Ted. *Jokes: Philosophical Thoughts on Joking Matters*. Chicago, IL: University of Chicago Press, 1999.

Cole, David and Jules Lobel. "Why We're Losing the War on Terror." *The Nation* (September 24, 2007): 11–18.

Collington, Philip. "Self-Discovery in Montaigne's 'Of Solitarinesse' and *King Lear*." *Comparative Drama* 35.3 (2001): 247–269.

Crane, Mary Thomas. *Shakespeare's Brain: Reading with Cognitive Theory*. Princeton, NJ: Princeton University Press, 2001.

Creaser, John. "Forms of Confusion." In Leggatt *Cambridge*, 81–101.

Crewe, Jonathan. "Outside the Matrix: Shakespeare and Race-Writing." *Yale Journal of Criticism* 8.2 (1995): 13–29.

Culler, Jonathan. *Flaubert: The Uses of Uncertainty*. Ithaca, NY: Cornell University Press, 1974.

Damasio, Antonio R. *Descartes' Error: Emotion, Reason, and the Human Brain*. New York: Avon, 1994.

Dardwall, Stephen. "Empathy, Sympathy, Care." *Philosophical Studies* 89 (1998): 261–282.

Davis, Lloyd "'Death-Marked Love': Desire and Presence in *Romeo and Juliet*." In White, 28–46.

Davison, Peter. *Othello*. Atlantic Highlands, NJ: Humanities Press International, 1988.

De Hooge, Ilona, Marcel Zeelenberg, and Seger Breugelmans. "Restore and Protect Motivations Following Shame." *Cognition and Emotion* 24 (2009): 111–127.

DeLong, Mahlon. "The Basal Ganglia." In *Principles of Neural Science.* 4th ed. Ed. Eric Kandel, James Schwartz, and Thomas Jessell. New York: McGraw Hill, 2000, 852–867.

DeSteno, David, Piercalro Valdesolo, and Monica Bartlett. "Jealousy and the Threatened Self: Getting to the Heart of the Green-Eyed Monster." *Journal of Personality and Social Psychology* 91.4 (2006): 626–641.

Dhanaṃjaya. *The Daśarūpa: A Treatise on Hindu Dramaturgy.* Trans. George Haas. New York: AMS Press, 1965.

Dijker, Anton and Willem Koomen. *Stigmatization, Tolerance and Repair: An Integrative Psychological Analysis of Responses to Deviance.* Cambridge: Cambridge University Press, 2007.

Doherty, Martin. *Theory of Mind: How Children Understand Others' Thoughts and Feelings.* New York: Psychology Press, 2009.

Döring, Sabine. "The Logic of Emotional Experience: Noninferentiality and the Problem of Conflict Without Contradiction." *Emotion Review* 1 (2009): 240–247.

Dovidio, John and Louis Penner. "Helping and Altruism." In Brewer and Hewstone, 247–280.

Dubrow, Heather. *Shakespeare and Domestic Loss: Forms of Deprivation, Mourning, and Recuperation.* Cambridge: Cambridge University Press, 2003.

Duckitt, John H. *The Social Psychology of Prejudice.* New York: Praeger, 1992.

Dutton, Denis. *The Art Instinct: Beauty, Pleasure, and Human Evolution.* Oxford: Oxford University Press, 2009.

Dykstra, Pearl and Tineke Fokkema. "Social and Emotional Loneliness Among Divorced and Married Men and Women: Comparing the Deficit and Cognitive Perspectives." *Basic and Applied Social Psychology* 29.1 (2007): 1–12.

Edmonds, J. M. *Lyra Graeca.* Vol. 1. Revised and augmented ed. Cambridge, MA: Harvard University Press, 1963.

Egberike, J. B. "The Carrier-Scapegoat Archetype and the Cult of Altruistic Suffering: A Study in the Mythological Imagination of *Hamlet, The Flies,* and *The Strong Breed.*" In *Proceedings of the 8th Congress of the International Comparative Literature Association.* Vol. 2. Ed. Béla Köpeczi and György Vajda. Stuttgart: Bieber, 1980, 293–302.

Ellis, A. B. *The Yoruba-Speaking Peoples of the Slave Coast of West Africa.* Ooserhout, Netherlands: Anthropological Publications, 1970 (1894).

Erber, Maureen and Ralph Erber. "The Role of Motivated Social Cognition in the Regulation of Affective States." In Forgas *Handbook,* 275–290.

Faust, Miriam. "Obtaining Evidence of Language Comprehension from Sentence Priming." In Beeman and Chiarello *Right,* 161–186.

Fearon, David. "The Bond Threat Sequence: Discourse Evidence for the Systematic Interdependence of Shame and Social Relationships." In Tiedens and Leach, 64–86.

Feeney, Brooke and Roxanne Thrush. "Relationship Influences on Exploration in Adulthood: The Characteristics and Function of a Secure Base." *Journal of Personality and Social Psychology* 98.1 (2010): 57–76.

Fehr, Beverley. "A Prototype Approach to Studying Love." In Sternberg and Weis, 225–246.

Fernie, Ewan. "Shame in *Othello*." *The Cambridge Quarterly* 28.1 (1999): 19–45.

Feyerabend, Paul. *Against Method: Outline of an Anarchistic Theory of Knowledge.* London: Verso, 1975.

Fiedler, Klaus. "Affective Influences on Social Information Processing." In Forgas *Handbook*, 163–185.

Fiedler, Leslie. *The Stranger in Shakespeare.* New York: Stein and Day, 1972.

Fiore, Stephen M. and Jonathan W. Schooler. "Right Hemisphere Contributions to Creative Problem Solving: Converging Evidence for Divergent Thinking." In Beeman and Chiarello *Right*, 349–371.

Fisher, Helen. "The Drive to Love: The Neural Mechanism for Mate Selection." In Sternberg and Weis, 87–115.

Fisher, Helen, Arthur Aron, Debra Mashek, Haifang Li, and Lucy Brown. "Defining the Brain Systems of Lust, Romantic Attraction, and Attachment." *Archives of Sexual Behavior* 31.5 (2002): 149–155.

Fiske, Susan T., Lasana T. Harris, and Amy J. C. Cuddy. "Why Ordinary People Torture Enemy Prisoners." *Science* 306.5701 (2004): 1482–1483.

Fitness, Julie, Garth Fletcher, and Nickola Overall. "Interpersonal Attraction and Intimate Relationships." In Hogg and Cooper, 219–240.

Flaubert, Gustave. *Madame Bovary.* Paris: Garnier-Flammarion, 1966.

Forgas, Joseph P. "Affect and Information Processing Strategies: An Interactive Relationship." In Forgas *Feeling*, 253–280.

   Handbook of Affect and Social Cognition. Mahwah, NJ: Lawrence Erlbaum, 2000.

   "Introduction: The Role of Affect in Social Cognition." In Forgas *Feeling*, 1–28.

   ed. *Feeling and Thinking: The Role of Affect in Social Cognition.* Cambridge: Cambridge University Press and Paris: Editions de la Maison des Sciences de l'Homme, 2000.

Freed, Peter, Ted Yanagihara, Joy Hirsch, and J. Mann. "Neural Mechanisms of Grief Regulation." *Biological Psychiatry* 66 (2009): 33–40.

Freedman, Barbara. "Errors in Comedy: A Psychoanalytic Theory of Farce." *New York Literary Forum* 5–6 (1980): 235.

Freud, Sigmund. *Group Psychology and the Analysis of the Ego.* In *Standard Edition of the Complete Psychological Works of Sigmund Freud.* Ed. James Strachey. Vol. 18. London: Vintage, 2001, 69–143.

   Jokes and Their Relation to the Unconscious. Trans. and ed. James Strachey. New York: W. W. Norton, 1960.

Frijda, Nico H. *The Emotions.* Cambridge: Cambridge University Press, 1986.

Frye, Northrop. *Anatomy of Criticism: Four Essays.* Princeton, NJ: Princeton University Press, 1957.

Galbraith, David. "Theories of Comedy." In Leggatt *Cambridge*, 3–17.

Gamino, Louis, Kenneth Sewell, and Larry Easterling. "Scott & White Grief Study: An Empirical Test of Predictors of Intensified Mourning." *Death Studies* 22 (1998): 333–355.

Garber, Marjorie. *Shakespeare's Ghost Writers: Literature as Uncanny Causality*. New York: Methuen, 1987.

Gardner, Daniel. *The Science of Fear*. New York: Dutton, 2008

Gaut, Berys. "Identification and Emotion in Narrative Film." In Plantinga and Smith, 200–216.

Gay, Peter. *Savage Reprisals: Bleak House, Madame Bovary, Buddenbrooks*. New York: W. W. Norton, 2002.

Ghose, Indira. *Shakespeare and Laughter: A Cultural History*. Manchester, UK: Manchester University Press, 2008.

Gil, Sandrine, Sylvie Rousset, and Sylvie Droit-Volet. "How Liked and Disliked Foods Affect Time Perception." *Emotion* 9.4 (2009): 457–463.

Gillath, Omri and Dory Schachner. "How Do Sexuality and Attachment Interrelate? Goals, Motives, and Strategies." In Mikulincer and Goodman, 337–355.

Gillies, John. *Shakespeare and the Geography of Difference*. New York: Cambridge University Press, 1994.

Godel, Armen and Koichi Kano, ed. and trans. *La Lande des Mortifications: Vingt-cinq Pièces de Nô*. Paris: Gallimard, 1994.

Goldberg, Jonathan. "*Romeo and Juliet*'s Open Rs." In *Queering the Renaissance*. Ed. Jonathan Goldberg. Durham, NC: Duke University Press, 1994, 218–235.

Gopalakrishnan, Radhamani. "The Christ Figure in Soyinka's Plays." In *The Writer as Myth Maker: South Asian Perspectives on Wole Soyinka*. Ed. Bernth Lindfors and Bala Kothandaraman. Trenton, NJ: Africa World, 2004, 113–122.

Gorski, Roger. "Sexual Differentiation of the Nervous System." In Kandel, Schwartz, and Jessell, 1131–1148.

Gould, Stephen Jay. *The Structure of Evolutionary Theory*. Cambridge, MA: Harvard University Press, 2002.

Graff, Gerald and James Phelan, eds. *William Shakespeare*, The Tempest: *A Case Study in Critical Controversy*. Boston, MA: Bedford/St. Martin's, 2000.

Greenblatt, Stephen. *Hamlet in Purgatory*. Princeton, NJ: Princeton University Press, 2001.

Will in the World: How Shakespeare Became Shakespeare. New York: W. W. Norton, 2004.

Greene, Ellen, ed. *Reading Sappho: Contemporary Approaches*. Berkeley, CA: University of California Press, 1996.

Gregory, Augusta. *Cuchulain of Muirthemne*. Gerrards Cross, UK: Colin Smythe, 1973.

Gross, James. "Emotion Regulation." In Lewis, Haviland-Jones, and Barrett, 497–512.

Hallett, Judith. "Sappho and Her Social Context: Sense and Sensuality." In Greene, 125–142.

Harris, Christine. "A Review of Sex Differences in Sexual Jealousy, Including Self-Report Data, Psychophysiological Responses, Interpersonal Violence, and Morbid Jealousy." *Personality and Social Psychology Review* 7.2 (2003): 102–128.

Hatfield, Elaine, John Cacioppo, and Richard Rapson. *Emotional Contagion.* Cambridge: Cambridge University Press, 1994.

Hatfield, Elaine and Richard Rapson. "Love and Attachment Processes." In Lewis and Haviland-Jones, 654–662.

Hauser, Marc. *Moral Minds: How Nature Designed Our Universal Sense of Right and Wrong.* New York: HarperCollins, 2006.

Hawkins, Harriett. "Disrupting Tribal Difference: Critical and Artistic Responses to Shakespeare's Radical Romanticism." *Studies in the Literary Imagination* 26.1 (1993): 115–126.

Heath, Stephen. *Gustave Flaubert: Madame Bovary.* Cambridge: Cambridge University Press, 1992.

Hirschfeld, Lawrence. *Race in the Making: Cognition, Culture, and the Child's Construction of Human Kinds.* Cambridge, MA: MIT Press, 1996.

Hodson, Gordon and Kimberly Costello. "Interpersonal Disgust, Ideological Orientations, and Dehumanization as Predictors of Intergroup Attitudes." *Psychological Science* 18.8 (2007): 691–698.

Hoefling, Atilla, *et al.* "When Hunger Finds No Fault With Moldy Corn: Food Deprivation Reduces Food-Related Disgust." *Emotion* 9.1 (2009): 50–58.

Hoffman, Martin. "Empathy and Prosocial Behavior." In Lewis, Haviland-Jones, and Barrett, 440–455.

"Empathy, Role-taking, Guilt, and the Development of Altruistic Motives." *Developmental Psychology Report No. 30.* Ann Arbor, MI: University of Michigan, 1973.

"Is Empathy Altruistic?" *Psychological Inquiry* 2.2 (1991): 131–133.

Hogan, Patrick Colm. *Affective Narratology: The Emotional Structure of Stories.* Lincoln, NE: University of Nebraska Press, 2011.

Cognitive Science, Literature, and the Arts: A Guide for Humanists. New York: Routledge, 2003.

The Culture of Conformism: Understanding Social Consent. Durham, NC: Duke University Press, 2001.

"For Evolutionary Criticism, Against Genetic Absolutism." *Style* 42.2/3 (2008): 202–206.

"Imagining What You Can Do: The Brain, Free Will, and Art." *PsyArt: An Online Journal for the Psychological Study of the Arts,* article 050718, http://www.clas.ufl.edu/ipsa/journal/2005_hogan01.shtml, July 18, 2005.

"Laughing Brains: On the Cognitive Mechanisms and Reproductive Functions of Mirth." *Semiotica: Journal of the International Association for Semiotic Studies* 165.1–4 (2007): 391–408.

"Literature, God, and the Unbearable Solitude of Consciousness." *Journal of Consciousness Studies* 11.5–6 (2004): 116–142.

The Mind and Its Stories: Narrative Universals and Human Emotion. Cambridge: Cambridge University Press, 2003.

On Interpretation: Meaning and Inference in Law, Psychoanalysis, and Literature. Athens, GA: University of Georgia Press, 2008.

"Othello, Racism, and Despair." *CLA Journal* 41.4 (1998): 431–451. Reprinted in *Shakespearean Criticism.* Vol. 53. Ed. Michelle Lee. Detroit, MI: Gale Group, 2000.

"Reading Tagore Today." In *Tagore's Best Short Stories*. Trans. Malobika Chaudhuri. London: Frontpage Publications, 2010.

"Sensorimotor Projection, Violations of Continuity, and Emotion in the Experience of Film." *Projections: The Journal for Movies and Mind* 1.1 (2007): 41–58.

Hogg, Michael and Joel Cooper, eds. *The Sage Handbook of Social Psychology (Concise Student Edition)*. Los Angeles, CA: Sage Publications, 2007.

Holland, Ashley and Glenn Roisman. "Adult Attachment Security and Young Adults' Dating Relationships Over Time: Self-Reported, Observational, and Physiological Evidence." *Developmental Psychology* 46.2 (2010): 552–557.

Holland, John, Keith Holyoak, Richard Nisbett, and Paul Thagard. *Induction: Processes of Inference, Learning, and Discovery*. Cambridge, MA: MIT Press, 1986.

Holland, Norman. *The Dynamics of Literary Response*. New York: Oxford University Press, 1968.

Laughing: A Psychology of Humor. Ithaca, NY: Cornell University Press, 1982.

Literature and the Brain. Gainesville, FL: The PsyArt Foundation, 2009.

Honeycutt, James and James Cantrill. *Cognition, Communication, and Romantic Relationships*. Mahwah, NJ: Lawrence Erlbaum, 2001.

Horberg, E., Christopher Oveis, Dacher Keltner, and Adam Cohen. "Disgust and the Moralization of Purity." *Journal of Personality and Social Psychology* 97.6 (2009): 961–976.

Hu Pin-ching. *Li Ch'ing-chao*. New York: Twayne, 1966.

Husserl, Edmund. *Cartesian Meditations: An Introduction to Phenomenology*. Trans. Dorion Cairns. The Hague: Martinus Nijhoff, 1970.

Husted, David, Nathan Shapira, and Wayne Goodman. "The Neurocircuitry of Obsessive-Compulsive Disorder and Disgust." *Progress in Neuro-Psychopharmacology & Biological Psychiatry* 30 (2006): 389–399.

Hutson, Lorna. *The Invention of Suspicion: Law and Mimesis in Shakespeare and Renaissance Drama*. Oxford: Oxford University Press, 2007.

Hyltenstam, Kenneth. "Critical Periods." In *The Cambridge Encyclopedia of the Language Sciences*. Ed. Patrick Colm Hogan. Cambridge: Cambridge University Press, 2011, 238–240.

Iacoboni, Marco. *Mirroring People: The New Science of How We Connect with Others*. New York: Farrar, Straus and Giroux, 2008.

Ickes, William and Jeffry A. Simpson. "Motivational Aspects of Empathic Accuracy." In Brewer and Hewstone, 225–246.

Ikegami, Eiko. "Shame and the Samurai: Institutions, Trustworthiness, and Autonomy in the Elite Honor Culture." *Social Research* 70.4 (2003): 1351–1378.

Immordino-Yang, Mary, Andrea McColl, Hanna Damasio, and Antonio Damasio. "Neural Correlates of Admiration and Compassion." *Proceedings of the National Academy of Sciences USA* 106.19 (2009): 8021–8026.

Issa, Kobayashi. "Thanatologue: A Record of My Father's Death." In Bolitho, 64–86.

Ito, Tiffany, Geoffrey Urland, Eve Willadsen-Jensen, and Joshua Correll. "The Social Neuroscience of Stereotyping and Prejudice: Using Event-Related

Brain Potentials to Study Social Perception." In Cacioppo, Visser, and Pickett, 189–208.

Iyer, Aarti, Colin Leach, and Anne Pedersen. "Racial Wrongs and Restitutions: The Role of Guilt and Other Group-Based Emotions." In Branscombe and Doosje *Collective*, 262–283.

Jacinto, George. "The Self-Forgiveness Process of Caregivers After the Death of Care-Receivers Diagnosed with Alzheimer's Disease." *Journal of Social Service Research* 36 (2009): 24–36.

James, Heather. "Dido's Ear: Tragedy and the Politics of Response." *Shakespeare Quarterly* 52 (2001): 360–382.

James, Henry. *The House of Fiction: Essays on the Novel*. Westport, CT: Greenwood Press, 1973.

Jankowiak, William. "Romantic Passion in the People's Republic of China." In *Romantic Passion: A Universal Experience?* Ed. William Jankowiak. New York: Columbia University Press, 1995.

Jauss, Hans Robert. *Toward an Aesthetic of Reception*. Trans. Timothy Bahti. Minneapolis, MN: University of Minnesota Press, 1982.

Jennings, Jerry and Christopher Murphy. "Male-Male Dimensions of Male-Female Battering: A New Look at Domestic Violence." *Psychology of Men and Masculinity* 1.1 (2000): 21–29.

Jones, Andrew and Julie Fitness. "Moral Hypervigilance: The Influence of Disgust Sensitivity in the Moral Domain." *Emotion* 8.5 (2008): 613–627.

Kagekiyo. In Shimazaki, 258–287.

Kandel, Eric, James Schwartz, and Thomas Jessell. *Principles of Neural Science*. 4th ed. New York: McGraw-Hill, 2000.

Kane, Julie. "Poetry as Right-Hemispheric Language." *Journal of Consciousness Studies* 11.5–6 (2004), 21–59.

Kant, Immanuel. *Critique of Judgment*. Trans. Werner Pluhar. Indianapolis, IN: Hackett, 1987.

　Critique of Pure Reason. Trans. Norman Kemp Smith. London: Macmillan, 1929.

Kastan, David Scott. "'The Duke of Milan/And His Brave Son': Old Histories and New in *The Tempest*." In Graff and Phelan, 268–286.

Keen, Suzanne. *Empathy and the Novel*. Oxford: Oxford University Press, 2007.

Kellerman, J., J. Lewis, and J. Laird. "Looking and Loving: The Effects of Mutual Gaze on Feelings of Romantic Love." *Journal of Research in Personality* 23 (1989): 145–161.

Khan, Zia Inayat. "Preface to the 1997 Edition." *The Story of Layla and Majnun*. By Nizami. New Lebanon, NY: Omega Publications, 1997, xix–xxi.

Kim, Ji-Woong, S.-E. Kim, J.-J. Kim, B. Jeong, C.-H. Park, A. Son, J. Song, and S. Ki. "Compassionate Attitude Toward Others' Suffering Activates the Mesolimbic Neural System." *Neuropsychologia* 47 (2009): 2073–2081.

King-Casas, Brooks, Damon Tomlin, Cedric Anen, Colin F. Camerer, Steven R. Quartz, and P. Read Montague. "Getting to Know You: Reputation and Trust in a Two-Person Economic Exchange." *Science* 308.5718 (April 1, 2005): 78–83.

Kirsch, Arthur. "Virtue, Vice, and Compassion in Montaigne and *The Tempest.*" *SEL* 37 (1997): 337–352.

Kosslyn, Stephen. *Image and Brain: The Resolution of the Imagery Debate.* Cambridge, MA: MIT Press, 1994.

Krendl, Anne, C. Neil Macrae, William Kelley, Jonathan Fugelsang, and Todd Heatherton. "The Good, the Bad, and the Ugly: An fMRI Investigation of the Functional Anatomic Correlates of Stigma." *Social Neuroscience* 1 (2006): 5–15.

Kristeva, Julia. "Romeo and Juliet: Love-Hatred in the Couple." In White, 68–84.

Kunda, Ziva. *Social Cognition: Making Sense of People.* Cambridge, MA: MIT Press, 1999.

Kupfermann, Irving, Eric Kandel, and Susan Iversen. "Motivational and Addictive States." In Kandel, Schwartz, and Jessell, 998–1013.

Lakoff, George. *Don't Think of an Elephant! Know Your Values and Frame the Debate: The Essential Guide for Progressives.* White River Junction, VT: Chelsea Green Publishing, 2004.

Langlois, J. and L. Roggman. "Attractive Faces Are Only Average." *Psychological Science* 1 (1990): 115–121.

Laroque, François. "Popular Festivity." In Leggatt *Cambridge,* 64–78.

Laudan, Larry. "Demystifying Underdetermination." In *Scientific Theories.* Ed. C. Wade Savage. Minneapolis, MN: University of Minnesota Press, 1990.

Leary, M. "The Self We Know and the Self We Show: Self-Esteem, Self-Presentation, and the Maintenance of Interpersonal Relationships." In Brewer and Hewstone, 204–224.

Leary, M. and D. Downs. "Interpersonal Functions of the Self-Esteem Motive: The Self-Esteem System as a Sociometer." In *Efficacy, Agency, and Self-Esteem.* Ed. M. Kernis. New York: Plenum, 123–144.

Lebel, Udi and Natti Ronel. "The Emotional Reengineering of Loss: On the Grief-Anger-Social Action Continuum." *Political Psychology* 30.5 (2009): 669–691.

LeDoux, Joseph. *The Emotional Brain: The Mysterious Underpinnings of Emotional Life.* New York: Touchstone, 1996.

Leggatt, Alexander. "Comedy and Sex." In Leggatt *Cambridge,* 139–155.
    ed. *The Cambridge Companion to Shakespearean Comedy.* Cambridge: Cambridge University Press, 2001.

Lehrer, Jonah. *Proust was a Neuroscientist.* Boston, MA: Houghton Mifflin, 2008

Lemerise, Elizabeth and Kenneth Dodge. "The Development of Anger and Hostile Interactions." In Lewis, Haviland-Jones, and Barrett, 730–741.

Levin, Harry. "Two Scenes from *Macbeth.*" In Miola *Macbeth,* 266–282.

Levy, Kenneth, Kristen Kelly, and Ejay Jack. "Sex Differences in Jealousy: A Matter of Evolution or Attachment History?" In Mikulincer and Goodman, 128–145.

Lewis, Michael. "Self-Conscious Emotions: Embarrassment, Pride, Shame, and Guilt." In Lewis, Haviland-Jones, and Barrett, 742–756.

Lewis, Michel and Jeannette Haviland-Jones, ed. *Handbook of Emotions.* 2nd ed. New York: Guilford Press, 2000.

Lewis, Michel, Jeannette Haviland-Jones, and Lisa Feldman Barrett, eds. *Handbook of Emotions.* 3rd ed. New York: Guilford Press, 2008.

Lickel, Brian, Toni Schmader, and Marchelle Barquissau. "The Evocation of Moral Emotions in Intergroup Contexts: The Distinction Between Collective Guilt and Collective Shame." In Branscombe and Doosje *Collective,* 35–55.

Lieberman, Debra and Elaine Hatfield. "Passionate Love: Cross-Cultural and Evolutionary Perspectives." In Sternberg and Weiss, 2006, 274–297.

Lindquist, Kristen and Lisa Feldman Barrett. "Emotional Complexity." In Lewis, Haviland-Jones, and Barrett, 513–530.

Lubbock, Percy. *The Craft of Fiction.* New York: Charles Scribner's Sons, 1921.

Lyonga, Lalova. "The Theme of Sacrifice in Wole Soyinka's *The Strong Breed.*" *Ngam* 1–2 (1997): 140–154.

Magnusson, Lynne. "Language and Comedy." In Leggatt *Cambridge,* 156–178.

Marder, Elissa. *Dead Time: Temporal Disorders in the Wake of Modernity (Baudelaire and Flaubert).* Stanford, CA: Stanford University Press, 2001.

Matsumoto, David, Dacher Keltner, Michelle Shiota, Maureen O'Sullivan, and Mark Frank. "Facial Expressions of Emotion." In Lewis, Haviland-Jones, and Barrett, 211–234.

McConachie, Bruce and F. Elizabeth Hart, eds. *Performance and Cognition: Theatre Studies and the Cognitive Turn.* New York: Routledge, 2006.

McGhee, Paul. *Humor: Its Origins and Development.* San Francisco: Freeman, 1979.

Mikulincer, Mario. "Attachment, Caregiving, and Sex within Romantic Relationships: A Behavioral Systems Perspective." In Mikulincer and Goodman, 23–44.

Mikulincer, Mario and Gail Goodman, eds. *Dynamics of Romantic Love: Attachment, Caregiving, and Sex.* New York: Guilford Press, 2006.

Mikulincer, Mario and Phillip Shaver. "Security-Based Self-Representations in Adulthood: Contents and Processes." In *Adult Attachment: Theory, Research, and Clinical Implications.* Ed. W. Steven Rholes and Jeffry Simpson. New York: Guilford Press, 2004, 159–195.

Mikulincer, Mario, Phillip Shaver, Omri Gillath, and Rachel Nitzberg. "Attachment, Caregiving, and Altruism: Boosting Attachment Security Increases Compassion and Helping." *Journal of Personality and Social Psychology* 89.5 (2005): 817–839.

Miller, Anthony. "Matters of State." In *Cambridge Companion to Shakespearean Comedy.* Ed. Alexander Leggatt. Cambridge: Cambridge University Press, 2002, 198–214.

Miller, William. *The Anatomy of Disgust.* Cambridge, MA: Harvard University Press, 1997.

Miola, Robert, ed. *Macbeth.* By William Shakespeare. New York: Norton, 2004.

"The Play and the Critics." In *The Comedy of Errors: Critical Essays.* Ed. Robert Miola. London: Routledge, 2001, 3–51.

"Roman Comedy." In Leggatt *Cambridge,* 18–31.

Moors, Agnes. "Theories of Emotion Causation: A Review." *Cognition and Emotion* 23.4 (2009): 625–662.

Msiska, Mpalive-Hangson. "The Politics of Identity and the Identity of Politics: The Self as an Agent of Redemption in Wole Soyinka's *Camwood on the Leaves* and *The Strong Breed*." *Journal of African Cultural Studies* 18.2 (2006): 187–196.

Murasaki, Lady. *The Tale of Genji*. Trans. Arthur Waley. New York: The Modern Library, 1960.

Myhre, Karin. "Wit and Humor." In *The Columbia History of Chinese Literature*. Ed. Victor H. Mair. New York: Columbia University Press, 2001, 132–148.

Nabokov, Vladimir. *Lectures on Literature*. Ed. Fredson Bowers. New York: Harcourt Brace Jovanovick, 1980.

Nagel, Thomas. "What Is It Like to Be a Bat?" *Mortal Questions*. Cambridge: Cambridge University Press, 1979, 165–180.

Nandy, Ashis. *The Intimate Enemy: Loss and Recovery of Self under Colonialism*. Delhi: Oxford University Press, 1983.

Ndiaye, Marième. "Female Stereotypes in Wole Soyinka's *The Strong Breed* and *The Lion and the Jewel*." *Bridges: An African Journal of English Studies/Revue Africaine d'Etudes Anglaises* 5 (1993): 19–24.

Neill, Michael. "Unproper Beds: Race, Adultery, and the Hideouts in Othello." *Shakespeare Quarterly* 40.4 (1989): 187–215.

Nordlund, Marcus. *Shakespeare and the Nature of Love: Literature, Culture, Evolution*. Evanston, IL: Northwestern University Press, 2007.

Nussbaum, Martha. *Hiding from Humanity: Disgust, Shame, and the Law*. Princeton, NJ: Princeton University Press, 2004.

"Patriotism and Cosmopolitanism." *For Love of Country*. Ed. Joshua Cohen. Boston, MA: Beacon Press, 2002, 3–27.

Nussbaum, Martha C. *Upheavals of Thought: The Intelligence of Emotions*. Cambridge: Cambridge University Press, 2001.

Oatley, Keith. *Best Laid Schemes: The Psychology of Emotions*. Cambridge: Cambridge University Press, 1992.

"Communications to Self and Others: Emotional Experience and Its Skills." *Emotion Review*, 1.3 (2009): 206–213.

Emotions: A Brief History. Malden, MA: Blackwell, 2004.

"An Emotion's Emergence, Unfolding, and Potential for Empathy: A Study of Resentment by the 'Psychologist of Avon.'" *Emotion Review* 1.1 (2009): 24–30.

"Suggestion Structure." In *The Cambridge Encyclopedia of the Language Sciences*. Ed. Patrick Colm Hogan. Cambridge: Cambridge University Press, 2011, 819–820.

"Why Fiction May be Twice as True as Fact: Fiction as Cognitive and Emotional Simulation." *Review of General Psychology* 3.2 (1999): 101–117.

Oatley, Keith and P. Johnson-Laird. "The Communicative Theory of Emotions: Empirical Tests, Mental Models, and Implications for Social Interaction." In *Striving and Feeling: Interactions Among Goals, Affect, and Self-Regulation*. Ed. L. Martin and A. Tesser. Mahwah, NJ: Erlbaum, 1995, 363–393.

"Towards a Cognitive Theory of Emotions." *Cognition and Emotion* 1 (1987): 29–50.

Oatley, Keith, Dacher Keltner, and Jennifer Jenkins. *Understanding Emotions*. 2nd ed. Malden, MA: Blackwell, 2007.

O'Connell, Michael. "The Experiment of Romance." In Leggatt *Cambridge*, 215–229.

Orgel, Stephen. "*Macbeth* and the Antic Round." In Miola *Macbeth*, 342–356.

Orkin, Martin. *Shakespeare Against Apartheid*. Craighall, South Africa: Ad Donker, 1987.

Ortony, Andrew, Gerald Clore, and Allan Collins. *The Cognitive Structure of Emotions*. Cambridge: Cambridge University Press, 1988.

O'Toole, Fintan. *No More Heroes: A Radical Guide to Shakespeare*. Dublin: Raven Arts, 1990.

Oveis, Christopher, E. Horberg, and Dacher Keltner. "Compassion, Pride, and Social Intuitions of Self-Other Similarity." *Journal of Personality and Social Psychology* 98 (2010): 618–630.

Oxford English Dictionary. 2nd ed. 20 vols. Oxford: Oxford University Press, 1989.

Page, Denys. *Sappho and Alcaeus: An Introduction to the Study of Ancient Lesbian Poetry*. Oxford: Clarendon Press, 1955.

Pandit, Lalita. "Emotion, Perception, and Anagnorisis in *The Comedy of Errors*: A Cognitive Perspective." *College Literature* 33.1 (2006): 94–126.

    "*Prophesying with Accents Terrible*: Emotion and Appraisal in Macbeth." In *Toward a Cognitive Theory of Narrative Acts*. Ed. Frederick Aldama. Austin, TX: University of Texas Press, 2010, 251–280.

Panksepp, Jaak. *Affective Neuroscience: The Foundations of Human and Animal Emotions*. Oxford: Oxford University Press, 1998.

Paris, Bernard. *Imagined Human Beings: A Psychological Approach to Character and Conflict in Literature*. New York: New York University Press, 1997.

Parker, Stephen and Rebecca Thomas. "Psychological Differences in Shame vs. Guilt: Implications for Mental Health Counselors." *Journal of Mental Health Counseling*. 31.3 (2009): 213–224.

Parkes, Colin Murray. *Love and Loss: The Roots of Grief and Its Complications*. New York: Routledge, 2006.

Parkinson, Brian and Sarah Illingworth. "Guilt in Response to Blame from Others." *Cognition and Emotion* 23 (2009): 1589–1614.

Paster, Gail Kern. *Humoring the Body: Emotions and the Shakespearean Stage*. Chicago, IL: University of Chicago Press, 2004.

    "The Tragic Subject and Its Passions." In *The Cambridge Companion to Shakespearean Tragedy*. Ed. Claire McEachern. Cambridge: Cambridge University Press, 2002, 142–159.

Paster, Gail Kern, Katherine Rowe, and Mary Floyd-Wilson, eds. *Reading the Early Modern Passions: Essays in the Cultural History of Emotion*. Philadelphia: University of Pennsylvania Press, 2004.

Penke, Lars and Jens Asendorpf. "Evidence for Conditional Sex Differences in Emotional But Not in Sexual Jealousy at the Automatic Level of Cognitive Processing." *European Journal of Personality* 22 (2008): 3–30.

Petit, C. and W. Savage. *Dictionnaire Classique Anglais-Français et Français-Anglais*. Paris: Hachette, 1950.

Pexman, Penny. "Verbal Humor, Development of." In *The Cambridge Encyclopedia of the Language Sciences*. Cambridge: Cambridge University Press, 2011, 899–901.

Philipse, Herman. "Transcendental Idealism." *The Cambridge Companion to Husserl*. Ed. Barry Smith and D. W. Smith. Cambridge: Cambridge University Press, 1995, 239–322.

Plantinga, Carl and Greg Smith, eds. *Passionate Views: Film, Cognition, and Emotion*. Baltimore, MD: Johns Hopkins University Press, 1999.

Porter, Laurence. "The Art of Characterisation in Flaubert's Fiction." In Unwin, 122–144.

Prinz, Jesse J. "Imitation and Moral Development." *Perspectives on Imitation: From Neuroscience to Social Science. Volume 2: Imitation, Human Development, and Culture*. Ed. Susan Hurley and Nick Chater. Cambridge, MA: MIT Press, 2005, 267–282.

Putnam, Hilary. "Quantum Mechanics and the Observer." *Realism and Reason: Philosophical Papers, Volume 3*. Cambridge: Cambridge University Press, 1983, 248–270.

Rando, Therese, ed. *Clinical Dimensions of Anticipatory Mourning: Theory and Practice in Working with the Dying*. Champaign, IL: Research Press, 2000.

Rexroth, Kenneth and Ling Chung, ed. and trans. *Li Ch'ing-chao: Complete Poems*. New York: New Directions, 1979.

Reynolds, Margaret. *The Sappho Companion*. New York: Vintage, 2001.

Rimé, Bernard. "Emotion Elicits the Social Sharing of Emotion: Theory and Empirical Review." *Emotion Review* 1.1 (2009): 60–96.

  Le partage social des émotions. Paris: Presses Universitaires de France, 2005.

Ritt, Nikolaus. "Memes and Language." In *The Cambridge Encyclopedia of the Language Sciences*. Ed. Patrick Colm Hogan. Cambridge: Cambridge University Press, 2011, 476–477.

Robinson, David. *Sappho and Her Influence*. Boston, MA: Marshall Jones, 1924.

Rohrmann, Sonja and Henrik Hopp. "Cardiovascular Indicators of Disgust." *International Journal of Psychophysiology* 68 (2008): 201–208.

Rottschaefer, William. *The Biology and Psychology of Moral Agency*. Cambridge: Cambridge University Press, 2008.

Royzman, Edward and Paul Rozin. "Limits of Symhedonia: The Differential Role of Prior Emotional Attachment in Sympathy and Sympathetic Joy." *Emotion* 6.1 (2006): 82–93.

Rozin, Paul. "Disgust." In Lewis and Haviland-Jones, 637–653.

Rozin, Paul, Jonathan Haidt, and Clark McCauley. "Disgust." In Lewis, Haviland-Jones, and Barrett, 2008, 757–776.

Rubin, David. *Memory in Oral Traditions: The Cognitive Psychology of Epic, Ballads, and Counting-Out Rhymes*. New York: Oxford University Press, 1995.

Russell, Emily and Helen Harton. "The 'Other Factors': Using Individual and Relationship Characteristics to Predict Sexual and Emotional Jealousy." *Current Psychology: Developmental, Learning, Personality, Social* 24.4 (2005): 242–257.

Rustomjee, Sabar. "The Solitude and Agony of Unbearable Shame." *Group Analysis* 42.2 (2009): 143–155.

Salovey, Peter, Brian Detweiler-Bedell, Jerusha Detweiler-Bedell, and John Mayer. "Emotional Intelligence." In Lewis, Haviland-Jones, and Barrett, 533–547.

Scarry, Elaine. *Dreaming by the Book.* New York: Farrar, Straus, Giroux, 1999.

Schachter, Stanley. In *Advances in Experimental Social Psychology.* Ed. Leonard Berkowitz. New York: Academic Press, 1964, 49–79.

Schacter, Daniel. *Searching for Memory: The Brain, the Mind, and the Past.* New York: Basic Books, 1996.

Schacter, D., D. Addis, and R. Buckner. "Remembering the Past to Imagine the Future: The Prospective Brain." *Nature Reviews: Neuroscience* 8 (2007): 657–661.

Scheff, Thomas and Suzanne Retzinger. *Emotions and Violence: Shame and Rage in Destructive Conflicts.* Lexington, MA: Lexington Books, 1991.

Schehr, Lawrence. "Flaubert's Failure." In Unwin, 208–219.

Schmidt, Ralph and Martial Van der Linden. "The Aftermath of Rash Action: Sleep-Interfering Counterfactual Thoughts and Emotions." *Emotion* 9.4 (2009): 549–553.

Sedikides, Constantine and Aiden Gregg. "Portraits of the Self." In Hogg and Cooper, 93–122.

Shakespeare, William. *The Comedy of Errors.* Ed. Charles Whitworth. Oxford: Oxford University Press, 2002.

    Macbeth: Texts and Contexts. Ed. William Carroll. New York: Bedford, 1999.

    Measure for Measure. Ed. S. Nagarajan. New York: New American Library, 1964.

    The Tempest. In Graff and Phelan, 10–88.

    The Tragedy of Hamlet Prince of Denmark. Ed. Sylvan Barnet. New York: New American Library, 1998.

    The Tragedy of Othello, The Moor of Venice. Ed. Alvin Kernan. New York: New American Library, 1986.

    The Tragedy of Romeo and Juliet. Ed. J. A. Bryant. New York: New American Library, 1986.

Shaver, Phillip and C. Hazan. "A Biased Overview of the Study of Love." *Journal of Social and Personal Relationships* 5 (1988): 473–501.

Shaver, Phillip and Mario Mikulincer. "A Behavioral Systems Approach to Romantic Love Relationships: Attachment, Caregiving, and Sex." In Sternberg and Weis, 35–64.

Shaver, Phillip and Caroline Tancredy. "Emotion, Attachment, and Bereavement: A Conceptual Commentary." In *Handbook of Bereavement Research: Consequences, Coping, and Care.* Ed. Margaret Stroebe, Robert Hansson, Wolfgang Strobe, and Henk Schut. Washington, DC: American Psychological Association, 2001, 63–88.

Sheikh, Sana and Ronnie Janoff-Bulman. "The 'Shoulds' and 'Should Nots' of Moral Emotions: A Self-Regulatory Perspective on Shame and Guilt." *Personality and Social Psychology Bulletin* 36.2 (2010): 213–224.

Shimazaki, Chifumi, ed. and trans. *Troubled Souls: From Japanese Noh Plays of the Fourth Group.* Ithaca, NY: Cornell University East Asia Program, 1998.

Shweder, Richard, Nancy Much, Manamohan Mahapatra, and Lawrence Park. "The 'Big Three' of Morality (Autonomy, Community, Divinity) and the 'Big Three' Explanations of Suffering." In *Morality and Health.* Ed. Allan Brandt and Paul Rozin. New York: Routledge, 1997, 119–169.

Siena, Kevin. "Pollution, Promiscuity, and the Pox: English Venereology and the Early Modern Medical Discourse on Social and Sexual Danger." *Journal of the History of Sexuality* 8.4 (1998): 553–574.

Simpson, Jane, Sarah Carter, Susan Anthony, and Paul Overton. "Is Disgust a Homogeneous Emotion?" *Motivation and Emotion* 30.1 (2006): 31–41.

Skura, Meredith Anne. "Discourse and the Individual: The Case of Colonialism in *The Tempest*." *Shakespeare Quarterly* 40 (1989) : 42–69.

Smith, Greg. *Film Structure and the Emotion System*. Cambridge: Cambridge University Press, 2003.

Snyder, Jane. *Lesbian Desire in the Lyrics of Sappho*. New York: Columbia University Press, 1997.

Sommers, Christina Hoff. "Filial Morality." *Journal of Philosophy* 83.8 (1986): 439–456.

Soyinka, Wole. *The Strong Breed*. In *Collected Plays 1*. Oxford: Oxford University Press, 1973, 113–146.

Spears, Russell and Colin Leach "Intergroup Schadenfreude: Conditions and Consequences." In Tiedens and Leach, 336–355.

Stanovick, Keith. *The Robot's Rebellion: Finding Meaning in the Age of Darwin*. Chicago, IL: University of Chicago Press, 2004.

Stehle, Eva. "Romantic Sensuality, Poetic Sense: A Response to Hallett on Sappho." In Greene, 143–149.

Stein, Dan and Bavanisha Vythilingum. "Love and Attachment: The Psychobiology of Social Bonding." *CNS Spectrums* 14.5 (2009): 239–242.

Sternberg, Robert and Karin Weis, eds. *The New Psychology of Love*. New Haven, CT: Yale University Press, 2006.

Stevenson, Richard, M. Oaten, T. Case, Betty Repacholi, and P. Wagland. "Children's Response to Adult Disgust Elicitors: Development and Acquisition." *Developmental Psychology* 46.1 (2010): 165–177.

Stevenson, Richard and Betty Repacholi. "Does the Source of an Interpersonal Odour Affect Disgust? A Disease Risk Model and Its Alternatives." *European Journal of Social Psychology* 35 (2005): 375–401.

Stowe, Harriet Beecher. *Uncle Tom's Cabin*. New York: Bantam, 2003.

Stroebe, Margaret, Henk Schut, and Kathrin Boerner. "Continuing Bonds in Adaptation to Bereavement: Toward Theoretical Integration." *Clinical Psychology Review* 30 (2010): 259–268.

Śūdraka. *The Little Clay Cart*. Adapted by A. L. Basham. Edited by Arvind Sharma. Albany, NY: State University of New York Press, 1994.

Tagore, Rabindranath. "I Won't Let You Go." In *I Won't Let You Go: Selected Poems*. Trans. Ketaki Kushari Dyson. Newcastle upon Tyne, UK: Bloodaxe Books, 1991, 82–86.

Takaki, Ronald. *A Different Mirror: A History of Multicultural America*. Boston, MA: Back Bay Books/Little, Brown and Company, 1993.

Tale of the Heike. Trans. Helen Craig McCullough. Stanford, CA: Stanford University Press, 1988.

Tangney, June Price. "Moral Affect: The Good, the Bad, and the Ugly." *Journal of Personality and Social Psychology* 61.4 (1991): 598–607.

Taylor, Kathleen. "Disgust is a Factor in Extreme Prejudice." *British Journal of Social Psychology* 46 (2007): 597–617.

Tesser, Abraham. "Self-Esteem." In Brewer and Hewstone, 184–203.

Tiedens, Larissa and Colin Leach, eds. *The Social Life of Emotions.* Cambridge: Cambridge University Press, 2004.

Tomasini, Floris. "Is Post-Mortem Harm Possible? Understanding Death Harm and Grief." *Bioethics* 23.8 (2009): 441–449.

Tutuola, Amos. *The Palm-Wine Drinkard and His Dead Palm-Wine Tapster in the Dead's Town.* New York: Grove Press, 1984.

Twain, Mark. *Adventures of Huckleberry Finn.* Ed. Thomas Cooley. 3rd ed. New York: W. W. Norton, 1999.

Unwin, Timothy, ed. *The Cambridge Companion to Flaubert.* Cambridge: Cambridge University Press, 2004.

Van Gulick, Robert. "Reduction, Emergence and Other Recent Options on the Mind/Body Problem: A Philosophic Overview." *Journal of Consciousness Studies* 8.9/8.10 (2001): 1–34.

van Leeuwen, Cees. "Perception." In *A Companion to Cognitive Science.* Ed. William Bechtel and George Graham. Oxford: Blackwell, 1998, 265–281.

Vygotsky, L. S. *Mind in Society: The Development of Higher Psychological Processes.* Ed. M. Cole, V. John-Steiner, S. Scribner, and E. Souberman. Cambridge, MA: Harvard University Press, 1978.

Waters, Everett, Nancy Weinfield, and Claire Hamilton. "The Stability of Attachment Security from Infancy to Adolescence and Early Adulthood: General Discussion." *Child Development* 71.3 (2000): 703–706.

Wheatley, Thalia and Jonathan Haidt. "Hypnotic Disgust Makes Moral Judgments More Severe." *Psychological Science* 16.10 (2005): 780–784.

White, R. S., ed. *Romeo and Juliet: Contemporary Critical Essays.* New York: Palgrave, 2001.

Willbern, David. "Shakespeare's Nothing." In *Poetic Will: Shakespeare and the Play of Language.* Philadelphia, PA: University of Pennsylvania Press, 1997, 125–142.

Williamson, Margaret. *Sappho's Immortal Daughters.* Cambridge, MA: Harvard University Press, 1995.

Wilson, E. O. *Consilience: The Unity of Knowledge.* New York: Vintage, 1999.

Wofford, Susanne. "A Critical History of *Hamlet.*" In *Hamlet.* Ed. Susanne Wofford. Boston, MA: Bedford Books, 1994, 181–207.

Wong, Roderick. *Motivation: A Biobehavioural Approach.* Cambridge: Cambridge University Press, 2000.

Worthen, W. B. "Drama, Performativity, and Performance." *PMLA* 113.5 (1998): 1093–1107.

Wypijewski, JoAnn. "Through a Lens Starkly." *The Nation* (May 18, 2009): 6, 8.

X, Malcolm, with the assistance of Alex Haley. *The Autobiography of Malcolm X.* New York: Ballantine Books, 1999.

Xuereb, Sharon, Jane Ireland, and Michelle Davies. "Developmental and Preliminary Assessment of a Measure of Shame, Guilt, and Denial of Offenders." *Journal of Forensic Psychiatry and Psychology* 20 (2010): 640–660.

Zajonc, Robert B. "Feeling and Thinking: Closing the Debate over the Independence of Affect." In Forgas *Feeling,* 31–58.

Index

332   *Index*

morality (*cont.*)
  ethics of complementarity and, 226, 254
  ethics of negation and, 226
  forced-choice scenarios, 231
  incidental emotional arousal, 229
  Indic tradition of, 232–233
  kāma and, 225
  in *Macbeth*, 176
  in *Measure for Measure*, sexual desire
      and, 243–254
  mokṣa and, 225–226
  obligational conflicts and, 234–237
  parameters of, 224–228
  perceptual projections and, 230
  pride and, 224
  rasa theory, 232–233
  semantic fields for, 225–226
  spontaneous empathy and, 177
  strict-father, 241
  Tagore on, 221–224
  thematic clusters for, 233, 239–240
  toward nonrelated persons, attachment
      and, 236–237
mourning, in Shakespeare works, 121–123
  ideology of, 128–129
multicomponent theories, of emotions, 7
Murasaki, Lady, 30
Myhre, Karin, 156–158

Nabokov, Vladimir, 288
Nectar in a Sieve (Markandaya), 287
neuroanatomy, emotional structure
      and, 42–43, 71–72. *See also* emotion
      systems
  circuit activation, perceptual causes
      of, 46–48
  for disgust, 43–44
  eliciting conditions for, 46
  emotion systems, 43–45
  regional specialization and, 42–43
neurochemical response
  for compassion, 262
  for emotion episodes, 52
  for empathy, 97
  for grief, 121
  mood and, 52
  for reward mediation, 83
  for romantic love, 82
  for romantic reunion, 83
  for trust, 80
neurons, emotional structure and, 41
  mirror, 49
  specialization of, 41–42

neurosciences
  artists and, 12
  emotion as study, 11
  Lehrer on, 11–12
Nordlund, Marcus, 201–202
normative empathy, 284
Nussbaum, Martha, 9

Oatley, Keith, 9, 68, 261, 301
obligations, conflicts and, 234–237
ordinary-language terms, 43
Othello (Shakespeare), 8, 199–215
  actional outcomes in, 210
  cistern symbolism in, 212
  disgust in, 199–200, 205–207
  emotional themes and, 220
  jealousy in, race as factor for, 201–202
  out-group categorization in, 199–201
  racial ideology in, 200
  racism in, 200, 205–207
  rationalization of behavior in, 212–213
  self-esteem in, 210–211
  shame in, 199, 201, 207, 213–214
  stigma endorsement in, 214–215
  suspicion in, 208–209
out-group identity. *See also* racism,
      in *Othello*
  in literature, empathy and, 277
  mirth and, 160–162, 172
  in *Othello*, 199–201
  scapegoating and, 172
  for Shakespeare, 160–162, 172
  stigma endorsement and, 214–215
oxytocin
  attachment and, 97
  empathy and, 97

Pandit, Lalita, 160, 175
Paris, Bernard, 288
Partage social des emotions (Rimé), 30–31
patriarchal ideology
  grief and, 143
  influence on emotional biases, 27
  misogyny and, 90
  in *Romeo and Juliet*, 90
perceptions, emotional activation and,
      46–48
  cortical activations as basis of, 47–48
  dominant appraisal theory and, 60
  dominant appraisal theory v., 46, 238
  eliciting conditions, 46
  emotion systems and, 48–49
  from inferences, 47